THE EMPLOYEE TERMINATION HANDBOOK

THE EMPLOYEE TERMINATION HANDBOOK

Edited by
Jeffrey G. Allen, J.D., C.P.C.

A Wiley-Interscience Publication
JOHN WILEY & SONS
New York • Chichester • Brisbane • Toronto • Singapore

This publication is designed to provide accurate and
authoritative information in regard to the subject
matter covered. It is sold with the understanding that
the publisher is not engaged in rendering legal, accounting,
or other professional service. If legal advice or other
expert assistance is required, the services of a competent
professional person should be sought. *From a Declaration
of Principles jointly adopted by a Committee of the
American Bar Association and a Committee of Publishers.*

Library of Congress Cataloging in Publication Data:

The Employee termination handbook.

"A Wiley-Interscience publication."
Bibliography: p.
Includes index.
1. Employees, Dismissal of—Law and legislation—
United States.   I. Allen, Jeffrey G., 1943–
KF3471.E43   1986   344.73′012596   86-7815
ISBN 0-471-82762-2   347.30412596

Printed in the United States of America

10 9 8 7 6 5 4 3 2 1

CONTRIBUTORS

JEFFREY G. ALLEN, J.D., C.P.C., has developed the specialty of placement law, with offices in Beverly Hills and Newport Beach.

Mr. Allen received his B.A. degree from California State University at Northridge and his J.D. degree from the University of West Los Angeles. He received the American Jurisprudence award for scholastic attainment and served as editor of the *UWLA Law Review*.

His combined experience as a certified placement counselor, personnel manager, and professional negotiator uniquely qualify him as an authority on the employment process.

Mr. Allen was appointed Special Advisor to the American Employment Association and is General Counsel to the California Association of Personnel Consultants. He writes a nationally syndicated column entitled "Placements and the Law," conducts seminars, and is regularly featured in television, radio, and newspaper interviews. Mr. Allen serves as Judge Pro Tempore of the Los Angeles Municiple Court. He is also author of the bestsellers *How to Turn an Interview into a Job* and *Finding the Right Job at Midlife*, (Simon and Schuster).

LOUIS J. BARNARD, M.B.A., J.D., is vice president, executive personnel of Lockheed Corporation in the Los Angeles area.

Mr. Barnard received his B.S. degree from Purdue University, his M.B.A. degree from the University of California at Los Angeles, and his J.D. degree from the University of San Fernando Valley.

He is responsible for the identification and development of management for the $5-billion Lockheed Corporation, including the implementation of management selection and succession programs.

He has also been responsible for labor negotiations, conciliation agreements and compensation design, benefit and affirmative action plans, and virtually all other human resources functions for exempt and non-exempt employees.

Mr. Barnard is a member of the State Bar of California and the Aerospace Industries Association Industrial Relations Committee.

ROBERT W. GILBERT, J.D., is the senior partner in the Beverly Hills law firm of Gilbert, Cooke & Sackman, specializing in representation of labor.

Mr. Gilbert received his A.B. degree from the University of California at Los Angeles with highest honors, and his J.D. degree from University of California at Berkeley where he was graduated Order of the Coif and served as editor-in-chief of the *California Law Review.*

He has over 40 years of experience representing international, national, and local trade unions and labor councils covering practically every major industry, and including public utilities and governmental units. He also serves as counsel for multiemployer benefit plans, and is active in the labor sections of the American Bar Association as well as various state and local bar associations.

Mr. Gilbert serves as Judge Pro Tempore of the Los Angeles Municipal Court. He has written many articles on labor law and procedure, and recently cowrote the supplement to the *Injunction Manual, Civil Procedure Before Trial* (University of California Continuing Education of the Bar).

JAMES G. JOHNSON, J.D., is a partner in the Los Angeles firm of Hill, Farrer & Burrill, specializing in management representation.

Mr. Johnson is a graduate of Georgetown University's nationally recognized master of laws program in labor law.

He is the author of "Selecting the Forum," the lead chapter on the subject of relations with organized labor in *Advising California Employers* (University of California Continuing Education of the Bar). He is also the author of "Albermarle Paper Company v. Moody—The Aftermath of Griggs and the Death of Employee Testing," which appeared in *Hastings Law Journal* (University of California) and "An Employer's Primer on Labor Relations." He is a frequent lecturer on labor law and related subjects before business groups and professional societies.

Mr. Johnson is a member of the labor law and litigation sections of the American Bar Association, the Committee on Practice and Procedure under the National Labor Relations Act, the Labor and Employment Law Section of the State Bar of California, and a member of the Executive Committee of the Los Angeles County Bar Association Labor Law Section.

STEVEN J. KAPLAN, J.D., is a partner in the Beverly Hills firm of Gilbert, Cooke & Sackman, specializing in representation of labor.

Mr. Kaplan graduated Phi Beta Kappa from the University of California at Berkeley, receiving his A.B. degree. Thereafter, he also received his J.D. degree from University of California at Berkeley where he served as editor of its *Industrial Relations Law Journal.*

He is former counsel for the National Labor Relations Board and represents international, national, and local unions in many industries, as well as public utilities and governmental units. He also serves as legal advisor for multiemployer benefit plans.

Mr. Kaplan recently contributed to the inaugural edition of *The Labor Lawyer* (American Bar Association). He is coauthor of the supplement to the *Injunction Manual, Civil Procedure Before Trial* (University of California Continuing Education of the Bar).

ROBERT N. MARX, J.D., is in the private practice of law in New York City, specializing in equal employment opportunity and related labor laws.

Mr. Marx graduated from Syracuse University, cum laude. Thereafter, he attended New York University, School of Law, from which he received his Juris Doctor degree in 1975.

He was formerly a Senior Trials and Appeals Attorney for the New York State Division of Human Rights. Mr. Marx prepared and litigated employment discrimination complaints, representing the Division of Human Rights through final decisions on appeal before the Appellate Division and the New York State Court of Appeals.

He is a member of the New York County Lawyers Association Civil Rights and Arbitration Committees, and the Association of the Bar of the City of New York.

Mr. Marx teaches law at Pace University, and has recently been appointed as an arbitrator for the Civil Court of the City of New York. He also serves on the American Arbitration Association Commercial Law and Discrimination Law panels.

BRUCE D. MAY, J.D., is an associate with Parker, Milliken, Clark, O'Hara & Samuelian in Los Angeles, specializing in representation of management.

Mr. May received his B.A. and J.D. degrees from the University of California. He was selected as a Distinguished Advocate in the University of California at Los Angeles' School of Law Moot Court Honors Program. His experience includes participation in wrongful termination, discrimination, unemployment insurance, wage and hour, unfair labor practice, grievance, and other proceedings.

He is editor of the *PMCO Labor Report* (published by his firm), has written articles for the *Personnel Journal* (Personnel and Industrial Relations Association), and has assisted in the preparation of other legal treatises.

Mr. May serves as Judge Pro Tempore of the Los Angeles Municipal Court. He is a member of the labor and employment law sections of the American Bar Association, State Bar of California, and Los Angeles County Bar Association.

ANTHONY T. OLIVER, Jr., J.D., is chairman of the Labor Department of Parker, Milliken, Clark, O'Hara & Samuelian in Los Angeles, specializing in representation of management.

Mr. Oliver received his B.A. degree and J.D. degree from Santa Clara University and served as vice president of its Law Society.

He has conducted labor relations programs for the American Arbitration Association, National Academy of Arbitrators, University of California, League of California Cities, and other organizations.

Mr. Oliver is active in the American Bar Association as Chair of its Subcommittee on Judicial Procedures Before and After Labor Arbitration, and he is an officer or member of the labor and employment law sections of the State Bar of California, Southeast District Bar Association and Los Angeles County Bar Association. He also participates in the Industrial Relations Research Association and Arizona Industrial Relations Association.

Mr. Oliver has written many articles on labor relations, and is a contributor to *Advising California Employers* (University of California Continuing Education of the Bar).

JOSEPH L. PALLER, Jr., J.D., is a partner in the Beverly Hills firm of Gilbert, Cooke and Sackman, specializing in representation of labor.

Mr. Paller graduated with honors from the University of California at Santa Barbara, receiving his B.A. degree, and from the University of California at Los Angeles, receiving his J.D. degree.

He is admitted to the California, New York, and Pennsylvania bars. Among his clients are international, national, and local labor unions, labor-management trust funds, and individuals discharged from employment.

BENNETT W. ROOT, Jr., J.D., is assistant chairman of the Labor Department of Latham & Watkins in Los Angeles, specializing in representation of management.

Mr. Root attended the University of Michigan and graduated with honors receiving his B.S. degree. He then attended Harvard University and graduated cum laude receiving his J.D. degree.

He has taught labor law at the University of California at Los Angeles, the University of Southern California, and Oxford University. He has been active in the American Bar Association and Los Angeles County Bar Association labor law sections and is a member of the State Bar of California. He was appointed to the American Arbitration Association Advisory Board and has served in many related positions.

Mr. Root's international experience includes review of human resources procedures to preserve the prerogatives of employers and development of a comprehensive program of standard operating procedures.

He is active in labor negotiations, representing employers and employer groups. In addition, Root regularly supervises the preparation and conduct of litigation concerning labor and employment matters.

CYNTHIA MADURO RYAN, J.D., is a partner in the Los Angeles firm of Macdonald, Halsted & Laybourne, specializing in management representation.

Ms. Ryan graduated from the University of Southern California cum laude, receiving her B.A. degree, and attended Loyola University of Los Angeles, where she obtained her J.D. degree. She is past president of the St. Thomas More Law Honor Society and a member of Blackstonians Legal Society.

She has appeared before the U.S. Labor Department, Equal Employment Opportunity Commission, Office of Federal Contract Compliance,

California Department of Fair Employment and Housing, and other federal and state agencies.

Ms. Ryan has served on several governmental regulatory boards and lectured to many industry trade associations on employment law. She has been active in the development of affirmative action programs and served as chairperson of the California Association of Life Insurance Companies' Legal Equality Committee.

A former insurance executive, Ms. Ryan has participated in the American Management Association, U.S. Chamber of Commerce, Joint Legislative Committee on Tort Liability, Los Angeles County Bar Association Insurance Committee, Mayor's Committee on City and County Government Growth, and is a founder of the Employment Council.

STEVEN M. SCHNEIDER, J.D., is a partner with Mitchell, Silberberg & Knupp in Los Angeles, specializing in management representation.

Mr. Schneider received his B.S. degree from Cornell University and his J.D. degree from Harvard University.

He has written or contributed to *The Unprotected Minority: Employers and Civil Rights Compliance* (Los Angeles County Bar Association), *Employment Discrimination Law* (Bureau of National Affairs), and *Advising California Employers* (University of California Continuing Education of the Bar).

STANLEY E. TOBIN, J.D., is chairman of the Labor Department of Hill, Farrer & Burrill in Los Angeles, specializing in management representation.

Mr. Tobin received his B.A. degree from Harvard College, graduating with honors, and his J.D. degree from Yale University, where he was editor of the *Yale Law Journal*.

He formerly taught at Stanford University Law School, where he now serves as an annual guest lecturer in labor law. He also regularly appears as a speaker before employer associations, attorney groups, and labor relations meetings throughout the country.

While Mr. Tobin practices in all phases of labor law, his emphasis is on the National Labor Relations Act, federal court labor litigation, and arbitration. In addition, he advises employers and management associations regarding benefit programs and strike-related operations.

ROBERT L. WENZEL, J.D., is the general counsel and administrative director of National Directory Company owned by Dun & Bradstreet Corporation in the Los Angeles area. His duties include responsibility for the overall legal, human resources, and training functions.

Mr. Wenzel received his B.A. degree from Carthage College, his J.D. degree from Western State University, and a Certificate in Industrial Relations from the University of California at Los Angeles.

He was formerly engaged in private law practice where he specialized in representing management in human resources and labor relations matters. He is a member of the State Bar of California, past president of the Personnel and Industrial Relations Association, and has served as Associate Director of the Merchants and Manufacturers Association.

PREFACE

When I was hired in my first human resources job 20 years ago, termination of an employee was considered largely within the discretion of the supervisor. Our function in the "Industrial Relations Department" was to document the reasons for termination to satisfy the unemployment insurance administrators and labor unions, and occasionally to justify firing a minority employee. While the management of our publicly held employer considered itself enlightened, it was motivated more by paternalism than protectionism.

With the rise of unions, passage of the federal Civil Rights Act, and birth of the Equal Employment Opportunity Commission, this absolute discretion was challenged. However, any human resources professional worth his or her title knew that the unwritten job description included objectively justifying the reasons for subjective dismissals. Affirmative action met with negative reaction. Slogans and statistics were the response to statutes and social change.

But now a steamroller has started, fueled by an increasing number of court decisions holding employers accountable for their firings. Those decided or pending include such household names as American Airlines, AT&T, ARCO, Atari, Avco, Bissell, Blue Cross/Blue Shield, Firestone, IBM, McGraw-Hill, and NCR. In fact, the list already reads like a *Who's Who in Corporate America*. Back pay, front pay, punitive and exemplary damages are the rule, often totaling hundreds of thousands of dollars. Over 75 percent of the awards are in favor of the former employee.

Since our offices have specialized for the past decade in the laws relating to employment, we have become involved in many wrongful termination cases. Unfortunately the problem with using civil courts to review management decisions is that judges and juries were not on the "firing line." There is very little objectivity in business . . . it is the intuitive ability of certain companies to choose between various options that has resulted in their success. This is why no two businesses are identical in products or services, size, marketing, distribution, or internal structure.

The public has the impression that a court is like a giant automated teller machine. Just plug in the right facts and law, and the cash will appear. Trial lawyers are disabused of this impression rather violently during their first court appearance. This is the difference between science and art in the practice of law. The *proof* and *interpretation* of the law are critical.

As a human resources professional, you have outgrown your record-keeping function and are now also becoming an indispensable advisor to management. Undoubtedly you have noticed that it is always safer to tell management *not* to terminate an employee. However, your function is to provide the guidance it needs so its business decision will be consistent with the law. Your advice may have direct financial impact and can directly affect employee morale, turnover, and productivity. When you are advising on *how* to accomplish severance of the relationship without an adverse result, you are performing one of your most important roles.

In editing the *Employee Termination Handbook,* I have chosen the most knowledgeable legal and human resources authorities in America. Our goal has been to develop a practical, systematic approach that gives you all of the answers you need when you're on the firing line. This handbook is intended to be your desk reference . . . your first source for fast, accurate, understandable information that you can communicate clearly and concisely to management.

It would take a thesaurus to list the different words for the same things, a dictionary to define them, and an encyclopedia to review their history. However, we have used only those definitions that are necessary . . . no more, no less.

If you work with this handbook on a daily basis, your thinking process will change. You will be transcending from reacting to acting. Your advice will no longer be relegated to warning about dire consequences: It will be a creative way to develop solutions to bottom-line business decisions.

This is our goal.

Best wishes for success,

JEFFREY G. ALLEN, J.D., C.P.C.

Beverly Hills, CA
May 1986

CONTENTS

1 WRONGFUL TERMINATION LAW: REPLACING EMPLOYMENT AT-WILL 1
Anthony T. Oliver, Jr., J.D., and Bruce D. May, J.D.

2 STATUTORY PROTECTION AGAINST WRONGFUL TERMINATION 41
Robert W. Gilbert, J.D., and Steven J. Kaplan, J.D.

3 DEFENDING AGAINST WRONGFUL TERMINATION BEFORE AND AFTER LITIGATION 61
Bennett W. Root, Jr., J.D.

4 EMPLOYER RULES AND POLICIES: BINDING CONTRACTS? 91
Anthony T. Oliver, Jr., J.D., and Bruce D. May, J.D.

5 THE PROTECTION OF EMPLOYEE PRIVACY 115
Steven J. Kaplan, J.D., and Joseph L. Paller, Jr., J.D.

6 EMPLOYMENT DISCRIMINATION LAW: WHAT IT SAYS 161
Louis J. Barnard, M.B.A., J.D.

7 DEFENDING EMPLOYMENT DISCRIMINATION CHARGES: THE INVESTIGATION 167
Robert N. Marx, J.D.

8 DEFENDING EMPLOYMENT DISCRIMINATION CHARGES: THE HEARING 207
Robert N. Marx, J.D.

9 TERMINATION WITHOUT TREPIDATION: A FAIL-SAFE APPROACH 243
Robert L. Wenzel, J.D.

10 TERMS OF TERMINATION: RESOLVING THE ISSUES 269
Bennett W. Root, Jr., J.D.

11 THE EMPLOYER'S SURVIVAL KIT: BASIC STEPS TO DEVELOP AN EFFECTIVE AFFIRMATIVE ACTION PLAN 299
Cynthia Maduro Ryan, J.D.

12 WRONGFUL HIRING? 353
Steven M. Schneider, J.D.

13 EMPLOYMENT CONTRACTS: HOW TO PREPARE THEM 367
Stanley E. Tobin, J.D., and James G. Johnson, LL.M.

Table of Cases 403

Index 407

THE EMPLOYEE
TERMINATION
HANDBOOK

Chapter 1

WRONGFUL TERMINATION LAW
REPLACING EMPLOYMENT AT-WILL

Anthony T. Oliver, Jr., J.D.
Bruce D. May, J.D.

"You're fired!"

Since the dawn of industrial society, the power behind these words has gone largely unquestioned in American jurisprudence. Under the time-honored doctrine of "at-will employment," courts and commentators starting in the nineteenth century have proclaimed time and again that employment for an indefinite duration may be terminated at will by either party without liability. To the vast numbers of white and blue collar employees who have neither a labor union nor a formal employment contract to safeguard their job security, the notice of termination has meant a judgment from which there was no appeal.

All of this has changed. Beginning inconspicuously with a California appellate decision in 1959 and proliferating dramatically in the past decade, courts throughout the land have recognized expansive new exceptions to the basic at-will doctrine. Most notably, a majority of the states have now endorsed an exception to the at-will doctrine where the discharge of an employee violates some clear public policy as reflected in civil or criminal statutes, administrative regulations, even professional codes of ethics in some cases. In still other decisions, the courts have fashioned new limits on the right to fire by rethinking traditional contract principles as applied to oral assurances of job security, personnel policies, and employee handbooks.

In an effort to curb the abuses that can flow from unbridled managerial prerogative, the courts have imposed liabilities unheard of at common law. Where once employees had not even a breach of contract claim for lost wages, they suddenly have standing to seek compensatory damages for mental distress, injury to reputation, and even punitive damages. In an area of decision making where the courts once dared not tread, judges and juries are now plunging head-on. Throughout this process, the law has shown little tolerance for the doctrinaire adherence to laissez-faire economics that the at-will rule embodies.

This surge in judicial activism has complemented existing state and federal legislation outlawing specific forms of wrongful discharge. Indeed, in this sense, exceptions to the at-will doctrine are nothing new. The National Labor Relations Act of 1935 and other federal labor laws prohibit the termination of at-will employees on account of union membership and other forms of concerted activity. Similarly, Title VII of the Civil Rights Act of 1964 and the Age Discrimination in Employment Act of 1967, together with corresponding state equal employment laws, forbid discrimination due to race, national origin, sex, age, and other illegitimate criteria. More recently the Employee Retirement Income Security Act of 1974, as amended, precludes discrimination that impinges on the rights arising from employee benefit plans.

But where these statutory limits proceed on clearly defined criteria, the new judicial limitations on at-will employment can expose an employer's conduct to almost unlimited review. Instead of simply determining whether an employer impermissibly relied on union activities, minority status, or pension rights in effectuating a termination, some courts are now asking whether the employer acted in good faith, obeyed public policy, or had proper cause. The vagueness inherent in some of these new theories allows the courts to reconsider every aspect of the employer's course of conduct.

Perhaps more importantly, the wrongful discharge doctrine often places this seemingly boundless discretion in the hands of a unique decision-maker: the jury. Employers accustomed to having their personnel actions reviewed either by no one, or perhaps by an arbitrator, unemployment board, or civil rights commission, are now finding themselves being second-guessed by civil juries.

One need not be a psychologist or a trial lawyer to appreciate what an employer is up against when facing a wrongful discharge jury. Virtually every juror has been employed in one capacity or another at some time and thus has a sense of how the employer controls one's working life. Countless jurors also have been victimized by an unjust dismissal or some other arbitrary personnel action, either personally or vicariously through a relative or close friend. The resulting institutional bias haunts every defendant employer, whether it is a mom and pop grocery store or a Fortune 500 conglomerate.

Some observers would suggest that the very idea of the at-will doctrine, whereby an employee can be discharged for any cause or even for no cause at all, simply does not seem fair to the average juror. Whether this springs from real life experience or ineffable notions of natural justice, most jurors find it hard to accept that an employee should suffer discharge without some tangible reason. In cases where the employer articulates a specific ground for discharge, jurors are often eager to substitute their own judgment and question the wisdom of the supervisor or personnel manager. And in cases where the reason is subjective or convoluted, jurors inescapably will sense a pretext and search for some sinister motive behind the termination. The results can be devastating.

In April 1985 a jury in San Jose, California, awarded a wrongfully terminated electronics sales representative more than $60 million, including some $54 million in punitive damages. Earlier that year, a jury in Los Angeles awarded a former insurance executive $20 million on the grounds that he was wrongfully discharged over a bonus dispute. In 1984 a jury in San Diego rendered a verdict of more than $6 million for the president of a retail chain who was unjustly fired for poor performance after less than six months on the job.

Not all of these staggering verdicts have involved top-level management. In January 1985 the Minnesota Court of Appeals upheld a jury verdict of more than $1 million to a group of insurance claims approvers who were fired after refusing to sign false expense reports. In 1983, a federal court jury in Michigan awarded more than $1.5 million to a sales employee who was terminated after a disputed transfer between Detroit and Cincinnati. And in November 1982, a former steel mill foreman in Fontana, California won a verdict for nearly $5 million on grounds of wrongful discharge.

This book is intended to help avert such disasters. In this chapter, the erosion of the at-will doctrine in its various forms will be addressed. We begin with a brief history of the doctrine itself and then turn to the body of case law concerning its many new exceptions. We should also mention what is not covered in this chapter. As noted, the laws concerning union activities and equal employment constitute two major inroads on the at-will doctrine. These are discussed extensively in Chapters 2 and 5. In addition the subject of personnel manuals and employee handbooks is left for Chapter 4. Beyond that, other chapters of this book discuss how to *defend* wrongful termination suits, and how to avoid them through "preventive" personnel practices.

As the reader will discover, contemporary theories of wrongful discharge can be divided into three basic categories, though some overlap does occur. First, is the public policy exception which forbids terminations that violate some established public policy. Second, is the category based on the implied covenant of good faith and fair dealing, whereby liability for wrongful discharge can stem from arbitrary or bad faith conduct. Third, we treat the category of cases in which the courts have enforced implied in fact limits on the right to fire arising from oral promises and formal personnel practices.

In each of these three sections we will review the facts and analysis from leading cases from the various states, but with a special emphasis on California law. This is fitting, for California was the very first state to codify the at-will doctrine, but is now among the leading jurisdictions seeking to circumscribe it. Nevertheless, our overview will be necessarily selective, since a thorough state-by-state summary would quickly exhaust this entire volume. While we will present an overall picture, the reader must remain acutely aware of the need for expert legal counsel on the law of each of the particular states.

In concluding our tripartite analysis we offer guidance for the employer in reducing its exposure to wrongful discharge liability. While no one of course can predict the course of litigation, or prevent it in all cases, our hope is that the reader will be better equipped to spot legal issues before they become lawsuits.

THE TRADITIONAL DOCTRINE
OF AT-WILL EMPLOYMENT

In its purest form the doctrine of at-will employment reflects an admirable simplicity: Employment for an indefinite duration may be terminated at any time by either party for any reason. California Labor Code section 2922, a typical statutory expression of the doctrine, states that "[a]n employment, having no specified term, may be terminated at the will of either party on notice to the other."

The core idea of at-will employment is that the parties have not agreed on how long the employment will last. This should not be confused with the question of whether or not the agreement is written or oral, although the typical at-will employee is hired on a handshake rather than a written contract. Even a written agreement, however, can provide that the employment is for an indefinite term, or that it may be terminated without cause; in either case the at-will doctrine generally applies.

An agreement by the parties as to specific duration might be expressed in terms of days, months, or years, or it may be clear from special circumstances. For example, courts have found a definite term where the parties agreed to employment "until normal retirement age," "for the full school year," or some other framework connoting a temporal element. A few courts have even reasoned that the pay period implies a specific term; thus a hiring at an annual salary may create a one-year term. Offers of "permanent" or "lifetime" employment, however, are traditionally deemed too indefinite to avoid the at-will rule.

Absent a definite term, the employment is said to be at will, and may be severed by either party without liability. The employee is free to quit and the employer is free to discharge. According to one rather emphatic phrasing of the doctrine, an at-will employee may be terminated "for good cause, for no cause, even for cause morally wrong." *Payne v. Western & Atlantic Railroad,* 81 Tenn. 507, 519–20 (1884). Though now hopelessly overbroad, this statement of the rule gives an idea of how staunchly the courts once defended managerial freedom.

THE HISTORY OF THE AT-WILL DOCTRINE

The historical origins of the at-will doctrine are clouded and rather dubious. No clear thread exists between the treatment that at-will employment received in early English law, and the eventual view adopted by early American courts. In feudal England rudimentary forms of employment were described as matters of "status" rather then "contract," which is to say persons were more or less born into the laboring class and remained so for life. The terms of employment reflected the social order rather than any freely bargained exchange between the parties.

In the fourteenth century, when the Black Plague decimated the population of Europe, and with it the ranks of labor, a series of laws known as the Statutes of Laborers were enacted to require all able-bodied persons to work at a reasonable wage under threat of criminal sanctions. Similar laws even found their way into the colonies, prompted by religious as well as economic ideals. Eventually the use of criminal sanctions and court injunctions proved unworkable, with the result that employment slowly came under the play of economic forces.

By the eighteenth century the British law of "master and servant" had begun to develop coherent principles for construing contracts of employment. In 1765 the great commentator Blackstone wrote that "[i]f the hiring be general, without any particular time limited, the law construes it to be a hiring for a year." This one-year presumption embodied the reality of the agrarian society as well as the slightly paternalistic notions of "master and servant." It prevented the harshness of hiring laborers for the harvest season and then "putting them away" for the winter, as Blackstone alluded.

This one-year presumption, however, could be rebutted by proof of an agreement for a different term or none at all. The evidence might consist of an explicit understanding as to the term of employment, or it could arise from the custom in the trade, the frequency of wage payments, or the length of notice required to terminate. This "totality of the circumstances" approach, which endured in British law as industrial society prospered, served to temper the at-will doctrine. Curiously, as we shall see, this same style of thought has been resurrected in the 1980s as the courts enforce implied contractual limits on at-will termination.

Against this backdrop, scholars have struggled to explain how the so-called American Rule of at-will employment came into being. Most commentators have erroneously asserted that the classic at-will doctrine was more or less invented by Horace Gay Wood, a prominent New York attorney and legal writer, in his 1877 publication, *A Treatise on the Law of Master and Servant* Section 134 (1877). Wood wrote that "[w]ith us, the rule is inflexible that a general or indefinite hiring is prima facie a hiring at will, and if the servant seeks to make it out a yearly hiring, the burden is on him to establish it by proof." Though Wood's contemporaries called him a "man of genius" and an "authority of high repute," modern commentators have criticized him for concocting a harsh doctrine without support in case law. In point of fact, however, some American courts had adopted the classic at-will rule more than 20 years before Wood's celebrated treatise.

One such case arose in Maine in 1851. In *Blaisdell v. Lewis,* 32 Me. 515 (1851), the plaintiff had agreed to perform work at daily wages in Hallowell, but was never called to duty. He sued and won a jury verdict, but the defendant's exceptions were sustained. The court's entire opinion was as follows:

An infirmity in this contract is, that it fixed no time during which the plaintiff's services should be rendered to the defendant. Suppose the plaintiff had gone to Hallowell, and tendered his services, there was nothing to prevent the defendant from discharging him at the end of a single day. In such a contract there is no value.

Blaisdell may well be the first reported decision in the United States to apply the at-will rule.

In *DeBriar v. Minturn,* 1 Cal. 450 (1851), the California Supreme Court ruled against a barkeeper who had been discharged from his job and ejected from his room at the defendant's inn. The court noted that he "was not hired for any definite period." In *Hathaway v. Bennett,* 10 N.Y. 108 (1854), the New York Court of Appeals ruled that a newspaper deliverer's contract for an indefinite period could be terminated "at pleasure" by the defendant. Though neither *DeBriar* nor *Hathaway* dealt exactly with the discharge of an employee, both cases were deemed to endorse the at-will rule long before Wood.

Other cases did so even more clearly. In 1871, the Wisconsin Supreme Court ruled in *Prentiss v. Ledyard,* 28 Wisc. 131 (1871), a breach of contract action, that "[e]ither party, however, was at liberty to terminate the service at any time, no definite period for which the service was to continue having been agreed upon." In 1874 Illinois reached the same result in *Orr v. Ward,* 73 Ill. 318 (1874), in which an employee was denied recovery because the contract "contain[ed] no undertaking . . . for a definite period." Perhaps most clearly, California enacted the first at-will statute, in the original California Civil Code, way back in 1872. For whatever reason, Wood never cited these authorities in his 1877 work.[1]

What Wood may have lacked as a researcher, however, he more than made up for as a prophet. Virtually every state eventually accepted his formulation of the at-will rule. The Court of Appeals of Maryland called Wood an "authority of great repute" when it adopted the at-will doctrine in *McCullough Iron Co. v. Carpenter,* 67 Md. 554, 11 A.2d 176 (1887), and New York's highest court noted in *Martin v. New York Life Insurance Co.,* 148 N.Y. 117, 42 N.E.416 (1895), that the at-will doctrine was "correctly stated by Mr. Wood."

Wood had pronounced a rule that was simple and consistent. It settled conflict among the lower courts, and spared judges and juries from undertaking complicated factual analyses. Most importantly the at-will doctrine fit the times. With the industrial revolution and the flourishing of laissez-faire economics, it dutifully served emerging notions of economic individualism.

For a time the at-will doctrine even assumed constitutional proportions. In *Adair v. United States,* 208 U.S. 161 (1908), the U.S. Supreme Court ruled that a federal statute prohibiting the discharge of certain employees for union membership was "an invasion of the personal liberty, as well as the right of property" protected by the Fifth Amendment. Justice Harlan's opinion endorsed the at-will doctrine in the loftiest terms:

In the absence, however, of a valid contract between the parties controlling their conduct towards each other and fixing a period of service, it cannot be, we repeat, that an employer is under any legal obligation, against his will, to retain an em-

---

[1] There is an interesting connection here between California and New York. The attorney for the unsuccessful employee in *Hathaway v. Bennett* (1854) was the famous New York attorney David Dudley Field, who was later commissioned by the State of New York to author the first comprehensive civil code. The so-called Field Code was the basis for the California Civil Code enacted in 1872 which, as noted above, contained the first statutory expression of the classic at-will doctrine. It may be that when Field set out to draft his civil code, he recalled the adverse holding in *Hathaway* and took it as the prevailing view. Ironically, in the 1980s, California is the leading state in eroding the at-will doctrine while New York is the leader in continuing to follow it.

ployee in his personal service any more than an employee can be compelled, against his will, to remain in the personal service of another . . . [The employee] was at liberty to quit the service without assigning any reason for his leaving. And the defendant was at liberty, in his discretion, to discharge [the employee] from service without giving any reason for so doing.

Though the ruling in *Adair* has lost all vitality, the vigor with which the courts endorsed the at-will doctrine well into the twentieth century has hardly a historical oddity. By subverting job security in the name of managerial prerogative, the courts assured the free play of market forces among the ranks of labor, a sentiment deeply imbedded in the spirit of capitalism. With the momentum of the times behind it, the at-will doctrine was understandably slow in yielding to exceptions.

JUDICIAL EROSION OF THE AT-WILL DOCTRINE

The Public Policy Exception

By giving the employer boundless authority to discharge, the traditional at-will doctrine makes the employer's motives irrelevant. An employer may terminate at-will employees "for good cause, for no cause, or even for cause morally wrong." In an ever growing number of jurisdictions, this is a dangerous misstatement of law.

The most dramatic new limitation on the at-will doctrine is known as the public policy exception. Under this theory, an employer may be liable in both tort and contract if it discharges an at-will employee for reasons that violate a specific statutory prohibition or a firmly established principle of public policy. In cases displaying a wide range of factual patterns, the courts have imposed liability precisely because of the employer's motives.

THE PETERMANN DECISION. The public policy exception originated in a 1959 decision by the California Court of Appeal, *Petermann v. International Brotherhood of Teamsters*, 174 Cal. App. 2d 184, 344 P.2d 25 (1959). Peter Petermann was a Teamsters' business agent who had been subpoenaed to testify before a committee of the California legislature. Petermann alleged that before his scheduled appearance, the secretary-treasurer who had hired him instructed him to make certain false statements before the Legislature. Petermann refused, testified truthfully before the committee, and was discharged the next day for no apparent reason.

Petermann sued for breach of contract, alleging that he was discharged because of his refusal to perjure himself as his superior had instructed. The Court of Appeal upheld his complaint and sent the case back for trial. In its landmark opinion, the Court of Appeal acknowledged the traditional at-will doctrine in California Labor Code section 2922, but held that the right to terminate could be limited by a specific statute or *"by considerations of public policy."* This statement in *Petermann* was unprecedented in modern jurisprudence.

The court recognized that "public policy" was an inherently "vague expression" which defied simple definition. Drawing on cases not involving employment, the court alluded to conduct which "has a tendency to be injurious to the public or against the public good." Noting that committing or soliciting perjury was unlawful under the California Penal Code, the court articulated the public policy exception:

It would be obnoxious to the interests of the state and contrary to public policy and sound morality to allow an employer to discharge any employee, whether the employment be for a designated or unspecified duration, on the ground that the employee declined to commit perjury, an act specifically enjoined by statute. The threat of criminal prosecution would, in many cases, be a sufficient deterrent upon both the employer and the employee, the former from soliciting and the latter from committing perjury. However, in order to more fully effectuate the state's declared policy against perjury, the civil law, too, must deny the employer his generally unlimited right to discharge an employee whose employment is for an unspecified duration, when the reason for the dismissal is the employee's refusal to commit perjury.

In the decades since *Petermann,* no court has better explained the public policy exception to the at-will doctrine. The eminently sound idea of that opinion is that society at large has certain fundamental interests which are weighty enough to override even a private employer's managerial privilege. What made *Petermann* such a dramatic change in the law is that the perjury statute in question said nothing about discharge from employment. While the legislature had enacted the ban on perjury, it was the judiciary that injected this statutory mandate into the terms of a private agreement.

WHAT CONSTITUTES "PUBLIC POLICY"? *Petermann* paved the way for a wealth of subsequent decisions applying the public policy exception. While later cases display a wide variety of factual settings, they ask the same ultimate question: What constitutes public policy? In *Petermann,* the California Penal Code flatly prohibited the commission or solicitation of perjury, and no one would question the compelling state interest in preventing false testimony. On the other hand, subsequent courts have often struggled with whether or not a cognizable public policy was implicated in a particular termination.

At one end of the spectrum, several courts have held that the employee must point to a specific statute embodying the public policy implicated in a particular discharge. For example, in *Brockmeyer v. Dun & Bradstreet,* 335 N.W.2d 834 (Wis. 1983), the Wisconsin Supreme Court flatly proclaimed that "[t]he public policy must be evidenced by a constitutional or statutory provision." Similarly, in *Shapiro v. Wells Fargo Realty Advisors, Inc.,* 152 Cal. App. 3d 467, 199 Cal. Rptr. 613 (1984), *hearing denied,* the California Court of Appeal found no statutory support for an employee's claim that his discharge violated the public policy of "promot[ing] job security and stability in the community." The strict view in *Brockmeyer* and *Shapiro* stems from the belief that only the legislature can capably ascertain the will of the electorate and thereupon articulate what is public policy.

At the other end of the spectrum is the view that any clear mandate of public policy, whether based on statute or simply judicial decree, will support a claim for wrongful discharge. The Oregon Supreme Court, in *Delaney v. Taco Time International, Inc.,* 297 Ore. 10, 681 P.2d 441 (1984), stated that a wrongful discharge claim can arise simply from the violation of some important "societal obligation." In *Novosel v. Nationwide Insurance Co.,* 721 F.2d 894 (3d Cir. 1983), a federal appellate court relied on the basic right of free speech in finding a public policy violation, even though the private employer in that case would not have been bound by the First Amendment.

The majority view, however, lies somewhere between these two extremes. Most courts would probably stop short of positively requiring a specific statute in every case, but would still "proceed cautiously if called upon to declare public policy absent some prior legislative or judicial expression on the subject." *Parnar v. Americana Hotels, Inc.,* 652 P.2d 625, 631 (Hawaii, 1982). Even the more judicially active courts will strive to pinpoint some statutory or constitutional underpinnings in an effort to avoid the appearance of usurping the legislative function.

In the search for public policy the courts have looked to state and federal constitutional provisions, criminal laws, general civil statutes, administrative regulations, professional codes of ethics, even the Hippocratic Oath—all with mixed results. In some cases the courts have isolated a specific statute on point, but have nevertheless rejected wrongful discharge claims because of the remote relationship between the operation of the statute and the discharge of the employee. In other decisions the employer has not violated any statute, but has behaved so unjustly that the courts have resorted to great ingenuity in finding a connection between the discharge and some legislative enactment.

The courts have also considered the *manner* in which a discharge can offend the public interest. On this account the public policy cases can be divided into three general categories. The first category, typified by *Petermann,* involves a discharge precipitated by the employee's refusal to commit an illegal act at the employer's behest. The second category, exemplified by cases where the employee is fired for filing a worker's compensation claim or complaining about workplace safety, involves terminations that come in retaliation for the employees' attempts to invoke their statutory rights. The third category, known colloquially as the "whistleblower" cases, it involves employees who are discharged when they attempt to publicize perceived wrongdoing by the employer. Each of these categories is discussed separately in the following.

Refusal to Commit an Unlawful Act

Probably the least controversial of the public policy cases are those involving employees who allege they were discharged for refusing to commit an illegal act. *Petermann* is the classic example of this type of case. In many other settings, where employees have refused to partake in conduct made unlawful by a statute or regulation, the courts have likewise found public policy violation.

PERJURY AND FALSE STATEMENTS. Numerous wrongful discharge cases stem from an employee's refusal to make a false statement. *Petermann* involved the solicitation of false testimony before a legislative committee, and the same result would follow where the perjury was to occur in a courtroom, in arbitration, or in any other forum where witnesses are placed under oath. In *Merkel v. Scovill, Inc.*, 570 F. Supp. 133 (S.D.Ohio 1983), the court refused to dismiss a public policy claim by an employee who refused to sign an allegedly false sworn affidavit that the employer had prepared for him in connection with a separate lawsuit.

A closer question arises in cases where the employee is discharged following the refusal to sign a statement that is false, but not under oath. The perjury laws would not apply to such unsworn statements, but the employer's conduct may be no less reprehensible, a fact that makes the courts reluctant to dismiss such claims outright. For example, in *Magnan v. Anaconda Industries, Inc.*, 37 Conn. Supp. 38, 429 A.2d 492 (1980), a Connecticut trial court denied the employer's motion to dismiss the public policy claim of an employee discharged after refusing to sign a false statement concerning the theft of refrigerators from the workplace. At the same time, however, the court reserved decision on whether it would require the violation of a particular statute to support a wrongful discharge claim.

On the other hand in *Delaney v. Taco Time International, Inc.*, 297 Ore. 10, 681 P.2d 114 (1984), the Oregon Supreme Court showed great ingenuity in upholding the public policy claim of a restaurant manager allegedly fired for refusing to sign a false, albeit unsworn, statement. The employer had terminated a black female waitress for apparently racist reasons. When she filed an unemployment claim, the employer concocted a false statement for plaintiff to sign accusing the waitress of soliciting sex and causing dissension when the request was refused. Plaintiff refused to sign the statement and was discharged.

In sustaining a public policy claim, the Oregon Supreme Court likened the case to *Petermann* and concluded that the discharge violated the "societal obligation not to defame others." The court acknowledged that the statement in question was only "arguably defamatory" under Oregon case law, and did not directly violate any specific statute. Nonetheless, the court alluded to two provisions of the Oregon Constitution, one which held every person responsible for abusing the right of free speech, and the other which proclaimed that every person shall have a remedy for injury to person, property, or reputation.

Admittedly the court's reliance on these constitutional provisions was rather attenuated, and one can seriously question whether other courts would carry the notion of public policy so far. But clearly the court in *Delaney* was swayed by the openly dishonest behavior of the employer. While the court's analysis may seem undisciplined, the tenor of the opinion comes as no surprise. No employer who suborns false statements, sworn or unsworn, should expect to find refuge behind the at-will doctrine.

EMPLOYEES WHO TESTIFY TRUTHFULLY AGAINST EMPLOYER. A more complex problem concerns employees who are discharged for giving or offering to give sworn testimony that is truthful, but adverse to the employer's interests. In *Montalvo v. Zamora*, 7 Cal. App. 3d 69, 86 Cal. Rptr. 401 (1970), the California Court of Appeal allowed a public policy claim by two farm workers allegedly discharged in part to prevent them from testifying before state agencies investigating the minimum wage. In that case, however, California Labor Code section 1196 specifically prohibited the discharge of employees who offer such testimony, and thus the court had no trouble finding a cause of action.

Similarly employee-witnesses usually enjoy specific statutory protection for testifying before equal employment agencies, state labor authorities, and workers' compensation or unemployment insurance boards. The same is true for federal labor and equal employment laws. Employees who testify truthfully before the National Labor Relations Board or in proceedings under Title VII of the Civil Rights Act of 1964 would have a statutory remedy for retaliatory discharge.

In the absence of such statutes, however, the law is uncertain. In *Meredith v. C.E. Walther, Inc.*, 422 So. 2d 761 (Ala. 1982), the Alabama Supreme Court rejected the public policy claim of an employee who testified in a lawsuit against his employer concerning the administration of an employee benefit trust. The court noted that plaintiff had not been solicited to commit perjury, and that his participation in the lawsuit offended no public policy.

The Supreme Court of Wisconsin reached the same result in *Brockmeyer v. Dun & Bradstreet*, 335 N.W. 2d 834 (Wis. 1983), in which a managerial employee alleged that he was terminated because he was prepared to testify truthfully in support of his former secretary's sex discrimination claim. The court flatly proclaimed that "[t]here is no clearly defined mandate of public policy against discharging an employee because his testimony may be contrary to an employer's interests."

Meredith and *Brockmeyer* notwithstanding, an employer should think twice about discharging an employee in retribution for giving truthful but adverse testimony, especially when the employee is subpoenaed, instead of volunteering. Some courts are bound to be receptive to employees who sacrifice their jobs in order to tell the truth. In egregious cases the courts may stretch a statute to find a public policy violation, or even invoke the implied covenant theory to redress what it perceives as bad faith by the employer.

Another approach the courts may take is to focus on the conduct of the employer that is the subject of the disputed testimony. In *Parnar v. Americana Hotels, Inc.*, 652 P.2d 625 (Hawaii, 1982), for example, the Hawaii Supreme Court ordered a trial for a hotel employee allegedly fired to prevent her from giving truthful testimony before a grand jury or in a criminal trial on antitrust violations by her employer. Rather than analyzing the public policy in truthful testimony, the court turned to the antitrust laws and found that a "retaliatory discharge in apparent furtherance of antitrust violations contravenes public policy."

ANTITRUST, TRADE REGULATION, AND CONSUMER PROTECTION LAWS. The Hawaii Supreme Court's decision in *Parnar* was neither the first nor the last decision to find an actionable public policy arising from the antitrust laws. In *Tameny v. Atlantic Richfield Co.*, 27 Cal. 3d 167, 164 Cal. Rptr. 839, 610 P.2d 1330 (1980), the California Supreme Court lent its imprimatur to the public policy exception in allowing a wrongful discharge suit stemming from a refusal to violate the antitrust laws.

The plaintiff in *Tameny* was a retail sales representative, whose duties included managing relations with certain ARCO stations in an assigned territory. Tameny alleged that for many years, ARCO had violated federal and state antitrust laws by conspiring to fix the retail gasoline prices of its independent dealers. Tameny claimed he was repeatedly pressured by his superiors to "threaten and cajole" independent dealers into conforming their prices to ARCO's wishes. When he refused to yield to such pressure, Tameny was terminated, allegedly in furtherance of the illegal price-fixing scheme.

Drawing on *Petermann*, the California Supreme Court encountered little difficulty finding a protected public policy emanating from the antitrust laws. Moreover, the court in *Tameny* ruled that a discharge in violation of public policy was not only a breach of contract—as held in *Petermann*—but also a common law tort for which the employee could recover compensatory and punitive damages. Although a few courts have limited public policy claimants to contract damages, *Tameny* reflects the emerging consensus that a wrongful discharge claim sounds in tort.

Other courts have concurred in *Tameny* where the discharge follows a refusal to commit conduct unlawful under applicable antitrust laws. In *Perry v. Hartz Mountain Corp.*, 537 F. Supp. 1387 (S.D.Ind. 1982), a federal trial court in Indiana allowed a public policy claim by an employee allegedly discharged for refusing to continue exclusive dealing and tying arrangements that violated federal and state antitrust laws. Similarly, in *McNulty v. Borden, Inc.*, 474 F. Supp. 1111 (E.D.Penn. 1979), a federal court in Pennsylvania refused to dismiss the wrongful discharge of a retail grocery products sales representative whose termination allegedly stemmed from a conspiracy to conceal special pricing arrangements that contravened federal antitrust laws.

A complex issue at stake in these antitrust public policy cases, as well as several other areas of wrongful discharge law, concerns the fact that the antitrust laws themselves provide for a cause of action for persons "injured in their trade or business." In general, the courts have found that only competitors "directly injured" by antitrust violations have standing to sue the perpetrators. Indeed, the employees in *Tameny* and *Perry* both sued under the antitrust laws themselves, only to have the claims dismissed for lack of standing.

Recently, however, in *Ostrofe v. H.S. Crocker Co.*, 740 F.2d 739 (9th Cir. 1984), the Ninth Circuit Court of Appeals broke with precedent and allowed an individual employee who was discharged for resisting his employer's unlawful bid rigging, price fixing, and market allocation, to bring suit directly under the antitrust laws. If *Ostrofe* is followed, employees who suffer discharge in retaliation for opposing unlawful trade practices may have both a common law remedy for wrongful discharge and a statutory remedy for antitrust violations.

This duality of theories for relief raises a crucial question: If a particular statute provides a statutory remedy for specific types of terminations, should the courts expand the parameters of relief by allowing common law wrongful discharge claims based on the public policy expressed in that statute? Or should the courts decree that the relief specified by the legislature is the employee's *exclusive* remedy? This issue holds special importance in cases where employees suffer termination after filing workers' compensation claims, protesting safety conditions, asserting rights under the fair employment laws, or engaging in union activities.

Antitrust violations are not the only form of unlawful business practices that have laid the basis for wrongful discharge claims. Other forms of trade regulation, particularly those concerned with consumer protection, can create compelling circumstances for a court to find an actionable public policy. In *Harless v. First National Bank of Fairmont*, 246 S.E.2d 270 (W. Va. 1978), the West Virginia Supreme Court of Appeals sanctioned a public policy claim by the office manager of the employer bank's consumer credit department who was discharged for his efforts at uncovering and preventing violations of the state consumer credit laws.

In *Sheets v. Teddy's Frosted Foods, Inc.*, 179 Conn. 471, 427 A.2d 385 (1980), the Supreme Court of Connecticut reached the same result in favor of a quality control director who endeavored to assure compliance with state food and drug laws at his employer's frozen food plant. Lastly, in *Garibaldi v. Lucky Food Stores, Inc.*, 726 F.2d 1367 (9th Cir. 1984), the Ninth Circuit Court of Appeals found a public policy violation in the case of a truck driver who refused to deliver a shipment of spoiled milk, an act that would have violated the California Agricultural Code.

These cases evince the willingness of the courts to find a public policy in any form of trade regulation that is infused with consumer welfare. Employees who are discharged for refusing to engage in acts that are prohibited in the interest of consumer health and safety will usually find ample support under even the narrowest definitions of public policy.

BRIBERY AND OTHER SHARP PRACTICES. The courts have also been receptive to wrongful discharge claims where the employee refused to partake in bribery, payoffs, or other plainly dishonest conduct. For example, in *Perry v. Hartz Mountain Corp., supra*, the plaintiff alleged that the antitrust violations he had resisted were effectuated in part by means of illicit payoffs, a fact which certainly enhanced the perception that a public policy had been offended. Other examples highlight the courts' natural hostility to unfair business practices such as bribery that have no inherent redeeming virtues.

In *Hansrote v. Amer Industrial Technologies, Inc.*, 586 F. Supp. 113 (W.D. Penn. 1984), a federal district court in Pennsylvania refused to set aside a jury verdict in favor of an employee whose employer had conditioned his tenure on "improperly influencing" his former employer into awarding a bid to the defendant. Noting that applicable state criminal statutes forbade commercial bribery, the court unhesitantly found the requisite offense against public policy.

In *Crossen v. Foremost-McKesson, Inc.*, 537 F. Supp. 1076 (N.D. Cal. 1982), a federal court in San Francisco denied the employer's motion for summary judgment in the case of an employee who allegedly resisted numerous forms of dishonest business practices. The plaintiff, managing director of defendant's Thailand dairy operation, alleged that he was discharged after embarking on a crusade to correct widespread illegalities, including false statements to the Thai government, violations of safety laws, and bribes to government officials. Although the court rested its ruling on the implied covenant of good faith and fair dealing as discussed later, rather than the public policy theory, these same allegations would easily sustain a public policy violation.

In *Thompson v. St. Regis Paper Co.*, 102 Wash. 2d 219, 685 P.2d 1081 (1984), the Washington Supreme Court recognized a public policy exception in a case where bribery was only secondarily the object of the plaintiff's insistence on compliance with applicable law. The plaintiff, a divisional controller, alleged that he was terminated after 17 years of service in retribution for his efforts to institute accounting procedures in conformity to the federal Foreign Corrupt Practices Act of 1977, which prohibits commercial bribes to foreign officials.

Finding a "clear expression of public policy that bribery of foreign officials is contrary to the public interest," the court deemed the act's accounting requirements to be an integral part of that public policy. While this may not be a classic example of a plaintiff who refused to commit an unlawful act, the decision in *Thompson* suggests how easily the courts will deduce a public policy where bribery is the target of the employee's crusade.

REFUSAL TO VIOLATE CODES OF ETHICS. A more enlightening search for public policy has arisen in a handful of cases where the employee resists a course of conduct as contrary to a professional code of ethics. These courts seem to rely on the inherent importance of the matters covered by the code, rather than on whether the code bears a legislative imprint. In the final analysis, the ethics cases require the court to engage openly in the balancing of interests that underlies the whole public policy doctrine.

In *Pierce v. Ortho Pharmaceutical Corp.*, 84 N.J. 58, 417 A.2d 505 (1980), the plaintiff was a medical doctor assigned to supervise the development and testing of a new drug which containing saccharin, a suspected carcinogen. The plaintiff and those under her were concerned with the controversy that the saccharin might cause, but over the plaintiff's objections, the decision was made to continue the research. The plaintiff advised her superiors that she considered any further participation on her part to be in violation of the Hippocratic oath. When efforts to reassign her failed, plaintiff resigned.

She alleged that Ortho had adopted a course of action which made it impossible for her to follow because of the Hippocratic oath, which provides in part: "I will prescribe regimen for the good of my patients according to my ability and my judgment and never do harm to anyone." Although her complaint alluded to state and federal regulations, the plaintiff did not specify any state or federal law which she believed would be violated by continued testing.

Taking a liberal view, the court decreed that "a clear mandate of public policy" could be found in administrative rules or decisions, court rulings, even professional codes of ethics in proper cases. On the subject of ethics, the court added that "a code of ethics designed to serve only the interests of a profession or an administrative regulation concerned with technical matters probably would not be sufficient."

On the facts before it, the court in *Pierce* concluded that the plaintiff had not shown an adequate public policy. "Viewing the matter most favorably to Dr. Pierce," said the court, "the controversy at Ortho involved a difference in medical opinions." The plaintiff had only insisted that saccharin was "controversial," not "harmful," and thus the case did not involve a clear risk of public harm. Instead, the court concluded that Pierce's dilemma stemmed from her "personal morals" rather than a refusal to commit "unethical conduct."

An interesting contrast to *Pierce* arose two years later when a New Jersey appellate court reached the opposite result in a case touching on the professional ethics of pharmacists. In *Kalman v. The Grand Union Co.*, 183 N.J. Super. 153, 443 A.2d 728 (1982), the plaintiff was a pharmacist employed at a pharmacy located within the defendant's grocery store. When the employer proposed to close the pharmacy on the July 4 holiday but to keep the rest of the store open, plaintiff balked and insisted that so long as the store remained open, the pharmacy had to remain staffed by a licensed pharmacist. The employer assured him that "no one would know," but plaintiff contacted the state Board of Pharmacy and had his beliefs confirmed. He then arranged to have the pharmacy kept open over the holiday, staffed by another pharmacist. Plaintiff was discharged for no stated reason the next day.

Applying the opinion in *Pierce*, the court in *Kalman* noted that a professional code of ethics could establish a public policy in the New Jersey courts. "The task of the court is to distinguish between public policy and the employee's own values; the latter would not entitle the employee to immunity from discharge." The court then proceeded to find that under a series of state regulations, the employer was indeed required to keep the pharmacy open and staffed whenever the store was open. The court also agreed with plaintiff that an unsupervised drug counter poses the risk of dispensing potentially dangerous substances without the aid of qualified personnel, as well as increasing the likelihood of theft.

The court concluded that plaintiff was "vindicating a clear mandate of public policy when he reported defendant's plan to the Board of Pharmacy." The court cited a provision from the Code of Ethics of the American Pharmaceutical Association to the effect that every pharmacist "should expose, without fear or favor, illegal or unethical conduct in the profession." Noting how the plaintiff's conduct fostered consumer welfare, the court remarked that "[t]his is an instance where a code of ethics coincides with public policy."

The reception that codes of ethics have received in *Pierce* and *Kalman* is by no means a unanimous view of the courts. Indeed, in *Suchodolski v. Michigan Consolidated Gas Co.*, 412 Mich. 692, 316 N.W.2d 710 (1982), the court rejected the claims of a senior auditor who purported to act under compulsion of the Code of Ethics of the Institute of Internal Auditors in publicizing his employer's questionable accounting practices. Dismissing the case as a "corporate management dispute," the Michigan Supreme Court opined that the regulation of utility accounting systems was not intended to confer rights on employees.

OTHER REFUSALS TO COMMIT UNLAWFUL ACTS. Other potential cases for invocation of the "refusal to commit an unlawful act" theory are as diverse as the various state statutes prohibiting specific acts of misconduct. Virtually any instance in which an employee is discharged for refusing to commit a criminal act will be actionable in a majority of jurisdictions, and the same result would follow in cases where a specific act of misconduct is outlawed but without any criminal penalty.

Retaliation for Exercising Lawful Rights

A second group of public policy cases involves employees who are discharged in retaliation for their exercising a lawful right. Rather than claiming that they refused to commit an illegal act at their employer's request, the claimants in these cases demanded their lawful entitlements at the workplace. To the extent the right in question is sufficiently infused with the public interest, the courts have allowed recovery in both contract and tort.

WORKERS' COMPENSATION CASES. The clearest example of this public policy theory are the numerous cases involving employees who were discharged in retaliation for having filed a workers' compensation claim. Beginning with the landmark decision by the Indiana Supreme Court in *Frampton v. Central Indiana Gas Co.*, 260 Ind. 249, 297 N.E.2d 425 (1973), the clear majority of cases recognize that allowing employers to retaliate for workplace injury claims would undermine the liberal remedial objectives of workers' compensation. As of Spring 1986, at least a dozen states have concurred in the *Frampton* holding, and nearly twice that number have enacted a specific statute barring such retaliation.

The only lines of dissent in this area turn on whether the legislature in a particular state has enacted a specific ban on retaliating against employees who file workers' compensation claims. A few courts have concluded that the absence of such a statute implies that the legislature has sanctioned, or at least failed to outlaw, retaliatory discharges. Indeed, in North Carolina, when the court of appeal refused to create a judicial exception to the at-will rule, the legislature promptly stepped in and enacted a protective statute. *Dockery v. Lampart Table Co.*, 36 N.C. App. 293, 244 S.E.2d 272 (1982), *cert. denied*, 295 N.C. 465; N.C. Gen. Stat. §97-6.1 (1982).

On the other hand, in a few of those states that have enacted a specific statutory remedy for aggrieved employees, some courts have reasoned that the legislature intended the statutory remedy to be exclusive. By thus preempting the field, the legislature has implicitly precluded the courts from imposing liability under common law.

In California, for example, Labor Code section 132a prohibits discrimination against workers' compensation claimants and provides aggrieved employees with reinstatement, backpay, and a significant increase in the underlying compensation award. In *Portillo v. G.T. Price Products, Inc.*, 131 Cal. App.3d 285, 182 Cal. Rptr. 291 (1982), *hearing denied*, the court of appeal ruled that section 132a constitutes the exclusive remedy for employees who suffer retaliation for filing a workers' compensation claim. Conceding the need for redressing such violations of public policy, the court responded that "the Legislature has decided the answer to that particular need by enacting Labor Code section 132a." Although only a handful of courts have adopted the view espoused in *Portillo,* the issue of exclusivity surfaces in other areas of wrongful discharge law.

OCCUPATIONAL SAFETY AND HEALTH. Another vein of public policy cases concerns employees discharged in retaliation for demanding workplace safety and health. The federal Occupational Safety and Health Act of 1970 (OSHA), 29 U.S.C. §654(a), and its numerous counterparts in the various states require in plain terms that the employer assure a safe and healthful workplace. These laws impose civil and criminal penalties for a vast range of unsafe practices and, in most cases, prohibit retaliation against employees who exercise their safety rights. Not surprisingly these rights have also been vindicated in common law wrongful discharge suits.

A unique usage of the public policy favoring workplace safety appears in *Cloutier v. Great Atlantic & Pacific Tea Co.,* 121 N.H. 915, 436 A.2d 1140 (1981), decided by the New Hampshire Supreme Court. In *Cloutier,* a store manager was ostensibly terminated for failing to make a bank deposit of store funds on a Saturday evening. This failure had resulted in a greater loss when the store was burglarized the next evening while plaintiff was off duty. The store was located in a high-crime area, and the evidence showed that the employer had at one time provided police protection to employees making bank deposits, but then stopped the practice for cost reasons. Worried employees were told they could leave deposits in the safe overnight and visit the bank during daylight hours.

The court reasoned that the employer had effectively condoned the plaintiff's failure to make timely deposits. Citing OSHA, the court found the employer breached its duty to provide a safe workplace by requiring bank deposits in a high-crime area without police protection. The court also found an offense to public policy in the employer's act of holding plaintiff responsible for a theft on Sunday, which was guaranteed as his day off under state law.

In a leading case from California, *Hentzel v. The Singer Company,* 138 Cal. App. 3d 290, 188 Cal. Rptr. 159 (1982), *hearing denied,* the Court of Appeal sustained a wrongful discharge complaint by an employee allegedly terminated for having demanded a workplace reasonably free of tobacco smoke. Under the California Labor Code, the court found ample foundation for the individual's public policy claim. The code obligated employers to provide a safe and healthful workplace and prohibited discrimination against employees who lodged complaints or refused work assignments they reasonably believed dangerous.

Taken together these provisions led the court in *Hentzel* to conclude that "an employee is protected against discharge or discrimination for complaining in good faith about working conditions which he reasonably believes to be unsafe, whether or not there exists at the time of the complaint an OSHA standard or order which is being violated." The court alluded as well to the "developing body of law in other jurisdictions which recognizes an obligation on the part of the employer to protect employees from health hazards which may be posed by cigarette smoking."

To uphold the employee's wrongful discharge claim in *Hentzel,* the court had to overcome two arguments based on the idea of preemption. First, the court rejected the claim by allowing employees to file discrimination claims with the responsible California agencies, the legislature had established the exclusive remedy for safety-related retaliation. The court reasoned that California's safety and health laws had merely created new statutory rights designed to supplement, but not supplant, existing common law remedies.

On this point other courts have ruled against employees who raised workplace safety objections but ignored their statutory remedies. In *Schwartz v. Michigan Sugar Co.,* 106 Mich. App. 471, 308 N.W.2d 459 (1981), a safety director who claimed he was terminated because he performed his job too zealously was denied relief in court because he had failed to bring his plight to the attention of responsible state agencies. Similarly, in *Trombetta v. Detroit, Toledo & Ironton Railroad,* 81 Mich. App. 489, 265 N.W.2d 385 (1978), the court denied relief to a truck driver who voiced his concern over a coemployee's alcohol abuse by refusing his work assignment rather than complaining to the state agency.

A second argument that the court in *Hentzel* rejected was that the National Labor Relations Act (NLRA), as amended, also preempted the employee's public policy claim. As explained in Chapter II, the NLRA protects employees who engage in "concerted" activity for their mutual aid and protection concerning wages, hours, and other terms and conditions of employment, including safety. Under traditional preemption rules, conduct "arguably protected" by the act falls within the exclusive jurisdiction of the National Labor Relations Board. In *Hentzel,* however, the court neatly avoided this preemption argument by noting that the employee had acted not in concert, but alone, in combatting workplace tobacco smoke.

Another interesting issue arising in workplace health and safety cases concerns the employee's state of mind. Should employees enjoy public policy protection simply because they subjectively believe that a workplace condition is unsafe? Or should they be required to prove by objective evidence that the condition violates a specific OSHA standard? In *Hentzel,* the court took its cue from pertinent antiretaliation statutes, and phrased the doctrine in terms of "a reasonable belief." While this would not require proof of an actual violation, it does incorporate an objective element, in that the employee must show some reasonable basis for the safety complaints.

Most courts probably would adhere to this "reasonable belief" standard. A purely objective standard would force employees to sacrifice their jobs at the risk that the employer had not actually violated a standard, but a purely subjective standard would be equally undesirable. Employees asserting the most frivolous or imaginary safety concerns would have a claim for wrongful discharge under the latter view. Several cases other than *Hentzel* reflect a preference for the middle ground.

In *Wheeler v. Caterpillar Tractor Co.,* 123 Ill. App. 3d 539, 462 N.E.2d 1262 (1984), the court dismissed the wrongful discharge claim of a laboratory technician who was fired for his complaints about allegedly unsafe x-ray equipment. Although a subsequent investigation by the U.S. Nuclear Regulatory Commission cited technical defects in the employer's safety program, the court found "no hard evidence of unsafe conditions, but rather only plaintiff's unilateral and subjective decision that such conditions did exist."

In a similar vein, an early wrongful discharge decision from Pennsylvania seemed sympathetic to an employee's safety-related complaints, but ultimately found no violation of public policy. In *Geary v. United States Steel Corp.*, 456 Pa. 171, 319 A.2d 174 (1974), a sales representative vociferously protested the proposed marketing of a high pressure steel casing he deemed untested and dangerous. The employee had no responsibility for "independent, expert judgment in matters of product safety," and had bypassed his immediate supervisors with his complaints. The court opined that despite laudable motives, the employee had "made a nuisance of himself" and was rightfully discharged.

The issues in *Hentzel, Geary,* and *Wheeler* can be expected to resurface as new matters of workplace safety come to the forefront. Concern over the handling and disposal of hazardous wastes, for example, has assumed a prominent place in the field of occupational safety, and while new regulatory efforts will continue under existing OSHA schemes, state and local regulations have begun to proliferate. Courts will have to address whether these regulations establish an actionable public policy, and whether any statutory remedies are to be deemed exclusive.

JURY DUTY. Another prime example of public policy claims based on statutory rights involves employees discharged for serving jury duty. In one of the earliest public policy cases, *Nees v. Hocks,* 272 Ore. 210, 536 P.2d 512 (1975), the Oregon Supreme Court broke new ground and allowed a tort suit by an employee discharged for missing work due to jury service. A federal court applying Michigan law more recently ruled in favor of an employee discharged for having been subpoenaed before a grand jury. *Miskotoni v. Michigan National Bank-West,* 716 F.2d 378 (6th Cir. 1983).

An earlier California decision, *Mallard v. Boring,* 182 Cal. App. 2d 390, 6 Cal. Rptr. 171 (1960), as well as a 1980 decision by the Alabama Supreme Court, *Bender Ship Repair, Inc. v. Stevens,* 379 So. 2d 594 (Ala. 1980), had reached the opposite result, but in both states, the legislature thereafter intervened and enacted a specific statute protecting employee-jurors from retaliation. At last count more than two-thirds of states have also passed statutes which either prohibit discrimination against employee on account of jury service or make such conduct a crime or contempt of court. The rule for employers in this area is simple: Do not discipline employees on account of jury service.

LIE DETECTORS AND RELATED TESTS. Cases involving discharge following the refusal to submit to a lie detector or similar test could produce a new wave of public policy cases. At least half of the states have enacted specific statutes either outlawing or severely limiting the use of lie detector tests as a condition of hiring or continued employment. These statutes could provide a firm foundation for wrongful discharge claimants who are denied their statutory prerogative and forced to undergo testing or else forego continued employment.

One federal appellate court decision, *Perks v. Firestone Tire & Rubber Co.*, 611 F.2d 1363 (3d Cir. 1979), reversed a summary judgment against an employee who had refused to submit to a lie detector test after being charged with accepting the services of a prostitute as a bribe from a customer. The court remanded for specific findings on whether the discharge stemmed from the acceptance of the bribe, which would constitute good cause for termination, or from the refusal to take the lie detector test. The court relied on a Pennsylvania statute making it a misdemeanor to require a "polygraph test or any form of a mechanical or electrical lie detector test" as a condition of employment.

Even without a statute, the West Virginia Supreme Court found a public policy violation in the case of an employee who refused to take a lie detector exam, even after signing a written consent to do so voluntarily. *Cordle v. General Hugh Mercer Corp.*, 116 LRRM 3447 (W.Va. Sup. Ct. App. 1984). And in *Jackson v. Kinark Corp.*, 282 Ark. 548, 669 S.W.2d 898 (1984), the Arkansas Supreme Court reversed a summary judgment against an employee discharged for refusing to take a polygraph test in connection with the disappearance of a television set from the hotel where he worked. Though the court did not elaborate, the polygraph refusal will no doubt raise troubling issues.

On the other hand, where the employer conducts its inquiry in conformity with applicable lie detector statutes, the claim of a public policy violation may be misplaced. California, for example, prohibits the mandatory use of lie detectors except in specified circumstances where the employee voluntarily consents after being apprised of the statutory right to refuse. A proper consent by the employee under the statute would comport with the legislative mandate and thus undercut any claim of wrongful discharge based on public policy.

In the absence of a lie detector statute claimants have met with little success. In a notable Arizona case, *Larsen v. Motor Supply Co.*, 117 Ariz. 507, 573 P.2d 907 (1977), the court denied relief to two employees who refused to sign a consent form and submit to a "psychological stress evaluation test." They contended that the form contained several false statements. Noting the absence of any statutory prohibition on the test itself, the court refused to find a public policy violation based solely on the form.

Nonetheless, employers should be wary of relying on polygraph and similar tests. Judging from the recent wave of state statutes on the subject, most of which flatly forbid the use of employee polygraphs, a strong public policy against such devices is in the wind. Legislators apparently recognize that lie detectors are far from infallible, and that the testing procedure itself can be a frightful experience. In cases of theft and dishonesty, the far safer course is to rely on other investigative techniques to document employee misconduct.

FAIR EMPLOYMENT LAWS. One obvious source of employee rights in the workplace would seem to be the wealth of federal and state laws banning employment discrimination on account of race, national origin, sex, age, physical handicap, religion, medical condition, marital status, pregnancy, and other impermissible criteria. By and large, however, when a state or federal equal employment law provides a full remedy for such discrimination, the courts will generally disallow recovery for wrongful discharge based on the same underlying facts. Though these statutory prohibitions unquestionably reflect compelling public policies, they typically also evince a legislative intent to create a comprehensive and exclusive remedial scheme.

In *Strauss v. A.L. Randall Co.*, 144 Cal. App. 3d 514, 194 Cal. Rptr. 520 (1983), for example, the California Court of Appeal rejected a wrongful discharge suit by a 17-year employee who alleged he was discharged because of his age of 55 years. Finding no preexisting common law right to sue for age discrimination, the court held that the plaintiff's sole relief was by way of the administrative complaint and conciliation process outlined in the California Fair Employment and Housing Act. Courts in Illinois, Massachusetts, Ohio, and Pennsylvania reached the identical conclusion respecting their states' age bias laws, and it seems clear the same result would follow in race, sex, national origin, and other types of employment discrimination cases.

Puzzling questions can arise, however, when the remedy customarily provided by applicable fair employment laws is unavailable to a particular claimant for one reason or another. This may be because the employer is not within the statute's jurisdiction, or because the claimant failed to satisfy prerequisites to suit by filing an administrative claim, or because the statute does not provide all of the relief the employee seeks. Title VII of the Civil Rights Act of 1964, for example, does not apply to employers with fewer than 15 employees. State statutes have similar, but lower jurisdictional thresholds. Some states also carve out exceptions for nonprofit employers and religious institutions. In such instances, the statute creating a potential public policy is in force, but the remedy creating the exclusivity bar is out of the picture.

Are these limitations simply matters of administrative convenience, or do they form an integral part of the public policy being expressed? Presumably the legislature exempted small employers simply to ease administrative burdens on state agencies, and not to sanction discrimination by these small firms. On the other hand, legitimate concerns over separation of church and state may have prompted the legislature to conclude that discrimination by churches does not implicate any firm public policy. Such questions will have to await case-by-case resolution.

UNION OR OTHER CONCERTED ACTIVITIES. Similar issues arise in cases where the discharge stems from union activities or other forms of collective organizing. In an early California case, *Glenn v. Clearman's Golden Cock Inn*, 192 Cal. App. 2d 793, 13 Cal. Rptr. 769 (1961), *hearing denied,* the Court of Appeal allowed a wrongful discharge action by several employees who were terminated after they applied for membership in the culinary workers union. The court found a public policy protecting union activities in Labor Code section 923, which makes it a misdemeanor to coerce any person not to join a union as a condition of employment.

The *Glenn* decision, however, is somewhat of an oddity, for the conduct involved in that case would customarily fall within the exclusive jurisdiction of the National Labor Relations Board. The *Glenn* decision failed to address the preemption issue. Though state right-to-work laws might be a likely candidate for a public policy theory, few reported cases deal with the subject, since these claims are brought before the National Labor Relations Board as unfair labor practice charges.

Section 7 of the NLRA guarantees the right of all workers to engage in "concerted activities for the purpose of collective bargaining or other mutual aid or protection." With or without a union involved, employees who act in concert to protest wages, hours, or other terms and conditions of employment would enjoy the protection of section 7. More importantly, they would fall under the exclusive jurisdiction of the National Labor Relations Board. Does this mean that employees who are discharged for engaging in "concerted activity" are relegated to the National Labor Relations Board and are barred from filing wrongful discharge suits?

For example, in the case of *Hentzel v. The Singer Co., Supra,* which involved an employee who was discharged for complaining about unsafe working conditions, the court was careful to note in passing that the plaintiff had acted alone. If he had been acting "in concert" with other employees, however, the court might have been constrained to find his wrongful discharge claims preempted by section 7, and thus deferred to the exclusive province of the National Labor Relations Board. The same issue could arise in any case where the discharge stems from the employee's participation in concerted activity over wages, hours, or other terms and conditions of employment.

PUBLIC POLICY SUITS BY UNION EMPLOYEES. The same concern for the primacy of federal labor law is intensified when an employee who is covered by a collective bargaining agreement seeks recovery for wrongful discharge. Although union employees may have standing to sue for breach of the labor agreement, the doctrine of preemption again requires that all such suits be governed by federal law exclusively. Pendent claims under state tort law are allowed only when their subject matter is peripheral to federal labor law and deeply rooted in local interests. Does this mean that a union employee cannot sue for wrongful discharge? The answer depends on the nature of the employee's suit.

In *Garibaldi v. Lucky Food Stores, Inc.,* 726 F.2d 1367 (9th Cir. 1984), the Ninth Circuit Court of Appeals allowed a union employee covered by a collective bargaining agreement to bring a suit for wrongful discharge. The employee claimed that he had refused to deliver a shipment of spoiled milk, which would have violated the California Agricultural Code, but instead notified local health authorities. Although the employee was protected by a labor agreement requiring just cause for discharge, and even though he had actually lost in a contractual arbitration, the court refused to find that his suit was preempted.

In the court's view, the "public policy" theory of wrongful discharge was designed to serve the state's interest in protecting any citizen who resists unlawful conduct, and was not concerned with the subject of job security per se, which federal law leaves to collective bargaining between labor and management. Thus finding no conflict between state interests and the federal labor laws, the court rejected the claim of section 301 preemption.

Complementing *Garibaldi* is the recent ruling of the Illinois Supreme Court in *Midgett v. Sackett-Chicago, Inc.*, 105 Ill. 2d 143 (1984), in which the court allowed a union employee to bring a public policy suit based on retaliation for having filed a workers' compensation claim. The Illinois court soundly rejected the employer's claim that the requirement of just cause and the existence of a grievance/arbitration provision in the employee's collective bargaining agreement provided a plenary remedy for such a vengeful discharge. The court openly stressed that relief under the labor agreement would not include punitive damages, which are central to the remedial objectives of the public policy exception.

On the other hand, in *Buscemi v. McDonnell Douglas Corp.*, 736 F.2d 1348 (9th Cir. 1984), and *Olquin v. Inspiration Consolidated Copper Co.*, 740 F.2d 1468 (9th Cir. 1984), the ninth circuit sustained the preemption defense where union employees brought suit for wrongful discharge based not on public policy, but on implied in fact contracts and the implied covenant of good faith and fair dealing, both of which are discussed later. In these cases the court recognized that allowing suit under state contract theories would directly subvert the federal interest in leaving job security to the collective bargaining process.

Later cases will require the courts to refine the contours of a union employee's right to sue for wrongful discharge. As *Garibaldi* and *Buscemi* reflect, the courts seem willing to allow such suits where necessary to redress clear public policy violations, but not where employees invoke implied contract theories in an effort to create job security. In the latter instance, the potential for conflict with the federal scheme of collective bargaining should lead the courts to find state law preempted.

PENSION AND EMPLOYEE BENEFIT RIGHTS. Yet another area where specific legislation may override state law wrongful discharge claims is in the area of pension rights. The Employee Retirement Income Security Act of 1974 (ERISA), as amended, sets forth a comprehensive federal scheme for regulating retirement and other employee benefit plans. State regulation of the same plans is explicitly preempted. Also ERISA prohibits an employer from discriminating against employees for the purpose of preventing them from attaining or exercising their rights under a benefit plan. In a leading decision from California, *Johnson v. Trans World Airlines, Inc.*, 149 Cal. App. 3d 518, 196 Cal. Rptr. 896 (1983), the Court of Appeal held that ERISA preempts any state law action for wrongful discharge flowing from the denial of pension rights covered by ERISA.

Other courts have also rejected public policy claims based on the matter of employee benefit plans. In *Price v. Carmack Datsun, Inc.*, 124 Ill. App. 3d 979, 464 N.E.2d 1245 (1984), the court found no public policy in support of an employee terminated for submitting a claim under the employer's group health insurance plan. In an earlier case, *Moore v. Home Insurance Co.*, 601 F.2d 1072 (9th Cir. 1979), the court rejected a claim under Arizona public policy where an employee was allegedly terminated to prevent his pension rights from vesting. Nonetheless, employers must realize that while state law is preempted, ERISA will provide a federal cause of action for employees who are discharged to prevent them from exercising their rights under employee benefit plans.

RIGHT TO SUE EMPLOYER. A handful of courts have addressed the question of whether public policy precludes the discharge of an employee who threatens or brings a lawsuit against the employer for reasons other than those forbidden by the cases discussed previously. Concerned with protecting citizen access to the courts, some courts have allowed the employee to recover in such circumstances. One such case was *Smith v. Atlas Off-Shore Boat Service, Inc.,* 653 F.2d 1057 (5th Cir. 1981), decided under maritime law. In *Smith,* an employee was allowed to recover for wrongful discharge when he was fired after informing his employer that he intended to sue for an injury suffered while he was on board ship. Analogizing to the workers' compensation cases discussed previously, the court refused to countenance a discharge designed to "intimidate the seaman from seeking legal redress."

Similar reasoning prevailed in a recent California decision, *Khanna v. Microdata Corp.,* 170 Cal. App. 3d 250, 215 Cal. Rptr. 816 (1985). In *Khanna,* a sales representative was terminated on the grounds that a lawsuit he had brought against the employer for unpaid commissions was "totally unfounded" and tantamount to "disloyalty." At trial, however, the employee presented evidence that the employer did not actually believe there was no merit to the lawsuit, and did not truly consider the suit to create a conflict of interest. Basing its decision on the implied covenant of good faith and fair dealing, which is discussed further in following sections of this chapter, the court of appeal held that the jury was entitled to decide whether the employee's lawsuit genuinely interfered with the employee's ability to do his job, or instead was an act of "bad faith retaliation" for having brought the suit at all.

Several courts, however, have ruled to the contrary, particularly when the employee works in a supervisory or managerial capacity. In *Meredith v. C.E. Walther, Inc.,* 422 So. 2d 761 (Ala. 1982), the Alabama Supreme Court flatly refused to find a public policy exception favoring an employee who was party to a lawsuit against his employer concerning the latter's handling of an employee benefit trust. Also in *Becket v. Welton Becket & Associates, Inc.,* 39 Cal. App. 3d 815, 114 Cal. Rptr. 531 (1974), *hearing denied,* the California Court of Appeal declined to find a public policy protecting an employee-stockholder who sued his employer and its board of directors for various acts of corporate misconduct.

A thoughtful analysis of the right to sue the employer appears in *Kavanaugh v. KLM Royal Dutch Airlines,* 566 F. Supp. 242 (N.D. Ill. 1983). In that case, a federal trial court summarily dismissed the claim of a management employee who threatened to sue his employer over an on-going pay dispute. The court observed that the pendency of litigation between employer and employee, especially at the management level, would necessarily undermine the required atmosphere of trust and cooperation. Beyond that a contrary ruling would allow employees to create self-protection simply by threatening suit, and "would penalize a company for discharging an at-will employee when the employment relationship has completely soured."

Apart from the case law, many statutes protect employees who become involved in litigation with their employers. Any employee who threatens to sue the employer for violating the wage and hour laws or other labor legislation would probably find protection under those laws themselves, if not in the state's public policy. In a unique ruling, *Montalvo v. Zamora*, 7 Cal. App. 3d 69, 86 Cal. Rptr. 401 (1970), the court found a public policy based on a state statute protecting organizing rights when two employees were fired after they designated an attorney to represent them in negotiations with the employer. Cases like *Zamora*, or any other in which groups of employees threaten to sue as part of *concerted* activity concerning wages and hours, could also be brought as unfair labor practice charges before the National Labor Relations Board.

Beyond that, the courts will allow recovery where an employee threatens or brings a lawsuit in the context of invoking some other public policy that has found protection in wrongful discharge law. For example, an executive who refuses to engage in illegal price fixing and threatens to sue the employer under the antitrust laws will have a valid claim because of the public interest in antitrust enforcement rather than simply the threat to sue. Thus, the cases discussed previously apply most clearly where the employee's threat to sue arises from a personal matter and does not implicate specific legislation governing employment.

FREE SPEECH, PRIVACY, AND OTHER CONSTITUTIONAL RIGHTS. Employees may also seek refuge in state and federal constitutional provisions as the courts expand on the notion of public policy. In one of the potentially most far-reaching public policy cases to date, *Novosel v. Nationwide Insurance Co.*, 721 F.2d 894 (3d Cir. 1983), the Third Circuit Court of Appeals allowed a wrongful discharge claim under Pennsylvania law by a district claims manager who was terminated for refusing to follow in his employer's orders to lobby in support of no-fault insurance legislation. Although the employer, as a private firm, would not be subject to the First Amendment, the appellate court concluded that "an important public policy is in fact implicated whenever the power to hire and fire is utilized to dictate the terms of employee political activities."

Whether other courts will so readily apply constitutional limitations on all private employers remains in doubt. In *Harmon v. La Crosse Tribune*, 117 Wisc. 2d 448, 344 N.W. 2d 536 (1984), for example, the court rejected the wrongful discharge claim of an attorney fired from his law firm after he issued a press release that accused a newspaper, a client of the firm, of printing falsehoods. The court noted that the attorney himself had breached an ethical duty of loyalty to the firm. And in *Redgrave v. Boston Symphony Orchestra*, 557 F. Supp. 230 (D. Mass. 1983), actress Vanessa Redgrave failed to persuade a federal court that the cancellation of her orchestra appearances because of her support for the Palestine Liberation Organization constituted a wrongful discharge. The court pointed out that Redgrave was only a short-term employee hired under a formal negotiated agreement.

The constitutional right to privacy, which is discussed in depth in Chapter 5, may come into play in wrongful discharge cases. In *Cort. v. Bristol-Meyers Co.*, 385 Mass. 300, 431 N.E.2d 908 (1982), two employees ostensibly discharged for poor performance, alleged that their terminations actually stemmed from their refusal to answer what they considered offensive personal questions on a personnel form. Although the court ultimately rejected the claim because the questions were relatively harmless, the opinion recognized a public policy arising from a Massachusetts statute banning "unreasonable, substantial, or serious interference" with any person's privacy.

While it remains to be seen whether other courts will go as far as Massachusetts, particularly in the absence of a privacy statute, there is another theory of wrongful discharge that could come to the forefront in such cases: the implied covenant of good faith and fair dealing. Two California cases have involved the implied covenant in the context of employer that touch upon employees' private lives. In *Crosier v. United Parcel Service, Inc.*, 150 Cal. App. 3d 1132, 178 Cal. Rptr. 361 (1983), the court rejected the bad faith claim of a senior manager discharged for fraternizing with an hourly employee, but in *Rulon-Miller v. International Business Machines Corp.*, 162 Cal. App. 3d 241, 208 Cal. Rptr. 524 (1984), the court upheld an implied covenant claim where the employer had discriminatorily applied its rule against employees dating competitors.

OTHER EXAMPLES OF PUBLIC POLICY. Other examples of wrongful discharge based on the exercise of employee rights are potentially as numerous as the wealth of state and federal laws safeguarding some interest of labor. We have noted the laws protecting employees who file workers' compensation claims, protest unsafe working conditions, or perform jury service, and we have seen how the courts gleaned a protected public policy from these expressions of legislative will. The same process could be applied to virtually any statute creating substantive rights in the workplace.

Examples of such provisions would include laws safeguarding employees who miss work in order to vote or to serve as election officers. Members of the National Guard, and veterans of the World War II and Vietnam eras enjoy special employment privileges by statute in some jurisdictions. Employees have a statutory right in many states to demand access to their personnel files, medical records, and safety reports, and to prevent their disclosure to unauthorized persons. Some states have even enacted laws protecting persons who participate in alcohol or drug rehabilitation programs, or who refuse to divulge their arrest records. In a few states, legislative protection has been afforded to employees who refuse to perform abortions. Lastly, employees who have their wages garnished are protected in a majority of states as they are under federal law, while a few jurisdictions have given similar protection to employees who file for bankruptcy. Each of these statutes raises the spectre of a public policy wrongful discharge suit.

As new cases arise under these statutes and other theories, the courts will continue to confront two major questions: (1) Has the plaintiff articulated some fundamental public policy deserving of judicial recognition? and (2) Has the legislature provided some exclusive statutory remedy for aggrieved employees? As we have seen, both these issues create ample opportunities for judicial creativity.

The Whistleblower Cases

The term "whistleblowing" aptly describes a third subcategory of wrongful discharge cases predicated on public policy. Roughly stated, these are cases of employees who are discharged in retaliation for attempting to publicize, internally or publicly, what they believe are illegal practices at the workplace. Instead of merely refusing to do the deed, the whistleblower threatens to go over a superior's head, or even "go public."

Whistleblowing has generated fewer decisions than our first two categories of public policy, but in a sense it represents the new frontier in wrongful discharge. Whistleblower statutes have been enacted in more than a dozen states, and the Civil Service Reform Act contains such a provision for federal employees. A few of the state statutes are restricted to public employees, or to specific types of violations, and some provide specific civil or criminal penalties without explicitly prohibiting discharge.

The significance of a whistleblower statute is that it supplies the vital legislative link between an employee's protests and the public policy implicated in the misconduct the employee seeks to publicize. In a sense a whistleblower statute injects the public policy into the very act of publicizing any apparent violation of law. For example, even if an employee was never asked to commit perjury, a whistleblower statute would afford protection if the employee sought to publicize perjury by other employees. Regrettably, whistleblower statutes are also susceptible to abuse. A marginal employee may commence a campaign of whistleblowing simply to create new "rights" to job security.

One of the first whistleblower cases provided the occasion for the Supreme Court of West Virginia to recognize the basic tort of wrongful discharge. In *Harless v. First National Bank of Fairmont*, 246 S.E.2d 270 (W. Va. 1978), the plaintiff alleged that he had been discharged in retaliation for having alerted his superiors as well as an outside auditor that his employer was violating state and federal consumer credit statutes. The court ruled that the clear public policy expressed in consumer credit regulation would be undermined if plaintiff were subject to discharge for his efforts at assuring compliance.

Other employees who sought to expose illegal or corrupt financial and management practices have also been vindicated in wrongful discharge suits. In *Petrik v. Monarch Printing Corp.*, 111 Ill. App. 3d 502, 444 N.E.2d 588 (1982), an Illinois appellate court sided with a corporate vice president who was fired after he had reported to the company president with evidence suggesting criminal embezzlement by fellow members of management. The court specifically rejected the trial court's ruling that the discharge was not actionable because the plaintiff had never gone public with his discovery. In *Adler v. American Standard Corp.*, 538 F. Supp. 572 (D. Md. 1982), a federal court in Maryland upheld the complaint of a high level executive who advised his superiors of numerous instances of bribery, falsification, and tax fraud. The executive alleged that he had threatened to disclose his findings to top management but was fired before he could do so.

One of the broadest pronouncements in favor of whistleblowers came in *Palmateer v. International Harvester Co.*, 85 Ill. 2d 124, 421 N.E.2d 876

(1981). Palmateer alleged that he was terminated for supplying information to local law enforcement officials regarding an undisclosed criminal act by a coemployee, and for agreeing to assist further in the investigation and any trial. The Illinois Supreme Court, relying simply on the state's interest in enforcing its criminal code, remanded the case for trial. Without citing a specific statute, the court concluded that "public policy nevertheless favors citizen crime-fighters."

Other corporate dissidents have been unsuccessful when they failed to expose actual criminal conduct. In *Suchodolski v. Michigan Consolidated Gas Co.*, 412 Mich. 692, 316 N.W.2d 710 (1982), a senior auditor at a public utility alleged he was discharged for reporting questionable accounting and management practices to his superiors. The Michigan Supreme Court rejected his public policy claim, finding that the state's regulation of accounting practices was not intended to confer employee rights, and that plaintiff in any event had failed to show actual illegal conduct.

Other cases involving public disclosure of unsafe products, impure food and drugs, or unethical medical practices have also yielded mixed results. In *Geary v. United States Steel Corp.*, 456 Pa. 171, 319 A.2d 174 (1974), the Pennsylvania Supreme Court rejected the claims of a sales representative who zealously protested the proposed marketing of a steel casing he deemed untested and dangerous. The employee had no independent judgment over safety matters as part of his job duties, and had departed from established reporting channels in publicizing his concerns. A similar result prevailed in *Wheeler v. Caterpillar Tractor Co.*, 123 Ill. App. 3d 539, 462 N.E. 1262 (1984), in which the court found no basis for the allegedly unsafe x-ray equipment about which the plaintiff had strenuously protested.

On the other hand, in *Sheets v. Teddy's Frosted Foods, Inc.*, 179 Conn. 471, 427 A.2d 385 (1980), the Supreme Court of Connecticut ruled in favor of a quality control director at a food processing plant who was discharged for communicating to his superiors his determination that the employer was violating state food processing and labeling laws. Without requiring actual proof that the statute had been violated, the court found a cognizable public policy. Similarly, in *Witt v. Forest Hospital, Inc.*, 115 Ill. App. 3d 481, 450 N.E.2d 811 (1983), the court ruled in favor of a nurse who had gone to a state commission with complaints about the employer's care of mentally ill patients. The court was aided by a statute designed to assure access to the commission by preventing reprisal against reporting employees.

New whistleblower statutes will undoubtedly produce new case law decisions. Recently enacted California Labor Code section 1102.5 prohibits an employer from discriminating against any employee for "disclosing information to a government or law enforcement agency, where the employee has reasonable cause to believe that the information discloses a violation of state or federal statute, or violation or noncompliance with a state or federal regulation." This statute is limited to employees who "go public," but it adopts a "reasonable belief" standard and thus would not require the employee to prove an actual violation of law.

The "reasonable belief" standard will also serve as the dividing line between legitimate whistleblowing, and conduct which amounts to harassment or insubordination. While an employee should not lose protection simply because a good faith complaint proves unfounded, the courts will have to sift out bad faith or frivolous claimants as lacking a "reasonable belief." These and other issues will require resolution on a case by case basis.

THE IMPLIED COVENANT OF GOOD FAITH AND FAIR DEALING

Apart from the public policy theory, a number of decisions have allowed at-will employees to recover for wrongful discharge based on what is called the implied covenant of good faith and fair dealing. This tacit promise to refrain from arbitrary conduct, which is said to arise by law in every contract, represents the most amorphous and thus most volatile theory of wrongful discharge liability. A few courts have used the implied covenant of good faith not only to redress arbitrary or malicious conduct, but also to create a general requirement of good cause for termination in situations where the at-will doctrine traditionally applied.

The implied covenant of good faith and fair dealing is implied in law, which is to say it does not depend for its existence on any agreement or conduct by the parties, nor can it be waived. And while its use in wrongful discharge cases is a fairly recent development, the implied covenant is well-known to the law. One can find decisions from the 1930s which purport to recognize the covenant in the employment context, and the Uniform Commercial Code adopted in virtually all the states long ago established the covenant in all contracts for the sale of goods.

It was in the insurance context, however, that the implied covenant came to fruition as an independent basis for recovery in both contract and tort. The courts invoke the implied covenant to impose liability on insurors who arbitrarily or in bad faith refuse to defend an insured or to accept a reasonable settlement within policy limits and thereby expose the insured to excessive liability. Although nothing in the insurance policy itself actually requires the insuror to refrain from such conduct, the courts find such an obligation arising by law via the implied covenant. A similar sort of judicial creativity has recently surfaced in the wrongful discharge context.

Two of the earliest wrongful discharge cases were predicated primarily on the implied covenant of good faith and fair dealing. In *Monge v. Beebe Rubber Co.,* 114 N.H. 130, 316 A.2d 549 (1974), the Supreme Court of New Hampshire allowed recovery by an at-will production employee who alleged that she was terminated maliciously by her supervisor after she had resisted his romantic overtures. In a potentially sweeping doctrinal innovation, the court held that the termination of an at-will employee which is "motivated by bad faith or malice or based on retaliation" constitutes a breach of contract. The court required no proof of a specific public policy.

Although *Monge* could have been brought under the fair employment laws prohibiting sexual harassment, the decision typifies how the implied covenant can support recovery based on seemingly vague notions of "bad faith" or "malice" on the employer's part. And while New Hampshire has retreated from an expansive reading of *Monge,* other courts have echoed its basic theme in expanding the covenant to require good cause in some instances, and in allowing recovery of tort as well as contract damages.

In *Fortune v. National Cash Register Co.,* 373 Mass. 96, 364 N.E.2d 1251 (1977), the Massachusetts Supreme Court dealt with a commissioned salesrepresentative whose written employment contract explicitly provided that he could be terminated at will. In sustaining the employee's claim that he was terminated in bad faith in order to avoid the payment of commissions he had substantially earned, the court invoked the implied covenant and ruled that the employer's express right to terminate at will was tempered by an implied in law obligation to deal in good faith. Although most subsequent courts have insisted that the implied covenant cannot be invoked to contradict the express terms of a negotiated contract, *Fortune* stands as a monument to judicial creativity in redressing perceived abuses by employers.

Fortune and *Monge* have been cited in countless cases, but their expansive use of the implied covenant has not enjoyed universal acceptance. A few states have permitted recovery based solely on "malice" or a "specific intent to harm," but the doctrinal basis for these decisions strikes most courts as too unprincipled for general application. Many other courts, while acknowledging its existence, have steadfastly refused to hold that the covenant alone creates a duty to discharge only for good cause.

The Supreme Court of Wisconsin held that imposing a general duty to discharge only in good faith would "unduly restrict an employer's discretion in managing the work force." *Brockmeyer v. Dunn & Bradstreet,* 113 Wis. 2d 561, 335 N.W.2d 834 (1983). Similarly, the Supreme Court of Hawaii concluded that "to imply into each employment contract a duty to terminate in good faith would seem to subject each discharge to judicial incursions into the amorphous concept of bad faith." *Parner v. Americana Hotels, Inc.,* 652 P.2d 625, 629 (Hawaii 1982). And the Court of Appeals of Arizona has criticized the *Monge* decision for "rewriting the employment contract" and judicially imposing "a substitute for a union collective bargaining agreement." *Daniel v. Magma Copper Co.,* 127 Ariz. 320, 620 P.2d 699 (1980).

Other states, however, have greatly expanded the use of the implied covenant. In the seminal California decision, *Clearly v. American Airlines, Inc.,* 111 Cal. App. 3d 443, 168 Cal. Rptr. 722 (1980), the court of appeal allowed recovery in tort based on the implied covenant by an 18-year airline employee who allegedly was fired unjustly on charges of theft, absence from work area, and threatening a fellow employee. The plaintiff pleaded that he had been denied the benefit of the employer's internal grievance procedures, which provided for an impartial hearing and independent review prior to discipline.

The court in *Cleary* reasoned that these internal procedures evinced the employer's recognition of its duty to "engage in good faith and fair dealing rather than in arbitrary conduct." Stressing the employee's history of satisfactory of service, the court ruled that substantial seniority, when coupled with the breach of "specific procedures for ajudicating employee disputes," operated as a form of estoppel that precluded any discharge "without good cause." Moreover, the court in *Cleary* pronounced that such a breach of the implied covenant would expose the employer to tort liability for actual and punitive damages.

A few subsequent decisions in California and elsewhere have picked up on this notion that substantial seniority combined with the employer's failure to abide by its internal policies can give rise to a tort action for breach of the implied covenant. In *Shapiro v. Wells Fargo Realty Advisors,* 152 Cal. App. 3d 467, 199 Cal. Rptr. 613 (1984), *hearing denied,* the Court of Appeal cited *Cleary* but rejected an implied covenant claim by a employee with three and half years seniority whose discharge allegedly stemmed from a desire to avoid paying him optimal benefits. The court deemed the employee's seniority insubstantial under *Cleary,* and also found no competent allegations that the employer had breached specific internal policies.

Without citing *Cleary,* the Supreme Court of Montana has adopted its basic reasoning. In *Gates v. Life of Montana Ins. Co.,* 638 P.2d 1063 (Mont. 1982), the court reversed a summary judgment for the employer and ordered that an employee's implied covenant claim be submitted to the jury. The plaintiff alleged that she was coerced into resigning for no good cause, and then further deceived by the employer when she sought to revoke her resignation. On a subsequent appeal, *Gates v. Life of Montana Ins. Co.,* 668 P.2d 213 (Mont. 1983), the court affirmed an award of compensatory and punitive damages, finding tort recovery appropriate under the implied covenant where the employer fails to follow its own internal disciplinary policies.

Still other California decisions seemed to have carried the implied covenant theory beyond the factual confines of cases like *Cleary* and *Gates.* In *Cancellier v. Federated Department Stores,* 672 F.2d 1312 (9th Cir. 1982), *cert. denied,* 103 S. Ct. 181 (1982), the Ninth Circuit Court of Appeals, applying California law, upheld an award of actual and punitive damages to a group of senior retail executives who were terminated on account of age and treated arbitrarily in breach of internal personnel policies. The plaintiffs in *Cancellier* had seniority ranging from 17 to 25 years.

In *Maddaloni v. Western Massachusetts Bus Lines, Inc.,* 386 Mass. 877, 438 N.E.2d 351 (1982), the Massachusetts Supreme Court followed *Fortune* and allowed recovery under the implied covenant by an employee under an incentive contract who was discharged to prevent him from receiving contractual commissions. The Supreme Court of Alaska reached the same result in *Mitford v. de Lasala,* 666 P.2d 1000 (Alaska 1983), even though the contract explicitly provided for discharge upon three months notice. In both cases, the courts found bad faith inherent in the employer's heavy-handed attempts to avoid contractual obligations.

The implied covenant took another step forward in *Rulon-Miller v. International Business Machines Corp.,* 162 Cal. App. 3d 241, 208 Cal. Rptr. 524 (1984) *hearing denied.* Rulon-Miller was terminated from her position as a marketing representative for office equipment due to her romantic relationship with an employee of one of IBM's competitors. In upholding a jury verdict for actual and punitive damages, the Court of Appeal relied heavily on an internal policy statement by IBM's chairman which drew a line between employee's personal and professional lives, and purported to allow discipline only when outside relations jeopardized on-the-job performance.

Conceding that IBM's policies preserved its right to terminate employee for conflicts of interest, the court seemed to suggest that IBM had condoned Rulon-Miller's activity, and had breached the implied covenant by applying its policies inconsistently. "The duty of fair dealing by an employer," said the court, "is, simply stated, a requirement that like cases be treated alike." While IBM could exercise the right to prohibit conflicts of interest as enumerated in its policies, the company was also obliged to assure employees of any benefits or protections that those policies bestow. On the evidence, the court found that the jury properly considered whether Rulon-Miller had actually violated the IBM policy on personal and professional relationships.

The ruling in *Rulon-Miller* provided an interesting contrast to the earlier Court of Appeal decision in *Crosier v. United Parcel Service, Inc.*, 150 Cal. App. 3d 1132, 178 Cal. Rptr. 361 (1983), in which the employer prevailed. *Crosier* dealt with a management employee who was discharged after refusing to sever his romantic relationship with a subordinate, nonmanagement employee. The court acknowledged the duty to act in good faith, but found that the employer's actions fairly served the legitimate interest in avoiding claims of sexual harassment and favoritism.

In one of the most recent California decisions involving the implied covenant of good faith and fair dealing, *Khanna v. Microdata Corp.*, 170 Cal. App. 3d 250, 215 Cal. Rptr. 816 (1985), the court of appeal carried the analysis one step further. The employee in *Khanna* had been terminated on the grounds that a lawsuit he brought against his employer for unpaid commissions was "totally unfounded" and tantamount to "disloyalty." The jury found, however, that the employer did not honestly believe that the employee's lawsuit was baseless or that it prevented him from faithfully performing his job.

The court of appeal affirmed the jury's verdict. Taking a fairly expansive view of the implied covenant of good faith and fair dealing, the court found it proper to let the jury decide whether the termination was actually based on genuine "dissatisfaction with services" or instead was a "bad faith action, extraneous to the contract." In *Khanna*, the jury decided that the employee had been wrongfully terminated in bad faith and in retaliation for having brought a bona fide lawsuit. Even without showing substantial seniority or the breach of internal policies, the employee in *Khanna* was entitled to have the jury review the employer's decision making.

It is difficult to predict where the implied covenant theory will go in California and elsewhere. Many courts seem reluctant to engraft a "good cause" requirement in every employment contract based solely on the implied covenant. If nothing else, judges do not want to review every personnel action as if they were a civil service commission. Some courts are also wary of the unfairness and inefficiency that unlimited punitive damages can spawn. Fear of massive jury verdicts might deter employers from discharging marginal employees, which thus engenders inefficiency.

On the other hand the courts reiterate time and again that the implied covenant arises in every contract, including those for employment. While the public policy exception is clearly ascendant, new factual patterns will arise where the employer's conduct was particularly reprehensible but not exactly a violation of public policy. In such instances, the courts might find the implied covenant to be the perfect vehicle for filling the voids in the public policy exception. As for the specter of excessive liability, some courts may rule, as a few already have, that breach of the implied covenant sounds only in contract and thus will not allow punitive damages.

CONTRACTUAL EXCEPTIONS TO THE AT-WILL DOCTRINE

A third category of wrongful discharge cases involves not so much a new exception to the at-will doctrine as a rethinking of the doctrine's analytical underpinnings. Without relying on public policy or implied-in-law covenants, courts have found contractual limitations on the right to discharge arising either expressly from the parties' agreement or impliedly from their overall course of conduct. Some cases in this vein are not "exceptions" to the at-will doctrine at all, but are based on orthodox principles of contract law that have been updated to reflect modern times. By these contractual means, the courts have managed to temper the at-will doctrine.

EXPRESS OR IMPLIED CONTRACTUAL LIMITATIONS ON THE RIGHT TO TERMINATE AT-WILL EMPLOYMENT. The pivotal condition triggering the at-will doctrine is that the parties have manifested no agreement as to the duration of employment. An often unspoken corollary is that even if the parties reach no agreement on the duration of service, they still can agree, expressly or impliedly, that the employment shall not be terminable at will. Some recent decisions have made it easier to prove such contractual commitments by relaxing or removing traditional elements of the burden of proof. While these cases are hardly the break from precedent that the public policy exception represents, they open the door to a new theory of wrongful discharge.

The question whether an implied agreement overrides the at-will doctrine crops up in cases where the employee is assured of continued employment "as long as your work is satisfactory" or "as long as you are doing your job." More recently, it has arisen in the context of implied assurances based on the overall conduct of the parties, or on the language of an employee handbook or personnel manual, a subject dealt with in Chapter 4. The issue has occasionally been joined in regard to offers of "permanent" employment or "employment for life," but traditionally such language is deemed only to create an at-will relationship.

THE RULE OF INDEPENDENT CONSIDERATION. The principal obstacle at common law to proving a contractual agreement not to terminate at will is the much debated rule of "independent consideration." A basic idea of contract law is that a promise is generally not enforceable unless the promisee gives some form of "consideration" in exchange, either by incurring some detriment or conferring a benefit on the promisor. An adjunct to this concept is that the value of the exchange is left to market forces. The courts, it is said, "will not inquire into the adequacy of consideration."

Traditionally the courts have refused to enforce promises not to discharge at will unless the employee provides some "independent consideration." It was not enough that the employee agreed to perform services, or to give up an existing job in exchange for the new employment. Even moving from out of state, enduring a longer commute, or agreeing to longer hours were typically deemed insufficient to overcome the at-will rule. Courts instead required proof that the employee sold a business, contributed trade secrets or patents, or bestowed some other substantial benefit on the employer. For reasons as dubious as those behind the at-will doctrine itself, early courts balked at the notion of obligating an employer to retain an employee who was free to quit at any time.

In modern decisions, however, the courts have begun to reverse this trend by liberally construing the "independent consideration" requirement or by discarding it altogether. More and more courts have recognized that the rule is contrary to the principle that the courts will not inquire into the adequacy of consideration. The emerging view is that an employee's promise to perform services will alone support an employer's express or implied promise not to discharge at will.

For example, in *Drzewiecki v. H&R Block, Inc.,* 24 Cal. App. 3d 695, 101 Cal. Rptr. 169 (1972), the California Court of Appeal dealt with the case of a branch manager for a national tax service who entered into a written employment contract which specifically limited the termination of his employment to instances where he "improperly conducted the business." The court soundly rejected the employer's claim that this contract was nonetheless terminable at will because of the lack of independent consideration. In the court's view, when the parties clearly state their intention to restrict at-will terminations, their agreement is enforceable based simply on the employee's commitment to provide services.

Whereas *Drzewiecki* rejected the independent consideration rule in the context of an express promise not to discharge at will, a subsequent California decision applied the same analysis to *implied* contracts of lasting employment. In *Pugh v. See's Candies, Inc.,* 116 Cal. App. 3d 311, 171 Cal. Rptr. 917 (1981), the Court of Appeal reversed a nonsuit granted the employer following a jury trial on the wrongful discharge claims of a managerial employee with 32 years seniority who was discharged without any apparent good cause. The employee in *Pugh* asserted that his discharge violated public policy in that it stemmed from his refusal to negotiate a labor contract on behalf of his employer which contained provisions that allegedly violated the antitrust, sex discrimination, and corporate responsibility laws. The court rejected these public policy claims as lacking in proof. Moreover, the court in *Pugh* declined to uphold the employee's claims based on the implied covenant of good faith and fair dealing, notwithstanding his length service, although the court did speak approvingly of that doctrine.

What the court did in *Pugh* was reject the requirement of "independent consideration" and allow the employee to prove an implied agreement not to terminate at will. Echoing a notion that thrived in nineteenth century British law long before the advent of the at-will doctrine, the court in *Pugh* invited proof of an implied contract based on the totality of the circumstances. The court suggested that an implied promise not to terminate at will could be inferred from the employee's length of service, commendations, promotions, raises, favorable performance reviews, lack of criticism, express or implied assurances of continued employment, the employer's past practices and policies, employee handbooks and personnel manuals, the custom in the industry, as well as "independent consideration." The court emphasized that this last element was simply one bit of evidence, and not a formal requirement of proof.

Other courts have also rejected the doctrine of independent consideration. In *Toussaint v. Blue Cross & Blue Shield of Michigan*, 408 Mich. 579, 292 N.W.2d 880 (1980), a leading case on the enforceability of employee handbooks, the Michigan Supreme Court held that an implied promise of job security was not dependent on proof that the employee gave consideration other than the mere agreement to perform services. As in *Pugh*, the court in *Toussaint* relegated the rule of independent consideration to an evidentiary function: If the employee did provide something more than a commitment to render services, this was evidence of "for cause" employment, but not a required element of proof.

Even New York, the leading state to reject the public policy doctrine, has looked favorably on implied promises of job security and abandoned any requirement of independent consideration. In *Weiner v. McGraw-Hill, Inc.*, 57 N.Y.2d 458, 457 N.Y. Supp. 193 (1982), the court found that implied promises in an employee handbook coupled with oral assurances of job security took the employment outside the at-will doctrine. The court concurred that the employee's agreement to perform services was sufficient consideration for all of the employer's promises, express and implied.

Similarly, in *Pine River State Bank v. Mettille*, 333 N.W.2d 622 (Minn. 1983), the Minnesota Supreme Court repudiated the independent consideration doctrine altogether. The court held that the employee's continued services supported implied promises of job security contained in a handbook circulated *after* the employee had been hired. The court condemned the independent consideration rule as a "forbidden inquiry into the adequacy of consideration."

Cases such as *Pugh, Toussaint, Weiner,* and *Pine River* remove the principal barrier to recovery on implied in fact contracts to terminate only for cause. Moreover, these decisions—*Pugh* in particular—suggest that any employee with substantial seniority and an accomplished work record could prove an implied promise not to terminate at will. They also underscore the importance of employment interviews, performance reviews, and personnel policies written and unwritten. Because the underlying theory sounds in contract, and thus would not support a claim for punitive damages, it will have greater appeal to courts concerned about excessive liability. Indeed it is already the case in many jurisdictions that wrongful discharge suits typically include a claim for breach of implied-in-fact contract.

THE STATUTE OF FRAUDS. If there is any doubt as to the vitality of unwritten contracts of employment, it is the statute of frauds, a law found in most state codes providing that certain types of agreements must be in writing to be enforceable. One typical such provision requires a written memorandum for any contract that cannot by its terms be performed within one year from the making. Most courts have applied this provision only where it was flatly impossible for the agreement to be performed within one year.

Thus unwritten agreements to employ a 40-year-old employee "until normal retirement" at age 65 would be unenforceable, as would an oral contract to provide vocational training for three full years. On the other hand, an agreement to employ "for life" could be enforced because the employee could die within one year. The same is true for contracts contingent on some happening, such as the closing of a business, which could occur within 12 months from the making. As discussed, contracts for "permanent" employment typically create only an at-will relationship terminable at any time, and this would not offend the statute of frauds.

In *Newfield v. Insurance Company of the West*, 156 Cal. App. 3d 440, 203 Cal. Rptr. 9 (1984), *hearing denied*, however, the California Court of Appeal held that an unwritten contract for employment terminable only for good cause was barred by the statute of frauds in California Civil Code section 1624(1) because it could not necessarily be performed within one year from the making. If followed, the ruling in *Newfield* would drastically undercut wrongful discharge claims based on express oral promises, or even implied in fact contracts as in *Pugh*.

It remains to be seen how other courts will apply the statute of frauds in employment cases. Some decisions flatly reject the reasoning in *Newfield* while other courts have taken a middle ground, and allowed the jury to determine whether the parties actually contemplated employment for more than one year. Still other courts may refuse to apply the statute where the employer promises to put the agreement in writing but then fails or refuses to do so.

Reducing the Risk of Wrongful Discharge

What can an employer do to reduce its exposure to wrongful discharge suits? The first step is awareness, not only of the regulatory environment in which the employer operates, but also of the judicial trends in the states where it does business. Beyond that, all employers should undertake a thorough revamping of all personnel policies and practices, written and unwritten, especially those that concern record keeping, employee performance, and disciplinary rules and procedures, all of which are touched on in Chapter 9 and elsewhere throughout this book. A complete analysis of employee handbooks, supervisory manuals, and similar documents is also a must as elaborated in Chapter 4. Furthermore, employers might consider the following guidelines pertaining to the three basic theories of wrongful discharge.

AVOIDING PUBLIC POLICY VIOLATIONS. It is neither enlightening nor completely accurate to say that the risk of public policy violations can be eliminated simply by assuring compliance with all applicable laws. Even the most scrupulous employers will encounter situations where they were unaware of specific laws, or took a good faith albeit erroneous position that their conduct was legal. Even in cases where the employer was decidedly correct, a disgruntled employee with the barebones of a public policy claim can put the employer to a costly defense or force a compromise settlement. Despite the increasing availability of wrongful discharge insurance, coverage will be denied where the employee alleges intentional or criminal conduct by the employer.

In most but not all cases the first notice of a public policy claim will come from the very employee to be discharged. Has the individual ever claimed that the employer has engaged in some form of illegal conduct? Has the employee complained to governmental or civic bodies, or otherwise publicly disclosed a belief that the employer is violating the law? In *Tameny v. Atlantic Richfield Co., supra,* the claimant alleged that he had resisted the employer's alleged antitrust violations *for several years* prior to his termination.

Public policy claims are more likely to arise where the employer's business or the particular employee's duties are heavily regulated by state or federal law. Does the employee have responsibility of any kind for assuring that the employer is in compliance with applicable laws and regulations? These could be laws concerning health and safety, equal employment, tax, payroll, finance, accounting, marketing, consumer protection, food and drug, licensing, export/import, hazardous waste, inventions and trade secrets, credit, collection, affirmative action, labor relations, governmental contracts, international trade and foreign investment, banking, investment, securities, antitrust, pricing, product safety, even community affairs. Is there any evidence of a disagreement involving the employee which touched in some manner upon compliance with these or any other laws?

Any such claim should be investigated fully prior to discharge, regardless of how frivolous it may seem. Legal counsel should be consulted to ascertain whether the asserted statutory provisions, or any other statute involved, was even arguably violated over the employee's objection. If the employer is satisfied after a thorough investigation that its conduct was fully legal, the results should be openly discussed with the employee. If the investigation reveals illegality, the employee should not be discharged or even disciplined.

The point of all these inquiries is to ferret out whether a public policy violation is even arguably applicable. Even when the employee's complaints seem frivolous, imaginary, or even outright fabrication, no employer should wait until a lawsuit is filed before assessing whether it has obeyed the law.

AVOIDING BAD FAITH OR ARBITRARY DISCHARGES. The nebulous nature of the implied covenant of good faith and fair dealing makes it difficult to formulate hard and fast rules for avoiding bad faith or arbitrary terminations. One basic precaution is simply to be consistent: Employees who engage in the same basic conduct must be treated in the same manner. A related notion is that if the employer has a specific policy or procedure for a particular situation, it should be followed in all cases without deviation.

Employers might do well to also consider adopting a simple disciplinary procedure that many companies used successfully before the advent of wrongful discharge. Under this procedure no supervisor may unilaterally discharge an employee. If an employee's conduct appears to merit termination the employee is "suspended pending investigation," and advised that discipline, including possible discharge, is under consideration. The matter is then referred to the personnel or labor relations department for investigation.

The investigation proceeds in roughly the same manner as if a lawsuit has been filed, but on an expedited schedule of no more than few days. All material witnesses, including those cited by the employee, are interviewed separately and a record is made of each individual's account. The investigator also uses this opportunity to review applicable employer policies to assure they have been consistently applied, and to consult with upper management where the employer's past practice is unclear. Legal counsel might also be contacted at this juncture, particularly when the employee has made claims of illegal conduct or threatened suit in some fashion.

The employee is then confronted with the results of the investigation and allowed to tell his or her story with the assurance that a final decision has not yet been made. Some employees will truthfully admit to their misdeeds when confronted with the statements of otherwise friendly witnesses, rather than the accusations of the responsible supervisor. Other employees might name new witnesses, or concede that there are none. In any event a clear record is made of the employee's side of the story at the earliest point in the process.

Once the investigation concludes the employer is in a position to make an informed disciplinary decision. If the employee is vindicated he or she is reinstated with back pay for work missed during the investigation. The employer should also explain the decision to the supervisor involved and perhaps to all supervisors. If the decision is made to impose discipline short of discharge, a similar process takes place. If the employer elects to carry through with the discharge the benefits of the investigative process can be substantial. Some employees, acknowledging the basic fairness of the employer's procedures, will acquiesce in the decision to discharge. Other employees, though still disgruntled, may be deterred from challenging the action if they realize that they have already made significant concessions in the disciplinary interview.

Even if the employee persists in protesting the decision to discharge—whether in a wrongful discharge suit, unemployment insurance proceeding, or any other forum—the record developed in the investigation can prove invaluable because it ties the employee to a particular position. Many times employees will have made statements during the investigation that are inconsistent with the position they are advised to take in litigation. The employer can then offer evidence of the employee's investigatory interview and attempt to show that the claims being made in litigation were concocted after the fact in order to build a case where none existed.

This procedure of suspending pending investigation will not eliminate the risk of wrongful discharge liability, and it will create new administrative burdens. But in effectively forcing the employer to deliberate every discharge decision and in building a record against the employee, its benefits surely seem to outweigh the costs. Even without the spectre of wrongful discharge litigation, such a procedure makes for good employee relations.

AVOIDING WRONGFUL DISCHARGE SUITS BASED ON IMPLIED CONTRACTS. Unlike in cases involving violations of public policy or the implied covenant of good faith and fair dealing, an employer has more effective means available to reduce the risk of losing a wrongful discharge suit predicated on an implied contract. The most direct approach is to have the employee sign a written acknowledgment that no cause is required for termination. As elaborated in Chapter 4 in the discussion of employee handbooks, several courts have upheld agreements containing language such as this:

In consideration of my employment at ACME Company, I understand and agree that my employment is for an indefinite duration and can be terminated at any time, with or without cause, and with or without notice, either by me or by the Company. I further understand and agree that no supervisor or other representative of the Company other than the President has any authority to enter into any agreement to the contrary.

Employers wishing to utilize such a disclaimer should include the same language on any employment application, personnel handbook, and other statements of company policy, and should delete any inconsistent language from the same documents. While some courts have upheld such agreements when signed by existing employees, the better practice is to have applicants execute the statement prior to any offer of employment.

This approach is not without its disadvantages. As the law develops some courts may find grounds for refusing to enforce such provisions, particularly where employees contend that they were effectively forced to sign or were misled as to the effect of the agreement. Moreover, such an agreement would not bar any claims based on the violation of public policy and in some courts, would not be a defense to a suit based on the implied covenant of good faith. Lastly, the employer has to consider the effect that such an agreement could have on employee morale, particularly in the context of a union organizing campaign. Nonetheless, it represents one technique for reducing an employer's exposure to liability based on implied promises of job security.

PERSPECTIVE

According to various sources, upwards of 65 percent of the American work force is composed of employees who would be deemed "at-will" under traditional doctrine. The remaining 35 percent enjoy the protection of a collective bargaining agreement requiring cause for termination, a civil service commission or similar tenure arrangement, or an individual employment contract. The fact that well over half the working population enjoys no tangible job security puts a powerful impetus behind the wrongful discharge movement.

The public policy exception is here to stay. A majority of the states have now adopted it, and the few that have declined to do so acted primarily out of concern that the task of tempering the at-will rule belongs to the legislature. As for the implied covenant of good faith, many courts may balk at construing it to create a general just cause requirement in all contracts, but the covenant seems well suited to cases where the employer's conduct is indefensible, albeit not in violation of public policy. Lastly, implied in fact contractual theories, particularly with respect to handbooks and manuals, could find widespread acceptance because they build on traditional contract principles and do not raise fears of massive punitive damage awards.

The wrongful discharge movement will also spur legislative efforts to undo the at-will rule. Even those states that have stood by the at-will doctrine may see renewed legislative concern to protect job security or, at least, to keep pace with the other states. Proposed statutes affirmatively requiring just cause to terminate any employment contract are under study in several states. Other legislative alternatives include a system of arbitration or mediation for employment disputes—in effect, a civil service commission for private industry—or a statutory presumption based on the payroll period.

We have offered suggestions on reducing the risk of wrongful discharge, but perhaps the best advice is to approach every termination from the view point of a prospective juror, rather than as a supervisor or human resource professional. As noted at the outset, there is a sense in which the at-will doctrine fails to reflect ordinary human experience and notions of fundamental fairness. Most people, judges and juries alike, tend to think that employees should be fired only for good cause. If an employer can adopt that frame of mind, and still feel justified in carrying out a discharge, then it should have little to fear if a jury ever comes to pass judgment on its conduct.

Chapter 2

STATUTORY PROTECTION AGAINST WRONGFUL TERMINATION

Robert W. Gilbert, J.D.
Steven J. Kaplan, J.D.

The most important statutory restrictions on an employer's right to terminate an "unsatisfactory" employee are contained in written laws which have evolved gradually over the last 50 years. Do not be misled by this fact and think that any of these laws are static and predictable in their results. Statutory protection against wrongful termination is in many ways just as challenging, just as uncertain, and just as capable of producing drastic and unexpected results as the newer, more dramatic, and apparently more unsettling development of "judge-made law" discussed in Chapter 1 of this handbook. Thus, U.S. labor and employment statutes relating to discharge can be a tangled web for the legally unwary.

The complicated American scene in this area differs sharply from that in industrialized European countries. In Europe wrongful dismissal statutes of general application are administered by a very few specialized agencies. Statutory protection against wrongful termination in this country is administered by both the courts and a host of governmental agencies, and partially as a result of this it is in an endless state of flux. There are obscure legalistic provisions hidden away among a plethora of Acts of Congress and state legislatures. What is even worse the helter-skelter array of scattered and uncertain legal limitations proclaimed by these statutes are being applied and interpreted by a bewildering variety of different federal and state courts and administrative agencies. This creates a myriad of constantly changing administrative and judicial decisions, rules, regulations, orders, and public policy pronouncements.

Only a neophyte among the human resource professionals who are confronted with problems involving statutory wrongful termination violations would hope that the answers can be found just by looking them up in this or any other book.

The specific questions raised by statutory wrongful discharge claims are much too complicated to be examined in this brief chapter. Rather, we will attempt here to outline and analyze for the reader's benefit the basic features of the most important legislation regulating employee terminations. We will also discuss some of the underlying factual situations and most frequent management policy decisions that give rise to wrongful discharge cases under these statutes. Finally, we will try to point out some valuable pragmatic steps that can be taken to avoid or at least minimize the risk of having to face such litigation.

Once a statutory wrongful termination case has reached the litigation stage, the most you can do is assist the attorney assigned to handle that case. You can help the attorney to obtain all the pertinent facts, provide possible witnesses to be interviewed, and supply the needed documents.

What else can you do, if you are really determined to avoid this type of litigation whenever possible? Where a contested case simply cannot be avoided, what can you do before it reaches court to assure a successful defense? The steps that can be taken by you for both these purposes are not that difficult.

1. Familiarize youself with the basic requirements of the most important protective laws pertaining to discharge, and learn to recognize and avoid the obvious pitfalls which are discussed in this chapter.

2. Resolve actual problems in work situations involving contemplated discharges or other progressive disciplinary action against employees (such as warnings, suspensions, and demotions) on a fair, even-handed, and objective basis, with appropriate documentation to support your actions.

3. Realize that the restrictions on the right to terminate employees found in these protective statutes have not completely abrogated an employer's prerogative to impose a discharge for good and sufficient cause. But discharge should follow appropriate warning, and may not be imposed for a prohibited discriminatory reason, such as characteristics or behavior which are unrelated to the employee's work performance or job qualifications, or in retaliation for legally protected conduct. (Of course, this general principle does not change any specific contractual obligations the employer may have relating to discharges under any applicable personal services or collective bargaining agreement.)

LEGISLATIVE HISTORY OF THE MOST IMPORTANT TERMINATION RESTRICTIONS

Until the 1930s, the nineteenth century American "at-will employment" rule was largely undisturbed by protective legislation. This doctrine said that an employee could be discharged by the employer for good cause, bad cause, or no cause at all, unless there was an express written contract for a definite term of employment.

It was only much later that the Supreme Court held that nineteenth century civil rights legislation adopted by Congress during the Reconstruction Era permitted federal lawsuits for racial discrimination in employment.[1] However, this judicial development did not take place until some 100 years after the passage of that legislation. It followed long after Congressional enactment of the 1935 Wagner Act (National Labor Relations Act) administered by the National Labor Relations Board (NLRB), forbidding discriminatory discharges for union activity. It even followed enactment of Title VII of the 1964 Civil Rights Act, administered by the Equal Employment Opportunity Commission (EEOC), forbidding discriminatory discharges because of race, sex, and other characteristics.

Like the American courts, for many years Congress and state legislatures apparently accepted the proposition that the successful operation of any business depends in large part on the employer's unlimited ability to manage and direct its labor force. The employer's ability to dispense with the services of what it considered to be "unsatisfactory" employees was accepted without question, over and above its right to make layoffs or reductions in force occasioned by business necessity during unprofitable periods. No statutory exceptions to the at-will rule were adopted until economic, social, or political changes in our society generated strong pressures for their creation.

In 1935 during the depths of an economic depression marked by widespread strikes, labor disputes over union recognition, and job discrimination because of union activities, Congress adopted the National Labor Relations (Wagner) Act, which is now Title I of the 1947 Labor Management Relations Act (LMRA). The NLRA forbids, among other proscribed unfair labor practices by employers, the discharge of employees for organizing, joining or belonging to unions or engaging in other such concerted activities. (In 1947 with the adoption of the Taft-Hartley amendments, unfair labor practices by unions were also forbidden by the NLRA, including causing or attempting to cause an employer to make such a discriminatory discharge.) The NLRA also expressly makes it a forbidden unfair labor practice for an employer to discharge an employee in retaliation for filing charges against it or giving testimony against it in proceedings before the NLRB.

These two features of the NLRA restricted the employer's previously unlimited discretion to terminate employees at will by prohibiting such discharges when based on collective employee conduct protected in the interest of society as a whole. The NLRA became the model for other later federal statutes prohibiting employee discharges based upon other types of protected conduct. It also gave rise to a whole host of similar state labor relations laws applicable to employers and employees who fall outside the coverage of the NLRA, such as agricultural employees and small businesses not involved in interstate or foreign commerce.

When the Fair Labor Standards Act (FLSA), another important piece of New Deal legislation, was adopted in 1937, that statute declared it unlawful to discharge an employee for filing a complaint, instituting a proceeding, or testifying regarding a violation of the minimum wage, overtime, or other provisions of the FLSA. It also authorized private as well as government lawsuits to remedy any such discharge.

---

[1] 42 U.S.C. §§ 1981 and 1985. See *Johnson v. Railway Express Agency*, 421 U.S. 454 (1975) and *Great Am. Fed. Sav. & Loan Ass'n v. Novatny*, 442 U.S. 366 (1979).

Legislation emerged from World War II to protect the reemployment rights of servicemen by protecting them against discharge without cause for one year after they had returned to their jobs. These laws continued in force until they were incorporated in the present Veterans Reemployment Act, administered by the Veterans Administration.

In 1946 the war-time Fair Employment Practices Committee established by President Roosevelt's Executive Order was terminated. This committee had been responsible for eliminating employment discrimination on the basis of color and race. One of the most controversial legislative issues before Congress after World War II was the campaign for legislation prohibiting employment discrimination because of race, color, religion, or national origin. The result was enactment of Title VII of the 1964 Civil Rights Act. This law not only made it a forbidden "unlawful employment practice" to dismiss an employee because of race, color, religion, or national origin, but because of sex as well. Title VII also protects against termination both because of participation in enforcement procedures under the Civil Rights Act, similar to the NLRA, and because of an employee's opposition to his or her employers' discriminatory employment practices that the employee believes in good faith to be unlawful under the Act.

Numerous state and local equal employment opportunity laws have also been adopted barring discriminatory discharges based on racial, ethnic, religious, or gender characteristics of employees. (In fact, Title VII expressly provides for initial deferral to a state or local agency having jurisdiction under such law, before the federal procedures take hold.)

In 1967 the Age Discrimination in Employment Act (ADEA) was adopted. It prohibits covered employers from discharging employees between the ages of 40 and 70, inclusive, because of their age. ADEA remedies are much like those provided under the FLSA, including both government action and private lawsuits. A number of similar state age discrimination laws have also been adopted.

Title IX of the Education Amendments of 1972 prohibits sex discrimination in employment in federally funded educational programs. In 1982 a private right to bring a lawsuit for violation of Title IX rights, which apparently could be available to a wrongfully discharged teacher or other school employee, was upheld by the U.S. Supreme Court.

The Rehabilitation Act of 1973 bars job discrimination by employers receiving federal contracts or grants against individuals having or regarded as having a nondisqualifying physical or mental handicap. The private right to bring a lawsuit and recover back pay made available to dischargees by amendment in 1978, was confirmed by a unanimous U.S. Supreme Court in 1984. State laws prohibiting terminations based on nondisqualifying handicap have also been adopted.

The Consumer Credit Protection Act, enacted in 1973, declares that no employer may discharge an employee because their earnings were subjected to garnishment for a single indebtedness. The question of whether a dischargee can bring a private lawsuit under that Act still is by no means clear.

The Employee Retirement Income Security Act of 1974 (ERISA) prohibits the discharge of an employee benefit plan participant because he or she exercised rights under ERISA or under a benefit plan, such as a pension or health and welfare plan covered by ERISA. A private lawsuit can be brought in U.S. district court to remedy this form of wrongful termination.

Section 1875 of the Jury System Improvements Act of 1978, entitled "Protection of Jurors Employment," provides for a civil penalty and damages, including back pay, and injunctive relief, against an employer who discharges or threatens to discharge a federal court juror or prospective juror by reason of his or her jury service. Affected employees can bring suit in U.S. District Court and recover attorney's fees.

A number of federal environmental statutes enacted within recent years forbid discharges or other employment discrimination for commencing a proceeding to enforce the particular statute, testifying in such a proceeding or otherwise assisting in carrying out the statutory purposes.[2] Only one of these statutes, the Clean Air Act, expressly permits a discharged employee to bring a private lawsuit. That dischargee may file a complaint with the U.S. Department of Labor to obtain an administrative order in his favor which may include reinstatement and compensation (including back pay). Then a U.S. district court action can be brought by the terminated employee to enforce that order.

Most of these environmental statutes are patterned after the Occupational Safety and Health Act of 1970 (OSHA) which prohibits employers from discharging employees because they file complaints; report unsafe conditions; request or assist federal inspection of the workplace; or aid in or bring court proceedings intended to correct or halt certain dangerous or unhealthy conditions. As in the case of OSHA, most of these environmental statutes provide that the discharged employee must file a complaint with the U.S. Labor Department, and on their face they do not authorize a private lawsuit for wrongful termination.

The Federal Employers' Liability Act makes it a crime, punishable by fine and imprisonment, to discharge an employee for furnishing information to an interested party regarding facts relating to an injury or death of any employee in a railroad accident. This is another statute where it is still not clear whether a private lawsuit can be brought. In contrast, the Federal Railroad Safety Act, which makes it unlawful for certain employers to discharge employees for filing complaints or testifying in proceedings under the Act, expressly allows a dischargee to elect either to settle his statutory claim by grievance arbitration under the Railway Labor Act or to seek the protection of "any other provision of law" that may be available.

The antiretaliation provisions of these various federal statutes have been followed in the last few years by numerous state statutes along similar lines. Popularly known as "Whistleblower Protection laws," they not only forbid terminations for reporting or testifying about employer violations of law, but also protect an employee's rights under state law to engage

---

[2] Drinking Waste Act, 42 U.S.C. § 300j-0(1); Water Pollution Control Act, 33 U.S.C. § 1367; Toxic Substances Control Act, 15 U.S.C. 2622; Solid Waste Disposal Act, 42 U.S.C. § 6771, Resource Conservation and Recovery Act, 42 U.S.C. § 6971; Energy Reorganization Act of 1974, 42 U.S.C. § 5851, and Clean Air Act, 42 U.S.C. § 7622.

in certain protected activities, such as serving on a jury, appearing as a witness, or filing an application for worker's compensation. There is considerable variation among these state laws as to whether they protect private sector employees or only state employees; as to what remedies are available; and whether or not a civil action may be brought by the dischargees.

All these federal statutes and matching state statutes, today provide many at-will employees with protection against wrongful termination by their employer because they possess certain characteristics, maintain certain beliefs, or engage in protected conduct. They contain legislatively imposed "public policy" exceptions to the traditional American rule that once gave employers unfettered discretion to discharge employees for any reason or no reason, as they saw fit.

The foregoing review of the legislative history of these most important statutory restrictions against wrongful termination should convince the labor relations specialist of the need to keep abreast of future developments in this constantly changing area of labor and employment law, in order to maintain his best capabilities as a human resource professional.

THE TWILIGHT ZONES OF IMPLIED PRIVATE REMEDIES AND PREEMPTION

Major federal statutes prohibiting wrongful terminations, like the NLRA and Title VII, either contain express restrictions against discriminatory discharges as such, or broadly restrict all forms of job discrimination which necessarily include discharges.

They establish specialized administrative agencies, like the NLRB or the EEOC and spell out the procedural framework for handling employment discrimination cases. Such statutes give the administrative agencies exclusive *primary* jurisdiction to hear, decide and provide remedies for claimed statutory violations, such as wrongful terminations. This is sometimes called "preemption."

The "Supremacy Clause" in Article VI of the U.S. Constitution declares federal statutes to be "the supreme law of the land." Based on that clause Congress has in some cases precluded private lawsuits from ever being brought to federal or state court to remedy employer misdeeds, like certain wrongful terminations that constitute violations of the federal statutes. This is also known as "preemption," and applies primarily to the NLRA.

Other federal statutes previously reviewed, like Title VII, the FLSA, and the ADEA, provide administrative remedies for discriminatory discharges which constitute statutory violations, but also authorize private lawsuits to remedy them.

Still others like the 1926 Railway Labor Act (RLA) covering railroads and now airlines, most of the federal environmental statutes, and some federal and state antiretaliation or "whistleblower" statutes, prohibit discriminatory discharges for engaging in protected conduct and occasionally may even provide criminal penalties for such violations, but do not expressly authorize private lawsuits by dischargees to obtain reinstatement and damages (including back pay).

Questions as to whether a private right to bring a lawsuit can be implied from the public policy against wrongful discharges contained in a federal or state statute are in many cases still open questions not yet decided by the courts. While the RLA preceded the NLRA by almost ten years, it was not until almost 46 years after its passage that the U.S. Supreme Court finally decided that section 2 of the RLA, which only provided criminal sanctions, was also privately enforceable.

In 1983 the Ninth Circuit Court of Appeals in San Francisco refused to imply that an employee terminated for wage garnishment can bring a private lawsuit under the wrongful discharge provisions of the Consumer Credit Protection Act. The court's refusal was based on a finding that Congress intended to allow only the U.S. Labor Department to enforce those provisions, not private individuals.

A significant number of recent court decisions have refused to imply the right to bring a private wrongful termination lawsuit under a statute not expressly providing for such a private right. These courts have principally relied on a 1975 U.S. Supreme Court decision requiring, as one of four tests to be met, that a court find Congressional intent, explicit or implicit, to allow such a result, before deciding to infer a private remedy from a federal statute.[3]

Preemption questions like implied private remedy questions, can be very perplexing to the lawyer as well as the nonlawyer. State court common law tort and contract actions for wrongful discharge due to an employee's union or other concerted labor activities will most likely be preempted by the NLRA. Section 301 of the Labor Management Relations Act, on the other hand, has been held by the Supreme Court to grant concurrent federal and state court jurisdiction over employee lawsuits against employers and unions for wrongful discharges involving an alleged breach of a union's duty of fair representation under a collective bargaining agreement.

Some implied RLA section 2 private court actions for wrongful dismissal have been held to be authorized by the ninth circuit. But in 1972, the U.S. Supreme Court reversed its own 1941 contrary precedent to decide that the RLA preempts common law court actions for wrongful dismissal by providing statutory arbitration remedies. State private lawsuits based on common law public policies, on the other hand, clearly are not preempted by federal antidiscrimination statutes such as Title VII, the Reconstruction Era civil rights statutes, and the ADEA.

Human resource professionals must be generally familiar with the existence of these legal issues as they relate to implied private remedies for wrongful dismissal and preemption of private wrongful dismissal lawsuits by federal administrative agencies and statutes. Difficult court litigation of wrongful dismissal lawsuits, exposure to the vagaries of jury trials, and the risk of large damages awards may be avoided by your attorneys if

[3] *Cort v. Ash,* 422 U.S. 66 (1975) discussed in more detail in Perritt, *Employee Dismissal Law and Practice* (Wiley, 1984), at pp. 59–61.

you are aware of these issues. Many of these difficult legal questions have not yet been decided by the U.S. Supreme Court, and may not be for many years. So from a practical standpoint, attorneys should try to give clients sound advice regarding the handling of dismissal problems that will minimize the risk of wrongful termination lawsuits, as well as statutory administrative proceedings.

NLRA GUIDELINES

Protected employee conduct under section 7 of the NLRA includes the exercise of statutorily guaranteed rights of employees to organize, bargain collectively, to engage in other concerted activities and, since the 1947 Taft-Hartley amendments, to refrain from such activities. Section 8(a)(1) of the NLRA makes it a prohibited unfair labor practice for an employer to interfere with, restrain or coerce employees in the exercise of their section 7 rights. Section 8(a)(3) similarly prohibits employment discrimination against employees to encourage or discourage union membership. This broad prohibition expressly applies to discrimination "in regard to . . . tenure of employment", that is, wrongful termination. Section 8(b)(2), adopted in 1947, makes it an unfair labor practice for a union to cause or attempt to cause an employer to discriminate in violation of section 8(a)(3). Section 8(a)(4) similarly prohibits employer retaliations against employees for filing charges with the NLRB or testifying in Board proceedings.[4]

NLRB jurisdiction includes all employers and employees engaged in interstate and foreign commerce, except those covered by the RLA, agricultural enterprises, and state and local governmental units. The Board limits the exercise of that jurisdiction to employers meeting certain dollar volume guidelines based upon direct and indirect commerce figures. Unless a company is very small or very localized it probably falls within this discretionary jurisdiction. The NLRB, which just celebrated its 50th anniversary, also has exclusive jurisdiction over discriminatory discharge cases arising under NLRA sections 8(a)(1), 8(a)(3), 8(a)(4), and 8(b)(2). The only court relief that interested parties can seek in such cases is to petition for judicial review of the NLRB's decision.

During the last half-century the NLRB has decided thousands of discharge cases and the U.S. Courts of Appeals have reviewed a substantial number of those decisions. The usual section 8(a)(1) or 8(a)(3) charge turns on a factual dispute over the employer's alleged anti-union or discriminatory motive or purpose. Under appropriate circumstances the Board, with judicial approval, has even found a violation without proof of anti-union animus or discriminatory motive where discouragement of union membership was the "natural consequence" of the employer's action.

---

[4] These sections of the Act are codified as 29 U.S.C. §§ 158(a)(1), 158(a)(3), 158(b)(2), and 158(a)(4). An enclyopedic legal treatise on these and all NLRA sections is Charles Morris, ed., *The Developing Labor Law*, 2d. ed., (ABA–BNA, 1983).

Section 8(c) of the NLRA affords the employer a broad right of "free speech" in commenting on labor relations and union problems. This does not mean that management and supervisory personnel can afford to be careless in making hostile comments of an anti-union character, or in interrogating employees about their union activities or support. Background evidence of this sort can be used before the Labor Board to raise an inference of an underlying antiunion motive or purpose in a subsequent discharge of a union advocate.

The burden of proof is on the party who filed the unfair labor practice charge and the NLRB General Counsel to prove the claim of unlawful discrimination. Pragmatically speaking, in the usual section 8(a)(3) case where a union supporter has been terminated, the employer must be prepared to convincingly prove a nondiscriminatory, nonpretextual reason for the termination. To prevail, the employer should demonstrate both an objective cause for discharge that was unrelated to the terminated employee's union activity, and that the employee would have been discharged regardless of such union activity.

To avoid or at least minimize the risk of losing wrongful termination cases under the NLRA and other protective statutes for which the NLRA is the prototype, it is suggested that the following defensive policies and practices be adopted by employers:

1. Be sure that all employees have been informed in writing of specific grounds for termination and the steps that will be taken by management in all cases before termination is imposed.

2. Carefully document the cause for every termination in the form of precise written records of all oral admonitions, complaints, warnings, probationary notices, remedial conferences, retraining efforts, and other steps taken to try to improve the employee's performance before termination was imposed.

3. Develop a well-defined system of progressive discipline that is strictly followed before termination takes place.

4. Make certain that all adverse performance evaluations and disciplinary actions short of termination are honestly justified. An abundance of petty and unwarranted criticisms, unprovoked warnings, ill-considered probationary notices, and harsh suspensions in an employee's personnel folder preceding termination will not serve to support a finding that the discharge was made for cause, and might even suggest unlawful discrimination.

5. Involve more than one supervisor or management official in the termination process, so as to avoid any inference of discriminatory personal bias or prejudice against the employee by a single supervisor or management official.

6. Avoid making terminations hastily or in a manner that will invite recrimination or create embarrassment, such as by terminating employees in front of the dischargee's fellow employees.

7. Conduct terminations and exit interviews in a fair, evenhanded and compassionate manner. Be even-tempered, but give the employee a clear

and objective written statement of the reasons for termination and explain them clearly at the exit interview. Be completely candid with the employee about the reasons for the termination.

8. In discussing the termination with the employee's coworkers, supervisors, or other management personnel, do not try to apologize for or minimize the reasons for the termination. Be careful about giving glowing letters of recommendation to dischargees that can be used as proof that the reasons advanced for their terminations were ill-founded and pretextual. The same is true about answering inquiries from prospective employers of the terminated employee.

9. Voluntary quits, as an alternative to termination, must be very carefully arranged, to avoid claims of constructive discharge for discriminatory reasons.

Under section 8(a)(1) the Board extends protection to other "concerted activities" by employees besides union-related conduct. Recent Board and court decisions in the area of discharges for nonunion activities have involved rather technical questions as to whether the activity in question was purely individual or "concerted." Concerted activity cases may involve such drastic action as walking off the job, refusing an assignment, or merely approaching management for the purpose of resolving a problem on behalf of a group of employees. Since this still remains a somewhat uncharted area, if confronted with this type of problem employers would be wise to investigate the actual circumstances quite carefully and use their best efforts to resolve the matter short of termination.

The antiretaliation provisions of NLRA section 8(a)(4) on their face appear to be much narrower than similar provisions under OSHA, the federal environmental statutes or even the FLSA. Only the filing of charges or the giving of testimony to the Labor Board are expressly protected. The U.S. Supreme Court expanded this narrow interpretation in 1972 by holding that section 8(a)(4) protects employees who give sworn affidavits to an NLRB agent investigating Board charges, but who have not themselves actually filed charges or testified at a formal unfair labor practice hearing. Since 1972 NLRB and the federal courts have liberally construed section 8(a)(4) to protect an employee who is scheduled or subpoenaed to testify at a Board hearing, but prevented from testifying.

Upon judicial review of a Board decision, an employee who deliberately filed false charges and gave false testimony before the NLRB was denied protection from discharge under section 8(a)(4). Conversely, a circuit court affirmed an NLRB finding that an employer violated this NLRA section by discharging an employee in part because of the dischargee's refusal to give possible false or misleading Board testimony in favor of the employer.

Both the NLRB and the federal courts have held that an employer's refusal to reinstate or rehire a discharged employee because of the employee's filing or refusal to withdraw a Board charge violates section 8(a)(4). This will be so even where the employee's original discharge for absenteeism may have been justified.

Great care should be taken whenever one considers discharging an employee who has filed an NLRB charge, testified at a Board hearing, given affidavits or statements to Board agents, or been served with a Board subpoena. Under circumstances where a colorable claim can be made that the discharge constitutes retaliation or reprisal, or was made for the purpose of discouraging employee complaints to the NLRB, it should be avoided.

Of course the reviewing courts have not gone so far as to require an employer to tolerate deliberately false charges and false testimony, or to suffer use of the Board's processes for malicious prosecution by continuous filing of meritless charges without probable cause. Moreover, the Board itself recognized that employees who voluntarily go AWOL to attend a Board hearing and fail to check out in violation of company rules can be discharged without violating section 8(a)(4) and are not entitled to the same broad protection as subpoenaed witnesses at such a hearing.

Section 8(a)(4) of the NLRA prohibits a retaliatory discharge by employers engaged to any extent in commerce, even one who falls outside the Labor Board's dollar volume discretionary jurisdictional standards, just as the antiretaliation provisions of section 215(a)(3) of the FLSA apply to "any person" and "any employee" regardless of the fact that the business is not covered by that Act.

TITLE VII GUIDEPOSTS

Title VII of the Civil Rights Act of 1964 is the most important of the series of federal and state statutes prohibiting employment discrimination based upon personal characteristics unrelated to job qualifications. They are race, color, religion, sex, national origin, age, and nondisqualifying physical handicap or mental impairment.[5] A comparison of Title VII with the NLRA shows a number of similarities and a number of differences. Both apply to employers and labor organizations in industries in interstate commerce, although unlike the NLRA, Title VII covers state and local governments. (Employers with less than 15 employees and labor unions with less than 15 members are excluded from Title VII coverage, but employment agencies are expressly covered.) Both are also administered by a specialized administrative agency: the NLRB in the case of the NLRA and the EEOC in the case of Title VII.

The statutes both enumerate a series of prohibited employer practices which are called "unfair labor practices" in the NLRA and "unlawful employment practices" in Title VII. Both include wrongful dismissal of an employee for a discriminatory reason among the proscribed practices enumerated in each statute, and each contains antiretaliation provisions that prohibit discharge of any employee for participating in enforcement

[5] An overview of Title VII and the other major employment discrimination laws referred to is presented in Chapter V and VI of this Handbook which follow and particular problems involved in such charges are discussed there in detail. For a comprehensive casebook and reference work about this entire subject see Schlei and Grossman, *Employment Discrimination Law*, 2d ed., (ABA–BNA, 1983).

procedures under the statute. Although Title VII goes further by extending such protection against discharge to other forms of opposition to unlawful employment practices.

The NLRB as a quasijudicial body is forbidden from performing conciliation functions, while the EEOC is expressly charged by its statute with seeking to obtain a conciliation agreement within stated time limits before filing suit against an employer. The NLRB has exclusive primary jurisdiction to hear and decide unfair labor practice charges which state and local agencies and courts are preempted from entertaining. In contrast, unlawful employment practice charges must initially be filed with the EEOC or referred by it to a state or local agency having jurisdiction before the courts can entertain such charges.

Under the NLRA, individual lawsuits to remedy unfair labor practices are preempted by NLRB jurisdiction from being maintained in a federal or state court. Under Title VII, if the conciliation efforts by the EEOC or the state or local agency having jurisdiction are unsuccessful, the Commission can itself file suit on behalf of the charging party or, if it chooses not to do so, must issue a "right-to-sue" letter to the charging party permitting him or her to file a private individual suit in the U.S. district court. Under appropriate circumstances, a state court can decide an employment discrimination claim that could have been brought before the EEOC and its decision will be binding in a later federal court action.

Apart from the procedural differences between these two statutes, the substantive issues in an unfair labor practice discharge case under the NLRA and an unlawful employment practice discharge case under Title VII are also very different.

Title VII prohibits an employer from dismissing any individual because of the previously enumerated personal characteristics (i.e., race, color, religion, sex, or national origin). So it is therefore necessary to establish a causal connection between the individual's dismissal and his or her personal characteristics in order to prove a violation. Establishment of a Title VII violation in a discharge case usually requires proof of the employer's intent to discriminate either by direct or circumstantial evidence. To this extent, proving such an intent to discriminate in a Title VII discharge case resembles proving an employer's discriminatory motive or purpose in an NLRA discharge case.

Proof of discriminatory intent in a Title VII discharge case may also be established under the "disparate treatment" theory. According to that theory, discriminatory intent may be inferred from indirect or circumstantial evidence showing that plaintiff employee was treated more harshly or given less consideration than other employees similarly situated with different racial, religious, gender, or ethnic characteristics. While a disparate impact theory is commonly used in class actions involving discriminatory hiring or promotion practices disproportionately disadvantaging the particular group to which plaintiffs belong, most Title VII individual discharge cases are not tried under that theory.

Where the plaintiff who has been discharged is able to meet his burden of proving a prima facie case of disparate treatment, the employer is required to articulate persuasive legitimate, nondiscriminatory reasons for plaintiff's termination in order to escape liability. Similar defensive policies and practices as those suggested to avoid losing an NLRA wrongful termination case would serve well in a Title VII discharge case. They will help demonstrate that legitimate business reasons rather than discriminatory intent motivated the plaintiff's termination.

Title VII provides certain narrow exceptions to its general prohibition against discrimination in employment where the employer's requirements or decisions are based on a "bona fide occupational qualification" (BFOQ) or a religious qualification imposed by an organization or school. For example, a motion picture producer lawfully may discriminate on the basis of race when casting for a role actually requiring a black or white person to portray that particular part. (BFOQ and religious qualification defenses are not usually applicable to Title VII termination cases, as distinguished from hiring cases.)

Another defense to the prohibition against discrimination is found when the employer's actions are based on a bona fide seniority or merit system. In recent years U.S. Supreme Court decisions defining and upholding bona fide seniority systems under this Title VII statutory exception suggest that this can be a viable defense particularly in an appropriate case involving selection of employees for lay-offs or reductions in force.

While court trials are available in Title VII discharge cases, unlike NLRA discharge cases, plaintiffs and defendants are not entitled to a jury trial. Both the NLRA and Title VII provide for back pay among the available remedies in discharge cases, but back pay under Title VII is limited to a maximum of two years prior to the filing of the charge. Unlike the NLRA under which attorney's fees are usually not recoverable, Title VII expressly authorizes recovery of reasonable attorney's fees as do most of the other wrongful termination statutes referred to in this chapter.

Section 704(a) of the 1964 Civil Rights Act prohibits discharges and other discrimination against employees either because they oppose unlawful employment practices of their employer or participate in Title VII enforcement procedures.

The same two procedural stages of administrative conciliation followed by individual lawsuits before a U.S. district court are applicable to claims for violation of the antiretaliation provisions of section 704(a).

One of the elements required to establish a prima facie case in a section 704(a) discharge case is a causal link between the termination and the discharged employee's protected conduct. In an opposition case, as distinguished from a participation case, the trend of authority is to merely require (1) a showing of the employee's good faith belief that his or her employer was violating Title VII, rather than proving an actual violation, and (2) a showing that the employee was in fact engaged in an appropriate form of protest of the employer's challenged policies, in order to demonstrate that statutorily protected expression of opposition was taking place.

ADEA GUIDELINES

Enacted in 1967, the Age Discrimination in Employment Act (ADEA) resembles Title VII in its basic approach. This statute prohibits still another form of employment discrimination because of a personal characteristic unrelated to the job qualifications of the protected group of employees, namely age.

Procedurally, and with respect to remedies, the ADEA incorporates a number of features of the FLSA which are not found in Title VII. The statute originally designated the secretary of labor as the administrator of the ADEA, just as the U.S. Labor Department provided FLSA administration. When the resemblance between the substantive aspects of ADEA and Title VII could no longer be ignored, responsibility for ADEA administration was transferred from the Labor Department to the EEOC by Reorganization Plan No. 1 of 1978.

ADEA covers all employers with 20 or more employees in an industry affecting interstate commerce, while Title VII covers such employers with 15 or more employees. Like Title VII, ADEA applies to state and local governments. The Act also prohibits all forms of age discrimination against "persons" between the ages of 40 and 70, inclusive. (At least one court has suggested that "persons" who are in that protected age group must be employees of the covered employers by holding that independent contractors who were allegedly discharged "because of age" are not covered by the ADEA. And like Title VII, exceptions to the antidiscrimination prohibition of the ADEA are afforded to employers who discriminate because of age based on a BFOQ or a "bona fide seniority system." Wrongful discharge is included within this statute's broad prohibition against employment discrimination, just as it is in Title VII. Section 623 of the ADEA expressly exempts from the scope of its prohibition discharges based "on a factor other than age" or based on "good cause."

The ADEA also authorizes U.S. district courts to remedy wrongful terminations in lawsuits filed by the EEOC or by the private individual claiming discrimination as does Title VII, but no "right-to-sue" letter is required under the ADEA. The limited form of private class action permitted under the FLSA whereby individuals can become joint plaintiffs by taking affirmative steps to "opt in" the lawsuit is expressly permitted by the ADEA.

An ADEA private lawsuit for wrongful termination, like a Title VII discharge case, can only be brought after the filing of charges with the EEOC or appropriate state agency within stated time limits. The ADEA has been interpreted to also require governmental conciliation efforts before a lawsuit is brought. Unlike Title VII, there are no time limits for conciliation set forth in the ADEA.

An employee allegedly discharged because of age may bring a lawsuit under the ADEA on his or her own behalf 60 days after that employee has filed an EEOC charge. The ADEA expressly allows jury trials in such lawsuits, which are not provided for by Title VII.

ADEA remedies for violations, like FLSA remedies, include back pay and an additional amount as liquidated damages where the violations are found to be willful. Most courts have refused to allow punitive damages or damages for pain, suffering and mental distress in ADEA cases. As in Title VII cases, broad injunctive relief is available in a proper ADEA lawsuit.

Courts have recognized the similarity between ADEA and Title VII wrongful termination cases in terms of the plaintiff's burden of proof required to make out a prima facie case and the defenses available to the employer. Both statutes prohibit an employer from dismissing any individual "because of" his defined personal characteristics. ADEA requires a plaintiff to prove the "causal connection" between the discharge and his or her age, just as Title VII requires a plaintiff to prove causation for the discharge because of his race or other enumerated personal characteristic.

As with Title VII, the plaintiff in an ADEA case may prove discrimination either by direct or circumstantial evidence. Usually a plaintiff in such a case lacks any direct evidence showing the employer's discriminatory intent to use age as at least one of the reasons for the challenged termination. The plaintiff most often is forced to rely on circumstantial evidence from which a judge or jury can infer that age was at least one determining factor in the employer's decision to terminate, such as evidence that the plaintiff was replaced by a much younger person. (It is not clear whether a "disparate impact" theory can be relied on in an ADEA discharge case.)

Where the plaintiff produces sufficient evidence of discriminatory intent to make out a prima facie case, the defendant employer must come forward with persuasive evidence of the existence of legitimate, nondiscriminatory reasons for the plaintiff's termination in order to prevail. Such reasons may include economic difficulties requiring a reduction in force or the plaintiff's poor work performance in comparison to other employees who were not terminated.

Once the employer raises such a defense and produces credible evidence tending to support it, in order to win the case, the plaintiff-dischargee must then meet his or her burden of proving that the employer's claimed reasons for the discharge were not legitimate and only a pretext. Employers can sometimes argue, depending on the particular job, that a correlation exists between the employee's age and the quality of his or her work performance or ability to perform the job in a satisfactory manner. For this reason, a BFOQ defense is more likely to be raised as an employer's defense in an ADEA age discrimination discharge case than in a Title VII discrimination discharge case.

In cases of jobs in industries involving important safety considerations, like airplane pilots or over-the-road truck drivers, efforts are sometimes made by the employer to argue that it was "reasonably necessary" to take the employee's age into consideration in deciding for or against termination. Plaintiffs may argue in rebuttal that strictly relying on management's fair and objective assessment of the quality of the individual's own work performance or present capabilities to do the job without regard to age is adequate.

The trial of a BFOQ issue of this kind in an ADEA discharge case may require resolution of a factual dispute created by the conflicting testimony of opposing medical experts on the state of the individual employee's health in reference to the requirements of the occupation involved, without taking the individual's age into consideration.

The ADEA, like the other statutes discussed in this chapter, contains a provision prohibiting retaliatory discharges for participating in enforcement procedures or protesting employer policies or practices believed to be violations under the statute. The ADEA provision is practically identical to section 704(a) of the 1964 Civil Rights Act.

RECONSTRUCTION CIVIL RIGHTS ACT GUIDEPOSTS

During the Reconstruction Era following the American Civil War, civil rights legislation was enacted by Congress in 1866 and 1871 that was aimed at preventing racial discrimination against either blacks or whites. Portions of those nineteenth century statutes are currently codified as sections 1981 and 1985 of Title 42 of the U.S. Code. They were held by the U.S. Supreme Court in 1975 and 1979 respectively to cover purely private acts of racial discrimination or purely private conspiracies to commit such acts in the employment context. Since those Supreme Court decisions were handed down, a number of employees who allegedly were wrongfully discharged have brought lawsuits under section 1981 and to a lesser extent under section 1985.

There are many reasons plaintiffs have chosen to sue under sections 1981 and 1985 rather then Title VII: (1) they can avoid Title VII requirements that they either exhaust agency administrative requirements or be barred from bringing suit, (2) the remedies under these sections are more favorable than those under Title VII, (3) the statutes of limitations applicable to a Title VII lawsuit and a Section 1981 lawsuit are different, and (4) a jury trial which is not available under Title VII may be available for certain legal issues under sections 1981 and 1985. Under the Civil Rights Attorney's Fees Award Act of 1976, attorney's fees are recoverable in actions brought under both these sections.

Section 1981

Title VII represents an exercise of power by Congress under the Constitution's "Commerce Clause" so that a substantial connection with interstate or foreign commerce is required in order to bring an employer or labor union under its coverage. In contrast, as an exercise of Congressional power under the Thirteenth Amendment, section 1981 can be applied to all employers or labor unions without regard to commerce data.

Like Title VII, section 1981 clearly applies to racial discrimination in employment, but according to the Supreme Court, it cannot be applied against sex discrimination which is covered by Title VII, or age discrimination which is covered by the ADEA.

Because there is no federal limitations period for bringing section 1981 lawsuits, the appropriate state limitations period applies. A discharged employee claiming racial discrimination can bring his or her lawsuit directly in the U.S. district court without seeking or awaiting the outcome of an administrative conciliation stage before any state or local administrative agency and/or the EEOC, or awaiting an EEOC "right-to-sue" letter, as is the case under Title VII. (Exhaustion of grievance and arbitration provisions of any applicable collective bargaining agreement is not required either, which is also true of Title VII.)

As under Title VII, a section 1981 action requires proof that a discharge was caused by intentional discrimination either by direct evidence or by proof of disparate treatment. Assuming a prima facie case satisfying that element has been made, the defendant employer can rebut it by producing evidence reflecting that a legitimate, nondiscriminatory reason existed for the termination, which was not a pretext.

Remedies under section 1981 include injunctive relief and monetary relief, with a possibility of punitive damages. Unlike Title VII, back pay is not limited to two years prior to initiating the action.

At least one U.S. court of appeals has ruled that section 1981 can be interpreted to prohibit retaliation against a white employee for protesting a black employee's allegedly discriminatory discharge. It does not appear, however, that section 1981 can be interpreted to prohibit retaliation for filing an EEOC charge in the same manner as section 704(a) of the 1964 Civil Rights Act.

Section 1985

Subsection (3) of section 1985 may provide a basis for lawsuits by discharged employees who allege racial and possibly other forms of discrimination of the sort prohibited by Title VII and ADEA under certain special circumstances. It broadly authorizes damage actions against parties to private conspiracies to deprive other persons of their basic rights given to them by the U.S. Constitution and other federal statutes.

Under decisions of the U.S. Supreme Court, section 1985(3) can be applied to such conspiracies arising in an employer-employee situation, such as wrongful discharge, if:

1. Plaintiff's injury was caused as the result of such a conspiracy
2. The conspiracy was intended to deprive the plaintiff of specific constitutional or statutory rights under the U.S. Constitution or other federal statutes
3. Plaintiff's discharge involves invidious, discriminatory animus against a class of persons of which plaintiff is a member, that Congress in 1871 intended to protect.

Insofar as section 1985 deals with deprivation of statutory rights, it does not cover violations of federal antidiscrimination statutes providing comprehensive administrative remedies, like Title VII and the ADEA, nor violations of state statutes.

In 1983 the U.S. Supreme Court held that the class-barred animus falling under the section 1985(3) prohibition could not be economic or commercial in nature. At the time the Court refused to limit section 1985(3) to conspiracies involving racial bias, without making clear what other types of group hatred might be covered. Since a conspiracy necessarily involves two or more persons, in a wrongful discharge case it might be argued that two or more officers or agents of the corporation where the plaintiff was previously employed formed a conspiracy to terminate his employment in violation of section 1985(3). The circuit courts of appeals are split on this question of whether there can be an intra-corporate conspiracy and until the Supreme Court decides it the question remains open.

Available remedies to a plaintiff-dischargee under section 1985(3) include compensatory damages, probably punitive damages, and injunctive relief. Section 1985(2) is much narrower in scope. In prohibits conspiracies aimed either at deterring, by force, intimidation or threat, any party or witness in a federal court from attending or testifying there, or at retaliating against such party or witness for having done so. Because animus against a protected class of persons is not required to bring a section 1985(2) lawsuit, any employee discharged for attending or testifying as a witness in federal court proceedings pursuant to such a conspiracy may be able to obtain a remedy under the antiretaliation provisions of this subsection.

HANDICAP DISCRIMINATION GUIDEPOSTS

Of principal significance to the field of wrongful termination legislation is the Rehabilitation Act of 1973, which created a new class of protected individuals known as "handicapped persons."

The statute does not apply to all employers. The group of employers prohibited by the statute from employment discrimination on the basis of handicap is restricted mainly to federal government contractors and recipients of federal grants.

The procedures, rights, and remedies provided to employees protected by the Rehabilitation Act are those applicable to certain employees of federally assisted programs who are discriminated against because of race, color or national origin under Title VII of the 1964 Civil Rights Act. Availability of back pay and the broad scope of private civil actions under the Rehabilitation Act were the subject of much litigation in the various U.S. courts of appeals until ultimately clarified and upheld by the U.S. Supreme Court in a unanimous decision handed down on February 1, 1984.[6]

The regulations adopted under this Act's broad definition of "handicap" define a "handicapped person" as one who has "a physical or mental impairment which substantially limits one or more major life activities", such as, a physiological disorder or condition, cosmetic disfigurement, or anatomical loss, or any mental or psychological disorder, such as mental retardation, organic brain syndrome, emotional or mental illness, and specific learning disabilities.

Experience with this protective legislation, including wrongful discharge, is still too limited to enable one to predict whether it will be extended by Congress to cover all employers generally.

OSHA GUIDELINES

Section 11(c) of the Occupational Safety and Health Act of 1970 (OSHA) sets forth a broad prohibition against retaliatory discharges and any other form of discrimination against an employee because he or she filed any

---

[6] *Consolidated Rail Corp. v. Darrone*, 465 U.S. 624, 79 L.Ed.2d 568, 104 S. Ct. 1248 (1984).

complaint, otherwise instituted a proceeding, testified in any OSHA proceeding or exercised on behalf of oneself or others any right under that statute.

Among the rights conferred upon individual employees by OSHA are the right (1) to inform the employer and the Occupational Safety and Health Administration of unsafe conditions, (2) to request an inspection, (3) to assist the inspectors, (4) to assist a court to determine whether imminently dangerous conditions exist, and (5) to bring an action to compel the U.S. Labor Department to seek injunctive relief against unsafe or unhealthy working conditions.

In a much discussed 1980 decision, the U.S. Supreme Court unanimously upheld the validity of the Secretary of Labor's interpretation of section 11(c)(1) to require an employer not to discharge or otherwise discriminate against employees who refuse to perform hazardous tasks which they reasonably believed confronted them with a real danger of death or serious injury, when there was insufficient time due to the urgency of the situation to eliminate the danger by seeking its correction from the employer or by resorting to regular statutory enforcement channels.[7] That broad decision construed OSHA as granting "an employee with no reasonable alternative, the freedom to withdraw from a workplace environment that he reasonably believes is highly dangerous." At the same time, the Court observed that an employee who refused to perform work "unreasonably or in bad faith" could be discharged without violating section 11(c) and noted that the sort of extreme circumstances that will justify a protected employee's refusal to perform work "will probably not often occur."

Where employees refuse to perform work on the basis of an asserted imminent danger, the employer should quickly but carefully obtain all the facts about the situation to assess the reasonableness of the employees' position. Several management officials besides the employees' immediate supervisor, and perhaps even safety experts, should evaluate the situation to determine the reasonableness of the refusal to perform assigned work before attempting to enforce the work assignment through threat of discharge or other discipline.

A discharged employee's administrative remedy for violation of section 11(c) can be invoked by filing a complaint with the Secretary of Labor, who is authorized to bring an action against the wrongful termination. While a number of discharged employees have brought private lawsuits based on section 11(c), the U.S. courts of appeals have held without exception that section 11(c) does not afford a private remedy, and that only the Labor Department may enforce section 11(c) rights.

---

[7] *Whirlpool Corp. v. Marshall*, 445 U.S. 1 (1980).

Chapter **3**

DEFENDING AGAINST WRONGFUL TERMINATION BEFORE AND AFTER LITIGATION

Bennett W. Root, Jr., J.D.*

Despite the tangle of legislated and court-created restrictions on an employer's "right" to terminate an employee's employment "at will," "for any reason" (stated or unstated), or "for no reason at all," employers which proceed thoughtfully at the outset of the employment relationship, and carefully when severing that relationship can minimize or eliminate significant risk of major liability for wrongful termination of employment. This chapter will focus on *how* to attain these results: Keeping the employer out of litigation generally, keeping out of the legal case books and seminar notes as examples of what *not* to do, and avoiding adverse court orders and jury verdicts destined for statisticians' record books. While there can be no guarantee of problem-free employment termination, taking deliberate steps now, and administering policies and procedures sensitively in the future, will materially reduce the risks associated with defending against wrongful termination lawsuits.

The evolution of protective legislation and the court-created demise of employers' rights, especially in the areas regarding severance of the employment relationship, place a substantial additional responsibility on the human resource professional. It is clearly not sufficient that the specialist in the human resource or personnel function has mastered the intricacies of federal and state legislative and regulatory requirements. Nor is it enough that the court-made case law of various jurisdictions be understood. Additionally, three basic tasks must be accomplished:

*The generous assistance of my partners and associates in the Labor and Employment Department at Latham & Watkins is gratefully acknowledged. Without their thoughtful analyses, written and oral, and gentle criticism, this chapter could not have been written.

Training and development of managers and supervisors to assure that line functions as well as staff functions are working within the developing law

Preparation of pro-active and reactive policies and procedures to minimize risks of wrongful termination litigation

Creation of post-termination devices to keep risks of litigation, and/or adverse results, within reasonable boundaries

Each of these requirements is considered in some detail following.

Anyone can file a lawsuit, and, increasingly, lawsuits are being filed by terminated employees. Some employers will lose such lawsuits. What you do now and in the future can keep you from being among those who lose. While no employer can fairly set a goal of never being sued, your employer can realistically prevent many such suits and can maximize the chances of winning the rest by taking the right steps. To paraphrase an old saying, pay now (through training and preparation), or pay much more later in adverse litigation results, paralyzed management, and derogatory publicity.

THE CRUCIAL FIRST STEP: MANAGEMENT AND SUPERVISORY TRAINING AND DEVELOPMENT

The big losers in wrongful termination litigation include an alarming number of corporate giants—sophisticated companies, with large and experienced human resource or personnel staffs. Why do *they* lose wrongful termination cases? Why should other employers expect to fare better? Why should other employers expect to fare better? What should be done that they did not think of or do?

In part, of course, some of the first big losers had no clear warning of the changes coming in the law. Be sure, however, that many of those corporate giants which were caught by surprise will not make the same mistakes again. As they have learned from misfortune, so should you and your employer.

The most sophisticated human resource staff cannot always expect to repair the mistakes of the line managers and supervisors. After all, their principal job is to manufacture, distribute, and service. They do not read cases on wrongful termination, nor do they effectively create tools to avoid litigation. Each employer must help its line management understand changes in the laws and cases so line management can effectively use the human resource/personnel staff functions. That is the first crucial step: Train the managers.

Most of corporate America is aware that first line supervisors of hourly employees need to proceed with caution when terminating employment. There are often rules under a union agreement or similar procedures for employers which presently are (and would like to remain) union free. Usually such supervisors are the least needy of the type of management development advocated here.

Put aside the legal and institutional distinctions between supervisors, managers, officers and so forth. All who direct the work of others, including senior executives, need development. Two major retailers, between them, were ordered to pay out almost $8 million for "wrongful" terminations of four senior management personnel. Although our current orientation is that the greater the discretionary responsibility and authority, the greater latitude an employer should have in dismissal, only one major court decision has recognized this principle to date. The lesson then, should be obvious: All who make decisions severing employment, or who effectively recommend such action, are exposed to scrutiny, and in some cases, even sanctions under the new rules. While you may well want to stratify your management development into say, direct supervision, middle management, and senior management to maximize the effectiveness of their training, all need to be familiarized with the changed laws regarding termination of employment.

Finally, some employers have been reluctant to engage in the necessary management development for fear of "educating" future terminee-plaintiffs in their very midst. More thoughtful employers, however, realize that a proper management development program is necessary, and the education of future plaintiffs is a lesser risk than the lack of education of future defendants. Moreover, a good management development program may actually dissuade future plaintiffs—they will know severance was done properly and move on to new horizons.

This text cannot serve as a detailed guide on the techniques of management and supervisory training, but it is recommended that the substantive points outlined below should (promptly) be included in your next training and development sessions.

Changed and Changing Rules

In many areas the law has already changed; in others it is in the process of changing or soon may change. Employers who historically simply took aim and fired employees today are shooting themselves in the foot. Even among the best run companies, management has too often discovered they had snatched defeat from the jaws of victory:

ARCO learned it could not fire an employee for disclosing facts supportive of antitrust claims

American Airlines discovered it could not summarily dismiss an employee without following its own internal procedural steps

IBM discovered it could not fire an employee romantically involved with an employee at a direct competitor

See's Candies was admonished that it could not fire a senior manager without disclosing to the court and jury its real reasons for termination

Sears was startled to learn that protective "at-will" termination language might not assure it the right to avoid trial regarding a termination "at will"

Cases that are lost may be *very* expensive. Increasingly juries are the final decision makers at trial, and they are awarding substantial damages, largely to punish the employer for its "wrongful" actions in the juries' retrospective view.

> A $1.9 million jury verdict for three senior managers against Federated Department Stores was upheld on appeal to a federal court.
>
> A $6 million verdict went against Fed Mart Corp. at trial on a wrongful discharge case brought by a chief executive.
>
> Over $60 million (mostly in punitive damages) was recently awarded a sales representative against NEC Electronics for a wrongful termination which included a defamation action.

While some such awards may be diminished by the trial court or reversed in appeal, the point is that managers' and supervisors' actions are being reexamined after the fact and are being found "wrongful." Not only is the risk of damages startling, but the costs are also great: Attorney's fees, lost executive time, damaged morale generally, and damaged careers for those managers and supervisors unlucky enough to be challenged. The details of these cases (and more) have been analyzed earlier and can be further developed for training materials. The message is clear, however; managers and supervisors ignorant of the changes in applicable laws and court decisions act at their peril and risk enmeshing their employer, in costly litigation.

Need for Balanced Approach

As expensive as wrongful terminations may be, an even greater risk attends those employers where management has become paralyzed, unable to properly terminate employment out of fear or excessive caution. Too often in such organizations, malingerers set the standards for conduct and a perceived impunity for malcontents undermines the morale and productivity of the majority. This type of calcification is likely to be at least as damaging to the employer and the individual careers of managers or supervisors as wrongful termination litigation. To draw an unpleasant metaphor, one is no less dead from slow, painless carbon monoxide poisoning than from being shot by a .357 magnum.

Those employers expecting to live through this period of change in the law of wrongful termination must take a new, balanced approach—not fearful or timid about termination of employment under proper standards adapted to their legitimate business needs, but only after careful assurance that the termination(s) are reasonable and fair under the provable circumstances of the case(s).

Now that you have the attention of the management and supervisory "trainees," you can proceed to reeducate them so the job of severing employment, when necessary, can be performed with a scalpel rather than a dull machete. The author has found this can best be accomplished by use of guidelines and checklists designed to force careful decision making by individuals more accustomed, thankfully, to manufacturing, distributing, and servicing than they are to terminating employees. While such guidelines and checklists obviously will need to be adapted to your organization's unique needs and objectives, several examples (touching different substantive points) are discussed in the next section.

Summary of Prohibited or Restricted Reasons for Termination

Because of the mechanics of our legislative and court system, there is no easy, comprehensive definition of "rightful" termination. The best that can be done is to avoid known land mines, and infer from what is known which analogous areas should be avoided. The following guidelines may provide managers and supervisors with a quick substantive review of the law as developed generally to date.

TERMINATION IN VIOLATION OF PUBLIC POLICY. For many years, the courts of most jurisdictions have held that a discharge gives rise to a cause of action when it violates "public policy" (as defined in various statutes, but not limited to employment matters, and sometimes beyond specific statutes). For example, an employee may not be discharged for refusing his or her employer's direction to commit perjury, or for refusing to participate in an illegal price fixing scheme. While such examples may seem obvious, other terminations in violation of "public policy" may be less clear. Also proscribed in many jurisdictions are:

Termination for exercising legal rights, such as declining polygraph testing, demanding to see one's personnel file, prosecuting an action against one's employer, or a third party action against a "valued customer," and so on

Termination for performing legal duties, such as serving on a jury

Termination for refusal to perform unethical actions, even though not expressly illegal

Termination for "whistleblowing" that is, for advising authorities of improper or illegal individual or corporate activities

Termination for failure to cover up a supervisor's misconduct

While the management will undoubtedly point out that this employer would never terminate anyone for these reasons, a closer look will reveal that some of the examples mentioned may be perceived by the employer as terminations for conflict-of-interest, or violation of "house" rules rather than violations of public policy. Yet the final decision on such a question is often left for a judge or a jury to decide. Legality or illegality, a violation of public policy or not, may be in the eye of the last beholder. Moreover, a reviewing judge or jury may later decide that a termination for, say, absenteeism, is really a "pretext" for violating a public policy of restricting one's right, say, to perform jury duty or to take a worker's compensation leave.

Because judges or juries are empowered to look for the "real reason" for termination and disregard the reason stated by the employer, where an employee's overall work record includes matters related to public policy, it is especially important for line management to work with human resources to assure that any termination decision is proper and defensible even if later reviewed by outsiders not beholden to, or perhaps even hostile to, the employer. Moreover, because the courts have held that discharges in violation of public policy many constitute torts which can serve as the basis for an award of unforeseen compensatory damages (*e.g.,* emotional distress) and punitive damages, special care in this area is warranted. The tools described later in this chapter should help to minimize risk.

IMPLIED-IN-FACT CONTRACTUAL LIMITATIONS. Lead by California, courts in over 35 other jurisdictions have recognized that certain implied-in-fact contractual limitations on the rights of employers to discharge employees at will may arise under various circumstances. Although the courts are continuing to refine what circumstances give rise to an implied contractual obligation not to terminate an employee without some "cause," and there is currently much disagreement among the various states, the following factors have contributed to a finding of such an implied obligation:

Long-term employment, especially where the employee is promoted from time to time, given positive reviews and significant (for the employer) increases in wages or salary.

Oral representations promising, or even alluding to, continuing job security. These may occur at any number of points in the employment process, including recruitment, performance reviews, promotional opportunities, and so on. Such "promises" may waive protective at-will language in the employers job applications. Also, such statements are heard, almost universally, to be a binding "promise" by the affected employee although the employer's representative was merely giving advice or generalizing from his or her own observations or experiences. Questions arising from such "misunderstandings" are usually left for a judge or jury to decide.

Written policies (formal or informal) and general practices which state or imply a commitment by the employer to treat the employee reasonably or fairly. Such policies and practices may appear in employee handbooks (which often are not intended to be universally applicable, but rarely say so), recruitment or publicity materials, memos, house organs, and a myriad of other places.

Changes in an employee's circumstances which is intended for, or has the effect of benefitting the employer. Passing up an alternative job opportunity, relocating (even at the employer's expense) and leaving another position have all given rise to implied-in-fact restrictions on an employer's "right" to terminate an employee at will. Such restrictions would appear to be the law in a majority of jurisdictions when the question has been squarely presented and the decision reported.

Although the issue is not yet clear in reported decisions, it is believed that the implied-in-fact contract theory should give rise only to damages for breach of contract. Such damages cannot be taken lightly, however, because the remedies may include reinstatement with back pay or even "front pay" if reinstatement is not appropriate. At least one court has also suggested attorney's fees may be part of the damages suffered.

IMPLIED-AT-LAW COVENANT OF GOOD FAITH AND FAIR DEALING. Some courts have considered the same factors listed above with respect to implied-in-fact contractual obligations in determining whether an implied-at-law covenant of good faith and fair dealing requires the employer not discharge an employee without "cause." The major unsettled legal question is whether a claim for breach of the implied covenant gives rise to compensatory and/or punitive tort damages. In the authors' view, tort liability should not exist unless there is some egregious mistreatment of the employee *apart* from the decision to discharge the employee. One need not review the legal debate here; the important point is that tort liability, with massive punitive damages possible, is still potentially available under the implied-in-fact covenant theory.

RELATED TORT THEORIES.[1] Most wrongful discharge plaintiffs also allege intentional infliction of emotional distress. In order to establish such a claim, the plaintiff must present evidence that the employer acted "outrageously" (i.e., beyond the bounds of conduct usually tolerated in a civilized community), that the employee suffered "severe" emotional distress (headaches and sleepless nights are usually not enough), and that the emotional distress was actually caused by the employer's outrageous acts. This is a difficult claim to establish—if the employer handles the actual implementation of the discharge decision properly. (See Chapter 10).

In addition to infliction of emotional distress, numerous other tort (and damage) theories are often alleged in wrongful termination cases. These would include:

> Defamation (libel or slander) allegations are often routine in wrongful termination cases. Where an employee is severed for reasons that could involve criminal conduct, publication (orally or in writing) of this outside a small "need-to-know" group can entitle the employee to recovery even if he or she cannot prove damages. Where the reasons for discharge are otherwise proof of actual damage is required for "compensatory" recovery, but in either case, punitive damages (almost without limit) can be awarded. (See, for example, the NEC Electronics case mentioned previously awarding $62 million in damages, mostly for defamation). Of course, truth is a complete defense, but that for the judge or jury to decide after the fact, and their perspective may be different than that of the employer. (*See* discussion of pretextual terminations.)

[1]Related tort theories are not, technically speaking, prohibitions on or restrictions of an employer's right to terminate at will. Rather, they are supplemental to the prohibitions and restrictions discussed previously. They do, however, add greatly to the potential cost of termination, and sometimes have the practical effect of making an otherwise essentially correct termination "wrongful." Because of their direct relationship with the theories considered, they are included here.

Interference with an advantageous employment contract or prospective employment, the latter being especially sensitive in matters regarding protection of trade secrets or other confidential business information.

Fraud, malicious (including retaliatory) discharge, negligent discharge (for example without regard to the real facts or all the facts) and invasion of privacy (See Chapter 5) are too often the basis for an employer to have an adverse verdict arising from wrongful termination.

PROBLEMS OF TIME AND LOCATION. Of course not all of the legal concepts previously referenced apply in any single state (with the probable exception of California), but for employers with multiple locations, especially where employees transfer or are transferred among them, the problems of wrongful termination are exponential. While a termination may occur in one state, and perhaps be tried in a local court there, the contract of employment might well have been made (or modified) in another state. An employer tort (or breach of public policy) in one state might be differently perceived elsewhere. Under some complex legal rules, the law of a state different than the one in which the termination occurred might apply. Thus, managers and supervisors of employees whose careers have spanned several locations must be generally familiar with the changed rules regarding employment termination even though they are not (now) located in one of the liberal states currently stretching the old law.

Difficult and confusing though it may be, line management must manage the new risks of employee terminations regardless of present location, and there is no meaningful relief in sight. Line management is certainly not helpless; rather it needs to update and coordinate its operating methods as in the following.

Guidelines for "Rightful" Terminations

It is impossible to list all the considerations necessary to assure fairness in all termination decisions for all employers in all cases. Fair treatment obviously depends upon individual circumstances which require careful assessment before a decision is made. Nevertheless, the following is a guideline of factors to be evaluated.

TERMINATION FOR MISCONDUCT. Fair treatment in cases of misconduct always depends on a careful investigation and assessment of the specific facts and circumstances, including:

1. The importance of the rule or standard of conduct allegedly violated
2. The degree of certainty that the employee in fact did what he or she is accused of doing
3. The employee's length of service, past performance, and conduct record
4. The employee's level of responsibility
5. The treatment of prior employees in similar situations
6. The employee's explanation of his or her conduct prior to making the decision (this is generally regarded by judges and juries as a

basic element of fairness, and it should be received in time to have an impact on the decision)

In certain situations, circumstances may require one or more of the following techniques.

1. Suspension of the employee pending an investigation where necessary to collect and evaluate all of the facts and circumstances.
2. Limiting the dissemination of information of the details regarding the employee's misconduct to those with a need to know. This will reduce potential exposure to a defamation claim.
3. Using progressive discipline if it is warranted by the nature of the offense and the level or length of service of the employee.

TERMINATION FOR POOR PERFORMANCE. Most courts and juries believe that it is unfair to discipline or discharge an employee for poor performance without first giving the employee some notice of his or her performance deficiencies and an opportunity to improve. The key procedure is a regular and effective performance appraisal program. In the author's experience, this is easy to establish but difficult to maintain effectively. The major problem is that managers are too often unwilling to identify and communicate performance deficiencies to higher level professional or management employees—and most wrongful discharge plaintiffs are higher level professional or management employees.

Many companies either fail to include executives and managers in the appraisal process, or believe that positive reinforcement is the only way to motivate good performance. Historically, if the employee failed to respond to positive messages, the simple answer was either to fire the employee or to wait until the mandatory retirement age. In light of the age discrimination laws and wrongful discharge claims, neither of these solutions is generally available anymore.

The performance appraisal process must be properly documented. It is also important to keep merit salary increases and bonuses in line with a true assessment of employee performance. Such compensation decisions can be and are used as evidence that the employee was performing well. Both appraisals and compensation history should be carefully reviewed prior to making any termination decision.

Whenever possible the employee should be specifically warned that the failure to improve performance could result in termination. A warning is more than "notice;" a warning includes a direct statement that failure to improve (to a specified amount in a defined time) will lead to termination (or other action if such is appropriate). A warning should be documented. Before a final termination decision is made, consider transfer or demotion as a possible alternative where warranted.

Finally in a situation involving inadequate performance, consider, together with the human resource or personnel staff, whether a separation agreement with a release is appropriate. With regard to separation agreements, first decide what the employer is willing (or committed to by policy or practice) to give the employee without a release (in terms of severance pay, time to look for another job, etc.). A reasonable, unconditional separation package will often avoid litigation, and may be an indication of "fair treatment" if a lawsuit is filed and if admissible as evidence. If the employee comes back and asks for more, it may then be appropriate to condition further separation benefits upon the signing of a release. In general, however, it is likely that something extra, above the normal severance benefit will be necessary to make the release valid, even as to nonstatutory claims.

PRIOR REVIEW OF TERMINATION DECISIONS.   Whether dealing with discharges for poor performance or misconduct, it is generally advisable to have a process of review and approval of the decision before it is implemented. Most companies *require* review of termination decisions by higher level line management and human resources or personnel professionals. The author highly recommends this type of review. In difficult cases, review by legal counsel prior to a termination decision may avoid serious potential litigation expense and liability. (This is discussed more fully later and this segment of your management training guidelines should be fleshed out when your review process is fully defined.)

IMPLEMENTATION OF THE TERMINATION DECISION.   An area that is often overlooked is the actual implementation of the discharge decision. Very few line managers and even human resources or personnel professionals have much experience in this area. There are two related pitfalls: in an effort to avoid the unpleasant confrontation, the manager often communicates the decision abruptly (e.g., by a written communication or a brief notification of the decision without any explanation). Alternatively, in the same effort to avoid a confrontation, the manager often expresses sympathy for and "sides with" the employee in communicating the decision. Either approach can substantially increase the risk of a lawsuit and liability. This matter is considered in greater detail in Chapter 10.

Pretermination Checklist for Management

In considering whether a proposed termination is more likely to be "rightful" rather than "wrongful," completing the following checklist may help. The person completing each step should initial the applicable section and note the date of completion; this will greatly facilitate review of the termination decision. Where answers are negative or steps incomplete, the supervisor should check with human resources or personnel before making or communicating a termination decision.

	Initials	*Date*
A. Establishing "Rightful" Termination (Misconduct and poor performance)		
1. *Get all the operative facts*	___	___
a. Conduct a full, fair, and impartial investigation of the facts. Get *objective* data.	___	___
b. Search out witnesses, don't rely on volunteers.	___	___
c. Be neutral, or get someone else to investigate.	___	___

    d. Give the employee a chance to explain or defend his or her actions or omissions.   _____ _____

    e. Review all mitigating factors.   _____ _____

    f. Consider a suspension during investigation as a cooling-off period.   _____ _____

    g. Key: Did the investigation reveal substantial evidence that the employee did what he or she was accused of? If "yes," proceed; if not check with human resources or personnel for assistance.   _____ _____

2. *Was the employee given prior warning of the disciplinary consequences of his or her conduct?*   _____ _____

    a. Assure the rules of conduct were communicated to the employee.   _____ _____

    b. Assure the rule which was violated is reasonable.   _____ _____

    c. Assure the employee was previously warned about the misconduct.   _____ _____

    d. Assure the warning clearly states the disciplinary consequences of further misconduct.   _____ _____

    (Note: certain offenses are serious enough that prior warnings may not be necessary. Check with human resources or personnel.)

    e. Key: Can you demonstrate that the employee knew what was expected and that he or she failed to follow the rules requirements?   _____ _____

3. *Were other employees treated similarly in the past?*   _____ _____

    a. Different levels of discipline may (but, may not) be appropriate for different employees. There must be a clear business justification for differential treatment.   _____ _____

    b. Avoid being (and also the appearance of being) arbitrary, discriminatory, or capricious in the imposition of discipline.   _____ _____

    c. Key: Can you demonstrate that the employee to be disciplined is not receiving harsher treatment or discriminatory treatment when compared to others? If "yes" proceed; if not, check with human resources or personnel for assistance.   _____ _____

4. *Special rules for terminations for poor performance.*   _____ _____

    a. Assure there are *objective* evaluations of the employee's performance which demonstrate clearly that the employee's performance is poor enough to warrant discharge.   _____ _____

b. Give the employee an opportunity to explain his or her performance problems. _____ _____

c. Establish that the employee knew what was expected. _____ _____

   i. Were performance standards communicated to the employee? _____ _____

   ii. Did those standards reflect the performance you have expected from your other employees? _____ _____

   iii. Were performance review or counseling sessions held with the employee? _____ _____

   iv. Review the overall performance reviews—don't just talk about the bad points. _____ _____

   v. Was it made clear to the employee that failure to improve could result in termination? _____ _____

   vi. Key: Can you prove that the employee knew what was expected and that he or she failed to meet those expectations? _____ _____

d. Review what was done before in similar situations including in other departments. _____ _____

   i. How does the employee's performance compare with others at the same level? _____ _____

   ii. Have others with similar performance problems been kept on? _____ _____

B. Have you followed any and all procedural guidelines relating to involuntary terminations? _____ _____

   1. Review *all* written policies, practices, procedures, handbooks, and so on, for information relevant to discipline or discharge. It is important to keep the written word. _____ _____

   2. Follow all required steps and document your compliance with procedures. _____ _____

   3. Check with human resources or personnel to assure that all steps have been properly completed. _____ _____

C. Confirm that "rightful" discharge has been documented. _____ _____

   1. Assure that warnings, disciplinary steps, performance reviews, and review conferences follow consistent written pattern. _____ _____

   2. Review memoranda to the file of counseling sessions and notes of meetings with the employee. If further documentation is necessary, assure that this is done accurately and promptly by those persons with direct, first-hand knowledge. _____ _____

3. Retain relevant documents and physical evidence   _____   _____
regarding an employee's performance or
misconduct: work samples, productivity data,
attendance records, empty beer bottles, and so on.

4. Assure that the termination notice is accurate and   _____   _____
complete.

5. Note: Remember an employee's right to inspect   _____   _____
personnel file and discoverability of documents in
litigation.

Based on my review of all the facts and circumstances and completion
of the above checklist, I recommend that _____ employment be
terminated effective _____.

Signed _____   Signed _____
         Line Management   Human Resources

Date _____   Date _____

Summary of Management and Supervisory Development

Just as a sow's ear can rarely be spun into a silk purse, the human resources
or personnel professional can rarely make a rightful termination out of
a case poorly handled initially by line management. Though you could
counsel, delay, and start again, such an approach loses time, deadens
general morale, and forces line management to see staff as the enemy
rather than the professional to assist when needed. Such circumstances
are obviously to be avoided, though it is very common.

The management development program sketched, when filled out by
reference to other chapters in this book and adapted to your own employer's unique needs and "corporate culture," will go a long way towards
preventing the conditions under which "wrongful-termination" suits can
get started. It will also make line and staff functions interdependent, not
antagonists. Training and development of managers and supervisors de-
serves top priority.

SPECIAL MEASURES TO BE INSTITUTED BY THE HUMAN RESOURCE AND PERSONNEL STAFF: THE SECOND LINE OF DEFENSE

Because an uninformed line management can at anytime make an informal or perhaps even formal wrongful termination decision, and because an uninformed management can say or do something, unwittingly,
which will make a timely, rightful termination virtually impossible, the
author regards the management and supervisory training outlined previously as the crucial, first step in preventing wrongful termination litigation. Yet almost as important, there is a broad counterpoint of measures
to be taken by the human resource/personnel staff. While the prophylactic

results of these measures will not be as immediate as a well-trained management and supervisory team, taking such measures now will have a very positive long-range protective value to the employer. They can, and should, be started simultaneously with the management training immediately.

The measures to be taken by the human resource/personnel professional will require rethinking, and often reformatting of the basic employment process and relationship. Your staff will need to adopt new rules and/or adapt existing policies and practices to assure that the institutional processes are "caught up" to the changed and changing law regarding wrongful termination of employment. This will require a detailed review of at least:

Hiring practices—formation of the employment relationship

Current policies and practices respecting continuing employment of existing and future employees

Pretermination decision making

The termination process itself

Each of these matters is discussed in detail in this section; other matters, generally post-termination in nature are discussed in the succeeding section.

Formatting New Employment Relationships

Too frequently the seeds of wrongful termination are sewn at the very beginning of the hiring process. Because changes in position of a prospective employee may give rise to an implied-in-fact contract, or in some jurisdictions to implied-in-law obligations, the breach of which could be tortuous, the entire recruitment and hiring process needs to be reviewed.

RECRUITMENT AND PREEMPLOYMENT INQUIRIES. Depending on the level and types of skills desired, the recruitment policies of the employer may range from responses to walk-in job seekers who complete a summary job application at one extreme to the use of outside recruiters, executive search firms or "head hunters" at the other extreme. At one time or another, most employers will utilize the full range of options available to staff its business. Hiring techniques nearer the first situation discussed can be dealt with in the application paperwork. Recruitment situations more like the latter situation, however, present special potential problems because even outside recruiters may become employer "agents" whose statements and promises, though technically unauthorized, could be binding on the employer.

While it is doubtful that an outside recruitment agency would deliberately make representations which would be contractually binding on an employer contrary to direction, where express limitations are not placed on an outside recruiter, there may be innocent statements or representations which nevertheless give rise to contract-type rights. Especially where the statements of a recruiter are not corrected before a recruit materially changes position in reliance on those statements, a future problem, in case of early termination, may have been created even before a hire decision has been made.

It is suggested that specific boundaries be set for recruitment, both inside and outside. Especially where executive search firms are engaged to do some screening of persons currently employed elsewhere, a frank and thorough discussion about the terms of any representations, and the limits thereof, should be a top priority. That is not to say that all contract-type inducements must be avoided, but the employer should clearly understand the scope of such representations made on its behalf. It may make sense, for example, for a recruiter to note an employer policy of not terminating employment except for (defined) cause, for a trial period or otherwise, but only if such representations are within the employer's job search authorizations.

Obviously, where particular executive, administrative, craft, or professional skills are necessary, recruiters may need more latitude to effectively search and screen candidates, but that latitude should be established in advance by the employer. A confirmation letter setting forth such latitude or any restrictions is advisable.

ENGAGEMENT LETTERS. Precisely because of the difficulties in controlling what is said, implied, or heard in the recruitment process, whether inside or outside, it is often prudent to confirm important details of the hiring arrangements in writing, usually in an engagement letter. This is especially true if no regular job application form is to be completed. Otherwise it is doubtful that an employer will be able to effectively rebut claims by a terminated employee that he or she was promised a minimum term of employment, employment as long as the work was satisfactory or any other of the permutations negating or undermining employment at will, or for that matter, employment on any other specific basis.

While an engagement letter presents an appropriate opportunity to clarify any misunderstandings and preserve the right of termination at will, it is possible that such a letter will confer contractual rights and that if it is vague or carries implications favorable to the employee, a judge or jury is *very* likely to construe the letter against the employer's interests. Such letters when properly done can provide an effective shield against potential employees suits for wrongful (contract) termination, but poorly done, such letters will surely give the employee a sword.

A letter agreement regarding employment prepared by Sutter Community Hospital came close to the mark, but left too much room for an example to wiggle according to a California appellate court. In the case of *Hillsman v. Sutter Community Hospitals,* 153 Cal. App. 3d 743 (1984), the court confirmed the basic principle that contract terms will not be *implied* which contradict *express* contract terms. However, the court in *Hillsman* found that a letter agreement providing that "termination of this letter of understanding by either party may be accomplished upon thirty day' notice" did not *expressly* preclude the employee's assertion that he had an implied-in-fact contract right to be terminated only in accordance with the procedures set forth in the employer's bylaws. The court noted that the express contract "does not state, for example, that termination of the agreement could be accomplished 'for any reason' or 'at will' or 'without cause' or 'without a hearing.' " 153 Cal. App. 3d at 755.

Given the rationale of the *Hillsman* decision, a more detailed engagement letter would appear appropriate. As a starting point, the following example may be helpful; it is suggested that it be adapted for your particular needs and reviewed by your counsel prior to use:

AGREEMENT REGARDING EMPLOYMENT RELATIONSHIP

This Agreement Regarding Employment Relationship ("Agreement") is effective as of _____, between _____, a _____ corporation (the "Employer") and _____ ("Employee").

1. The Employer will employ Employee in the initial position of _____ and at the initial salary rate of _____ . Employment benefits shall be provided the Employee, from time to time, in the Employer's sole discretion, as it does for employees of like positions.

2. Employee's future salary rate and position(s) shall be determined by the Employer, in its sole discretion.

3. Employee's employment with the Employer is not for any specified term and may be terminated by Employee or by the Employer at any time for any reason, stated or unstated, with or without cause.*

4. Paragraphs 2 and 3 above constitute the complete agreement between Employee and the Employer regarding the matters referred to in said paragraphs and supersede any and all prior written or oral agreements or understandings on such matters. Employee understands that no representative of the Employer has been authorized to enter into any agreement or commitment with Employee which is inconsistent in any way with the terms of paragraphs 2 and 3.

5. The terms set forth in paragraphs 2 and 3 above may not be modified in any way except by a written agreement signed by Employee and by an authorized representative of the Employer which expressly states the intention of the parties to modify the terms of this Agreement.

Dated: _____   Dated: _____

_____   _____

_____

         "Employee"   "Employer"

By _____

Title _____

*Additional text may be added here to "soften" this text or provide notice, and so on.

Engagement letters are not panaceas. They have practical and legal limitations (as to the latter, you and your management should assure that you understand specific limitations in your state through discussions with your counsel). As a practical matter, some employers stay away from such letters as morale breakers or recruitment inhibitors. The author believes this is overstated—most good employment prospects are more anxious to get at the job than to negotiate their severance arrangements. Each employer, however, must balance those practical considerations in its own employment market.

Legal limitations are more pervasive, but perhaps less critical. First, engagement letters are only effective for new hires; forcing present employers to sign such an agreement "in consideration of" keeping their jobs is likely to be ineffective.[2] Use of such an agreement as part of the overall arrangements in a major promotion (for example from nonexempt to exempt status for wage and hour purposes), however, may pass muster. Secondly, the language does not, and should not in the author's opinion, attempt to eliminate exposure for tortious (mis)conduct by the employer in the termination process. If an employer attempts to override or waive future defamation claims or other tortious conduct, the employer increases the chances that such a letter will be found to be an unenforceable contract against public policy or of adhesion. Finally, the author believes there is risk in wholesale use of such letters, especially where the employer has overwhelming "bargaining power," the employee is unsophisticated or reasonably cannot understand the meaning of such a letter, and so on. These issues should be considered with your counsel.

Despite their limitations, the author recommends engagement letters, at least for exempt employees. For those concerned about the abruptness of paragraph 3 of the example text, the following addition of text might be considered:

[u]pon [90 calendar days] advance written notice, or pay in lieu thereof, or without any advance notice in the event Employee violates any rule or policy of Employer; fails to fully, promptly and properly complete any task or responsibility assigned to [him/her]; otherwise engages in misconduct; or for any other honest business reason thought sufficient by the Employer.

Although you may experience some cost in terms of pay in lieu of notice under this approach, it provides the tools for a negotiated severance with, perhaps, a release, (discussed in the next section) and is supported by the old adage, "An ounce of prevention is worth more than a pound of cure."

EMPLOYMENT APPLICATIONS. Many employers regard employment applications, after they have been sterilized by equal employment and affirmative action dictates, as a relatively unimportant management tool. Such a view may be shortsighted. Appropriate language included in an employment application may be enough to preserve at-will termination rights.

The California courts, often criticized for bad decisions regarding at-

---

[2]In attempting such a course, there is an obvious risk that a long-term employee will refuse to sign an express at-will agreement and will claim that there is no legal "consideration" to support the agreement. Such an employee may claim that he or she already has an implied contractual right (which has "accrued" over years of service in reliance on prior policies and practices) not to be discharged without cause. Such an employee might claim that the requirement to sign such a document as a condition of future employment is itself a breach of implied contractual rights. The author is not aware of any judicial decisions which have dealt with such contentions. There is no legal risk in *requesting* the employee to sign the agreement. Whether an employee who refuses to sign the agreement should be terminated is a question which should be carefully considered in light of the specific circumstances. Obviously, requesting (or requiring) current employees to sign such agreements may create serious problems from an employee relations perspective which outweigh the benefit, and if exceptions are made for one or more employees, problems of discrimination may arise.

will termination, have recently produced some helpful decisions, at least at the appellate level. In *Shapiro v. Wells Fargo Realty Advisors,* 152 Cal. App. 3d 467 (1984), the court rejected a claim by a former treasurer and vice president of Wells Fargo that there was an implied promise by Wells Fargo to discharge him only for good cause. The court held that an express at-will provision in a stock option agreement signed by Shapiro precluded his wrongful discharge claim based on a theory of implied contract. The relevant language provided that

[n]othing in this Stock Option Agreement . . . shall confer upon the Employee any right to continue in the employ of the Trust or the Advisor or shall interfere with or restrict in any way the rights of the Trust or the Advisor, which are hereby expressly reserved, to discharge the Employee at any time for any reason whatsoever, with or without good cause. *Id.* at 475, n.3.

The court in *Shapiro* specifically rejected the employee's claim that the stock option agreement was an unlawful contract of adhesion, noting that "the provision merely expresses the intention of the contracting parties and defines their employment relationship." *Id.* at 482, n.10. Although *Shapiro's* Stock Option Agreement may be distinguished from the mass of employment applications by hourly or salaried nonexempt employees, the case makes it clear that those employers wishing to preserve at-will termination rights should put such language in the job applications. The language of paragraph 3 of the example text of the engagement letter should provide a model from which to start.

Sears, Roebuck had solid language in its employment application stating that applicant Conboy could be terminated at will. At trial, however, Conboy testified that there had been an oral modification of the at-will language. Something to the effect that Conboy need not worry about that language, as long as he did a good job. . . . The exact language of the waiver is hardly relevant; the point is, the court permitted oral testimony to the effect that the protective language Sears had so carefully included was waived and therefore of no protective value. Although *Conboy* was later reversed on other grounds, it is suggested that language be included in your employment application stating that no one can waive or modify the at-will language, and in fact that such language cannot be modified except by a subsequent written agreement, signed by the parties which is expressly designed to change the at-will agreement. See paragraphs 4 and 5 of the example text of the engagement letter for suggested language.

Finally, to avoid the applicant testifying that he or she was rushed and did not read all that fine print at the end of the application, just above the signature line (the author does not intend to imply any such testimony should constitute a legal defense to the effect of such language), it is suggested that each major statement be initialed by the applicant expressly indicating his or her assent. At least for the vast majority of hourly, and salaried nonexempt applicants, this procedure should provide a valid, admissible memorandum of intent that their employment be at will.

EMPLOYMENT AGREEMENTS. While the use of employment agreements is still limited, the author believes judicious use of such agreements makes sense especially in those areas of employment where the terms and conditions may be necessarily different than those the 12 people behind you at the supermarket might understand or think are reasonable. Examples of such employment conditions might include: The proper use of judgment and discretion by senior managers; the right to transfer employees (with or without their families) to new and perhaps undesired locations, especially overseas; the right to radically change assignments, eliminate job responsibilities, titles and/or perquisites, and so forth. Were an employer to terminate a long service employee for declining an overseas transfer, a judge or jury might well conclude that the employment relationship would not reasonably have included that right and that the termination was therefore wrongful, pretextual, retaliatory and so forth. (Even a resignation under such circumstances might be regarded as a "constructive termination" entitling the employee to sue for wrongful termination in spite of resignation.)

While employment agreements cannot preclude a suit based on public policy wrongful termination, for example, whistle-blowing or statutory grounds, or age or sex discrimination, they can provide several advantages:

Provide for term or project employment

Define special facts, rights, and responsibilities

Protect trade secrets and confidential information

Provide proper language about termination

Provide an alternative dispute resolution procedure for example arbitration or fact finding as an "exclusive remedy"

Limit "damages" in terms of type or amount

Provide for posttermination consulting and/or a noncompete covenant.

Employment agreements are not for everyone, and they are discussed in detail in Chapter 13. Do not fail to consider this approach, however, because it has not been to your employer's advantage previously. Changing rules may require changed approaches.

Reformatting Continuing Employment Relationships

Various courts and commentators have stated that employer policies and practices are part of the employment agreement and give rise to enforceable contract rights. Despite differences in the federal courts of appeal, the Employee Retirement Income Security Act (ERISA) may well have lent its support to such a concept, even for unfunded "plans" like sick leave, vacation policies, holiday, and severance pay. Compare *Scott v. Gulf Oil Corp.* 754 F.2d 1499 (9th Cir. 1985), *Abella v. Foote Memorial Hospital, Inc.,* 740 F.2d 4 (6th Cir. 1984) and *Blau v. Del Monte Corp.,* 748 F.2d 1348 (9th Cir. 1985). Although this subject is considered in detail in Chapter 4, the author here assumes that such policies and practices may already have contract right status, and/or the employer may want exactly such a result in certain cases. What is considered briefly in the following section are techniques for achieving or avoiding that result as part of reformatting the continuing employment relationship.

LOCATING AND PRESERVING SEGMENTS OF THE EMPLOY-MENT AGREEMENT. It is embarrassing: So often, employers cannot even locate the various segments of the alleged employment agreement. Old handbooks were not retained or the dates of their effectiveness were not recorded. Policy memoranda have been superseded and prior rules and regulations discarded. Only the plaintiff and his or her lawyers have copies.

Where is the (possible) employment agreement? The answer will vary from employer to employer (and state to state) but the following list should get your thinking started:

Employee handbooks

Supervisor's manuals

Insurance and retirement plans and trust agreements

Summary plan descriptions

Union contracts/Antiunion campaign literature

Policy statements

Memoranda regarding employment matters (general)

Memoranda regarding a specific employee's responsibilities and rights

Stock option agreements and other deferred compensation plans

Patent and noncompetitive agreements

Corporate bylaws (usually as to directors and officers, only)

Locate these documents, including superseded documents and the notice that they were superseded. Date all documents. Determine what language might bear on the employer's right to terminate employment and to whom such language is applicable. Develop a procedure so future documents are correct, coordinated, retained, and indexed. Good luck.

Revising the Employee Handbook and Supervisor's Manual

The employer's written employment policies, manuals, and handbooks must be reviewed and usually revised to assure that they do not create unwanted implied contractual obligations and that they are consistent. The objective here is *not* to make policies or practices uniform or consistent among employers, and thus, no recommended text can be given. Rather, the purpose is to make your documents *precise:* Say what you mean because a judge or jury is likely to believe you meant what you said, and they will hold you to it. See for example, *Cleary v. American Airlines,* 111 Cal. App. 3d 443 (1980) where the court found a wrongful termination because of failure to follow stated procedures, not because of any ruling that the termination itself was faulty.

A small library could be filled with books on writing employee handbooks. They need not be repeated here. In reviewing policies, manuals, and handbooks, however, consider the following points as examples of what may not be discussed in the books about handbooks:

1. What does completing any probationary period really mean? Does an employee become "permanent?" Or regular? Are there different standards for termination, depending on probationary or regular employment status? If your employment relationship is at will does probationary status make sense? Consider whether more frequent reviews are appropriate at the outset of the relationship if you do not intend to create rights because the "probationary" period is completed. Recall that use of such terms in union agreements often means a regular employer cannot be terminated except for proven cause after completion of the probationary period.

2. Consider deleting any vague assurances of "fairness" or "job security." For example, the statement that "it is company policy to treat all employees fairly" may be good public relations, but it may also create an implied contract right of "fair treatment." As a practical matter (in the absence of an express at-will contract), such statements leave you vulnerable to the conclusion by a jury that you were not fair or reasonable in *their* judgment. Say what you mean. If you only terminate for violation of rules or other misconduct, say so. If there is not a standard you wish to be held to, do not allude to general "fairness," unless of course, you want jury review after the fact. Be precise.

3. Add brief, general disclaimers to those policies and segments of manuals which are not intended as contractual rights that say so: These segments are merely guidelines for management, are not required to be followed in all circumstances and are not intended to confer contract rights on any employee. Separate out ERISA plans where you may want contract protection and preemption options. If you want a mandatory internal review of termination decisions, separate that also. The following language may be appropriate for the guideline portions (say promotional considerations or salary adjustments).

The policies, practices, and procedures set forth in this section [describe document] are guidelines for supervision. They are not intended to confer contractual rights of any kind upon any employee, or to create contractual obligations of any kind for the Employer. The Employer may revise, delete or supplement any policy, practice, or procedure in this [describe document] at any time in its sole discretion.

The employee handbook can still be an integrated whole, but identify with particularity which segments are guidelines and which are contractual in nature.

4. Take a close look at any written policies relating to employee discipline and termination. Again, be sure that the procedures are clearly described as guidelines if that is what you intend, and clearly provide that appropriate discipline depends on the particular facts and circumstances and on the discretion of management. Be sure that descriptions of specific progressive discipline procedures in such policies cannot be read to apply to all employees in all circumstances as a matter of right. If discipline, termination, or other policies are intended to apply only to nonmanagement or nonexempt employees, be sure to express that lim-

itation. This is one of the most common pitfalls in wrongful discharge litigation. A typical case involves an executive claiming wrongful discharge because he or she did not receive certain prescribed verbal and written warnings prior to discharge as set forth in a personnel manual. Although most managers would agree that such policies were not intended to apply to executive management, this can become an issue of fact to be decided by a jury if it is not stated clearly in the written policy.

5. Include a statement that management reserves the right to change its policies at any time in its sole discretion. Change may well include, revoking, discontinuing, reducing or substituting alternative benefits which may or may not be equivalent or comparable, and so forth. If that is what you intend, say so. Otherwise someone may claim a "vested" right in or reliance on an old policy or procedure.

6. Consider specifying rules (not all inclusive) with penalties so a judge or jury cannot substitute a later judgment about reasonableness. If any theft, no matter how small, is a dischargeable offense, say so. If "no drugs" means not even marijuana where it is decriminalized, say so. This will help consistent enforcement as well as reduce the risk that other's judgments about what should cause termination would take precedence over yours.

7. Be sure to include the at-will language and no modification thereof as discussed if you mean to use this concept. As a practical matter, this reiteration discourages lawsuits and helps dispose of the few that may be filed.

SPECIAL PROVISIONS FOR SPECIAL EMPLOYEES.   There are employees in special positions that may require special attention when formatting or reformatting their employment relationships. If not otherwise covered by an employment agreement, supplementary language should be developed for the types of employees referenced in the following and other employees with employment conditions out of the ordinary. Precise language will vary among employers and should be reviewed with your counsel before being implemented. Generally, as with engagement letters, such agreements should be entered into at the beginning of the employment relationship, or when otherwise supported by "consideration."

1. Many executives may be required to perform duties which could create a real or apparent conflict of interest. The traditional prohibition against accepting gifts from vendors may leave an employer unable to cope with more sophisticated and dangerous problems. Even a "passive" investment interest in a major supplier, or any such investment by a family member, or close relative may create problems of impartiality and sound business judgment. Without a policy expressly prohibiting conflicts of interest, or even the appearance of conflicts, the employer may be unable to resolve apparent problems of self-dealing. Unless the employer may prove, probably beyond a reasonable doubt, that employee actions are criminal, termination of employment for conflict of interest, without an express prohibition, is at best risky. A broad prohibition of conflicts, real or apparent is appropriate for decision makers who could be in a conflict position.

In addition to a policy prohibiting conflicts, a questionnaire should be circulated periodically requiring disclosure of investment interests in and payments received from, directly or indirectly, persons or entities doing business with, and perhaps competing against, the employer. Such a questionnaire should have prophylactic effects as well as making a record in any case of concealment.

2. Employees whose job location or responsibilities may change radically in the employer's discretion should be required to acknowledge this condition of employment in advance. The concept of "constructive discharge," for example, a quit instead of accepting an unwanted transfer, may permit the quit to be deemed a termination and found to be wrongful in certain situations. Therefore, where involuntary transfer is possible, the employer's transfer policy should be accepted by the employee and memorialized in writing before he or she is hired or promoted.

3. Employees receiving stock options, stock appreciation rights or other deferred compensation should acknowledge that such rights do not restrict the employer's right to terminate at will. *See, Shapiro v. Wells Fargo,* supra. Recitation of the employer's right in such documents is important to counter the argument that the employee was implicitly engaged for the period of the deferred compensation grant. Also assure that the corporate papers (articles and especially bylaws) provide that officers and directors can be removed or terminated at will.

MID-COURSE CORRECTIONS. Although courts have prohibited stranger things, employers have generally been believed to have the right to modify wages, salaries, benefits, and the terms and conditions of employment (rules, policies, procedures, standards, etc.) unless restricted by law or contract. Certain formalities are, however, required and/or advisable.

1. Broad-scale or general changes should be effected by publication of a notice to all affected employees communicating the new rule, procedure, or practice. Though actual notice may not be required, lack of notice must be the employee's fault rather than defective communication by the employer. The notice should be explicit in stating the effective time and date of the change, in revoking the prior rule, procedure or practice and in specifying a resource for answering any questions about interpretation or application. Any language barriers should be bridged by the employer so the job requirements are clearly communicated. Finally, the consequences of failure to accept the change should be anticipated, whether termination of reticent employees (sometimes risky), discussion, waiver, or otherwise.

2. Job performance or other work-related behavior of an individual employee may be corrected, in lieu of termination, by effective notice of objective standards to be met within a reasonable time period. The required standards must be job related and not discriminatory. They should be corrective, not punitive. Excessive requirements often cause juries to award punitive damages against the employer.

Goals and/or objectives for individual employees are often set in performance review conferences. They should be clearly documented. Though it takes more time in the conference, goals and objectives that are set by the employee or jointly are much more helpful should there be a wrongful termination action when those goals or objectives are not met. At a minimum, in a problem case, solicit and obtain the employee's agreement that the goals and/or objectives are reasonable. Secondly, apply progressive discipline where it makes sense. Finally, do not single an employee out as the only one with objectives or with materially different objectives than his or her counterparts. Differential treatment will create a wrongful termination as surely as anything. (See Management Checklist.)

PRETERMINATION REVIEW. Before deciding on termination of employment, it is advisable to have the recommended decision reviewed in detail by a line superior and a human resource/personnel specialist. Persons reviewing a termination recommendation should review the facts and circumstances (see Management Checklist), as well as the overall reasonableness of the termination. If the matter of removal from the workplace is immediately critical, the employee should be suspended pending investigation so a proper decision can be made. If exonerated, the suspended employee should be returned to work with no loss of pay or benefits. Otherwise, he or she should be promptly notified of the decision to terminate employment. In particularly difficult cases, or where litigation is likely, your counsel should be involved in the pretermination decision process.

COMMUNICATION OF THE TERMINATION DECISION. How the termination decision is communicated to and received by the affected employee seems to correlate more directly with the prosecution of an agency or court action than does the legal or moral correctness of the decision. Given this apparent relationship, the reader is directed to Chapter 10 for a discussion of the mechanics of implementing the termination decision.

Audit and Refinements

Severing employment is normally a significant and deliberate act. Much can be learned from understanding the reason(s) for the decision to separate. All voluntary departures should be given an exit interview. Involuntary terminations should be interviewed also by human resources/personnel not line management, especially if their employer's system excludes or minimizes their involvement or if the reasons for termination are not clear for any other reason. This final interaction can assuage emotions (thus controlling or eliminating agency or court actions), evaluate and document reasons for severance and clean up final details (collect ID, assure proper payment of accrued benefits, provide a proper postemployment reference point, etc.).

Employee turnover is expensive. Seldom do employers evaluate the costs of recruitment, orientation, and lost efficiency during training. Therefore, understanding the reasons for severance, involuntary or voluntary, can help refine your procedures to meet your objectives of a stable workforce or a targeted turnover. In addition to avoiding or winning any wrongful termination suits, the proactive measures suggested previously should help you reduce costs of staffing your business as well as improve morale and productivity.

POSTTERMINATION RISK MANAGEMENT: OPPORTUNITIES AND PITFALLS

After a termination decision is made and communicated to the employee, there are a number of important steps that can be taken by the human resource or personnel professional to limit the risk of wrongful termination litigation in the first instance or an adverse result should a suit be filed. The items discussed in the following should all be reviewed when there is a hostile separation from employment. The human resource/personnel department must keep abreast of posttermination matters in order to protect the employer from being set-up for a wrongful termination liability.

Internal Review and Dispute Resolution

Internal review is a posttermination procedure that an employee may (sometimes must) invoke to challenge his or her termination. The procedures at various employers take many forms, but for those employers which have meaningful internal review, there is an opportunity to see and evaluate an employee's wrongful termination claim prior to agency or court litigation, and if appropriate, make adjustments promptly and at a relatively low cost. It may be possible, in some jurisdictions, to make an internal review procedure a mandatory first and perhaps last step.

It is the author's opinion that internal review serves an employer well; an effective system should reduce external dispute resolution procedures and expenses associated therewith, as well as enhance morale. A very brief comment on several common internal review systems follows.

OPEN DOOR POLICY. The traditional "open door policy" may have some very limited efficacy in very small businesses, but otherwise it is generally ineffective as an internal review procedure. It is rarely used and even less often provides meaningful review.

GRIEVANCE AND ARBITRATION PROCEDURES. Although generally associated with union contracts, grievance procedures and in some cases neutral arbitration systems have been adopted by some employers for nonunion employees. Such grievance or complaint procedures are effective only if employees are skilled at or assisted with presentation of their position and there is a perceived fairness in the results. The employer must decide whether the employee can be represented by outsiders—a chance for both sides to explore the other's case—and whether the decision in the final step of the procedure will be made by an employee or an independent arbitrator.

Arbitration procedures are faster, simpler, and more private than most court procedures. Arbitration can be made mandatory and exclusive by contract, although statutory claims, for example, age discrimination, may survive. Employees and employers may elect, on a case-by-case basis, to proceed to arbitration; if this election is done carefully, it may waive employee suits other forums. Thus, an employer has a variety of options in adopting an effective complaint procedure; with or without arbitration, establishing or rejuvenating such at procedure should reduce the risk of legitimate wrongful termination actions.

ALTERNATIVE TECHNIQUES OF DISPUTE RESOLUTION. For these employers reluctant to give away their absolute right to terminate at will by agreeing to arbitration, there are some alternatives. Mediation by inside professionals or outside specialists permits the parties to explore mutually satisfactory results without giving away any authority to make decisions. Mediators explore the disputants' interests or needs, often finessing the stated issues, and try to fashion a compromise that each can accept. Unlike arbitration, however, the mediator has no power to impose a settlement; rather he or she works to effect an agreement that meets both sides' needs.

Fact finders, as their title implies, resolve factual disputes, but make no decisions. If properly engaged, their findings may be final, possibly eliminating jury issues. Though not widely used, they permit credibility issues to be solved quickly and inexpensively. From that base, disputes can often be resolved without resort to full-blown court processes.

Finally, some employers have adopted a system of peer-group review. While such a process takes the ultimate decision from the employer, peers are often able to cut to the heart of the matter and are rarely mislead by fantastic excuses. Employees sloughing their work, whether by absenteeism or poor performance, are often going to get a fair result from their peers. And such a procedure may get great deference, obviating or reducing factual matters to be tried.

An effective internal review procedure may, in certain circumstances, eliminate your exposure to courts and juries, but in virtually all cases, it will give the employer an opportunity to eliminate weak cases and the exposure inherent in such cases to massive punitive damages.

Explanations, References, and Placement

Almost universally, there are conflicting needs after terminating an employee: A need to rationalize internally, and a need to reconcile externally. This creates a tendancy to explain the termination internally in the harshest possible light—certainly there was abundant cause. But externally, the normal reaction is to minimize the fault, do a good turn for the employee you are now rid of—give him or her an exaggerated recommendation. Both reactions, though instinctive, are wrong in terms of potential litigation. The harsh statements internally may create a valid defamation claim, or at the least an active sympathy on a jury. Either result can be very costly. To compound the problem, when you give a good report externally, you butress the plaintiff's case that the termination was improper. Yet you get a bad report, you defame your former employee.

The only proper answer is employment dates, jobs performed, and with authorization, ending wage or salary. When you go beyond those bare-bones facts, you increase the risk of an action for bad-mouthing or for wrongful; termination bolstered by the esteem and value placed on the employee's services in the reference check. The high road and the low road being risky, take the middle and give only objective data about which there can be no argument. In this context "name, rank, and serial number" translates into dates of employment (starting and ending dates), classifications held and, if authorized, wage/salary earned at the time of separation. Nothing more; do not comment on the employee's reason for leaving; work record in a qualitative sense, that is beyond classifications held; or his or her eligibility for rehire. Name, rank and serial number only. And tell your supervisors to say the same thing or, better yet, refer all calls regarding former employers to human resources or personnel.

Because terminated employees have an obligation to minimize any damages resulting from termination (the obligation to "mitigate" damages), the employer has an obvious interest in the placement of former employees, both from a moral and a pecuniary viewpoint. Often the placement process can be hastened, and the negatives inherent in litigation can be properly evaluated with an experienced outplacement service. Outplacement specialists do not find a match between candidate and job opening as a search firm would; rather they teach the art of finding an appropriate job for those cast off by a particular employer. Few of us make a habit of searching for jobs. Most of us are in the job market only occasionally. As a result, we are awkward at finding a job. We do not mitigate because we are untrained and unprepared. Outplacement can reduce or alleviate the problem. It is considered in greater detail in Chapter 10.

File and Document Review

In the terminated employee's file is a potential gold mine or a potential land mine. It should be reviewed again (the first review should have been pretermination) to assure that it is complete and accurate. It will be put into evidence by the employee or the employer, depending on which contentions it supports. Rarely is the file a neutral. Thus, it should be reviewed again posttermination to make sure that the investigation of the reason for termination is complete and completely documented. The file should be reviewed against the termination checklist. Documentation should be complete, including written statements from all witnesses.[3] Such statements should be made as contemporaneously as possible, should be in the witness' first language and should be executed under penalty of perjury. Physical evidence should be saved with a chain of custody clearly established in writing. Where appropriate, medical and/or pharmacological evidence should be included. Similarly, reports from experts or

---

[3] Some counsel may wish to keep such material in a separate litigation file. Because the author believes preventing a lawsuit is better than winning it, inclusion is often preferred. There are numerous considerations, however, and this matter should be discussed **promptly** with your counsel.

professionals that were relied on in making the termination decision should be included.

Occasionally there is evidence of wrongdoing that comes to light after the termination. Most arbitrators and judges will not permit newly discovered evidence to support the original termination decision (although it should be considered when any remedy—particularly reinstatement—is considered). The proper approach to this situation may be to terminate the employee a second time based on the newly discovered evidence. Though this may seem cumbersome and unnecessary, it will permit the newly discovered evidence to be admissible in support of a termination decision rather than only for remedy purposes.

Finally, review the file from the point of view of an adversary. Though it is improper and unwise to destroy or delete evidence supportive of an adversary's position such a review may require that additional evidence be collected to explain the points that may be raised adversary.

Collateral Proceedings

In many jurisdictions, there are several possible agencies and procedures that an employee may go to after separation from employment for example, unemployment insurance, workers' compensation, the EEOC, the NLRB, and so forth. The classified ads in many major newspapers often carry solicitations for terminated employees or those near termination; such solicitations may promise to secure unemployment compensation, stress-related disability payments, and even reinstatment. At many companies, such claims are handled by outside contractors (insurers for instance), and such claims are often given minimal attention because of their presumed low cost, or are compromised at nuisance value. Often the human resource/personnel professional may not even know, or be responsible for, the results.

Even if such an approach once made sense, such complacency today may be very expensive and very painful. Legal concepts of collateral estoppel and/or *res judicata* may allow a terminated employee to bootstrap a cheap victory in, say an unemployment compensation case, into a major win in a wrongful termination case.

Collateral estoppel prevents parties from relitigating *facts* finally determined in a prior proceeding. *Res judicata* prevents parties from relitigating *legal matters* finally determined in a prior proceeding. Thus if there is an agency determination (quasi-judicial in nature) that termination from employment was not "rightful," that determination may foreclose relitigating the matter in court of the reasons and propriety of the termination, and permit the wrongful termination plaintiff to proceed directly to litigating damages—the amount of employer liability only.

As might be surmised, California and New York courts have lead the way in this dubious development. Under the California unemployment insurance laws, for example, an employee who is separated from employment will get unemployment compensation unless he or she voluntarily left without good cause or was terminated for misconduct of a deliberate type which tended to injure the employer's interest. These are factual matters, often decided in a short administrative hearing where technical rules of evidence are rarely applied and traditional litigation safeguards are unheard of. Yet an adverse result to an employer may well undermine any real chance to defend against a wrongful termination suit later brought in a civil trial.

Given such results, the traditional employer complacency characterizing most incidental agency proceedings must now be reexamined. After considering the exposure with your counsel to collateral estoppel and *res judicata* in your state, review:

Who handles your agency proceedings: Rookies and inexperienced outsiders may no longer be sufficient.

Is your best case put forward in the agency proceeding: Slipshod case preparation and presentation holding out the "good" evidence for a later trial may now be counterproductive.

Who coordinates your agency proceedings with human resources/personnel risk management for terminated employees.

Increasingly, failure to revamp management of these issues may compromise your ability to defend wrongful termination cases. Where you have induced a "resignation" and agreed not to contest unemployment compensation, you may have allowed a potential plaintiff to present facts proving a wrongful constructive discharge. The following civil case may become a slam-dunk winner for your former employee.

Wrongful termination litigation is here to stay. Your company can be part of it, or can shy away from it by not terminating employees. Either approach is likely to be very detrimental to your business health. It is suggested a better course would be to spend the time and resources to educate your human resource/personnel staff and your executive and supervisory line management about the techniques (developed and developing) to minimize risk to wrongful termination suits, including posttermination risks. Reviewing the concepts discussed in this Handbook will give you a picture of today's current law and some guesses about law which is still developing.

History teaches, and it is clear, that some future changes in laws, cases and techniques will be important to integrate into your policies and procedures. Only change is constant. Therefore, the author suggests you establish a periodic policy review and update for your management development, say once a year. Consult with a legal specialist in this area to assist with your review and management development so your company stays far from the maddening courthouse crowd.

Chapter 4

EMPLOYER RULES AND POLICIES
BINDING CONTRACTS?

Anthony T. Oliver, Jr., J.D.
Bruce D. May, J.D.

Most employers tend to generate a fair amount of paperwork when it comes to employee relations. The hiring process usually begins with written employment applications, followed by one or more interviews at which applicants receive a sheaf of documents detailing their duties and entitlements. A great many employers publish employee handbooks or personnel manuals that outline the company's policies on everything from absenteeism to workers' compensation. Other personnel policies concerning discipline, performance reviews, or compensation may appear as employee bulletins or supervisor memoranda. Yet as all this paper proliferates, how many employers stop to think that these documents might reappear one day as trial exhibits in a wrongful discharge suit?

Traditionally courts have paid little attention to employee handbooks, personnel manuals, and the like. Except in cases where the employer promised a definite benefit to employees, such as a guarantee of severance or vacation pay, the courts have tended to treat an employee handbook or similar internal guidelines as mere expressions of general policy, gratuitous proclamations of what the employer will probably do in given situations. In recent times, however, the courts have been raising some difficult questions on how an employee handbook might affect the employer's right to terminate at-will employees.

Do an employer's personnel policies and procedures constitute a binding contract? If an employee handbook says that employees will be deemed "permanent" if they perform satisfactorily during a three-month probationary period, does this mean the employer then must have just cause to terminate? If an employer's rules of conduct sets forth specific offenses warranting discharge, does this preclude the employer from firing for other reasons? What about a standard operating procedure that provides for a corrective warning prior to discharge for poor performance, does this have to apply in every case? And what of the memorandum from the company president discussing whether employees will be disciplined for conduct outside the office, could the employer be held liable for failing to follow such guidelines? These are the sorts of questions that this chapter hopes to answer.

In the past decade or so, as part of the boom in wrongful discharge law that we reviewed in Chapter 1, many courts have elevated an employer's internal policies and procedures to a stature that might surprise even the employer that promulgated them. Courts that once considered employee handbooks and personnel manuals unenforceable expressions of general intent are now concluding that an employer's internal policies can indeed become integrated into the employment contract itself. Instead of loose talk, an employer's policy statements are now words to live by in many courts.

In decisions from numerous states, the courts are rethinking traditional contract doctrine in the employment context, and abandoning dubious common law strictures that have prevented employees from enforcing personnel policies. Even though an employee gives nothing in exchange for the promises contained in employee handbooks other than the commitment to render services, many courts have found the elements of a valid contract. And even when the policies are announced or amended after hiring, employees are being afforded contractual protection for their legitimate expectations.

In still other cases, the courts have pointed to the employer's breach of internal policies as evidence of bad faith in wrongful discharge suits based on the implied covenant of good faith in fair dealing. As discussed in Chapter 1, this implied covenant, which arises by law in every contract, is violated by bad faith or arbitrary conduct, which can take the form of an employer's failure to follow its own announced policies. Though still a minority view in the law of wrongful discharge, the implied covenant theory, when coupled with the employer's breach of its policies and practices, can expose an employer to liability in tort as well as for breach of contract.

In the following we take a close look at how the courts have treated employee handbooks and internal personnel policies in the context of wrongful discharge suits. Following that, we scrutinize some of the more important provisions found in employee handbooks, with notes on what an employer might avoid or at least think twice about in drafting such documents. Though the law is still developing in this area, every employer is well-advised to take its internal policy statements seriously.

DOES AN EMPLOYEE HANDBOOK OR PERSONNEL POLICY CONSTITUTE A BINDING CONTRACT?

When an employer offers to hire an employee for a specific job at a certain wage, and the employee accepts, the law has little trouble recognizing that a contract has been formed. The employer has promised to provide work and to pay the stated wages, and in consideration the employee has promised to perform the requested services. In terms of the mutual promises, the exchange of consideration, and the meeting of the minds, this simple transaction exhibits all the earmarks of a common law contract.

For reasons both historical and logical, however, the law had great difficulty in readily applying these concepts to employee handbooks and other formal statements of personnel policy. The principal historical reason, elaborated in Chapter 1 in our discussion of the at-will doctrine, stems from the law's traditional reluctance to tread on managerial prerogative. Given a long-standing rule that employment for an unspecified duration may be terminated at will, the courts have been hesitant to construe an employer's internal pronouncements as self-imposed limitations on the power to terminate.

The logical reason for the law denigrating employee handbooks is that they simply do not arise in the manner typically contemplated by the law of contracts. Instead of being negotiated by the parties at arm's length, employee handbooks are drafted solely by the employer and issued more or less perfunctorily to the employees. An employee might haggle over the wages the employer is offering, but how many employees have ever bargained over a particular provision in an employee handbook or personnel manual? Beyond that, the promises in an employee handbook seem gratuitious on the surface of things. Employees usually give nothing in exchange for the handbook except for their services, which they had already agreed to provide.

This sort of thinking had led some courts to conclude that an employee handbook is a unilateral statement of policy which the employer is free to change at will, and which is not enforceable as a contract. Alluding to the lack of "mutuality of obligation" or the "inadequacy of consideration," these courts have refused to enforce employee handbooks as contracts because of the perception that the employees had given nothing other than their services in exchange for the employer's promises.

One example of this view is *Gates v. Life of Montana Insurance Co.*, 638 P.2d 1063 (Mont. 1982), decided by the Supreme Court of Montana. The employer in that case had issued a handbook which listed certain types of misconduct for which employees would be "subject to reprimand or dismissal *with prior warning*." An employee discharged for poor performance and absenteeism brought suit for wrongful discharge, contending that the handbook created a contractual obligation to issue a corrective warning notice prior to discharge. The court rejected her claim that the handbook created an express contract:

The employee handbook was not distributed until about two years after Gates was hired. It constituted a unilateral statement of company policies and procedures. Its terms were not bargained for, and there was no meeting of the minds. The policies may be changed unilaterally at any time. The employee handbook was not a part of Gates' employment contract at the time she was hired, nor could it have been a modification to her contract because there was no new and independent consideration. . . . Therefore the handbook requirement of notice prior to termination is not enforceable as a contract right.

The Supreme Court of Kansas took the same view in *Johnson v. National Beef Packing Co.*, 220 Kan. 552, 551 P.2d 779 (1976). In that case, a terminated employee brought suit for breach of an employee handbook provision stating that "no employee shall be dismissed without just cause." In rejecting the claim for breach of contract, the court replied:

[T]he manual was not published until long after plaintiff's employment. It was only a unilateral expression of company policy and procedures. Its terms were not bargained for by the parties and any benefits conferred by it were mere gratuities. Certainly, no meeting of the minds was evidenced by the defendant's unilateral act of publishing company policy.

The Supreme Court of Delaware recently expressed similar sentiments. In *Heideck v. Kent General Hospital, Inc.*, 446 A.2d 1095 (Del. 1982), the employee handbook contained a list of serious offenses for which discharge would result. An employee terminated for misconduct not specifically mentioned on the list brought suit, arguing that the handbook operated as a contractual limit on the employer's freedom to fire at will. The court disagreed, and characterized the handbook as a "unilateral expression" of the employer's policies which "does not grant to any employee a specific term of employment and does not, therefore, alter plaintiff's 'at-will' employment status."

This sort of reasoning has fallen into disfavor in many other jurisdictions. As we pointed out in discussing implied-in-fact contracts in Chapter 1, the law of employment contracts has often distorted traditional notions of contract law, due largely to the belief that an employee gives nothing of value simply by promising to render services. We noted, for example, the numerous older cases that refused to enforce a contract for permanent employment unless the employee supplied some "independent consideration" other than the commitment to work. As with such promises of job security, however, the courts have started to rethink the whole idea of consideration in applying contract law to employee handbooks.

This process of undoing long-standing precedent has manifested itself in different ways. Some courts have simply rejected antiquated notions of employment contract law as contrary to the fundamental notion that the courts "will not inquire into the adequacy of consideration." These courts reason that an employee's promise to work will alone support all of the employer's promises, whether they be oral assurances of continued employment or handbook provisions requiring just cause for termination. The logic is, since at-will employees are free to quit, their act of remaining in employment means they have incurred a detriment to themselves and bestowed a benefit on the employer.

Other courts have reached the same result by stressing the benefits that flow to an employer when employees comply with the provisions in employee handbooks. By laying down basic guidelines and reporting necessary information, an employee handbook can help increase productivity, reduce misunderstandings, and promote employee morale. Some courts have opined that an employer reaping such benefits must reciprocate by assuring employees of any privileges conferred by the employee handbook.

The landmark decision of the Michigan Supreme Court in *Toussaint v. Blue Cross & Blue Shield of Michigan,* 408 Mich. 579, 292 N.W. 2d 880 (1980), typifies the modern approach that some courts have taken in analyzing handbooks. In that case, the court concluded that an enforceable contract arose from the following statement contained in a manual of personnel policies that Blue Cross had distributed to employees: "It is the policy of the company to treat employees leaving Blue Cross in a fair and consistent manner *and to release employees for just cause only.*"

After exhaustively reviewing the traditional rule of at-will employment, the court in *Toussaint* reasoned that an enforceable agreement to terminate only for cause could arise from an employer's internal policy statements, even if the term of employment remains indefinite. As the court remarked, "[w]e see no reason why an employment contract which does not have a definite term—the term is 'indefinite'—cannot legally provide job security."

With the traditional at-will doctrine thus put to one side, the court in *Toussaint* explained how traditional contract principles could support a jury's finding that the employee handbook was fully enforceable. Expounding on the reasons why an employer would issue a handbook in the first instance, the court recognized that a handbook can produce substantial benefits for the employer. And if the employer is to reap the benefits of a handbook, so too should the employees. As the court wrote:

While an employer need not establish personnel policies or practices, where an employer chooses to establish such policies and practices and makes them known to its employees, the employment relationship is presumably enhanced. The employer secures an orderly, cooperative, and loyal workforce, and the employee the peace of mind associated with job security and the conviction that he will be treated fairly. No pre-employment negotiations need take place and the parties' minds need not meet on the subject; nor does it matter that the employee knows nothing of the particulars of the employer's policies and practices or that the employer may change them unilaterally. It is enough that the employer chooses, presumably in its own interest, to create an environment in which the employee believes that, whatever the personnel policies and practices, they are established and official at any given time, purport to be fair, and are applied consistently and uniformly to each employee. The employer has then created a situation "instinct with an obligation."

The Supreme Court of Minnesota also has taken a very progressive approach to the contractual status of employee handbooks. In *Pine River State Bank v. Mettille,* 333 N.W.2d 622 (Minn. 1983), the court rejected traditional barriers to the enforcement of employee handbooks and allowed a former loan officer to proceed on a counterclaim for wrongful discharge. But unlike the court in *Toussaint,* which emphasized the countervailing benefits that an employer reaps from an employee handbook, the court is *Pine River,* relied on orthodox rules of offer and acceptance.

The employee in *Pine River* had been terminated after a year and a half of service for poor performance and other shortcomings. A few months after he was hired, the employee had been given a printed employee's handbook which contained provisions on many company policies, including job security and disciplinary policy. The latter section set forth a progressive disciplinary procedure whereby employees were to be given an oral reprimand, written reprimand, and suspension prior to discharge. The employer's president, who had drafted the handbook by adapting forms obtained from a trade association, testified to no avail that he never intended the handbook to become part of the employee's employment contract.

The court turned to basic notions of offer and acceptance in analyzing the promises an employer makes to employees through a handbook. It reasoned that a handbook provision, if "definite in form" and communicated to employees, constitutes a unilateral offer by the employer to follow a specified procedure or policy. In requiring a reasonably definite offer, the court excluded what it termed "an employer's general statement of policy." In the *Pine River* case, the handbook contained a loosely worded preamble discussing how employment in the banking industry was stable, and how the bank had few layoffs. This provision was deemed too vague to constitute an offer.

The handbook provision on employee discipline, however, set forth a very specific multi-step procedure to be applied whenever an employee violated company policy. This, said the court, was definite enough to constitute a unilateral offer by the company to its employees. The court then found that the bank's at-will employees, by continuing in their employer's service, impliedly accepted the employer's handbook offer. As at-will employees, they would have been free to quit, and their act of remaining in employment supplied valid consideration for the employer's undertaking. Thus, a contract was formed even though the handbook was issued long after hiring.

The employer argued that the employee's mere act of remaining employed did not suffice as valid consideration. The court, however, refused to inquire into the adequacy of consideration. Applying an ancient rule of contracts, the court decreed that it would not undertake to evaluate the employee's commitment to remain employed. If the employer was willing to issue the handbook without receiving anything tangible in return other than the employees' continued service, then the law would look no further into the bargain between the parties.

Like the Minnesota Supreme Court in *Pine River,* other courts have enforced employee handbooks by applying traditional rules of offer and acceptance. In an earlier ruling, the Oregon Supreme Court in *Yartzoff v. Democrat-Herald Publishing Co.,* 281 Ore. 651, 576 P.2d 356 (1978), upheld a wrongful discharge claim based on the employer's failure to provide corrective warning letters prior to discharge as spelled out in its employee handbook. As for the fact that the handbook was not distributed until after the employee had commenced work, the court reasoned that her continuing in service constituted valid consideration and made the handbook an enforceable *modification* of the original oral employment pact.

The Supreme Court of Nevada concurred in *Southwest Gas Corp. v. Ahmad,* 668 P.2d 261 (Nev. 1983), in which it upheld a finding that the employer had breached provisions of its handbook requiring good cause and prior warnings in order to discharge. "The fact that the company issued such handbooks to its employees," said the court, "supports an inference that the handbook formed part of the employment contract of the parties." And by continuing in employment after receiving the handbook, an at-will employee supplies good consideration for any promises of job security.

In another influential opinion, the Court of Appeals of New York held that provisions in an employee handbook coupled with oral promises of job security at an initial interview can suffice to create a contractual exception to the at-will rule. In *Weiner v. McGraw-Hill, Inc.*, 57 N.Y.2d 458, 443 N.E.2d 441 (1982), a publishing executive had been recruited with oral promises that McGraw-Hill would discharge only for good cause. He signed an employment application which stated that his employment would be subject to the provisions of the employer's handbook on personnel policies and procedures. This handbook established a policy of terminating only for just and sufficient cause, and only after all practical steps toward rehabilitation had failed.

In allowing the employee to proceed with his breach of contract claim, the court rejected the argument that his act of merely remaining employed was an illusory promise of no benefit to the employer. Adhering to the traditional rule that courts will not inquire into the adequacy of consideration, the court found the employee had bestowed sufficient consideration, even while retaining the freedom to quit at will. Since the employer found enough incentive to issue the handbook in the first place, the court was unwilling to require anything more than what the employee had already provided.

Other courts have taken approaches that differ somewhat from *Toussaint*, *Pine River*, and *Weiner*, but the results generally favor the employee. Some decisions, for example, have focussed on the intent of the employer in determining whether a handbook or other formal policy statement constitutes a contract. In *Hepp v. Lockheed-California Co.*, 86 Cal. App. 3d 714, 150 Cal. Rptr. 408 (1978), the plaintiff was a laid off employee who alleged that his employer breached a "well-established policy" of offering new jobs to qualified persons on layoff, rather than hiring or promoting other employees.

In reversing a summary judgment for the employer, the court of appeal in *Hepp* reasoned that the jury should decide whether the alleged policy statements were "management guidelines only and not intended for the benefit of the employees," or instead were intended as a "positive inducement for employees to take and continue employment with defendant." In the latter instance, the employee's act of remaining in service with knowledge of the policy constituted valid consideration and thus formed a binding contract.

Similarly in *Hedrick v. Center for Comprehensive Alcohol Treatment*, 7 Ohio App. 3d 211, 454 N.E.2d 1343 (1982), the appellate court reversed the dismissal of a suit by an employee who claimed to have been discharged without good cause or a pretermination hearing. The plaintiff contended that she was guaranteed such protections by the terms of an employee handbook, various policy statements, a formal discharge procedure, a staff distribution form, and an employment confirmation form. The court decreed that the enforceability of these provisions turned on the intent of the parties, and implied that a contract would arise if the policy in question "clearly was intended by both to form the basis of the relationship between employer and employee."

While no one mode of analysis predominates, the clear trend in the case law is toward enforcing employee handbooks through the use of ordinary contract principles. Thus, the cautious employer must recognize that it may be creating contractual obligations when it sets out to circulate an employee handbook. The question then becomes which provisions rise to the level of contractual promises.

WHICH OF THE PROVISIONS IN AN EMPLOYEE HANDBOOK ARE ENFORCEABLE AS CONTRACTUAL PROMISES?

The provisions typically found in employee handbooks vary widely in their scope and specificity. A handbook might contain a firm commitment to discharge only for just cause, or it might simply include a flowery recital of how the firm looks forward to long service from each employee. In other cases, the handbook might contain an express requirement of corrective notices prior to termination, or perhaps just a general statement that the employer will strive for fairness and consistency in discipline. The question is, when does a statement in an employee handbook constitute an enforceable promise?

A sensitive analysis of this point appears in *Pine River State Bank v. Mettille, supra.* In proposing that certain statements in a handbook constituted unilateral offers from the employer to its work force, the court drew a basic distinction between "an employer's general statement of policy," and an offer "in definite language." As the court explained, "general statements of policy are no more than that and do not meet the contractual requirements for an offer." But when an employer proposes "in definite language" to follow a particular guideline or procedure, the employees can create an enforceable contract by continuing to work. For example, one provision in the handbook in *Pine River* was the following language on job security:

Employment in the banking industry is very stable. It does not fluctuate up and down sharply in good times and bad, as do many other types of employment. We have no seasonal layoffs and we never hire a lot of people when business is booming only to release them when things are not as active. The job security offered by the *Pine River State Bank* is one reason why so many of our employees have five or more years of service. In return for this, Management expects job security from you. That is, the security that you will perform the duties of your position with diligence, cooperation, dependability, and a sense of responsibility.

The court in *Pine River* found that this provision amounted to a mere "general statement of policy" which could not form the basis for a breach of contract claim. The court analogized this language to statements that an employee had a "great future" and was in a "career situation." None of this language is specific enough to bind the employer to some particular course of action. On the other hand, the handbook in *Pine River* also contained the following language on disciplinary procedure:

In the interest of fairness to all employees the Company establishes reasonable standards of conduct for all employees to follow in his employment at *Pine River State Bank*. These standards are not intended to place unreasonable restrictions on you but are considered necessary for us to conduct our business in an orderly and efficient manner.

If an employee has violated a company policy, the following procedure will apply:

1. An oral reprimand by the immediate supervisor for the first offense, with a written notice sent to the Executive Vice President.
2. A written reprimand for the second offense.
3. A written reprimand and a meeting with the Executive Vice President and possible suspension from work without pay for five days.
4. Discharge from employment for an employee whose conduct does not improve as a result of the previous actions taken.

In no instance will a person be discharged from employment without a review of the facts by the Executive Officer.

The court in *Pine River* had no trouble finding this language enforceable as a contract because it "set out in definite language an offer of a unilateral contract for procedures to be followed in job termination." Most courts would agree. In *Yartzoff v. Democrat-Herald Publishing Co., supra*, the Oregon Supreme Court enforced a similar disciplinary procedure which called for a corrective letter and one-day suspension prior to termination for misconduct.

Other courts also recognize the need for distinguishing between the specific and the general when construing an employee handbook. In *Thompson v. St. Regis Paper Co.*, 102 Wash. 2d 219, 685 P.2d 1081 (Wash. 1984), the Washington Supreme Court stated that language appearing in an employee handbook creates contractual rights only if it "promises *specific treatment in specific situations*." Echoing the *Pine River* opinion, the court in *Thompson* agreed that "general statements of company policy" are not binding. The Court of Special Appeals of Maryland adopted the same distinction in *Staggs v. Blue Cross of Maryland, Inc.*, 486 A.2d 798 (Md. App. 1985), in which the court remarked, "we caution that not every statement made in a personnel handbook or other publication will rise to the level of an enforceable covenant."

When the language in an employee handbook is ambiguous, the courts have tended to let the trier of fact, usually a jury, decide what the language means. The results are often surprising, particularly where the disputed language deals with probationary periods, seniority, or disciplinary rules. In many cases, the courts have taken vague or subjective language and construed it in a way that probably was never intended by the employer who drafted it.

For example, in *Chamberlain v. Bissell, Inc.*, 547 F. Supp. 1067 (W.D. Mich. 1982), the employer had promulgated a set of specific reasons for discharge, without actually specifying that just cause was required in all cases or that the list was intended to be exhaustive. Still the court reasoned: "Although not specifically limited to the reasons for discharge listed on the form, the procedure as a whole implied a policy of discharge only for good cause, that is, those reasons listed on the form or some other equivalent and equally good reason."

In *Walker v. Northern San Diego County Hospital District*, 135 Cal. App. 3d 896, 185 Cal. Rptr. 617 (1982), the court was faced with a series of amended employee handbook provisions dealing with the probationary period of new hires. In various versions, these provisions contained the following language: "If [your probationary period] is satisfactory, you will be promoted to 'permanent employee status, . . . if your overall performance is unsatisfactory, the Hospital reserves the right to terminate employment at any time within the probationary period," and "If satisfactory, as a full-time employee you will be eligible for all benefits." The court held that the jury should be permitted to review these provisions and determine whether they created an implied contract to terminate only for good cause.

The importance of probationary clauses was underscored in *Arie v. Intertherm, Inc.*, 648 S.W.2d 142 (Mo. App. 1983). The employee in *Arie* signed an employment application ostensibly for a temporary position, and was supplied a temporary employee handbook. At her initial interview, however, the plaintiff was told she would be a "full-fledged employee" after successfully completing a 90-day probationary period. The temporary employee handbook stated only that employees who passed the probationary period would be placed on a "permanent seniority list." On this evidence, the court allowed the plaintiff to proceed with her claim that once she worked for 90 days, she became a permanent employee and could be terminated only for good cause.

In *Tiranno v. Sears, Roebuck & Co.*, 99 A.D.2d 675, 472 N.Y.S.2d 49 (1984), a New York appellate court took an equally indulgent view of an employer's disciplinary policy. The personnel manual in that case provided that "[t]he Company may terminate an individual's employment at any time that his/her work . . . does not measure up to Company standards." In affirming the denial of the employer's motion for summary judgment, the court ruled that "[t]his language is susceptible to being interpreted as requiring 'just cause' since it indicates objectivity in employee evaluation and termination." Despite the employer's apparent attempt to reserve its discretion, the court decreed that "a jury could find, based on the 'totality of the circumstances' that good cause was required for plaintiff's termination and, if so, whether such good cause existed."

Needless to say, these cases demonstrate the need for careful drafting if an employer wishes to avoid implied limits on the right to terminate by virtue of its employee handbook. In the last section of this chapter, we offer guidelines on drafting and revising the more important provisions of handbooks and personnel manuals.

EMPLOYEE HANDBOOKS AND THE IMPLIED COVENANT OF GOOD FAITH AND FAIR DEALING

All of the cases discussed thus far applied the law of contracts, and successful claimants recovered lost pay and benefits, that is, traditional contract damages. Another line of cases, however, raises the prospect that an employer could be liable in tort for failing to abide by its employee handbook or other formal policy. This is significant, for in a tort action an employee may recover punitive damages. These cases rely on the implied covenant of good faith and fair dealing, which is a tacit promise by every party to a contract that it will not in bad faith subvert the basic bargain between the parties. The implied covenant theory thus poses a risk that an employer must consider in drafting employee handbooks.

In a case called *Cleary v. American Airlines, Inc.*, 111 Cal. App. 3d 443, 168 Cal. Rptr. 722 (1980), a California appellate court ruled that a long-term employee, allegedly discharged without good cause and in violation of the employer's formal procedures for resolving employee disputes, could bring a tort action against the employer for breach of the implied covenant of good faith and fair dealing. *Cleary* demonstrates how a discharged employee could pursue a tort cause of action based on the employer's failure to follow internal policies.

Claiming that he was precipitiously terminated following a workplace incident, the employee in *Cleary* alleged that the airline had adopted "specific procedures for ajudicating employee disputes." These procedures, set forth in a formal policy statement, apparently provided for a disciplinary hearing prior to termination with a limited right of review to higher management. Remarkably, the text of the procedures was not put into the record on appeal, and yet the court still found them to have vital legal effect.

The court in *Cleary* reasoned that the employer's adoption of specific disciplinary procedures evinced an awareness of the duty to act in good faith. The court held that the employee's 18 years of service, coupled with the airlines' breach of its own regulations, operated as a form of estoppel that precluded termination without good cause. What is more, the court held that such misconduct constitutes a tortious breach of the implied covenant of good faith and fair dealing, for which the full range of compensatory and punitive damages were available.

In a later California case, *Rulon-Miller v. International Business Machines Corp.*, 162 Cal. App. 3d 241, 208 Cal. Rptr. 524 (1984), an employer was held liable in tort for arbitrarily discharging a sales employee because of her romantic relationship with an employee of a competitor. The court relied heavily on IBMs own policy of avoiding work restrictions that invaded an employee's personal life and privacy. In describing the employer's implied duty of good faith, the court noted: "Implied in this, of course, is that the company, if it has rules and regulations, apply those rules and regulations to its employees as well as affording its employees their protection."

An even more remarkable use of the implied covenant appears in *Gates v. Life of Montana Insurance Co.*, 638 P.2d 1063 (Mont. 1982). The employer in *Gates* had issued an employee handbook which listed two categories of disciplinary offenses, the more serious of which was said to warrant discharge without prior warning. The plaintiff contended that she had not engaged in any such serious misconduct, but still was discharged without receiving any prior warning. The Montana Supreme Court refused to find that the handbook created an enforceable contract. Suprisingly, however, the court opined that the employer could be liable for breach of the implied covenant of good faith and fair dealing if it wrongfully denied plaintiff the due process promised in the employee handbook.

As explained in Chapter 1, most courts have not yet expanded liability under the implied covenant theory into the employment context. Cases like *Cleary, Rulon-Miller,* and *Gates,* however, cannot lightly be cast aside. They are significant for three reasons: First, they could expose an employer to tort liability, including punitive damages, in employee handbook cases. Second, as *Gates* demonstrates, the implied covenant could form the basis for relief even if the court refuses to find that the handbook constitutes an express contract. Third, the implied covenant could provide a potential theory of recovery even if the handbook language falls short of a "promise of specific treatment in specific situations."

For example, in *Rulon-Miller,* the court of appeal relied heavily on an internal memorandum from IBMs chairman to all managers. In clear but rather literary language, the memorandum discussed the subject of when employees should be disciplined for conduct away from the office. It stated in part:

I have seen instances where managers took disciplinary measures against employees for actions or conduct that are not rightfully the company's concern. These managers usually justified their decisions by citing their personal code of ethics or by quoting some fragment of company policy that seemed to support their position. Both arguments proved unjust on close examination. What we need, in every case, is balanced judgment which weighs the needs of the business and the rights of the individual. . . .

We have concern with an employee's off-the-job behavior only when it reduces his ability to perform regular job assignments, interferes with the job performance of other employees, or if his outside behavior affects the reputation of the company in a major way. When on-the-job performance is acceptable, I can think of few situations in which outside activities could result in disciplinary action or dismissal. . . .

IBM's first basic belief is respect for the individual, and the essence of this belief is a strict regard for his right to personal privacy. This idea should never be compromised easily or quickly.

These lofty ideals, so eloquently expressed by the chairman's memorandum, came back to haunt IBM in the *Rulon-Miller* case. The court ruled that these and other internal policies, coupled with the company's overall behavior in terminating the plaintiff, were properly considered by the jury. Although the court recognized IBM's right to terminate employees for conflict of interest, the jury was entitled to decide whether the employee had in fact violated the company's policies.

Rulon-Miller demonstrates how a claim based on the implied covenant of good faith and fair dealing could find support in an employee handbook, even one phrased in terms as generalized as the chairman's memorandum at IBM. Employers who profusely promise "fair treatment" or commit to some other laudable objective could be held to their word under the implied covenant, even if their language falls short of a promise of specific treatment.

DOES THE EMPLOYEE HAVE TO BE AWARE OF SPECIFIC POLICIES OR PROCEDURES TO ENFORCE THEM?

Several of the cases previously noted allowed recovery based on employee handbooks that had been distributed after the employee was hired. The logic was that the employer reaped benefits by offering specific treatment, and the employees reciprocated by continuing to work despite being free to quit at will. Thus, an employee need not know of a specific policy at the time of hiring in order to enforce compliance if it is still in effect at the time of firing.

A better question arises when the employee does not learn of a policy until after discharge, perhaps not until discovery in litigation. An employee can hardly be said to have been induced by promises of specific treatment, or to have conveyed any corresponding benefit to the employer, when the employee is not even aware of the supposed policy. Can an employee sue for breach of contract in such circumstances? This issue was lurking in the *Toussaint* case, in which the court remarked:

An employer who establishes no personnel policies instills no reasonable expectations of performance. Employers can make known to their employees that personnel policies are subject to unilateral changes by the employer. Employees would then have no expectation that any particular policy will continue to remain in force. Employees could, however, legitimately expect that policies inforce at any given time will be applied to all. . . . Having announced the policy, presumably with a view to obtaining the benefit of improved employee attitudes and behavior and improved quality of work, the employer may not treat its promise as illusory.

Under this theory of "legitimate expectations," it would seem that an employee must be aware of an employer's basic policy at some time prior to discharge in order to enforce it after discharge. Only if the employee knew of the policy and thereby formed an "expectation" would the court have a basis for finding acceptance and consideration. Curiously, however, the court in *Toussaint* also remarked at one point in its opinion that it did not matter whether the employee "knows nothing of the particulars of the employer's policies and practices."

Does this comment in *Toussaint* mean that the court would enforce promises set out in policy statements even when the employee has no idea of what those promises are? Probably not. More likely, the court was only referring to the specific terms, or, as it said, the "particulars" of individual policies, rather than the basic existence of the policy. For example, an employee might know of a policy providing for progressive discipline prior to discharge, without knowing whether the policy requires one warning, two warnings, a suspension, or some other specific progression. In such a case, the employee nevertheless has a legitimate expectation of some prior notice, and the employer presumably is receiving the benefits of a more secure worker. Thus, the courts, at least under *Toussaint,* would enforce the contract.

This reasoning may have played a part in the decision in *Salimi v. Farmers Insurance Group*, 684 P.2d 264 (Colo. App. 1984). The employee in that case alleged that he was wrongfully demoted in breach of the employer's personnel policies and procedures. Curiously, however, one allegation in the employee's complaint was that the employer had refused to give him a copy of the policies and procedures manual at the time of his demotion. Presumably then, *Salimi* was a case in which the employee knew generally of formal personnel policies but not of their "particulars," and yet was still allowed to sue for breach of contract.

If a policy was never officially conveyed to an employee, a court might have to create new doctrine in order to find a contract. In the *Pine River* case, for example, the court implied in a footnote that a "control copy" of the employer's policies, if not disseminated to employees, would not constitute a contract but only a "policy guide for supervisors." Similarly in *Speciale v. Tektronix, Inc.*, 38 Ore. App. 441, 590 P.2d 734 (1979), the court dismissed a breach of contract claim by an employee who failed to allege that he was aware of certain personnel policies during his employment.

An issue closely related to the employee's knowledge is whether the policy was even intended to apply to persons in the employee's position. This question will arise in cases involving different levels of management. An internal policy for top management, for example, should not redound to the benefit of front-line supervisors when that policy does not by its terms apply to them. In such instances even full awareness by the plaintiff would not suffice to establish a contract.

WHO DECIDES WHETHER AN EMPLOYEE HANDBOOK OR PERSONNEL POLICY HAS BEEN VIOLATED?

Those courts that have found contracts arising from employee handbooks have generally allowed the trier of fact, be it judge or jury, to determine whether the particular policy was complied with. Thus, if an employee handbook creates a contract to terminate only for good cause, the jury can decide whether the grounds for termination offered by the employer constitute just cause. Needless to say, this undercuts the employer's traditionally unbridled discretion to terminate.

In *Toussaint*, the employer argued unsuccessfully that the court should have given a jury instruction which instead of tendering the issue of just cause per se, only allowed the jury to decide whether or not the employer's decision was "reasonable." As the court replied, "[w]here the employee has secured a promise not to be discharged except for good cause, he has contracted for more than employer's promise to act in good faith or not to be unreasonable." Most other courts have given the trier of fact similar discretion.

At least one court has taken an alternative view. In *Simpson v. Western Graphics Corporation*, 293 Ore. 96, 643 P.2d 1276 (Ore. 1982), the Oregon Supreme Court ruled that while a provision for "just cause" in an employee handbook was enforceable, it was to be reviewed by the trier of fact from a very limited perspective. The employer was held to a just cause standard, but the employer alone was to decide whether just cause was present. As the court stated, "a trial court reviewing the discharge need only find that there was substantial evidence to support the employer's decision and that the employer believed the evidence and acted in good faith." The court explained how this deferential standard would comport with the unique nature of the handbook:

The handbook was not negotiated. It is a unilateral statement by the employer of self-imposed limitations upon its prerogatives. It was furnished to plaintiffs after they were hired and the evidence affords no inference that they accepted or continued in employment in reliance upon its terms. In such a situation, the meaning intended by the drafter, the employer, is controlled and there is no reason to infer that the employer intended to surrender its power to determine whether facts constituting cause for termination exist.

The opinion in *Simpson* represents a well thoughtout but still minority view. Most courts have not been so deferential to employers. In *Crosier v. United Parcel Service, Inc.*, 150 Cal. App. 3d 1132, 178 Cal. Rptr. 361 (1983), where a just cause requirement was imposed under the implied covenant of good faith and fair dealing, the court refused to adopt the "business judgment rule" which would have prevented the courts from ever reviewing the legitimacy of an employer's decision to discharge. As the court stated:

An implied in fact or implied in law promise to dismiss an employee for cause would be illusory if the employer were permitted to be the sole judge and final arbiter of the propriety of the policy giving rise to the discharge. If we were to adopt such a rule, an employee would implement a patently absurd business policy carapaced from judicial inquiry.

HOW MUCH DISCRETION CAN AN EMPLOYER RETAIN IN HANDBOOKS AND PERSONNEL POLICIES?

Even the most liberal courts have made clear that the employer is free not to promulgate any policies, or to change existing policies at any time with notice to employees. The court in *Toussaint*, for example, reiterated that "an employer need not establish personnel policies or practices," but once a policy is put in force, the employer is bound to follow it. The question becomes, can an employer draft a handbook provision that affords employees some assurance of job security but without surrendering all of the employer's traditional disciplinary powers?'

The court in *Toussaint* seemed to forecast great discretion for the employer in drafting suitable language. As the court stated, "[t]he employer's standard of job performance can be made part of the contract." Thus, a handbook could list specific acts of misconduct and provide that any such violation constituted grounds for discharge. Under *Toussaint*, the jury in such a case would only decide whether the employer had consistently applied the underlying rules of conduct, and not whether the violation amounted to "just cause."

A better question would arise if the handbook reserved the company's right to discharge for "any other conduct not in the best interests of the company," or "other just cause as determined by the personnel manager." As the Washington Supreme Court noted in *Thompson v. St. Regis Paper Company,* an employer's policies can be written "in a manner that retains discretion to the employer." Taken at face value, this would allow an employer to retain the discretion to decide when discharge is appropriate.

On the other hand, we have seen how subjective language, even when clearly slanted in the employer's favor, can take on new and unexpected meaning when submitted to a judge or jury. For example, in *Tirrano v. Sears, Roebuck & Co., supra,* the court allowed the jury to decide whether just cause was required under a personnel manual allowing termination where the employee's work "does not measure up to Company standards." One has to wonder whether the employer in that case ever intended to limit its right to discharge by using such phraseology.

Moreover, some courts might invoke the implied in law covenant of good faith to find new limits on the power of termination, even when the handbook purports to retain managerial discretion. This was revealed in *Gates v. Life of Montana Insurance Co., supra,* in which the court held that a set of disciplinary rules, while not a valid express contract, nevertheless created an implied obligation to provide disciplinary due process. Thus, the use of oblique language in employee handbooks in order to retain employer discretion poses an unavoidable risk that a judge or jury will effectively rewrite key provisions.

RESERVING THE RIGHT TO TERMINATE AT WILL

If an employer is unwilling to assume any contractual limits on its right to terminate at will, it should consider adopting a formal personnel policy that clearly retains the employees' at will status. As the Michigan Supreme Court commented in *Toussaint,* "[e]mployers are most assuredly free to enter into employment contracts terminable at will without assigning cause." Similarly, the court in *Pine River* conceded that "[l]anguage in the handbook itself may reserve discretion to the employer in certain matters." An express provision reserving the right to terminate at will might be phrased as follows:

In consideration of my employment at ACME Company, I understand and agree that my employment is for an indefinite duration and can be terminated at any time, with or without cause, and with or without notice, either by me or by the Company. I further understand and agree that no supervisor or other representative of the Company has any authority to enter into any agreement to the contrary.

A provision like this led to the dismissal of an employee's wrongful discharge claims in *Ledl v. Quik Pik Food Stores, Inc.,* 133 Mich. App. 583,

349 N.W.2d 529 (Mich. 1984). After nearly eight years of service, the employee in *Ledl* signed an employment agreement which disclaimed any guarantees of job security and explicitly acknowledged her at-will status. Citing *Toussaint,* the court rejected the employee's claim that the agreement was a contract of adhesion foisted on her without any meaningful negotiations.

Similarly in *Hillsman v. Sutter Community Hospitals,* 153 Cal. App. 3d 743, 200 Cal. Rptr. 605 (1984), the defendant had hired the plaintiff under the terms of a letter agreement that was explicitly subject to termination or renegotiation upon thirty days' notice. The letter concluded, however, with the salutation that "[w]e look forward to a long, pleasant, and mutually satisfactory relationship with you and the Sutter Community Hospitals." The court rejected the plaintiff's contention that this letter language overcame the provision allowing termination without notice. The court remarked that the employer's closing language was "simply to add a touch of personal warmth to an otherwise businesslike letter."

Express statements of the right to terminate at will have their costs and risks. First and foremost, many employers simply would not want such a provision as the backbone of their personnel policy. They are the antithesis of job security, and they hardly foster good morale or help in recruiting top applicants. In the context of a union organizing campaign, they could become the pivotal point for employee sentiment.

Beyond that, from a legal perspective, there is no guarantee that such a provision will be upheld in every case. Courts might be amenable to finding an oral or written modification of the policy in order to avoid the harshness of the at-will rule. In *Schipani v. Ford Motor Co.,* 102 Mich. App. 606, 302 N.W.2d 307 (1981), for example, the court allowed a 25-year employee to proceed with his claim that an at-will agreement he signed in 1952 was modified by the employer's subsequent policy statements. Thus, employers determined to preserve at-will status must include a provision like the one in our example, that only the president or other designated officer can modify the employer's stated policy.

In other settings the courts might turn to equitable doctrines to overcome even the clearest disclaimer. Under the doctrine of unconscionability, courts have struck down so-called contracts of adhesion where one party, by virtue of clearly superior bargaining power, has effectively forced the other party to sign a lopsided agreement. This doctrine could be invoked in the employment context. Beyond that, employees who are intimidated or deceived into signing might seek relief under common law fraud and other tort theories.

The courts will also have to sort out whether an express statement of the at-will doctrine would rule out all wrongful discharge claims. It seems clear that employees who are discharged in violation of public policy—because they refused to commit perjury, for example—would not be barred by an express at-will provision. As for claims based on the implied covenant of good faith and fair dealing, the matter is less clear. The courts have disagreed on whether an express provision for termination at-will bars suit based on an implied-in-law covenant.

In *Crossen v. Foremost-McKesson, Inc.,* 537 F. Supp. 1076 (N.D. Cal. 1982), an executive had signed a written employment contract which either party could terminate by giving 60 days' written notice. Finding that this preserved the individual's at-will status, the court rejected his claim that the implied covenant of good faith and fair dealing required good cause for termination. As the court stated, "[t]here cannot be a valid express contract, and an implied contract, each embracing the same subject but requiring different results."

On the other hand in *Mitford v. DeLasala*, 666 P.2d 1000 (Alaska 1983), the Alaska Supreme Court reached a contrary result. The plaintiff had entered into a written agreement that assured him a percentage of the employer's profits, but which also provided for termination by either party on 3 months' notice. Despite this at-will provision, the court ruled that the employee could sue for wrongful breach of the implied covenant discharge based on the allegation that the employer had discharged him in a bad faith attempt to deprive him of future profits.

In other situations like *Mitford*, arbitrary or underhanded conduct by the employer may induce a court to allow an implied covenant claim, even if the employee handbook or employment agreement explicitly reserves the right to fire at will. Nonetheless, if an employer acts in good faith, and does not violate public policy, an express reservation of at-will status represents one possible means of preventing a wrongful discharge suit based on the provisions of an employee handbook.

PERSPECTIVE

If the courts seem eager to enforce employee handbook provisions in specific situations, it is largely due to two motivations. First, courts recognize the internal benefits that an employer can reap when employees comply with personnel policies; the law is simply trying to assure employees of their side of the bargain. Second, the courts are naturally hostile to any employer that says one thing in its policy statements, but another thing by its actions. As we will further elaborate, the basic message for employers in all this is simple: Do not adopt any personnel policy that you do not intend to live by.

DRAFTING AND REVISING EMPLOYEE HANDBOOKS TO MINIMIZE THE RISK OF WRONGFUL DISCHARGE

No court has ever held that an employer has an obligation to publish an employee handbook, or to adopt any firm personnel policy. Even in the most progressive courts, the only obligations that arise from an employee handbook are ones the employer has *voluntarily* assumed. Why then, should an employer bother to issue an employee handbook in the first place?

The simple response is that employee handbooks can do a lot of good. By laying down basic guidelines and reporting necessary information about how the business operates, an employee handbook fosters stability and good will in the workplace. By describing employee benefits and privileges and by projecting the company's unique image, the handbook enhances morale and serves as a useful recruiting tool. Similarly, supervisory manuals and other formal policy statements help assure consistency and continuity in personnel administration. The challenge in drafting or revising an employee handbook lies in achieving these benefits without unduly or unwittingly restricting managerial freedom.

In the wrongful discharge cases discussed previously employee handbook provisions have often been construed to impose two basic limitations on the employer's right to terminate at-will employees. The first limitation is a *substantive* requirement that the employer must have just cause or good cause in order to discharge. The second limitation is a *procedural* requirement that the employer issue prior warnings or progressive discipline of some type, or, in a few cases, conduct a pretermination hearing.

In most cases, these obligations were more or less spelled out in the employee handbook, and the only innovation of the court was in treating them as a binding contract. In other cases, however, it seems clear that despite the handbook language, the employer never *intended* to submit to such substantive or procedural limitations on its power to discharge. Without realizing it, many employers have written their way into wrongful discharge lawsuits by not scrutinizing the statements in employee handbooks.

The following is a brief outline of some of the handbook provisions that have come back to haunt the employer as contractual limits on the power to terminate. Our purpose in reviewing these provisions is limited in several respects. The decision to promulgate a policy of firing only for just cause or utilizing progressive discipline prior to discharge is one that should be based on an employer's business judgment, and not solely on advice of counsel. Many employers, for good reason, voluntarily choose to adopt a policy of terminating only for cause.

Our objective is not to dissuade employers from assuming a just cause standard, but rather, to prevent an employer from doing so unintentionally. Moreover, we offer the following guidelines as an alternative to an express reservation of at-will status, which some employers would deem unacceptable. We are trying to assist employers who do not want to adopt a just cause limitation, but are unwilling to tell their employees emplicitly that they can be dismissed at will.

Beyond that, no employer should undertake to write a personnel handbook simply by copying another employer's handbook or forms supplied by a trade association or management consultant. Every handbook should reflect the unique personality of the company publishing it. Employee handbooks also touch on matters other than discharge, and many of these other areas are governed by independent bodies of law. Handbook statements as to overtime pay, workers' compensation, or jury duty, for example, must comport with the law of a particular jurisdiction. Every employer should thus consult local law before issuing a handbook.

Introduction

Most employee handbooks begin with an introductory statement, often in the form of an open letter to employees from the owner, president, or general manager. The language is upbeat, informal, and reflective of the pride and character of the company. Though most courts would be hard pressed to construe such language as creating a contract, employees will often cite statements in the introduction to bolster wrongful discharge claims based on other handbook provisions.

An employer concerned about such adverse implications should refrain from comments like "We at ACME Company provide the highest degree of job security in the industry," or "We believe in the principle of seniority for employees who do their jobs well," or "We are glad you have chosen to make your career with us." Statements like this seem inconsistent with the notion of at-will employment. As an alternative the introduction could focus on the stature of the company itself, its leadership in the industry, its reputation for quality, or its history of growth and progress. Or the introduction could stress the firm's high expectations for its employees with statements like "We owe our success to the hard work and dedication of all our local employees."

Probationary Clauses

Employee handbooks typically contain some form of probationary period for new employees. From a wrongful discharge standpoint the establishment of a probationary period implies that once the period has been satisfied, good cause or something more is needed to terminate the individual. A carefully drafted statement can mitigate this undue inference.

Employers who wish to avoid a just cause obligation should avoid language such as "During your probationary period, the company reserves the right to terminate you for any cause," or "If your performance is unsatisfactory, the company reserves the right to terminate your employment at any time within the probationary period." Phrased in this way, a probationary clause strongly implies that the standard for discharge changes once the employee survives the probationary period. Similarly, employers should be careful about using the term "permanent employees" to describe those who pass their probationary period. For example, a just cause requirement could be inferred from the statement that "If you demonstrate during the probationary period that you can perform your job satisfactorily, you will become a permanent employee."

Avoiding such language is fairly simple. With respect to the first type of phrase, employees really do not need to be told what will happen if they perform unsatisfactorily. Mere use of the term probation implies a conditional or trial status. Instead, the handbook might refer to what happens if the employee does perform adequately, for example, "Once you complete your probationary period, you will become a regular employee. Your seniority will date back to your hire date and you will become eligible for employee benefits as explained elsewhere in this handbook."

Note how the word "regular" is used in place of "permanent" to avoid the connotation of guaranteed employment. Yet another approach is to use either of these terms, but then to include a specific definition of the term that sets forth the at-will rule. For example, the handbook might refer to "permanent" employees, but then define them as "Employees hired with the expectation that their services will be for an indefinite duration." By using some of these ideas, the employer might end up with a probationary clause like the following:

The first 90 days of employment will be considered a probationary period for every new employee. During this period, you will have an opportunity to get adjusted to your job and new surroundings, and to demonstrate your ability and desire to perform assigned work. Following successful completion of the probationary period, your original date of hire will become your seniority date for purposes of determining your eligibility for employee benefits and privileges.

Seniority Clauses

Seniority has the greatest meaning for employee benefits, layoffs/recalls, transfers, and promotions. Some employers, however, have unwittingly adopted a just cause standard by specifying in their handbook that employees will forfeit their seniority in the event of "discharge for just cause," "involuntary termination for good cause," or similar language. Obviously any employer who wishes to avoid a just cause obligation should delete such phrases from the seniority provision. The handbook can simply state that seniority will be forfeited "upon involuntary termination," or "upon discharge."

Performance Reviews

Most employers make use of periodic performance reviews for employees of all levels. From a wrongful discharge perspective, handbook provisions describing performance reviews raise issues similar to those concerning probationary clauses. Adverse inferences could conceivably arise if the performance review provision inflates the expectations an employee might have from a positive review. For example, employers should be wary of statements like, "If you are doing anything that jeopardizes your continued employment, your supervisor will use the performance review as an opportunity to tell you what you are doing wrong." Such language could be construed to require prior corrective warnings before an employee may be discharged.

Discipline and Discharge

Handbook provisions under this heading are obviously the heart of the matter when it comes to wrongful discharge. As previously noted, there are two basic extremes an employer could adopt in formulating its disciplinary policy. One is to require just cause for termination, and the other is to preserve the right to terminate "with or without cause at any time." Those employers, however, who wish to retain the at-will freedom without heavy-handed statements to that effect will have to be somewhat vague in phrasing their disciplinary policies.

The discipline provision should not attempt to cover every possible situation. Even when the handbook includes a list of specific acts of misconduct, it should be made clear that the list is not all-inclusive, and that the company will impose discipline in other settings. In phrasing this "catch-all provision," the employer should be careful about using terms like "other good cause," "other just cause," or even "for similar reasons." These terms all imply that the conduct leading to discharge must be at least as serious as the listed violations. Instead the employer should openly, but diplomatically, reserve the final word on what conduct will lead to discharge. One possible format for a discipline section might be as follows:

In order to run a safe and orderly business, the company retains the right to discipline and discharge employees whose conduct disrupts the work of others, causes a hazard or interruption, or fails to live up to the company's expectations. It would be impossible to list all of the situations in which discipline or discharge would be appropriate, but the following are some examples of conduct that will subject employees to discipline, including discharge, if the company feels it is proper in the circumstances:

(The handbook would then list rules of conduct and safety rules suited to the employer's operation, and would conclude with the following "catch-all provision:")

The following list does not cover every situation, and the company will impose discipline, including discharge, for any other conduct which, in the judgment of the company, is not in its best interests.

Another of the many possible approaches to disciplinary policy is an abbreviated statement that conveys general standards, rather than specific acts of misconduct, and retains discretion with management. For example:

We at ACME Company operate with a minimum of formal rules and regulations. We rely on the good judgment of our employees to act in manner fully consistent with their responsibilities to their jobs, their fellow workers, and the community in which we live. Unfortunately, discipline including discharge may be required as a result of poor work performance, poor attendance, disregard of company rules, failure to follow orders, safety violations, dishonesty, indecency, breach of confidence, or in other instances in which the company determines that discipline or discharge is appropriate. Since it is necessary to consider all the facts and circumstances in each case, the final decision on whether to discipline or discharge shall be made solely by the company.

The language on discipline in an employee handbook can also create procedural limits on employer freedom. Many employers choose to adopt a formal progressive discipline system of one type or another. Some handbooks explicitly set forth a disciplinary progression to be followed in all cases, such as "First offense—oral reprimand; second offense—written warning; third offense—suspension; and fourth offense—discharge." There is nothing inherently wrong with such procedures, and indeed they are highly desirable in most companies.

The problem arises when an employer either adopts such a requirement unknowingly, or commits to follow it in every case, even when the employees' conduct is such that prior warnings would be futile. Thus, an employer should be wary of lightly referring to a practice of warning or suspending employees before they are discharged. Some employers fall into this trap by drafting an elaborate list of offenses, some of which are classified as serious and subject to discharge, while the others are less serious and will be met first with a corrective warning. Such lists should be accompanied by a "catch-all" provision in which the employer reserves the right to discharge without prior warning when it deems necessary.

The point is, an employer should draft such requirements with full awareness of how they will restrict managerial freedom. Even though progressive discipline makes good sense, employers are well-advised to include a provision stating that in appropriate cases, the company will exercise the right to discharge immediately without prior warnings.

Merger Clauses

Once an employer has drafted a suitable handbook, it should consider including a clause which prohibits any unauthorized supervisor from modifying the employer's policies or agreeing to additional committments. The same provision might also reserve the employer's right to modify or revoke any policy in the future, and to promulgate new ones. An example of such a clause is as follows:

In no circumstances may the policies described in this handbook be changed except through a written agreement signed by the president. In the event of a contradiction between the terms of this handbook and any statement made to you by any supervisor or other representative of the company, the terms of this handbook shall control in all cases. Any agreements or assurances governing the terms of your employment must be in writing and signed by the president of the company. The company reserves the right to modify, revoke, or add to the policies described in this handbook at any time without prior notice. If you have any question about this handbook, please ask your supervisor or the personnnel department.

Conforming Other Documents

Even the most carefully drafted handbook will serve little purpose if it is contradicted by an employment application, personnel manual, or any other formal statement of company policy. The final step in drafting or revising a handbook is conforming all other writings that touch on related personnel policies. This is particularly important if the employer has elected to include an express statement of the at-will doctrine. In such cases the employment application should include language to the effect that applicants acknowledge their at-will status. For example, "I understand and agree that my employment at ACME Company is for an indefinite duration and can be terminated at any time, with our without cause, and with or without notice, either by me or by the company."

The Fundamental Rule

The simplest and most important rule of drafting an employee handbook or other personnel policy is to include only those provisions that you intend to comply with consistently. If you have any doubts about a provision in a handbook, leave it out. A handbook should be written in plain English, and its terms should be analyzed from the perspective of a potential juror, rather than a supervisor or human resource professional. If an employer can live up to its word without exception, it faces little risk of breaching any contract that might arise from an employee handbook.

Chapter 5

THE PROTECTION OF EMPLOYEE PRIVACY

Steven J. Kaplan, J.D.
Joseph L. Paller, Jr., J.D.

Although most people believe they have a right to personal privacy, they would be hard pressed to explain it. A working definition of privacy has long proved elusive, even for judges and scholars.

The concept itself embraces a wide variety of concerns, ranging from interests in seclusion (such as sexual intimacy), to protection from the unnecessary gathering and disclosure of personal information, and beyond that to resistance to unwarranted demands made by persons in authority.

In private sector employment, privacy concerns are linked to the concept of intrusion. From the moment an individual first walks through his or her employer's doors, an employee gives up many privacy rights. As a condition of employment, employees must reveal personal facts about their background, and thereafter submit to continuing employer scrutiny. Beyond that he or she may face an employment physical, a polygraph examination, a psychological test, or even an antibody test for AIDS. Physical intrusion may also be involved: Some employers frisk employees as they leave work or search their lockers, even where there is no reasonable suspicion of employee theft.

Privacy interests are also implicated where an employer conducts routine surveillance and monitoring of employees. Employers have been know to operate video cameras in employee restrooms, and some companies have installed computers to monitor the performance of video display terminal operators. It has been said by critics that such activities subject employees to constant stress, prevent them from working at their own pace, and make them feel that their every move is being observed.

The privacy invasion in employment extends also to efforts by employers to gather personal information about employees that is not job-related. Employers have a legitimate need to know certain things about

115

their employees, including their work abilities, reputations for honesty, and past employment experiences. But some employers want to know much more. They assert, however mistakenly, that everything about an employee is relevant to the job; that it is necessary to examine the "whole person" in order to determine whether he or she is suited for employment. If the employee smokes marijuana at home, or is a homosexual, or socializes with the "wrong" kind of people—the employer wants to know.

Finally, privacy rights are implicated when employers disclose information about their employees to third parties. Such disclosures are primarily made to other prospective employers in the form of job references. An employer may also disclose an employee's confidential medical records to those who have no business seeing them; or may publicize negative private facts about an individual out of spite or a misplaced desire for revenge. These acts are also intrusive in that they may cause embarrassment to an employee, subject him or her to scorn and ridicule from friends and acquaintances, or ruin their reputation and job prospects.

Should the law be concerned with the protection of privacy rights in the workplace? While it is true that employers have legitimate business interests that sometimes require intrusions on the privacy of employees, there are compelling reasons to place limits on the ability of an employer to trespass on employee privacy rights where no overriding business necessity exists.

First and foremost, many privacy invasions undermine the integrity of the individual. Strip searches and restroom surveillance, for example, are degrading and dehumanizing. Second, critics have argued that there are sound societal reasons for protecting privacy in the workplace. Protection operates as an important check on abuse of authority. Life in the corporation demands conformity and substantial suppression of one's personal lifestyle. These critics contend that corporate life makes demands on the way an individual lives, thinks, and socializes that arguably rival the demands made by authoritarian governments, and therefore that enforcement of privacy rights operates to inhibit the arbitrary abuse of authority by irresponsible employers.

Third, protection of privacy is essential for free and frank communication. The development of ideas requires the opportunity to express thoughts about policies and persons at all levels without fear that one's private remarks will become public property or a source of embarrassment. The elimination of confidential communication among employees inhibits invention and creativity, and may stifle the success of the business venture.

A growing number of employers now recognize that in the long run they are better off if they respect the privacy rights of their employees. Many of America's major corporations maintain internal privacy guidelines even though these policies give employees more than the law requires. This development may be explained by the fact that the beneficiaries of these new policies are primarily middle- and upper-level management personnel. These are individuals whose greater interest in confidentiality in business-related communications, and more sophisticated and complex lifestyles, make them especially concerned that the company will excessively monitor their working time or pry too deeply into their personal lives. This chapter reviews the current state of employee privacy rights and its implications for the emerging law of wrongful termination. In the past 10 years there has been a tremendous expansion of the legislation regulating privacy in private employment. Literally hundreds of statutes have been enacted, and the courts have become much more receptive to privacy claims under judicially created common law. Curiously, however, there has been relatively little employee activism to enforce these emerging legal rights. There seem to be two reasons for this dearth of litigation. First, some laws, although ostensibly designed to protect employees, frequently leave employers with considerable discretion to disregard privacy concerns when gathering or releasing information about their employees.

Second, most privacy violations occur during the job application process or before employment has terminated. The adversely affected individual must usually suppress their objections in order to get a job or keep it. This reluctance to initiate legal proceedings explains why privacy litigation most often occurs where a privacy invasion has led to a discharge, when the employee is no longer dependent on the employer for his or her livelihood.

With the recent development of wrongful termination law has come the prospect that many employment disputes that begin as protests over an invasion of personal privacy will end in a suit for wrongful discharge. An employee may be terminated in retaliation for protesting a policy that arguably violates his or her privacy interests. Or a discharge that is indisputably lawful may become an actionable privacy violation if the employer wrongfully publicizes the cause of termination. In such cases the employee may invoke public policy, found either in the privacy statutes or common law, to support a termination action of the type discussed in Chapter 1. A job applicant may even be able to sue for the wrongful refusal to hire, if the individual discovers that the hiring decision was based on information obtained in violation of their privacy rights.

A wrongful termination action may also be based on an employer's violation of the privacy provisions of its own personnel policies. As Chapter 3 discussed, the abrogation or inconsistent application of personnel policies may give rise to wrongful termination actions based on a contractual theory or a breach of the covenant of good faith and fair dealing. Where the policy breach involves employee privacy (such as, for example, termination resulting from surveillance in violation of such a policy) an action may lie.

This chapter addresses three basic areas of employee privacy rights. We first answer the frequently asked but rarely understood question whether private sector employees have a constitutional right of privacy. The remaining sections discuss the two basic areas of privacy violations— legal limitations on an employer's ability to gather private and personal information about its employees, and legal limitations on an employer's ability to disclose such information. We have tried to draw an overall picture, emphasizing federal law wherever possible. Because most regulation in the privacy field consists of state law, however, we have also included extensive discussion of this subject, focusing on the similarities among the states. This chapter discusses the privacy rights of employees in the private sector. It does not address those statutes, such as the Privacy Act of 1974, the Freedom of Information Act, and their state and local counterparts, which affect the privacy rights of public employees, and the government's ability to disclose information about private citizens.

The statutes which will be discussed deal directly with the issues of intrusion and privacy. This article does not discuss privacy rights as they indirectly arise under general employment statutes. For example, state and federal discrimination laws and the National Labor Relations Act guarantee employees that their employers will not inquire into certain matters, such as religious convictions and union sympathies. These matters are beyond the scope of this chapter, but are discussed elsewhere in this handbook.

DO EMPLOYEES HAVE A CONSTITUTIONAL RIGHT TO PRIVACY?

The U.S. Constitution does not contain the word "privacy." But the Supreme Court has held that the Bill of Rights contains implicit privacy protections, from the right to be free from unreasonable searches by law enforcement officers to the right of a woman to obtain an abortion.

Constitutional rights, however, may be asserted only when there is some governmental involvement in the objectionable conduct. This involvement is known as "state action." For example, a city or state may not deprive individuals of free speech by censoring publications, but a private business acting without government involvement or compulsion is free to prevent its employees from distributing literature or wearing campaign buttons in the workplace.

State action is generally not present in private employment. Therefore, although the U.S. Constitution does recognize a right to privacy, it is not a right that private sector employees normally can assert against their employers.

Several years ago, commentators and legal scholars argued that private sector employees should be entitled to certain constitutional rights in the workplace, including the rights of free speech and privacy. These commentators noted that private businesses, especially the nation's large corporations, hold vast power over the lives of individuals, as well as over American economic life in general. In addition corporate power is initially derived from the state, which issues corporate papers, licenses businesses, and regulates many business activities.

These ideas were popular in the 1960s and 1970s, but have gradually lost much of their appeal to lawyers and legal scholars. More important, they have been spurned by the Supreme Court, which has so far refused to subject most private business activity to constitutional limitations. Employees and their lawyers have thus had to look elsewhere to find legal support for employment privacy claims. One place they have turned is to state constitutional law. At least 10 state constitutions contain provisions expressly guaranteeing privacy rights. But most of these state constitutions, like the U.S. Constitution, require state action and, therefore, do not constitute a source for private employment rights.

The principal exception is California. In 1972, article I, section 1 of the California Constitution was amended by popular vote to create an "inalienable right" of "pursuing and obtaining privacy." No state action is required under this section. It applies to both government and private business. Although the language of the amendment is somewhat vague, it has been interpreted by the California Supreme Court to entitle individuals to very specific rights of privacy:

The right of privacy is the right to be left alone. . . . It prevents government and business interests from collecting and stockpiling unnecessary information about us and from misusing information gathered for one purpose in order to serve other purposes or to embarrass us.

This constitutional amendment has the potential to greatly extend legal privacy rights. Because the amendment does not require state action, every employee has a colorable legal basis to use his or her employer for a perceived privacy breach. This potential for unlimited expansion of privacy protection is illustrated by a recent case. In *Payton v. City of Santa Clara*, 132 Cal. App. 3d 152, 183 Cal. Rptr. 17 (1982), an employee discharged for dishonesty claimed that the employer had posted a memorandum to that effect on a bulletin board for other employees to see. There was no statutory or common law right against this kind of public disclosure. Nevertheless the court decided that the employer's actions constituted an actionable privacy breach under the California Constitution, permitting a suit for damages.

A California employee's privacy rights are not absolute. They may have to give way to employer policies which, though intrusive, are nevertheless important. Although the California Supreme Court has not announced a test for ascertaining when an individual's interest in personal privacy must give way, it is likely the court will rely on analogous constitutional principles and permit an invasion of individual privacy when justified by compelling or overriding business interests. This means that the intrusion must be both necessary for the employer's continued successful operation of its business and carefully structured so that privacy intrusions are minimized.

To date California is the only state whose constitutional provision on privacy has been interpreted to extend individual privacy rights beyond their development under previous law. There are other state constitutions, including Montana, Hawaii, and Illinois that have privacy protections which have been interpreted to apply in the private sector. Unlike California, these sections have been construed to embody only such rights of privacy as already existed under the common law. The constitutional privacy provisions in these states have not yet become a source for the expansion of employee privacy rights, as in California.[1]

---

[1]Some states, including Massachusetts, have enacted general privacy statutes that limit the right of private business to trespass on personal privacy rights. But these statutes, like Illinois' constitutional privacy section, have not expanded the protections already available under the common law.

INFORMATION GATHERING

A growing number of state laws restrict employer inquiries into the personal lives and backgrounds of employees and job applicants. These statutes can be costly traps for uninformed employers. Many not only permit lawsuits for civil damages (and, in some cases, criminal penalties), but may expand protections against wrongful termination. Thus, if an employee or job applicant can show that their discharge or the refusal to hire resulted from the employer's acquisition of information prohibited by the law, the employer may be liable, even if the job applicant or employee was the source of the information.

Additionally, employers are facing an increasing variety of novel lawsuits based on traditional invasion of privacy theories, even in the absence of a statute prohibiting the employment test or inquiry.

RESTRICTIONS ON EMPLOYEE TESTING

Lie Detectors and Other Truth Verification Devices

Twenty-four states and the District of Columbia now have laws limiting employer use of lie detectors and other truth testing devices.[2] Twenty-six states require that polygraph operators who test employees meet strict licensing requirements. With the possible exception of defamation cases, no other area of state privacy law has yielded as rich and bountiful a harvest of lawsuits against employers.

In June 1985, a Maryland court of appeals upheld a jury verdict awarding $1.3 million to an employee who was forced to resign because she had refused to submit to a lie detector test intended to ferret out the source of inventory shortages. In Florida an assistant store manager recently won $250,000 in damages for negligence and libel against a discount department store when he was fired after failing a poorly administered polygraph test falsely implicating him in the theft of $500 from the company safe. In Connecticut, 22 employees were awarded a total of $220,000, the largest judgment in New London County Court history, for being forced to take lie detector tests. Sixteen of these employees were fired for refusing or failing the tests. Six others recovered damages simply because they had been forced to take the tests against their wills.

Despite the ever increasing number of lawsuits and judgments against employers, between 500,000 and 2 million polygraph tests are administered every year to job applicants and employees across the nation. The American Polygraph Association estimates that 30 percent of Fortune 500 companies, including many of the nation's largest department store chains, use lie detectors in employment, primarily to prevent theft among low level employees with access to cash and inventory.

The Association, a polygraph industry lobbying group, also claims that polygraphs are 90 percent accurate in employment situations. Some critics, however, rate the accuracy of lie detectors in employment as "no better than flipping a coin." Nevertheless, these devices remain popular because

[2]Nevada's law was repealed July 31, 1985.

they are cheaper and quicker than other forms of employee background checks and have an aura of scientific legitimacy. Some employers also maintain a practice of administering such tests simply to discourage thieves from seeking employment.

But concerns are frequently expressed over the instruments' reliability, examiner competence, and their unquestionable intrusion into personal privacy. Polygraphs probe a person's innermost thoughts and feelings. Examiners commonly inquire into employees' or job applicants' personal finances, medical histories, accident experiences, drug and alcohol use, personal problems, underlying motives for seeking employment, and sexual habits. Examiners also frequently ask questions that are forbidden by state law, such as about arrest records. The questioning itself is dehumanizing because the subject is effectively prevented from refusing to respond to a question; once a question is asked, the device automatically records nonverbal, physical responses to the question before the subject has time to object.

The testing procedure creates an atmosphere that leads people to confess. Subjects believe that the machine will discover attempts to evade questions or conceal the truth. This eagerness to appear honest and truthful often leads subjects to disclose private facts about themselves that they would not otherwise willingly reveal.

Employees also have little choice but to consent to take the examination. As one New Jersey Court has stated: "By merely 'requesting' the employee to take the test, the employer is in fact offering the employee an ultimatum—either he takes the test or he puts their character in doubt among management as well as his fellow workers." *State v. Community Distributors, Inc.*, 123 N.J. Super. 589, 304 A.2d 213, 218–19 (1973), *affirmed*, 64 N.J. 479, 317 A.2d 697 (1974).

Although there is little empirical evidence, polygraph tests are considered less accurate in employment situations than in criminal investigations. For example, the questions asked in a criminal investigation usually relate to a specific event in the immediate past ("Did you rob the First National Bank last Friday night?"). In employment situations, questions are often by their very nature so broad as to make any generalized response misleading or inaccurate ("Have you ever stolen anything?"). The subject may truthfully respond "no" while feeling irrational guilt for failing to return a pencil to his seventh-grade teacher, creating the inaccurate recorded impression that he is lying.

The attitude or condition of the subject often leads to inaccurate test results. Stress caused by the pressure of the examination, such as headaches, fatigue, illness, or anger and embarrassment created by the questions themselves, frequently leads examiners to mistakenly conclude that a truthful answer is a lie. By the same token, the lie detector will not expose the dishonesty of persons who can lie without guilt or fear, or the lies of those who erroneously believe that their answers are true. An employee who honestly but mistakenly believes that he or she saw another person steal company property is likely to be believed when their statement registers as true in a polygraph examination, causing an innocent employee to suffer. The coercive nature of lie detection in employment is also frequently cited as a source of polygraph inaccuracy.

Even assuming that lie detectors yield accurate information, many critics have questioned whether a job applicant's honesty or future behavior can reliably be tested from answers to general questions about past conduct, particularly where the test examinee has never worked with money or inventory in the past.

Finally, lie detector results are still largely a matter of interpretation. It is the examiner, not the machine, that detects lies. The device merely measures observable physiological responses to stress and anxiety. The examiner must interpret this data in an effort to determine whether responses are based on truth or lies, or perhaps on truth masked by deep-seated guilt feelings or traumatic childhood incidents. As polygraph examiners candidly acknowledge, lie detection is not a science, but rather the subjective application of several disciplines, including psychology and physiology. Although the success of a lie detection test may turn on the examiner's skills in these areas, many examiners have little formal training beyond learning to operate the instrument itself.

Ultimately the test results depend on the personal judgment of the examiner, to the same extent that results of a job or disciplinary interview depend on the personal judgment of the interviewer. Indeed, studies conducted by researchers at the U.S. Army Land Warfare Laboratory and the University of Utah suggest that visual observations during questioning are more accurate indicators of truth or falsity than raw polygraph data.

STATE AND FEDERAL REGULATIONS. There is no federal law today restricting the use of polygraphs in private employment. But the intrusive nature of polygraph testing and doubts about its accuracy have led federal legislators to propose a number of bills over the years to ban or regulate the use of lie detector tests by private employers. In the House of Representatives one bill has been introduced to bar polygraph examiners from inquiring into an individual's religious beliefs, racial background, political or union affiliations, and sexual practices or preferences. Other bills would ban use of polygraphs in most private-sector employment entirely.

State statutes restricting employer use of polygraphs or other truth verification devices are numerous, and differ radically. (Statutes restricting employer disclosure of the results of lie detector tests are discussed near the end of this chapter.) To be safe from lawsuits or criminal prosecution, it is vitally important that every employer consult an attorney who is familiar with state law in this area before administering any form of truth verification test. But certain generalizations about these laws can be made because they tend to follow similar patterns.

BASIC RESTRICTIONS ON EMPLOYER USE. Roughly half the state statutes prohibit employers from *requiring* or involuntarily *subjecting* employees to so-called truth tests. An employer is liable only if it administers a lie detector test after the employee or job applicant has resisted taking it, or if it discriminates against the individual for refusing. California, the District of Columbia, Hawaii, Idaho, Iowa, Maryland, Montana, Nebraska, Oregon, Pennsylvania, Rhode Island, Utah, and Washington have laws of this type.

In these states an employer may still *request* or *suggest* that the employee or job applicant take the examination. For example, an employer can tell an employee that he or she is suspected of stealing, but that the employee will not be fired if his or her innocence can be proven through a lie detector test. Job applicants who are asked to submit to such a test will be concerned that their chances of getting the job are slim or none if they refuse. But if applicants or employees refuse to submit to the test, they can sue or initiate criminal charges against the employer if they can show that the employer's decision not to hire or to discharge them resulted from their refusal to take the test.

Many of these laws obligate employees or job applicants to consent to the test in writing, and some of these further require that the written waiver contain certain mandatory language advising the employee of their right to refuse to take the test without fear of retaliation by the employer. A sample consent form, modeled after one used by many polygraph services in California, appears at Appendix A of this chapter. Employers should beware that use of a form of this kind may not immunize them from liability since in some states, including California, courts have been sympathetic to claims that written waivers of statutory rights were obtained in coercive circumstances by a person or corporation with superior bargaining power.

Other states forbid employers to *request, solicit,* or *suggest* that employees and prospective employees take lie detector tests. These states include Alaska, Connecticut, Delaware, Maine, Massachusetts, Michigan, New Jersey, New York (psychologic stress evaluators only), Vermont, West Virginia, and Wisconsin.

These stricter state laws attempt to minimize employer influence and coercion by precluding employers from even suggesting that a truth test be taken. An employer cannot *ask* employees to prove their innocence, or job applicants their honesty, by taking a lie detector test. Nevertheless these states permit *employees to request* the opportunity to take a polygraph test to prove their innocence. This right has been subject to abuse by employers, leading in some cases to massive judgments against them.

Finally, both the "require" and the "request" laws frequently exempt certain industries, such as manufacturers, distributors, and retailers of drugs and narcotics, by permitting those employers to require the test as a condition of employment. New Jersey, Pennsylvania, Vermont, Washington, and West Virginia are among the states that have exceptions of this type.

TYPES OF TESTS. The polygraph examination is but one form of lie detector test. Psychologic stress evaluators and voice stress analyzers test vocal reactions, retinoscopes test eye movements, and lie detector chairs (so-called wiggle seats) register muscle pressure and movement. Many state laws prohibit one device while permitting others. New York, for example, prohibits the use of psychologic stress evaluators while leaving the use of all other test devices unregulated. Other state laws broadly restrict the use of all forms of mechanical or electrical truth verification devices. The California, Connecticut, District of Columbia, Iowa, Maine, Minnesota, Nebraska, Oregon, Utah, West Virginia, and Wisconsin laws appear to do so.

RESTRICTIONS ON QUESTIONS. At least 11 states limit the types of questions that an employer may ask. The Arizona, Georgia, Illinois, Maine, Michigan, Maryland, Nebraska, Nevada, New Mexico, Tennessee, and Virginia laws variously prohibit questioning involving sexual practices or orientation, medical or psychological conditions, and religious, political, or union sympathies and affiliations. As discussed in greater detail later, many states have other blanket restrictions on certain employer inquiries, such as questions concerning arrest records, that are not contained in their lie detector statutes. Where such inquiries are prohibited generally, they are also prohibited when asked during a lie-detector test. It is vital that an employer make sure that its questioning of employees and job applicants does not intrude in these areas or into subjects forbidden by state and federal civil rights laws.

LICENSING. Many states prohibit employers from using polygraph operators who are not licensed by the state. The 26 states with such licensing laws are Alabama, Arizona, Arkansas, California, Georgia, Illinois, Indiana, Kentucky, Louisiana, Maine, Michigan, Mississippi, Montana, Nebraska, Nevada, New Mexico, North Carolina, North Dakota, Oklahoma, Oregon, South Carolina, Tennessee, Texas, Utah, Vermont, and Virginia. Some of these laws specifically state that an employer is not liable for the wrongful acts of a polygrapher of which it is not aware.

PENALTIES AGAINST EMPLOYERS. Most of the state laws restricting employer use of polygraphs and other truth verification devices treat violations as crimes, prescribing fines, imprisonment, or both for violations. Others specifically permit the employee to sue. Both types of laws provide fertile ground for suits by discharged workers as well as job applicants who are denied employment as a result of a lie detector test.

At least 10 state statutes expressly permit employees or job applicants to sue employers for damages for violating lie detector statutes. The damages allowed are potentially devastating. West Virginia will award a successful employee triple the actual damages, while Michigan permits double damages. Both these states, as well as Minnesota, Oregon, and Washington, award attorney's fees and a wide variety of costs to successful employees and job applicants. Vermont law permits the court to order an employee to be reinstated in his or her job; Oregon authorizes the Commissioner of the Labor Bureau to seek orders reinstating discharged employees or requiring an employer to hire an unsuccessful job applicant. Statutes in California (voice stress analyzer violations only), the District of Columbia, Maryland, New York, Vermont, and Washington allow either the employee or the State Labor Commissioner to bring suit for lost wages. Many of these states also allow suits for injunctions to prevent future abuses by an employer.

Moreover, in many states whose statutes do not specifically provide for civil suits, the courts have allowed employees to sue for wrongful discharge when the termination decision was based on a prohibited lie detector test. But in states, such as Missouri, where there is no law regulating employer use of lie detectors, the courts have been reluctant to permit wrongful discharge suits for lie detector abuse.

It should come as no surprise that juries generally abhor lie detector use in employment. The plaintiff in a polygraph suit may be a long-term, church-going employee with an unblemished character who was discharged after failing or refusing to take a lie detector test. Where these facts exist, a jury is likely to be more sympathetic to a live and suffering plaintiff than to a cold machine, and six figure judgments against employers in these cases are not uncommon.

LABOR ARBITRATION. A labor union may challenge an employer's lie detection program through the grievance procedure contained in most collective bargaining agreements. Under most union contracts, an employer may not unilaterally or arbitrarily implement policies that impinge on employee rights or adversely alter working conditions. Arbitrators universally acknowledge, however, that even under a union contract, employers retain certain "management rights" that enable them to promulgate reasonable rules necessary to efficiently and safely operate their businesses.

A union may successfully challenge rules and regulations promulgated by the employer only if they are arbitrary, serve no reasonable work-related purpose, or undermine working conditions and protections obtained through collective bargaining.

Unlike other privacy issues, arbitrators are unreservedly hostile to the use of lie detector tests in employment discipline cases. Even in the rare instance where a collective bargaining agreement specifically provides that a company could require employees to submit to polygraph tests, arbitrators have ruled not only that the results of the tests are not admissible as evidence of guilt, but that an employee's refusal to take a test does not constitute just cause for discharge. And the courts have affirmed such decisions. (See, *Amalgamated Meat Cutters, Local 540 v. Neuhoff Brothers Packers, Inc.,* 481 F.2d 817 (5th Cir. 1973).) Many more arbitrators have held that uniform work rules requiring employees to submit to polygraph tests are inherently unreasonable and unenforceable, and that an employee's refusal to comply with such a company policy is not insubordination and should not prejudice him or her in any way.

"Under the overwhelming weight of arbitral authority . . . where an employee does submit to lie detector testing, the test results should be given little or no weight in arbitration." Elkouri & Elkouri, *How Arbitration Works* 315 (4th ed. 1985). Arbitrators share the courts' distrust of the accuracy of lie detector tests. They have also expressed repugnance over the intrusive nature of the testing procedure, finding it to be an unwarranted invasion of privacy. In addition, arbitrators have objected to the fact that employee consent is usually coerced, if not explicitly, then by fear of appearing dishonest by refusing to submit to the procedure.

Drug and Alcohol Tests

Baseball players, Olympic athletes, and race horses are not the only ones being asked to submit to drug screening. Alcohol and drug testing of job applicants and workers is spreading rapidly throughout the nation. The U.S. Drug Enforcement Administration estimates that 25 percent of Fortune 500 companies, including such giants as IBM, General Motors, and American Airlines, routinely administer urinalysis tests as an inexpensive method of ferreting out drug users among their workers and prospective employees. Unfortunately these tests often produce a rather painful side effect—employee lawsuits.

In Los Angeles two nurses filed suit against a hospital after they were fired for refusing to submit to drug tests. In San Francisco, an electrical engineer filed suit against Southern Pacific for damages for wrongful discharge and invasion of privacy, when she was fired the day after she refused to submit to a urinalysis test uniformly administered to 500 other employees. She refused the test because she wished to keep her recent pregnancy a secret from her employer and co-workers. In both of these lawsuits the discharged employees were not suspected of drug abuse.

Criticism of these tests has increased in proportion to their expanded use. Respected medical researchers have challenged the accuracy of these tests. Courts have recognized that breathalyzer, blood, and urinalysis tests for alcohol are frequently administered improperly by law enforcement agencies, leading to inaccurate results. The error rate for drug urinalysis tests may be as high as 25 percent, even when they are properly administered. Some retail cold medicines, for example, test positively as amphetamines. In addition, some experts have concluded that an individual who has passively inhaled smoke from a marijuana cigarette smoked by another may test positively for marijuana use. The 25 percent error rate can increase alarmingly in the laboratory. The Center for Disease Control researchers recently reported a *66.5 percent* false positive rate from one surveyed facility.

Even when test results are accurate, they do not discriminate between the occasional or Saturday night user and the hardened addict. The tests do not show who is intoxicated on the job and whether the measurable drug residue has resulted in any work impairment. Thus, an accurate test result may punish off-premises conduct that creates no risk of harm to the employer.

Like polygraph tests, drug tests infringe on privacy interests. For most people, the act of giving a urine specimen is repulsive or embarrassing. It becomes even more degrading when submission to the test is coerced by an employer. For many, blood testing for alcohol is even more unpleasant. In addition, job applicants and employees often are not even informed that a routine medical examination may also contain a drug or alcohol screening test. In these circumstances, the subject is deprived of all choice to refuse the test or to verify whether it was properly administered.

Needless to say, the consequences of a failed drug or alcohol test can be disastrous. Not only can an employee or applicant lose their livelihood, but may also be blackballed by other companies that share the employer's test results. Many critics believe that this is too high a price given the demonstrated inaccuracy of the tests.

But the stakes are high for employers as well. Drug and alcohol induced accidents have led to lawsuits and worker's compensation claims. Internal studies frequently link absenteeism, high insurance costs, and declining productivity to drug and alcohol abuse. Employers tell tales of drug-dependent employees stealing money and selling confidential information to support their habits. Although background checks and more comprehensive programs may be more reliable methods for detecting and detering alcohol and drug use, they are also far more expensive than urinalysis and similar tests.

With few exceptions, laws controlling employer drug and alcohol testing are virtually nonexistent. A recent San Francisco Ordinance restricts employer drug testing. Oregon's lie detector law prohibits employers from requiring employees and job applicants to take breathalyzer tests, blood-content tests, and any other tests "to detect the presence of alcohol in the body through the use of instrumentation or mechanical devices." The law does not address drug testing, and contains two broad exceptions. An employee can consent to alcohol testing, and an employer is permitted to administer alcohol tests if it has "reasonable grounds to believe" that an individual is intoxicated. But an employee is not considered intoxicated unless his blood alcohol content exceeds the amount specified in an existing workrule or collective bargaining agreement.

Some state polygraph laws restrict the use of lie detectors "and other similar tests" by employers, and some plaintiffs are claiming that these laws prohibit drug and alcohol tests in the workplace. Unfortunately there are no reported court decisions on this issue, and in those states employers have no clear guidelines to govern administration of these tests.

As will be discussed later, California and other states forbid employers from asking job applicants and employees whether they have participated in a drug or alcohol diversion program as a result of an arrest, or whether they have been arrested for or convicted of certain drug abuse offenses. Other states permit employees to deny the existence of arrests that have not resulted in convictions, or to deny convictions where the court records have been sealed or expunged, without fear of employer retaliation.

Challenges to drug and alcohol testing have arisen far more frequently in labor arbitrations than in the courts; however, there are still few guidelines. In general arbitrators have been reluctant to uphold disciplinary penalties for refusing to consent to random or blanket drug or alcohol tests, absent a contract provision or established work rule requiring submission to such tests. Even where a test was demanded based on the employer's suspicion that a particular employee was intoxicated, arbitrators have frequently overturned a discharge based simply on the employee's refusal to take the test, absent strong corroborating evidence that the employee was in fact intoxicated, such as erratic behavior or alcoholic breath. However, some arbitrators have upheld or imposed lesser penalties than discharge for such a refusal.

Arbitrators are far more willing to uphold discharges where the employer has promulgated a rule requiring compliance with testing procedures, and the test has been fairly administered in compliance with the rule. Discharges are also upheld where an employee consents to take but then fails an alcohol or drug test. Even in these circumstances, though, arbitrators frequently require other corroborating evidence of the employee's intoxication. Arbitrators have also been sympathetic to evidence that a drug or alcohol test was inherently inaccurate or improperly administered.

Particulary in cases involving allegations of illegal drug or narcotic use, arbitrators are divided as to the standard of proof necessary to sustain a discharge or suspension. A survey by the American Arbitration Association shows that more than half the responding arbitrators require the employer to prove a marijuana offense by clear and convincing evidence or by proof beyond a reasonable doubt, rather than by a mere preponderance of the evidence, the usual standard in discipline cases.

New Privacy Problems in the Workplace: AIDS and Genetic Testing

In September 1985 Florida's Dade County tentatively approved an ordinance requiring all restaurant and other food workers to obtain and carry certificates that they are free from AIDS, venereal disease, and tuberculosis. Newark, New Jersey also considered such a law. In contrast, although Pentagon medical experts recently issued a report disputing recommendations by top military leaders that all military personnel be immediately subjected to AIDS testing, such testing was ordered and AIDS carrying personnel were discharged.

The AIDS crisis is spawning panic in the workplace. Civil liberties groups report that homosexuals are being fired or denied employment because of employer fears that they may be AIDS carriers, while some prominent industrial leaders have publicly discussed initiating AIDS testing in the workplace. AIDS discrimination lawsuits have already been filed against Columbia University, United Airlines, and other major employers.

In response to concerns about employment discrimination against homosexuals and intrusions into individual privacy rights, California and Wisconsin have recently passed laws which mandate AIDS testing in blood donations, but forbid disclosure of the test results to third parties, including employers and health insurers. The California law also prohibits undisclosed AIDS testing in employment physicals by requiring that the applicant give written consent before antibody testing is conducted.

New laws of different kinds are being considered in a number of jurisdictions. The difficulty facing state legislatures and local governments is to strike a balance between competing concerns for public health and safety, and unjustified discrimination and privacy intrusions in the workplace. The California and Wisconsin statutes, and the proposed Dade County and Newark ordinances, fall on opposite sides of the fence on this issue. Employers that are considering or conducting AIDS testing must be watchful as the courts and legislatures begin to address these problems.

The issue of genetic testing is less well-publicized. Recent scientific data suggest that there may be a link betwen inherited genetic traits and occupational disease caused by exposure to chemicals. But a firm connection between certain genetic traits and increased health risks has yet to be established. Nonetheless, at least 18 major corporations have begun administering genetic tests to workers and job applicants, while many more are considering the use of such tests. Privacy groups have complained that employees in some cases were not made aware of the purposes or potential impact of the tests, and therefore had no opportunity to refuse or have their representatives monitor their proper administration. Employees are also being denied both access to test results, and assurances that they will not be disclosed to other employers.

A few state statutes and one OSHA regulation provide for employee access to medical records in their employers' possession, and others protect their confidentiality. These laws, which are discussed in later parts of this chapter, provide little comfort to those who object to genetic testing. Like AIDS testing, genetic testing is a thorny privacy issue that has not yet been fully confronted by legislatures and the courts.

RESTRICTIONS ON ELECTRONIC SURVEILLANCE

Statutory Limits

Employers are increasingly using electronic surveillance and monitoring devices to keep tabs on employee conduct during the workday. These devices are primarily designed to combat theft and pilferage, although some employers have used them to obtain personal information about their workers.

Technological developments have enhanced employers' surveillance capabilities. Infrared devices permit photographs to be taken through walls, miniature microphones can be hidden in virtually any location, and entire buildings can be wired to listen in on employee conversations and identify the speakers. It was recently reported that the owner of one small factory installed microphones in the women's restroom. He became known around the plant as the "crapper-tapper." In industries with heavy use of video display terminals (VDTs), some employers have installed new computers to monitor employee work performance, to record when they come, when they go and how fast they operate their machines.

As yet there are no federal laws prohibiting employers from filming or video monitoring employees in the workplace. Nor are there any federal statutory limits on VDT monitoring, which fulfills much the same purpose. Only one state clearly prohibits closed circuit audio and video surveillance of employees. A Connecticut law prohibits employers from operating any electronic surveillance device, including sound recording and closed circuit television cameras, in employee lounges, restrooms, and locker rooms. Surveillance is not prohibited in actual work areas. Video surveillance is at present unlimited in all other states.

There are significant federal and state laws restricting employer eavesdropping on telephone conversations and other voice communications. Title III of the Omnibus Crime Control and Safe Streets Act of 1968, the only federal law on the subject applicable to private employers, prohibits most deliberate and surreptitious eavesdropping. The law is primarily directed against wiretapping and other methods of intercepting telephone conversations. But it also prohibits the interception of oral communications between employees when uttered with "an expectation that such communication is not subject to interception under circumstances justifying such expectation." When employees speak confidentially at times and in places where they reasonably can expect privacy (e.g., in an employee restroom), their employer cannot eavesdrop without violating the statute.

In businesses with heavy VDT use (e.g., insurance companies, newspapers, the communications industry), employees often communicate by sending each other messages through the computer or word processing network. These types of communications may also constitute wire communication within the meaning of Title III, and eavesdropping on them may therefore be prohibited.

There are certain exceptions set forth in Title III that allow an employer to eavesdrop on oral conversations or tap telephone conversations. Among these are monitoring activities which are part of the normal course of business of the employer, and where one of the parties to the wire or oral communication has given prior consent to the interception involved ("single party consent").

It has been suggested that this last exception allows an employer to tap its own telephones. This is probably an incorrect interpretation. No automatic consent should be implied simply because an employee is using a company telephone. But because an employer can often obtain the prior consent of at least one party to a telephone communication *within* the company, it is not as difficult for it to engage in extensive intracompany monitoring of telephone or oral conversations.

The recent case of *Watkins v. L.M. Berry & Co.*, 704 F.2d 577 (11th Cir. 1983), illustrates the scope and limits of employee monitoring. In that case the employer was accused of illegally eavesdropping, and was sued for damages, *even though the conversation it monitored was arguably business-related.*

The company ran a "boiler room" from which employees telephonically solicited Yellow Pages advertising. Watkins was one of the solicitors. The employer regularly monitored solicitation calls with a standard extension telephone as part of its ongoing training program. Employees were permitted to make personal calls and were told that such calls would not be monitored except to the extent necessary to determine if a particular call was of a personal or business nature. At one point Watkins received a personal call from a friend who asked Watkins if she was interested in a job with another company. Watkins said that she was interested. Without her knowledge, Watkins' boss listened in on the entire conversation. Watkins was fired soon after, and sued the company for violation of Title III.[3] The court rejected the company's argument that Watkins' knowledge of the monitoring policy constituted "consent." Because Watkins only consented to the policy of monitoring business calls, the company was required to hang up as soon as it determined that her call was of a personal nature. "[K]nowledge of the *capability* of monitoring alone cannot be considered implied consent."

---

[3]Watkins took the other job as soon as she was fired. She therefore did not sue for wrongful discharge but merely for violation of Title III. It would seem, however, that the termination, resulting from the company's illegal eavesdropping, would have constituted an actionable discharge in violation of public policy. This type of action is discussed in Chapter 1.

The court also rejected the employer's contention that the monitoring was in the ordinary course of business. The company had argued that it could monitor the conversation because the topic of the conversation—Watkins' search for a job with a different employer—was of great interest to the business. But the court said her interest in another job was a personal matter:

To expand the business extension exemption . . . would permit monitoring of obviously personal and very private calls on the ground, for example, that the company was interested in whether Watkins' friends were "nice or not."

Implicit in this important decision is a broad concept of employee privacy rights. An employer does not have a legal right to listen every time his or her employees talk about work. Its legitimate business interest is limited to work performance itself.

Many states have enacted anti-eavesdropping and wiretap laws that are essentially identical to the federal statute and contain the same "single party consent" exception. Among the states that have such laws are Colorado, New York, and Texas. Other states have enacted laws that are more restrictive than federal law. California and Massachusetts, for example, strengthen the consent exception by forbidding interception of oral or wire communication unless all parties to the conversation have given their consent. These laws make it virtually impossible for employers to lawfully engage in surreptitious eavesdropping.

Employers should take note that if the electronic surveillance law in their state imposes greater restrictions than Title III, they must comply with the requirements of both Title III and the stricter state law.

Electronic Surveillance in Labor Arbitration

Arbitrators generally hold that among the management rights retained by employers is the right to monitor and supervise employees. In one case where the union protested overzealous observation by supervisors that created employee "fear and apprehension," the arbitrator held that "[a]lthough emotional tranquility is a condition much to be desired in labor relations, it is not one of the rights guaranteed . . . by the contract between the parties." *Picker X-Ray Corp.*, 39 LA 1245, 1246 (1962).

Arbitrators have generally been unsympathetic to employee protests against electronic surveillance. They very often admit into evidence tape recordings made in violation of Title III or state antiwiretap laws, even though those same tape recordings would be inadmissible in a court or governmental proceeding.

Arbitrators usually uphold an employer's intrusive surveillance, by video monitoring, wire interception, and other eavesdropping techniques, so long as the employer can point to a particular problem which it is trying to remedy. In one case where an employer installed closed circuit television monitors, the employer established that the surveillance was designed to combat major theft problems. The arbitrator not only upheld the practice, but denied that employee privacy interests were even implicated. He noted that all employees work with the knowledge that they may be observed by supervisors. Video monitoring was regarded as merely a "difference in degree, not a difference in kind." *FMC Corp.* 46 LA 335, 338 (1966).

Other arbitrators recognize the obvious fact that electronic surveillance does impinge on privacy interests, but comment that these interests normally are subordinate to the employer's right to engage in surveillance to fight theft. Where the employer cannot show that the intrusive surveillance is a necessary response to a real problem, arbitrators have been known to order surveillance or monitoring devices removed. Of course employees can expand their protection from electronic surveillance through collective bargaining. Although arbitrators are unlike to forbid surveillance absent an express contractual prohibition, they will enforce bargained-for surveillance restrictions.

As American business continues its advance into the computer age, efforts by organized labor to protect their members from intrusive surveillance have increased. For example, in recent collective bargaining negotiations, the Service Employees International Union opposed VDT monitoring by special computers. The employer would not agree to discontinue the practice altogether, but granted the union a contractual right of access to the data accumulated by the computer.

In the long run, collective bargaining offers both employers and employees a less expensive and more efficient forum to resolve employee privacy concerns than the courts. At the same time collective bargaining permits employers to obtain rather than lose the cooperation of employees in implementing and enforcing a consensual antitheft monitoring program.

LIMITATIONS ON EMPLOYER INFORMATION GATHERING IN CONSUMER PROTECTION LEGISLATION

One of the most serious and intrusive invasions of privacy in modern American society is also the most common—the accumulation and dissemination of personal and often intimate information about individuals by private credit reporting agencies and consumer investigative services. Often an employer will want to know more about an employee than he or she can learn from a job application or letter of reference. When this is the case, the employer may hire an outside agency to provide the company with additional information about the background and personal habits of the job applicant or employee. There are clearinghouses that do nothing but gather information about employees and share it with employers. It has been estimated that over five million consumer[4] reports are made every year, and that there are over 200 million credit and in-

---

[4] Under the fair credit reporting laws, the term "consumer" includes employees and prospective employees.

vestigative reports sitting in the data banks of these agencies. These agencies maintain sophisticated computer data banks, which contain detailed information on the private lives of millions of people. Their reports may include financial information, intimate details of sexual proclivities and orientation, arrest and conviction records, employment histories (including information on discharges and discipline), and virtually any other subject into which an investigative agency may choose to delve.

There is an obvious danger in the proliferation of these data banks. Inaccurate and damaging information can be collected and disseminated to prospective and current employers. Employers can also obtain highly confidential and intimate information about their employees which is not job-related and which the employer has no justifiable interest in knowing.

In 1970 Congress enacted the Fair Credit Reporting Act (FCRA) to regulate the gathering and disclosure of information by these investigative agencies. The FCRA was ostensibly designed to protect the private interests of consumers and employees, but the protections it affords are minimal. As one commentator has put it, since "the law was virtually written by the very industry it purports to regulate, its teeth are not very sharp."

Many states have also enacted fair credit reporting laws. Most of these laws mirror the federal act and do not enlarge the rights available to employees. For example, the fair credit laws in Connecticut, Kansas, Pennsylvania, Texas, and Virginia are nearly identical to the FCRA insofar as the rights of employees are concerned.

Some states have passed fair credit reporting laws with more teeth. They restrict the kind of information that may be placed in a consumer report and sometimes eliminate some of the immunities from civil liability contained in the FCRA.[5]

Types of Reports Available

There are essentially two types of reports that an employer may purchase from an investigative or credit agency. The first is a standard "consumer report." This is a report bearing on an employee's credit status, character, arrest record, general reputation, personal characteristics, employment history, and the like. The second is known as an "investigative consumer report." It goes much further, involving interviews with friends, neighbors, or business associates. An investigative report necessarily involves a greater intrusion into the private life of the employee, as it may include opinions of the subject's acquaintances concerning the employee's lifestyle, drinking patterns, medical condition, sexual orientation, or general habits. It is also more likely to contain inaccuracies based on the false or misleading impressions of the interviewees.

[5] Consumer investigative agencies have challenged the constitutionality of some of the more restrictive state laws on the ground that they are inconsistent with, and therefore superseded or "preempted" by the federal law. But for the most part, courts have upheld the right of states to enact legislation which is more protective of privacy rights than federal law, so long as compliance with the state law would not involve an actual violation of the FCRA or its general purposes.

Limitations on the Kind of Information that May Be Placed in a Report

The FCRA contains a prohibition against reporting certain obsolete information. For example, a report may not include bankruptcy cases older than 10 years, and arrest and criminal records as well as other adverse information older than seven years.

In one New York case, the employer fired a 17-year-old girl when it learned from a consumer report that she had been accused of, but not arrested for, shoplifting at Gimbels when she was just 12 years old. The information was not obsolete, so the court found that the agency had an absolute right to report it and the employer to use it. *Goodnough v. Alexanders,* 82 Misc. 2d 662, 370 N.Y.S.2d 388 (1975).

The FCRAs "obsolete information" provision does not apply to reports about employees earning $20,000 or more annually. Some states, including California and New York, have raised the $20,000 limit to higher levels.

Some states have expanded the number of subjects which cannot be addressed in a consumer report. In New York no consumer report can contain information about an employee's race, religion, color, ancestry, or ethnic origin. In both New York and California, criminal charges which did not result in conviction may not be included in the report, unless the charges are still pending.

These restrictions are primarily of interest to the consumer agencies that prepare reports, and not to the employers that order them. Nevertheless employers should be aware of these limitations. Attempts to obtain such prohibited information may pose liability problems. Employers should also not assume that reporting agencies will always keep strictly to the letter of the law. And employers using out-of-state investigative agencies should confine their requests to fit the requirements of their respective state laws, with which that agency may be unfamiliar.

Employer Use of Reports

All credit reporting laws expressly permit employers to purchase a standard consumer report or a more detailed investigative consumer report. Thus, these laws implicitly authorize employers to use such reports in making employment decisions. Since there are few limits on the type of information that can be requested, employers are generally free to use any type of information they can obtain from a reporting agency, including information which is not job-related.

Disclosure to Employees

The FCRA does not require an employer to notify the employee or prospective employee when it orders a *standard* consumer report. Thus, an employer may order a consumer report on all job applicants without informing them it is doing so. Most state laws are identical. In New York, however, the employer must disclose to job applicants that it *may* request a standard consumer report on them, and if such a report is ordered, it must, on request, tell the applicant the identity of the reporting agency.

Apart from rare exceptions like New York, there are only two situations when disclosure is mandated under the FCRA and most state credit reporting laws.

INVESTIGATING CONSUMER REPORTS. First, an employer must notify the employee when it orders an *investigative* consumer report. The disclosure must be in writing and given the employee within three days after the report was ordered. The employer must also notify the employee or job applicant that he or she can make a written request for a complete disclosure of the "nature and scope" of the investigation requested. If such a request is made, the employer must provide this information within five days. Under the FCRA and most state laws the employer does not have to tell the employee precisely what information was requested and, most significantly, which investigative agency was used. The employee thus may never be able to obtain a copy of the report itself, because he or she will not know what agency prepared it. Some states, including California, require the employer to disclose the identity of the agency used.

There is a "headhunter's" exception to this disclosure requirement. An employer does not have to warn applicants who have not "specifically applied" for a position that an investigative consumer report about them has been ordered. This exempts employers who use executive search firms (which are themselves clearinghouses of employment information concerning millions of professionals and executives) from having to notify persons who are being considered for job offers. Thus, if an employer simply goes to a headhunter or similar clearinghouse for job prospects, rather than advertising for them, he or she can totally circumvent this FCRA disclosure requirement.

Unless the employee applied for the position, employers are also free from the disclosure requirement when they investigate a *current* employee for promotion or reassignment. But if the employee has specifically applied for the promotion or change of assignment, disclosure is required.

ADVERSE ACTION. The employer must tell the employee or job applicant that a report was obtained if it discharges or denies the individual employment based on the contents of a standard or investigative consumer report. In these circumstances both the FCRA and state laws also require the employer to give the employee the identity of the investigative agency or clearinghouse that was used.

Under the FCRA and most state laws, the disclosure requirement applies only if "employment is denied." This probably means that an employer who denies a current employee a promotion based on information obtained in a consumer report has no disclosure duty.

Once the employee or applicant learns the name of the reporting agency, he or she may contact it to verify the accuracy of the information given to the employer. But by then it is usually too late. Neither the FCRA nor state laws require the employer to hire or reconsider hiring the employee or applicant if inaccuracies in the information given to the employer are subsequently discovered.

Liability

An employer that fails to comply with these disclosure requirements is liable to the employee or applicant for actual damages and reasonable attorney's fees. If the noncompliance was deliberate or willful, the employee or applicant may also recover both punitive damages and damages for humiliation and mental distress.

Despite this potential for devastating damages awards, few if any employers have yet been severely penalized for violating this requirement. For example, in *Alexander's, Inc.,* FTC Dkt. No. 2892 (1977), a New York City department store denied employment to several job applicants based on adverse information in consumer reports, and then failed to tell them why they were rejected. The Federal Trade Commission ordered Alexanders's to cease and desist from this unlawful practice, and to give written notice to all applicants denied employment in the previous two years. The employer was not assessed any damages, however, nor was it required to reconsider applications on an employee's showing that the consumer report information was incorrect.

Limits on Liability

Apart from liability imposed for wrongful nondisclosure, most fair credit reporting laws, including the FCRA, prohibit an employee from suing an employer for defamation or invasion of privacy. In effect under the guise of consumer protection legislation, the FCRA has given employers carte blanche to intrude into the personal lives of their employees through a reporting agency.

Only a few states allow invasion of privacy claims in actions under their reporting laws. For example, Maine does not immunize employers from suits for invasion of privacy. California prohibits actions for invasion of privacy arising from standard consumer reports, but permits them in connection with investigative consumer reports.

Peller v. Retail Credit Co., 359 F. Supp. 1235 (N.D. Ga. 1973). *affirmed,* 505 F.2d 733 (5th Cir. 1974), illustrates some of the difficulties facing employees suing employers for invasions of privacy based on credit reporting violations. In that case the plaintiff was rejected for employment when a lie detector test administered by the company indicated that he had previously smoked marijuana. A second company subsequently hired the plaintiff, but dismissed him when it obtained a background credit report containing the results of the lie detector test. The plaintiff sued both employers. The court found that absent employer malice or willful intent to injure the employee on the basis that the FCRA forbids libel or invasion of privacy suits based on intrusive consumer reports. The court concluded that the minimal statutory restrictions imposed on users of credit reports do not support an action against either employer.

Future Trends

There is little likelihood reporting laws will soon be changed to increase employee privacy rights. In 1980 the Federal Privacy Commission recommended amendments to the FCRA to expand requirements of disclosure to employees, but these recommendations were not enacted.

Creative employees (or their attorneys) may find indirect methods to compel disclosure of consumer reports outside the fair credit laws. For example, as will be discussed, many states require that employees be given access to their personnel files, and a consumer report is certainly the type of personnel document to which employees have access. Employees may also have legal claims against their employers if they discover that the employer sought information from a reporting agency that employers are not legally permitted to ask directly of employees.

The public policies underlying credit reporting laws may become a source for much important employment litigation in the future. Job applicants who are denied employment on the basis of consumer report information which is not job-related, or which the employer knows or believes to be false, may bring actions for the wrongful refusal to employ. Thus, employers should not think that strict adherence to the FCRA or state consumer credit laws will immunize them from all possible liability relating to the use of consumer credit reports. Nor can they necessarily rely on the reporting system as a way to circumvent other laws restricting their ability to gather information.

THE COMMON LAW TORT OF INTRUSION

Traditional Analysis

Until now we have discussed statutory rights against the invasion of employee privacy. In addition to these specific statutes, there is a body of judge-made law, known as common law, that protects some employee privacy interests. Violation of these privacy interests is a type of tort, treated more like an automobile accident case than a breach of contract. In fact, all 50 states recognize some form of protection against invasions of privacy. Although the elements of this tort differ slightly from state to state, there is unusual uniformity.

One of the privacy rights recognized in most states is protection against intrusion. This tort is defined as unlawful meddling in the seclusion, solitude or private affairs of an individual. To state a cause of action for intrusion, an employee must prove at minimum that the information sought by the employer is private and that the manner in which it is obtained was unduly intrusive. There has been relatively little litigation of the intrusion tort in the employment setting. There seem to be two reasons for this dearth of legal activity. First, employees usually submit to intrusiveness for fear that voicing opposition will lead to discharge. Second, the courts have generally been unsympathetic to employee claims. They have frequently absolved employers from liability on the ground that the employee has consented to the intrusions or that the employer's right to conduct its business in the manner it sees fit should prevail over the employee's legitimate, but less important, privacy interests.

In deciding "intrusion" cases, most courts have applied a rough balancing test. Where the employer's actions are intrusive to an abusive degree and are lacking in any kind of business justification, it is more likely that a court will protect the employee's privacy interest. Asking an employee questions that are not job-related is not enough to create a possible privacy tort unless the questions are also intrusive. Likewise the more sensitive the employee's privacy interest, the more it will be found to be deserving of protection.

The case of *Cort v. Bristol-Myers Co.*, 385 Mass. 300, 431 N.E.2d 908 (1982), exemplifies this balancing test. Three drug company sales representatives were fired when they refused to properly answer questions in a written questionnaire asking about their medical histories, off-the-job problems, principal worries, and long-range plans. They sued for invasion of privacy and wrongful discharge. The court held that the employer had not violated any public policy by demanding answers to these questions, but acknowledged that in other circumstances the intrusion could become so great, and the relevancy to work so slight, that a common law privacy action would be successful. The court also made the interesting comment that high level and confidential employees have fewer privacy rights in the company than lower level employees.

Despite this and other defeats, privacy-minded employees have had some success in protesting some employer intrusions. As the previous discussion makes clear, an abusive or outrageous intrusion may overcome what might otherwise be a legitimate business interest. In one Oregon case, *Bodewig v. K-Mart, Inc.*, 54 Or. App. 480, 635 P.2d 657 (1981), a well-intentioned but reckless managerial decision led to damages against an employer for invasion of an employee's personal privacy and integrity. In that case a K-Mart department store cashier was accused by a customer of pocketing money that the customer claimed to have left on the sales counter. The customer made such a commotion that the store manager searched the cashier's jacket pockets, and then ordered the employee to the ladies' room to disrobe in the presence of the irate customer. The employee was stripped down to her underwear by a female assistant manager, at which point the customer allowed her to stop because she could "see through [her] underwear anyway." The court held the store liable for putting the employee through this degrading and humiliating experience. The court noted that any employee consent was coerced by the fear of losing employment.

Intrusive Searches in Labor Arbitration

As discussed previously, a labor union may challenge an employer's intrusive policies through grievance procedures in its collective bargaining agreement. The majority of arbitrators have held that a company may properly establish reasonable rules permitting random searches of employees and their personal property, including purses, packages, and lockers, absent an express contractual prohibition. However, arbitrators have cautioned that the right to search employees is not absolute and should be exercised only within certain limits. For example, in a leading locker-search case the arbitrator ruled that a broad management rights clause permitted the employer to conduct locker searches in response to recent thefts, because the employer provided these protections: the search was conducted in the presence of a union official; the personal property of employees was not examined; and no disciplinary action was taken against employees when company property was found in their lockers. *International Nickel Co.,* 50 LA 65 (1967).

Generally speaking, employer search policies will be upheld if they contain the following:

1. The policy is a response to a real business problem
2. The policy is clear and unambiguous
3. Employees are notified of the rule by posting or other written means
4. Employees are warned of the disciplinary consequences of noncompliance with the rule
5. The rule is strictly enforced on a nondiscriminatory basis
6. The rule is fashioned to limit privacy intrusions and to protect employees' dignity to the greatest extent possible

Arbitrators will generally not countenance a forcible search of an unwilling employee, however. Where the employee refuses to consent, the proper company response is to impose the discipline threatened in the rule rather than use physical means to force the employee to submit.

Where a particular employee is reasonably suspected of theft, arbitrators have relaxed these guidelines. Thus, even in the absence of a search rule, arbitrators have upheld the search of an employee's locker or personal property where the employer can demonstrate a legitimate suspicion of theft.

New Horizons: Expansion of the Rights Against Intrusive Surveillance Under the California Constitution

As noted the California Constitution's protection of privacy has been interpreted as expanding common law privacy rights. Thus, it may provide a new basis for lawsuits for intrusive searches or demands for personal information that are not available under traditional tort principles. There is no California decision addressing this issue. But California employers should be aware that intrusive information gathering, be it by electronic surveillance, demands for personal, nonjob related information, or employee searches, may be subject to constitutional attack.

False Imprisonment

Frequently coupled with unlawful intrusion is the tort of false imprisonment. This tort permits an individual to sue if, in the course of an interrogation, he or she is restrained or confined by force or threat of force, thereby depriving the individual of liberty.

It is no defense that the employee was detained during working hours.

In a Maryland case, *General Motors v. Piskor,* 277 Md. 165, 352 A.2d 810 (1976), security guards detained an auto worker leaving the plant because they suspected that he was carrying auto parts. As the court found, the guards yelled at the employee, "nudged and shoved him" and then confined him during interrogation. Eventually the employee won $1500 in compensatory damages and $25,000 in punitive damages in a successful action for defamation, assault, and false imprisonment.

Only where an employee is caught in the act of stealing may an employer forcibly detain him or her with impunity. In these circumstances, the detention must be tailored to accomplish the goal of stopping the theft. Forcible confinement should not continue after the basic interrogation is complete for the sole purpose of extracting a confession.

ACQUISITION OF MEDICAL INFORMATION

Although many state laws prohibit the unauthorized *disclosure* of a patient's medical records, a subject that will be discussed later in this chapter, few prohibit or penalize the unauthorized *acquisition* of medical information. In Colorado the unauthorized acquisition of medical records or information is punishable as felony theft. In Maryland an employer cannot inquire into physical or mental conditions of a job applicant which do not bear a "direct, material and timely relationship" to their ability to do the job. But a physician selected by the employer may nonetheless conduct a medical examination of a job applicant.

Some state laws require that an employee not be charged the cost of a physical or that they be given a copy of the results. Although a mandatory medical examination is the most intrusive form of medical information gathering, there are virtually no legal controls on these procedures. In some states, such as California, the physician must obtain the job applicant's or employee's written consent before disclosing examination results to the employer, but this is as far as the regulation goes. (A sample consent form tailored to California law appears at Appendix B). An employee may still be required to sign the release as a condition of employment. In the few reported cases where a worker has refused to undergo such an examination or to answer medical inquiries in employer questionnaires, the courts have generally upheld the employer's refusal to hire or its decision to discharge the reluctant individual, so long as the examination or questions were important to determine the employee's fitness to perform their job duties effectively.

There is little arbitral precedent concerning employer requests that employees furnish medical records or otherwise consent to their disclosure. In one case, the arbitrator ruled that an employee was justified in refusing to sign a form authorizing the release of medical records to the employer, where the form was so broad as to be "a license for a fishing expedition into his private affairs." *Bondtex Corp.,* 68 L.A. 476, 478 (1977). Cases of this type serve to caution employers that medical record requests and the scope of physical exams should in some manner be relevant to the employee's job.

CRIMINAL ARREST AND CONVICTION RECORDS

Most employers believe that a job applicant's arrest and conviction history is critical or at least relevant to the hiring decision. No pharmacy wants to hire a job applicant who was once a thief or drug pusher, no matter how earnest their claim to have reformed. Yet critics of employment decisions based on criminal backgrounds warn that they breed recidivism and defeat rehabilitation goals. If a criminal, after paying his debt to society, cannot support himself by lawful means, he will have no choice but to return to crime. Moreover, they penalize the innocent suspect who was arrested but acquitted of any criminal wrongdoing.

State legislators have reacted in conflicting ways to these competing interests. On the one hand, many states have made records of arrest or convictions freely available to private employers. Georgia, New York, Oregon, Pennsylvania, and Washington require an employer to advise a job applicant that it has sought such information from a law enforcement agency or used a criminal record as a basis for a decision not to hire. Georgia and Washington further require the employer to tell the employee of the contents of the criminal records it has obtained.

Other states have established procedures to seal or expunge records of arrests and criminal charges that did not result in conviction, as well as records of certain misdemeanor convictions and stale felony convictions. Illinois, Maryland, New York, Ohio, and Virginia prohibit employers from asking job applicants about arrests that did not result in convictions and about certain expunged criminal records. Massachusetts and Rhode Island forbid retaliation against a job applicant for falsely stating that they have no criminal record or were never convicted, if the record has been sealed or expunged.

California law is far and away the most restrictive. An employer is guilty of a misdemeanor if it even *seeks* information from *any* source (including the applicant or employee, or the police or an investigative reporting agency) concerning arrests that did not result in conviction. It also prohibits inquiry into the employee's or job applicant's participation in a drug diversion program, or of conviction of violating certain marijuana laws. Limited exceptions are provided for certain employers, in particular those in the health care industry.

The penalties for a California employer's violation of this law are severe. If an employer uses such information as a factor in hiring, promotion, or termination decisions, the affected employee or job applicant can sue for damages, attorney's fees, and costs of suit. An "intentional" violation is punishable by an award of *triple* the actual damages suffered by the employee or applicant.

Some state laws that prohibit inquiry into arrests that did not result in conviction do not tell the employer what it can or cannot ask if an arrest has been made and the case is still pending. In most states, employers do have a right to know this information, but in states in which the law is less clear they should refrain from making any adverse employment decisions until final disposition of the criminal case.

INFORMATION AS TO NONEMPLOYMENT ACTIVITIES

Illinois' and Michigan's personnel records acts prohibit employers from gathering or maintaining information regarding an employee's off-premises political, associational, and other "nonemployment activities," unless the employee has consented in writing. Employees and former employees can inspect their employers' personnel files for such information and sue if any is found. Violations are punishable by purging the employee's personnel file of the information and paying him or her damages and court costs. For a willful and knowing violation, the employer must pay the employee an additional $200 fine and the employee's attorney's fees.

EMPLOYER DISCLOSURE OF PERSONAL AND PRIVATE FACTS ABOUT EMPLOYEES

Employees today are as concerned with the harm that can be done by the disclosure of private facts about themselves to third parties as they are about their employers' ability to obtain personal information. While an employer may legitimately acquire abundant information about an employee, that does not give the employer the right to disclose sensitive facts to the outside world.

There is a growing body of law that limits employers' rights to disseminate information about employees. These limits apply not only to information that is obviously personal, such as medical records, but to data generated by the employer, such as job evaluations and reports concerning the causes of discipline and discharge.

This section describes the various avenues available to employees to redress privacy violations resulting from wrongful disclosure of information, and suggests how employers can avoid liability in this area.

WRONGFUL DISCLOSURE OF FALSE INFORMATION

Employees have two legal avenues available to redress the wrongful disclosure of false information. First, they may sue under the common law for defamation. Defamation is the communication of false information that injures another's reputation. In order to constitute defamation, the false statement must be communicated to someone other than the defamed person. Second, in some states, employees have a statutory right to recover damages from their employer under a "service letter" statute. Defamation may not, at first glance, appear to constitute an invasion of privacy, because it means the communication of *untrue* facts. Nevertheless defamation is a privacy violation because it invades people's interest in their good name and reputation and thus intrudes into and damages their private life.

There is a growing fear among employers that certain communications, made routinely in the course of business, may give rise to defamation or "service letter" liability. Employers are especially worried about job references. To avoid this potential liability IBM stopped giving formal job references in the 1960s, and hundreds of other large and small enterprises have followed suit.

Failure to give a job reference, however, may also pose risks to the employer. In a recent Massachusetts case, a doctor who was accused of rape in one hospital left his job for a position at second hospital. When the second hospital called the first for a reference, it complied without mentioning the rape charge. The doctor committed a rape in the second hospital. The second hospital then sued the first for its negligent failure to mention the doctor's suspected criminal proclivities in its reference.

Defamation in Employment

Defamation is governed by state common law or statute. State defamation laws are not entirely uniform, although all states recognize at least some right against defamation. There are two types of defamatory communications. If the communication is recorded in some tangible or material medium, such as a letter or a video tape, it is *libel*. If it is only an oral statement, or some type of physical or transitory gesture, it is *slander*.

An ambiguous statement can be defamatory if it *tends* to injure one's reputation. For example, a statement which falsely insinuates that an employee has participated in a criminal act is probably defamatory. In conducting an investigation of continued theft, an employer may interrogate an employee by saying: "We are investigating a serious theft problem in the plant and want to ask you a few questions about your coworker." If the allegation was false, the coworker probably has been slandered.

 An employer may even commit libel or slander by doing nothing, so long as the omission reasonably suggests false information about the employee. In the case of *Lewis v. Equitable Life Assurance*, 361 N.W.2d 875 Minn. App. 1985), three women were fired by the company for submitting disputed expense vouchers. Their employer refused to give job references explaining the discharges to their prospective employers, thereby shifting the responsibility to the employees to explain why they had been discharged. The court held that the employer slandered the employees, even though it had made no communication whatsoever, because its silence forced the employees themselves to communicate the libelous information.

The Employer's Privilege under
Common Law Defamation

In general, a person who defames another is liable for compensatory damages, even where false information is transferred negligently. Employers, however, are not subject to this traditional rule. The common law provides employers with a limited immunity called the "qualified privilege." This privilege was fashioned by the courts many years ago, and in some states such as California, it has been enacted into statute.

The qualified privilege protects statements that are made in the course of legitimate business dealings. A job reference to a prospective employer is such a protected communication because employers need such information to make informed hiring decisions. Communications among supervisory employees concerning suspected employee theft, even if false, are also protected by the qualified privilege, because employers must be allowed to investigate conduct which is damaging and perhaps unlawful.

An employer can lose the qualified privilege by acting with "malice." As the word implies, a malicious communication is one made with spite or ill-will. But malice also exists where a false statement is made with knowledge of its falsity, or with reckless disregard of its possible untruth. The privilege can also be lost if abusive or vitriolic language is used, if persons with no need to know the information are told, or if information which is not job-related is disclosed in conjunction with the communication of privileged information.

Defamation and Job References

There has been little litigation in this field, primarily because most employers promulgate and enforce cautious job reference policies, and most employees do not learn about libelous job references. Even in states with broad employee personnel record inspection rights, including California, Connecticut, Illinois, and Michigan, an employee has no legal right to inspect job references in his or her personnel file.

One Texas decision illustrates the typical employment defamation case where the qualified privilege was used to absolve an employer from defamation liability. In *Duncantell v. Universal Life Ins.*, 446 S.W.2d 934 (1969), the plaintiff was fired for suspected theft, which he had not committed. The employer told prospective employers "not to fool with" the plaintiff because he "couldn't be trusted." Although the employer could not prove that the plaintiff had in fact been guilty of wrongdoing, the court ruled that the communications were privileged because the employer believed the plaintiff was a thief, and the communication was made in the regular course of conducting business.

Recently some courts have rejected the common law qualified privilege where employees have been seriously harmed by the employer's false statements. The recent case of *Carney v. Memorial Hospital*, 64 N.Y.2d 770, 485 N.Y.S.2d 984 (1985) is indicative of this trend. In that case a prospective employer was told by the defendant hospital that the plaintiff doctor had been dismissed "for cause." New York's court of appeals held that the term "for cause" could be interpreted as implying that the doctor was incompetent, and therefore the doctor had stated a cause of action of libel.

The most far reaching case is *Harrison v. Arrow Metal Products Corp.*, 20 Mich. App. 570, 174 N.W.2d 875 (1970). There an employee was falsely accused of theft and subsequently discharged. The employer responded to reference requests by telling prospective employers that the employee had been fired for theft. The court held that the employer's communication was not protected by *any* privilege. The court looked at the serious effect of the employer's charge, saying that this one "unproved accusation could . . . become the basis for permanently depriving a man of his dignity, good name, self-respect and right to earn for the support of himself and his family." Whether the employer publishes with malice or without it, as the court noted, the "effect on the employee is exactly the same."

Potential Employer Liability under State Service Letter Statutes

Many state legislatures have enacted antiblacklisting and service letter statutes that go far beyond the common law by mandating that employers give only truthful oral and written job references when an employee quits or is discharged.

Pure antiblacklisting statutes punish employers for maliciously or willfully attempting to prevent former employees from finding work. Pure service letter statutes, on the other hand, require an employer to furnish an employee with a written statement of the cause for their dismissal or, in the case of many such laws, the reasons for their resignation. The employer cannot furnish prospective employers with reasons for dismissal that deviate from those in the service letter.

Arkansas, California, Connecticut, Florida, Indiana, Iowa, Kansas, Maine, Missouri, Montana, Nebraska, New Hampshire, New Mexico, North Carolina, Ohio, Oklahoma, Texas, Utah, Virginia, and Washington are among the states that have laws of these types. Many of these state statutes are an amalgam of antiblacklisting and service letter laws.

Service letter laws require an employer to give a truthful letter of reference if a former employee so requests. Some of the states with laws of this type are Florida, Indiana, Kansas, Maine, Missouri, and Montana. The majority of these statutes require no more than the former employer state the reason for the employee's departure. Missouri and Kansas require that the employer state the nature and character of the employee's services as well. Kansas law mandates that the employer state the employee's length of employment, job classification, and wage rate. Some of the service letter statutes punish *truthful* as well as untruthful statements of the reasons for an employee's discharge or resignation. The former are discussed in the section entitled "Disclosures of Truthful Information to Other Employers and Third Parties." This section addresses only false communications.

Some of these laws, such as those of Florida and Idaho, state that a service letter need only be given if the employee was discharged. The Indiana, Maine, Montana, and Nebraska laws also require service letters after an employee's voluntary resignation.

Whether a letter of reference is mandatory, such as the service letters discussed, or permissive, as with antiblacklisting laws, most states provide penalties for their violation. (The Florida law is unusual in that it precludes an employee from suing for libel if the letter was furnished at his or her request, even if the letter is libelous.) The advantage to an employee of suing under an antiblacklisting or service letter statute is that the common law employer privileges frequently are not defenses in such actions.

Arkansas, Maine, Nebraska, New Mexico, and Utah punish untruthful job references as crimes. Missouri permits civil actions against employers for compensatory damages for untruthful statements. The following states provide for criminal penalties, civil damages actions by former employees, or both: California, Florida, Iowa, Kansas, Montana, North Carolina, and Texas. The California and Kansas statutes provide for an award of *triple* an employee's damages in certain circumstances, while the Montana and North Carolina statutes provide for punitive as well as actual damages.

Most of the antiblacklisting and service letter laws prescribe penalties for sending letters with the purpose of preventing a former employee from obtaining new employment. California law is unusual in stating that a letter of reference will be presumed to have such an improper purpose if it is sent when neither the former employee nor a prospective employer has requested it.

Defamation Liability for Intracompany Communications

Internal company communications may create defamation liability. Potentially libelous or slanderous communications within the company include untruthful performance evaluations, false off-hand remarks, and disclosure of unwarranted theft investigations.

Under the common law employers have the same qualified privilege with respect to these types of communications as they do with respect to job references, because the courts acknowledge that broad managerial discretion is necessary to operate a business, and because free communication within the business should be encouraged. One Georgia court has gone so far as to say that "publication of allegedly defamatory information in the course of an employer's investigation of an employee's job performance is not 'publication' within the meaning of the law." *Monahan v. Sims,* 163 Ga. App. 354, 294 S.E.2d 548 (1982). Thus, in Georgia at least, an employer may be entitled to communicate any defamatory information within the company, even where common law malice is present. Even in Georgia, however, this entitlement is limited to communications between persons with a reasonable, job-related interest in the information.

There is no hard and fast rule governing defamation liability for intracompany communications. If a defamatory statement is made in response to a serious business problem, courts will tend to expand the privilege. In one case an employer arguably defamed an employee while investigating a bomb scare. The court ruled that the serious nature of the threat made the employer's slanderous statements privileged. In another case, an employer was found privileged to tell employees about a coworker's misconduct in order to let them know that they themselves had been exonerated following a plant-wide investigation. The opposite result was reached in another case, however, where the court held that the goal of boosting morale did not justify defamation.

An employer may be subject to defamation liability for physical acts alone. In *General Motors Corp. v. Piskor*, 277 Md. 165, 352 A.2d 810 (1976), an employee was suspected of theft when leaving the premises. He was grabbed by guards in full view of employees, and interrogatd in a glass-enclosed room where he was visible to 5000 employees as they entered and left work. Piskor, the employee, sued for defamation, claiming that the mere act of arresting his movement and publicly interrogating him communicated to other employees that he was a thief or had committed some other wrongdoing. The court upheld his claim, and awarded him $25,000 punitive damages.

WRONGFUL DISCLOSURE OF TRUTHFUL BUT PRIVATE INFORMATION

Common Law Privacy Actions for the Wrongful Disclosure of Truthful but Private Information

It is an invasion of privacy to disclose true but embarrassing private facts to persons having no legitimate business interest in learning those facts. This tort is known as "public disclosure of private facts." To be actionable under the common law, the offending disclosure must contain three characteristics.

1. *It Must Be Made to the Public at Large.* This means broad disclosure to a large number of people.
2. *The Facts Disclosed Must Be Private Ones.* For example, although some information in medical records may be private, there are many matters, such as one's age and number of children, which are available to the public and thus not protected.
3. *The Facts Must be Highly Offensive to a Person of Ordinary Sensibilities.* Thus, while the contents of medical records have been considered potentially embarrassing, other information in personnel records may be so innocuous as not to cause embarrassment to the average person.

As with defamation actions, there are certain qualified privileges that give employers greater leeway when it comes to the disclosure of private information. Like defamation, an employer will not be held liable for private disclosures justified by business necessity, unless motivated by malice or ill-will.

Expansion of the Tort of Public Disclosure of Private Facts under the Common Law

Although many commentators expected that the tort of "disclosure of private facts" would become the basis of most invasion of privacy actions brought by employees, this has not occurred. This should not be surprising. Employers generally have no interest in disclosing private facts about employees to the public at large; where disclosure is made, it is generally made to a limited group of persons whom the employer believes should be told. For example, an employer might, in the course of terminating an employee for misconduct, disclose private facts about the discharged employee to other employees in the plant in order to deter them from similiar misconduct. Disclosure of this truthful information even to a large number of employees would probably not qualify as sufficient "publicity" to establish a disclosure tort.

Thus, this tort does not pose a major threat to employers. At the same time employees are often inadequately protected by traditional common law from disclosure which, while not necessarily tortious under the "public disclosure" theory, are nonetheless damaging. Some courts, in apparent recognition of this deficiency, have found additional legal grounds to remedy the unreasonable and offensive disclosure of private information about employees by their employers.

One of the earliest examples of this is a New Hampshire case, *Huskie v. Griffen,* 74 A. 595 (1909). In that case, the plaintiff employee asked his employer for a raise and was rebuffed. His employer told him that if he thought he could do better elsewhere, he should leave. The plaintiff employee then found a higher paying job with another company, and so gave notice to his employer. The employer paid the departing plaintiff employee his final wages, and then called his new employer, suggesting that his departure from work at mid-day was dishonorable. The plaintiff was then fired by his new company. The New Hampshire Supreme Court held that the employer's "statement of the truth [to the new employer] made for the sole purpose of damaging the plaintiff . . . is actionable if damage ensues." The court noted that the employer's ill-will could be established not only by proving the existence of spite or malice, but by merely showing that "there was no good reason for doing the act."

A more recent case expanding employee's privacy rights is the Michigan case of *Tipton v. Gigantico Food Stores,* 271 N.W.2d 284 (1979). After terminating a cashier for theft, the store informed its supervisory personnel of the reason for the discharge. The court recognized that, under the common law of privacy, an employer has a limited privilege to disclose private information. But the court held that the employer had abused the privilege by releasing the information to an unnecessarily broad extent. In effect the Michigan court admonished employers to limit the disclosure of private, embarrassing facts—even if true—to those who have a reasonable need to know them.

To date, no courts outside of Michigan have adopted this "unnecessary disclosure" test. But we expect that, in the future, courts will be guided by this precedent to establish new grounds for employees to defend themselves against unwarranted truthful disclosure of personal information.

Expansion of the Right Against Public Disclosure of Private Facts under California Constitutional Law

As noted California's elevation of the privacy right to constitutional status marks an expansion beyond common law legal rights. This constitutional right is also a vehicle to expand statutory protections regarding disclosure of information. The leading case on this subject is *Payton v. City of Santa Clara,* 132 Cal. App. 3d 152, 183 Cal. Rptr. 17 (1982). After the plaintiff was terminated, the employer posted a memo for all employees to see stating that Payton had been discharged for "unauthorized absence, failure to observe departmental rules, and dishonesty." Payton did not sue for defamation, and perhaps wisely so because, as we have seen, the qualified privilege would probably have protected the employer even in the event the memo was false. Nor did he sue for tortious publicity, and again his decision was probably wise, because disclosure to 40 or 50 employees probably does not qualify as disclosure to the public at large.

Rather, Payton claimed that his former employer violated his constitutional right of privacy. The court upheld his claim. It said that the employer had made improper use of the information; and that such improper use and disclosure to third parties was one of the "principal mischiefs" the privacy amendment was designed to eliminate.

The *Payton* case is significant for two reasons. First, although it involves a public employer, the case is equally applicable to private businesses in California, because no "state action" is required. Second, the case recognizes that information about the cause of termination, which relates not to the employee's private life but to his or her job performance, nevertheless constitutes *private facts* about the employee, in which the employee has a right of privacy that he may invoke against the employer.

California employers may still disclose private information about their employees, but only if such disclosure is justified by a *compelling interest.* Unfortunately the courts have not yet defined what such a "compelling interest" might be, and employers are as yet left to guess where the line will be drawn.

In the meantime, California employers would be well advised to observe cautious, common sense rules when it comes to disclosing private information about an employee, including job performance information generated by the employer:

1. If an employee is led to believe that information about him or her will be kept confidential, the employer should keep it confidential unless the employee consents in writing to the disclosure.

2. Disclosure of private information should be limited to the fewest persons possible. If, for example, only two or three people need to know the reason an employee was terminated, the employer should make sure that no broader disclosure is made.

3. If the employer believes that disclosure is necessary to achieve a legitimate or compelling business purpose, he or she should determine whether there is a way to accomplish their goal with minimal disclosure of private facts. For example, in *Payton* the employer might have felt that posting the memo on the bulletin board was useful as a warning to all employees, to deter severe attendance or performance problems. This reasoning would not excuse the constitutional violation, however, because the employer could have posted a general warning about attendance, or told employees that some unidentified individual had been terminated for these reasons, without also telling them of Payton's personal problems.

4. The preparation and contents of job references should be carefully circumscribed. The employer should assure itself that inquiries come from legitimate prospective employers, perhaps by insisting on written requests. Then, a written assurance of confidentiality from the prospective employer should be obtained. Only essential, job-related information should be disclosed. A policy of disclosing only the dates of employment, position, and salary, which many companies have now adopted, is probably the most liability-proof approach.

Statutory Limitations on Disclosure of Truthful Information to Other Employers and Third Parties

An expanding number of states have enacted statutes severely restricting employer rights to disclose information from employees' personnel and medical files. Most of these laws have teeth, permitting employees to sue for civil damages. Some statutes also provide for criminal penalties against culpable employers. New grounds for lawsuits against employers may be emerging as a result of these laws. In some states an employer may face liability even if a letter of reference is truthful, if the informational basis for the letter was contained in employer files that were not shown to the employee or if the employer failed to timely furnish the letter to the employee on his or her request. Thus, an employee need not prove the traditional elements of defamation or invasion of privacy in order to recover damages.

Increasingly, employers must also face the unwelcome prospect of defending lawsuits challenging their disclosure of stale disciplinary actions; or for failure to give timely notice to an employee that personnel records were disclosed; or for disclosure of an employee's off-premises political and other nonemployment activities. In addition, an employer can now be sued for disclosing medical records without the employee's authorization or, on the other hand, for failing to disclose them when an employee has authorized disclosure.

These statutory developments have resulted from an expanding recognition of the sensitive and confidential nature of much that is contained in personnel files. Employment records typically contain information that an employee might not wish to reveal to his or her closest friends, or even family members, such as true wages and the results of evaluations and performance tests. Medical records and psychological evaluations often contain intimate details of an employee's diseases, habits, and social life, including alcohol or drug use, and sexual activities. Much of this information may have been provided by the employee with the added expectation or assurance that it would be maintained in confidence. If disclosed to others, embarrassment, and loss of reputation could result.

The differences among state privacy and disclosure statutes is bewildering. As will be discussed in detail, recognition of these privacy interests has led many states to enact legislation permitting employees to inspect, and frequently to challenge or rebut the contents of their personnel and medical files.

On the other hand some courts and state laws have also recognized an employer's privacy interest in protecting certain employment records from disclosure to the employee. Letters of reference from former employers, for example, are frequently given with the assurance that their contents will remain confidential. Absent protection from employee inspection, former employers may refuse to speak with candor or provide negative information about a prospective employee's character and qualifications. Other states by contrast, recognizing the potentially devastating impact of untruthful job references on future employment, have legislated an affirmative duty on the part of employers to disclose the contents of references given to prospective employers.

Additionally some states recognize that the employee might suffer from knowledge of the contents of sensitive records, such as psychological profiles or examination notes, and have therefore restricted employee access. But other states give employees a nearly unqualified right to inspect psychological data in the employer's possession.

Because of these competing privacy interests, state statues frequently interweave the subject of disclosure of personnel and medical records to third parties and the subject of their disclosure to the affected employee. For the sake of clarity, these subjects are discussed together in the section that follows.

PERSONNEL RECORDS. Limitations on release of employment data vary widely from state to state. Some states, most prominently New York, place no restrictions on an employer's dissemination of the truthful contents of personnel files. Connecticut has enacted the strictest limitations on employer disclosure of information to prospective employers and other third parties. Absent an employee's written permission to do so, an employer may not disclose any employment records or data, with the narrow exceptions of dates of employment, position and salary. No civil remedy or criminal penalty is specified for an employer's violation of the law.

Illinois and Michigan have enacted twin laws prohibiting employers from divulging *disciplinary* information, including information concerning a disciplinary discharge, unless a copy of the statement is mailed to the affected employee. An employer need not furnish the employee with a copy of the statement if the former employee has given their prospective employer a written authorization to obtain the information. In addition references to disciplinary action more than four years old must be deleted from any disciplinary information released to a third party.

A number of states have enacted legislation permitting employees and, in some cases former employees, to inspect personnel files maintained by employers. These states include California, Connecticut, Delaware, Illinois, Maine, Michigan, Nevada, New Hampshire, Ohio, Oregon, Pennsylvania, Washington, and Wisconsin. Some of these states also permit inspection by a representative designated by the employee. These laws, however, prohibit employees from inspecting such confidential items as letters of reference, records of investigations of losses, information about misconduct or crimes that have not been used adversely against the employee, and confidential information about other employees.

The Connecticut, Delaware, Illinois, Michigan, New Hampshire, Washington, and Wisconsin laws permit employees to insert written rebuttal statements in their personnel files. That is, if an employee disagrees with any statement in the file and the employer will not agree to delete it, the employee may insert his or her own explanation which must thereafter be kept in the file. All but the last two states require the employer to forward these rebuttal statements when it sends any corresponding information of its own to other employers or third parties.

The Illinois and Michigan laws contain yet more pitfalls for the unwary employer. If a personnel file contains information that is known by the employer to be false, an employee can bring legal proceedings to expunge the false information. The employer has the same right to bring suit if the employee has inserted false information in a rebuttal statement, but it cannot, without a court order, remove it or prevent the employee from inserting it in their personnel file.

More importantly, except in limited circumstances, employment data which was not subject to employee inspection cannot be used in any judicial or quasi-judicial proceeding except at the *employee's* request. Thus, an employer cannot use undisclosed information to defend itself in a suit by the employee.

Finally, as discussed in connection with information gathering, Illinois and Michigan prohibit employers from gathering or keeping records of their employees' off-premises political, associational, and other nonemployment activities that do not interfere with their work duties, unless the employees have consented in writing. Disclosure of information concerning such activities is also impliedly prohibited.

If employers violate any provision of the Illinois or Michigan act, they may be compelled to comply with the law by court order, and a civil action may also be filed by the employee for damages and court costs. If a "willful and knowing" violation of the statute is found, employers will be charged with an additional $200 in damages, plus the prevailing employee's attorney's fees.

Employers in all of the states mentioned may soon face new and novel lawsuits for wrongful termination and other damages actions, for such things as denial of employee access and rebuttal rights, or for retaliatory dismissal for attempted exercise of these rights. Employees may also sue for damages for harmful disclosure of information to prospective employers to which the employee has been denied access, or for failure to disclose rebuttal statements to prospective employees. In Connecticut, employers may soon see suits against them for forwarding harmful information to others without the employee's written permission. In Illinois and Michigan, employers may face damages actions for injuries resulting from their providing stale disciplinary information to others, for failing to mail employees copies of disciplinary information given to prospective employers, and for disclosing information regarding political or associational activities that the employees never authorized their employers to maintain.

The Michigan law has already prompted a United Auto Workers local union to file a class action lawsuit for damages because an employer gave the buyer of its plant its old personnel files. The contents of these files, including disciplinary information, were then used to make hiring decisions. The case ultimately settled for $50,000 and an agreement not to further transfer disciplinary records without proper notice to the affected employees.

Personnel records statutes are becoming increasingly popular with state legislatures. Although the law in this area is in its infancy, employers must be vigilant in view of the courts' growing attention to employee privacy rights.

SERVICE LETTER LAWS AND PERSONNEL INFORMATION DISCLOSURE. Almost all the state laws discussed in the preceding subsection restrict employees' access to letters of reference contained in their employers' personnel files. These restrictions are based on employers' needs for candid assessments of prospective employees. But confidentiality creates an opportunity for vindictive employers to retaliate against their former employees by issuing biased letters of reference. Some legislatures, in states other than those discussed, have attempted to solve this problem by requiring employers to give former employees, on their request, letters of reference truthfully stating the causes for their discharge (and in some states, the reasons why they resigned). Most of these laws also require the former employer to stick to what was said in this letter in later communications with the former employee's prospective employers.

As discussed in the section on defamation, these "service letter" statutes give employees a right to bring suit for untruthful statements in an employer's letter of reference or subsequent communications. But many of these laws also punish employers for failing to provide the employee with a service letter on request, or for thereafter *truthfully* disclosing to others the reasons for the employee's discharge or resignation.

For example, Florida law requires an employer to give a discharged employee a truthful statement of the reasons for his or her dismissal within 10 days of the employee's written request. If the employer fails to timely provide the service letter, it is forever prohibited from giving prospective employers any oral or written statement of the cause of the discharge. If an employer violates this duty of perpetual silence, the discharged employee can sue for damages and the employer may be found guilty of a criminal misdemeanor. Montana law is similar.

Florida also imposes a unique obligation on a prospective employer who receives a service letter or any oral communication from a former employer concerning the reasons for the employee's discharge. The prospective employer must give the terminated employee a copy of the letter or the substance of the oral communication within 10 days of the employee's demand. If the new or prospective employer fails to do so, they too can be sued for damages or found guilty of a misdemeanor.

MEDICAL RECORDS. The Connecticut and Michigan personnel records laws discussed previously also restrict disclosure of medical records and medical information in an employer's possession. Connecticut's law defines "personnel records" to include medical records "that are work-related or on which such employer relies to make any employment-related decision." An employee may not inspect their own medical records, however. The act restricts inspection to a physician chosen by the employee or former employee, or to a physician chosen by the employer with the employee's consent. The same rebuttal rights and limitations on disclosure as exist with respect to other personnel records are applicable to medical records, with the additional requirement that where an employee's written authorization to disclose medical records or information is requested, the employer must "inform the concerned employee of his or his physician's right of inspection and correction, his right to withhold authorization, and the effect of any withholding of authorization upon such employee."

Michigan's personnel records act provides that medical records are subject to employee inspection and rebuttal rights if they are not available from the employee's doctor or medical facility. Thus, if the employee can get these records from his or her doctor, the employer does not have to show them to the employee. The Illinois act, which resembles the Michigan act in so many respects, is silent with respect to medical records.

California places the most stringent restrictions on an employer's disclosure of employee medical records and information. A California employer and his or her agents may not disclose or "use" employee medical records and information without first obtaining a signed and dated authorization from the affected employee. To be valid, the written authorization must comply strictly with detailed statutory requirements as to form and content. (A sample authorization tailored to California law appears in Appendix B at the end of this chapter.) Employers are specifically forbidden from discriminating against employees for refusing to sign an authorization. However, a loophole permits an employer to "take such action as is necessary" because of the absence of medical information caused by an employee's refusal to sign an authorization. Thus, it appears that an employer may fire an employee in a job involving heavy lifting if the employee refuses to consent to the release of medical records in the possession of their orthopedist.

California employers are also required to establish "appropriate procedures" to ensure the confidentiality of medical records. Responsible employees must be instructed on how to maintain the confidentiality of medical records, and "security systems" must be created to restrict access to files containing such information. "In addition to any other remedies available at law," an employee who has suffered "economic loss or personal injury" because of an employer's violation of the California statutes may recover compensatory damages, punitive damages not to exceed $3000, attorney's fees not to exceed $1000 and costs of suit, and the violation is also punishable as a criminal misdemeanor.

Colorado law is also strict. If an employer discloses employee medical records or information without employee authorization, the act is punishable as felony theft.

Finally, OSHA regulations and some state laws permit employee access to medical records in the hands of their employer. It is mandated by OSHA that employers permit their employees and employee representatives or attorneys to inspect medical records and records of employee exposure to toxic substances. The states with these laws include Delaware, Maine, Ohio, and Wisconsin. All but the Maine law permit an employee to rebut medical records in the employer's file. The Delaware and Wisconsin statutes further mandate that these rebuttal statements accompany any disclosure of the rebutted medical records by employers to third parties.

DISCLOSURE OF LIE DETECTOR TEST RESULTS AND ARREST RECORDS. Surprisingly few state laws limit an employer's disclosure of the results of lie detector tests to consumer investigative and credit agencies, other employers, and third parties. In one widely publicized 1973 case, a Georgia job applicant was denied a job because he failed a preemployment polygraph test. The polygraph operator then supplied the test results to a credit reporting agency. The applicant got another job, but was fired when his new employer obtained the polygraph results from the credit agency during a routine background check of the employee. The employee sued the first employer for wrongful disclosure, but lost because there was no statutory basis for his lawsuit. His suit against his new employer was also dismissed. *Peller v. Retail Credit Co.*, 359 F. Supp. 1235 (N.D. Ga. 1973), *affirmed*, 505 F.2d 733 (5th Cir. 1974).

Since then Georgia, Michigan, Minnesota, Nevada, and Virginia have passed laws that require employers to maintain the confidentiality of test results and prohibit their disclosure to third parties without the employee's consent. Some state licensing statutes now also require that the polygraph examiner keep results in confidence from all but the employer and the examination subject.

SOME RECOMMENDATIONS AND CONCLUSIONS

In 1979 Louis Harris took a poll of employees and employers to find out what they thought about privacy rights in employment. The survey found that 75 percent of employers and 80 percent of employees believed there should be some limits on the type of personal information an employer can seek from its employees. Over 85 percent of employees and 80 percent of employers thought it was "very important" that an employer should notify employees before releasing any personal information from their files. Fifty-one percent of employers, as opposed to 77 percent of employees, objected to closed circuit television monitoring of work areas.

An overwhelming 90 percent of employers and employees supported the idea that all employers should have specific privacy policies. Although the percentage of employers that have promulgated such policies is not that high, hundreds of companies, including most of those in the Fortune 500, have incorporated privacy rights into their personnel policies.

The benefits of a privacy policy are obvious. In this constantly evolving area of the law, clear written guidelines, uniformly enforced at all levels of the enterprise, will minimize unnecessary intrusions and reduce the risk that private information will be wrongfully disclosed. Policies containing an internal grievance procedure will give employees a place, other than court, to air complaints that their privacy was invaded. This mechanism also provides a convenient vehicle for reducing or avoiding damages and limiting liability.

If employees are represented by a labor organization, the policy should be planned jointly with the union, as many major corporations have done. Union representation in the drafting process, perhaps with employee participation, is the surest way of accurately learning employee sentiment, of obtaining informed employee input, and of ensuring employee co-operation instead of resistance.

In Chapters 1 and 3 it was learned that there is always some risk in promulgating a written personnel policy of any kind. Discharge of an employee in violation of a personnel policy may give rise to an action for damages in contract, or for breach of the implied covenant of good faith and fair dealing. In fact, one of California's leading wrongful discharge cases involves the violation of an internal privacy policy. In *Rulon-Miller v. IBM,* 162 Cal. App. 3d 241, 208 Cal. Rptr. 524 (1984), an IBM employee was fired for dating a competitor's employee. IBM had promulgated a privacy policy guaranteeing that it would not take an interest in employees' outside activities so long as they did not interfere with work. Rulon-Miller's termination appeared to violate the policy, which had also been enforced inconsistently. A jury awarded her $100,000 compensatory and $200,000 punitive damages.

IBM was under no legal obligation to promulgate the policy, and the policy may have guaranteed employees more privacy rights than they had under law. By enacting the policy, the company ran the risk that the policy would be turned against it in the event of a violation. Indeed, after the *Rulon-Miller* case was decided. IBM was reported to have modified its policy to cut back on privacy rights. But the *Rulon-Miller* case should not deter employers from maintaining privacy policies. A cautious policy will likely have little impact on the way the employer gathers and maintains information about its employees. It should have no adverse effect on general matters of managerial discretion, because privacy restrictions generally place limits only on those things which are not genuine business concerns. And in most cases it will prevent privacy suits by forestalling privacy invasions in the first instance.

In designing a privacy policy employers should begin by reviewing their job application process. Employers should inquire only about past job performance and the candidate's suitability to the new job. Obviously what is job-related differs with the nature of the industry and the responsibilities of the job. Drug and arrest histories are more relevant to many positions in a health care facility than they are to switchboard operator positions. Employers should avoid using polygraphs, voice stress analyzers, and urinalysis drug tests. These are demonstrably inaccurate, unnecessarily intrusive, and often illegal.

Full disclosure should be the watchword at all stages of the employment process. If a consumer credit report is sought, the job applicant or employee should be informed of the name of the agency to be consulted. Requests should be limited to job-related information, and no questions should be asked that could be construed as violations of the National Labor Relations Act, state and federal discrimination laws, or other laws limiting employer inquiries. If reasonable doubt exists as to the accuracy of information, the prospective employee should be given an opportunity to inspect the report before a decision is made with respect to his or her employment.

The employer's next step should be a review of its record keeping practices. Only relevant information should be maintained. Employees should be told what records are maintained. Reasonable procedures should be adopted to assure the accuracy, timeliness, and completeness of the information. Employees and former employees should be given an opportunity to see, copy, and (on proper proof), correct and amend records maintained about them.

The employer should also review its practices in monitoring employee performance. Employees should have an opportunity to see their performance evaluations. If electronic monitoring is to be done, it should not be surreptitious. Moreover, if data is maintained based on electronic surveillance, employees or their union representative should have an opportunity to examine it.

The policy should contain a procedure for correcting errors. The best source for correcting inaccuracies is the employees themselves. If there is a dispute concerning any record, the employee should at least be given an opportunity to place a rebuttal statement in his file. Equally important, as recommended by the Federal Privacy Commission, any corrections made by the employer should be reported to all individuals and organizations that were furnished the information within the previous two years. If the wrong information originally came from a consumer reporting agency, the agency should be notified.

Finally, strict limitations on disclosure are the best assurance that private as well as false information is not wrongly publicized. Not every managerial employee within the company needs to have a right of access to all employee data. Systems should be instituted to secure employee files from prying eyes, and procedures established to limit disclosure of potentially embarrassing disciplinary information to those who have a legitimate reason to know.

Appendix **A**

SAMPLE CALIFORNIA POLYGRAPH CONSENT FORM

_____   Start: _____

[Employer Name]

Date: _____   Time: _____

Stop: _____

Subject: _____   Social Security #: _____ - _____ - _____

Client: _____   Address: _____

Sex: _____ D.O.B. _____   Zip: _____ Length of Empl.: _____

Occupation: _____   Test: _____ Examiner: _____

This examination is by request (as opposed to a demand or requirement). A subsequent examination may also be requested to correct future company irregularities when necessary. Applicants, employees, or others may agree to decline this examination in accordance with the California Labor Code, Section 432.2, which provides:

> No employer shall demand or require any applicant for employment or prospective employment or any employee to submit
> to or take a polygraph [lie detector] or similar test or examination as a condition of employment or continued employment.

Prior to administration of the examination, and regardless of the reason for the examination, each person will be informed of all questions to be asked. In line with our policy of not invading the privacy of applicants, employees, or private individuals, no immaterial or extraneous subject matter will be covered.

"I am taking this polygraph examination without any promise of reward or hope of immunity. I am making all statements freely and voluntarily without any threats, either physical or mental, and understand my rights against self-incrimination under the Constitution of the United States and the State of California, and my right to refuse to take this polygraph examination without retaliation against me by my employer or prospective employer for exercising these rights."

"I have read the above statement and understand the polygraph examination must be conducted on a voluntary basis and is not a condition of my employment or continued employment. I hereby consent to the polygraph examination, voluntarily and without any reservation. I hereby release and forever hold harmless from any and all liability, [name

of polygraph service], the examiner _____, their agents and employees, and

_____, their agents and employees."

[name of employer]

"I have no objection to this interview and examination being recorded."

Dated: _____

Witness: _____   Signature: _____

****

I, _____, have read and agree with the above and give my consent for my

[Parent or Guardian]

_____, _____, to be examined on the polygraph

[Son, Daughter, Ward]   [Name]

as requested by his employer, prospective employer or attorney.

Date: _____   Signature _____

[Parent or Guardian]

Appendix B

CALIFORNIA MEDICAL CONSENT FORM

[Addressee]
[Address]

Re: [Name of Employee or Applicant]
Social Security No.: _____

Dear Sir or Madam:

This shall authorize you to furnish [name and address of employer] any and all records in your possession, with the exception of bills or statements for services, concerning my physical condition and examinations or treatments therefor, for its review in connection with my employment. I have been given a copy of this authorization. After sixty days of the date hereof, you are no longer authorized to divulge any medical information to that employer.

Dated:

_____
(Signature of Employee)

Chapter 6

EMPLOYMENT DISCRIMINATION LAW
WHAT IT SAYS

Louis J. Barnard, M.B.A., J.D.

For the past 50 years there has been some statutory regulation of the employment relationship by state and federal legislatures. In the past 15 years the number of regulations has been escalating at an increasing rate. The statutes can generally be grouped under laws respecting labor relations or statutes which specifically address equal employment opportunity.

The first category started with the passage of the National Labor Relations Act (NLRA), 29 U.S.C. EE 141-197. The Act contains restrictions on discharges in sections that define unfair labor practices. Sections 8(a)(1), 8(a)(3), and 8(a)(4) provide as follows:

(a) It shall be an unfair labor practice for an employer—
(1) to interfere with, restrain or coerce employees in the exercise of the rights guaranteed in {Section 7} of this {Act};...
(3) by discrimination in regard to hire or tenure of employment or any term or condition of employment to encourage or discourage membership in any labor organization....
(4) to discharge or otherwise discriminate against an employee because he has filed charges or given testimony under this subchapter.

Thus the NLRA prohibits the discharging of an employee on account of the union membership, union organizational activities, the filing of an unfair labor practice charge, or testifying in any proceeding before the Board. However, an employer is not precluded from taking disciplinary action including discharge for poor performance or conduct which would otherwise result in an employee being disciplined.

Specific prohibition against discharge is in section 11 of the Occupational Safety and Health Act (OSHA), 29 U.S.C. EE 651-678. The pertinent section provides:

No person shall discharge or in any manner discriminate against any employee because such employee has filed any complaints or instituted or caused to be instituted any proceeding under or related to this chapter or has testified or is about to testify in any such proceeding because of the exercise by such employee on behalf of himself or others of any right afforded by this chapter.

Thus, OSHA prohibits the discharge of an employee because of filing a complaint or providing testimony. There are also restrictions on the employer's actions when the employee is exercising rights under this act, such as refusing to work in an unsafe workplace.

The Fair Labor Standards Act (FLSA), 29 U.S.C. EE 201-219, generally applies to hours and wages of covered employees, but specifically bans discharge based on filing or causing a complaint to be filed or about to or testifying in any proceeding.

Similar prohibitions against discharge for exercising a right provided by law are found in The Employee Retirement Income Security Act (ERISA), 29 U.S.C. EE 1001-1381. The Consumer Protection Act, 15 U.S.C. EE 1671-1677 relates to discharge because of a garnishment, and the Protection of Jurors' Employment Act, 28 U.S.C. EE 1875.

There are also many state laws which are in the general category of labor relations. For example, the labor code found in most states provides the same protection against discharge when exercising a statutory right. The subjects include: participation in a proceeding before the State Labor Commissioner, Workers Compensation Appeals Board proceedings, jury or witness duty in a state court, engaging in political activities or serving as an election officer on election day.

With a multistate employer, it is very important to know how the state law impacts the employment relationship in each location. Each state has jurisdiction over the persons employed in the state. Therefore, knowledge of only the federal statutes is not enough.

The second major category is equal employment laws and started with the passage of the Civil Rights Act of 1964. Title VII of the Act, 42 U.S.C. 2000e–2000e–17 specifically restricts the basis for discharge or other adverse employment action taken by an employer. The Act prohibits an employer, employment agency, or labor organization from discharging or otherwise discriminating against employee on account of race, color, religion, sex or national origin. In addition Section 704 of the Act contains a specific ban on discharging or otherwise adversely impacting an employee or applicant for employment on account of filing a charge, testifying, or participating in any manner in an investigation, proceeding, or hearing.

There has been civil rights legislation dated 1820, 1866, and 1871, but those were concerned with general areas of right to contract, holding personal property, and using any statute, ordinance, and so on to deprive any person a right secured by the Constitution of the United States. Some litigation has been based on these old statutes; however, the first major legislation dealing specifically with the employer/employee relationship was in 1964.

The Act, as amended, specifically provides that nothing in the legislation requires an employer to grant preferential treatment to any individual or group on account of an imbalance which may exist with respect to the total members or percentage of persons of any race, color, religion, sex, or national origin. This section is the basis for claims of "reverse discrimination."

The Act created the Equal Employment Opportunity Commission (EEOC), composed of five members, empowered to prevent any person from engaging in any unlawful employment practice. A member of the Commission may file a complaint alleging an unlawful employment practice as well as any person. The charge must be in writing under oath or affirmation setting forth sufficient facts to initiate an investigation. If the Commission determines, after an investigation, that there is not reasonable course to believe that the charge is true, it shall dismiss it and notify the persons involved.

If the Commission determines there is reasonable cause to believe the charge to be true, it must try to eliminate such unlawful employment practice by informal methods of conference, conciliation, and persuasion. This presents the first and perhaps the best opportunity to resolve the complaint. A complete investigation of all the facts is essential. One technique which has proven successful provided for a complete investigation of the facts surrounding the complaint. A meeting was held when the investigator presented the findings. Attendees included the manager and functional head of the organization where the employee worked plus the company Equal Employment Opportunity (EEO) officer, legal counsel, and the head of the human resource function. This process resulted in a timely review of all the facts and the involvement of the policy makers of the company. A company position was developed at the meeting which gave general guidance to those charged with the responsibility of meeting with representatives of the EEOC and resolving the case. Direct contact with the complainant was not made without concurrence of the EEOC representative.

In determining whether reasonable cause exists, substantial weight will be given to final findings and orders made by state or local authorities acting in accordance with a state or local law prohibiting the unlawful employment practice alleged and has the authority to grant or seek relief or to institute criminal proceedings. While it is not possible to review, at this time, all state or local laws regarding employment discrimination, it is important to know these laws in addition to the federal legislation when a complaint is filed. How the state and local complaints are resolved can impact a subsequent charge filed with the EEOC.

A charge shall be filed within 180 days after the alleged unlawful employment practice; however, certain extensions may result in lengthening the period for another 120 days for a total of 300 days. If a timely charge is filed, the Commission may bring a civil action against the respondent if a satisfactory conciliation agreement has not been obtained. If a charge is dismissed or the Commission has not filed a civil action or obtained a conciliation agreement, the complainant may, within 90 days after receiving such notice, bring a civil action against the respondent. If the charge was filed by a member of the Commission, the civil action may be brought by any person whom alleges was aggrieved by the alleged unlawful employment practice.

The Act requires certain relevant employment records be mentioned and certain reports be made. Employment records should be retained during the period a person may file a timely charge or until final resolution of a charge once it is filed.

For each major protected class (i.e., race, religion, sex, etc.), specific interpretations have developed. With the increase of females in the workforce, the number of EEOC complaints based on sex has increased. Sexual harassment is a difficult issue for employers to resolve, since it can often be one employee's word against another. Sexual preference has also been included under the general issue of sexual harassment. These discrimination issues, as well as others, require a careful review of employment policies and practices to eliminate potential sexual harassment complaints.

It is difficult to generalize about a specific instance. Each situation should be judged on its merits. For example, a long-service employee announces he is in the process of a sex change to become a female. What should the management do to preclude a complaint? Issues include: reaction of peer employees and subordinates, if a supervisor; is there a material adverse impact on the effectiveness of the employee; how much time off will be required; which rest room will the person use, and so forth. When circumstances raise possible discrimination issues it is best to anticipate the problem areas and develop a sound approach for everyone to follow. After the fact actions may be too late.

The Age Discrimination in Employment Act of 1967 (ADEA), as amended, 29 U.S.C. 61-34 combines a general prohibition on employment discrimination on the basis of a specific status, that is, age. Currently persons aged 40 through 69 years are members of the affected class protected by this legislation. There are meaningful exceptions to ADEA. These include:

1. When age is a bona fide occupational qualification reasonably necessary to the normal operation of the particular business.

2. To observe the terms of a bona fide seniority system or employer benefit plan which is not a subterfuge to evade the purpose of the Act.

3. May require compulsory retirement of an employee who has attained 65 years of age provided for the two-year period immediately before retirement is employed in a bona fide executive or a high policy-making position and is entitled to a minimum level of benefit from deferred compensation plans, such as pension, profit sharing, savings, or any combination of such plans.

4. The mandatory retirement exclusion between age 65 through 70 years of age is also extended to institutions of higher education.

Several states have passed age discrimination legislation. In some states, such as California, the law is more liberal than federal law and in such cases state law will prevail.

Since the general purpose of the Act is to "promote employment of older persons based on their ability rather than age," the exceptions have been narrowed over the years. For example, the level of deferred compensation required to qualify for exemption as an "executive" was raised from $27,000 to $44,000 per year. Accordingly the exceptions should be viewed in light of the purpose of the Act and judgement made accordingly.

The Pregnancy Discrimination Act of 1978 was added to Title VII and expands the coverage of the Act. Employers are required to consider pregnancy, childbirth, or related medical conditions the same as any other disability for all employment-related purposes (42 U.S.C. 2000e (K)). Health insurance benefits for abortion are specifically not required except where life of the mother would be endangered.

The Vietnam-Era Veterans' Readjustment Assistance Act of 1974, 38 U.S.C. 2011–2026 prohibits an employer from refusing to reemploy an inducted person who satisfactorily completes military service of at least 180 days during any part of the Vietnam Era and who remains qualified to perform the job. There are further restrictions requiring "good cause" for discharging a Vietnam Era veteran during the first year of reemployment.

While the foregoing applies to all employers, those employers have added responsibilities if they are a prime contractor or subcontractor with the U.S. government with 50 or more employees and have a single contract or annual billings of $50,000 or more. In addition, such an employer who serves as a depository of government funds or who is a financial institution issuing or redeeming U.S. Savings Bonds and savings notes are also covered. The added responsibility is set forth in Office of Federal Contract Compliance Programs, Revised Order Number 4, which was created by President Johnson in Executive Order 11246.

Revised Order Number 4 requires a good faith effort to take affirmative action to correct any deficiencies in the full utilization of minorities and females at all levels and in all segments of the workforce. The Department of Labor has the responsibility to audit plans and receive complaints from persons. The enforcement agency (Office of Federal Contract Compliance) will review individual complaints with specific emphasis on systemic issues and pattern and practice discrimination.

If an employer is found to be not in compliance, a "show cause" notice may be issued which could ultimately result in an employer being excluded from current and future U.S. government contracts.

Our society has experienced rapid change in recent years, and our laws have been changed with increasing frequency. Employment discrimination laws will continue to change as our society struggles to accommodate current and future social issues. Also, current laws will be interpreted to meet new applications. All this activity requires a responsible employer to keep abreast of the changing legal aspects of employment discrimination law.

Chapter 7

DEFENDING EMPLOYMENT DISCRIMINATION CHARGES
THE INVESTIGATION

Robert N. Marx, J.D.

The purpose of this and the following chapter will be to provide the reader with the knowledge and tools with which to effectively and successfully respond to the filing of a complaint of unlawful discrimination. This chapter will focus on administrative agency treatment of a complaint filed by an employee charging unlawful discrimination by the employer, from the time the initial complaint is filed through the disposition of the complaint at the investigatory level. The chapter will describe the administrative procedures that are followed and that an employer should be aware of, and will offer suggestions for how an employer should proceed.

A disposition favorable to the employer at the investigatory level ends the process and would make unnecessary any reference to the following chapter. However, administrative investigation of complaints sometimes results in a finding of "probable cause." As I will discuss more fully later, probable cause means that a determination has been made that the employee's complaint of discrimination has merit, and will be examined further. A probable cause finding is significant because it precipitates further administrative agency action and requires an employer to direct additional attention to refuting the allegation of discrimination.

The following chapter describes the procedures resulting from a finding of probable cause and outlines suggested responses. As a consequence of a finding of probable cause, it is likely that the employer will be required to defend himself or herself at an administrative hearing on the complaint. Accordingly, the following chapter deals extensively with pre- and posthearing procedures before the agency.

A preliminary discussion of terminology is in order at this point. The law of employment discrimination is created by a series of state and federal statutes known generically as "fair employment laws." The complexity of the law in this area is a result of the existence of both federal and state discrimination laws and the intermeshing of administrative agency enforcement of these laws on the state and federal level.

On the federal level, the Equal Employment Opportunity Commission (EEOC) is the administrative agency that enforces the major federal fair employment legislation. More specifically, the EEOC enforces Title VII of the 1964 Civil Rights Act, as amended, and the Age Discrimination in Employment Act (ADEA).

In addition to the federal laws, most states have enacted their own fair employment laws, and have created state agencies to enforce these state laws. These state agencies will be referred to as "state EEO agencies." The EEO acronym stands for Equal Employment Opportunity.

A complaint filed with the EEOC or with a state EEO agency, is also known as a "charge," and the complainant is similarly referred to as the "charging party." When a complaint is filed with the EEOC, that agency will initially ascertain whether or not the state in which the complaint was filed has its own state EEO agency. If the state has its own EEO agency, the EEOC will send, or "defer," the complaint to the state EEO agency. This intricate procedure between similar state and federal EEO agencies will be described in greater detail later in this chapter. For the present time, the reader should be aware that the complaint sent or deferred to the state EEO agency, is known as a "deferred complaint" or as an "EEOC-deferred complaint."

EEOC-deferred complaints comprise a substantial number of the total complaints handled by the state EEO agencies. Indeed, one of the hallmarks of EEO law is the interrelationship between state and federal laws and agencies. One might accurately assert that the bulk of administrative investigation and resolution of federal EEO complaints is accomplished not by the EEOC, but by various state EEO agencies.

As most employers are aware, modern federal EEO law begins with Title VII of the 1964 Civil Rights Act. Title VII—or Part Seven—of the 1964 Civil Rights Act, makes unlawful employment discrimination on the basis of one's race, color, creed, or national origin. In 1965 the Act was amended to also make unlawful employment discrimination on the basis of one's sex.

Procedurally, Title VII of the 1964 Civil Rights Act, as amended, must be considered one of the more complicated statutes on the books. To make matters as simple as possible, we will refer to the statute as Title VII. Under most federal statutes, such as the Bankruptcy or Copyright Acts, a person who wishes to sue under the federal law may go directly into federal court with a summons and complaint. However, a Title VII plaintiff may not go directly into federal court. First, complaint must be filed with the EEOC and a wait of at least 180 days while that agency tries to resolve the complaint. Only thereafter, may a Title VII plaintiff request what is called a "right to sue" letter in order to bring his or her action in federal court. A more detailed explanation of the "right to sue" letter is included later in this chapter. In addition, before a Title VII plaintiff can even file his or her complaint with the EEOC, our potential plaintiff must first file a complaint with the state EEO agency where the complainant lives or works, if that state has an EEO agency.

As a matter of federal law, when a complaint is filed with a state EEO agency, that agency has exclusive jurisdiction over the complaint for 60 days. This means that for 60 days after the complaint is filed, only the state agency can consider the complaint. Only after 60 days from the time the compliant is filed with the state EEO agency, may the complaining employee then file a complaint with the federal EEOC. This legal requirement is based on the theory that the state agency should be given the first opportunity to resolve the complaint, thus hopefully eliminating the need for involvement on a federal level. Whether or not the theory is persuasive, the fact is that in practice the EEOC defers to the state EEO agency in most, if not all cases, and for periods of time well in excess of 60 days.

Most, if not all, state EEO agencies have ongoing contracts with the EEOC under which contracts the state EEO agencies are paid an amount of money for each EEOC-deferred complaint that is handled by the state EEO agency. Although the EEOC has the right to assert jurisdiction over, or to "take back" an EEOC-deferred complaint after 60 days, this is rarely done. Instead the EEOC allows the state EEO agency to take as much time as it needs, while the complaint is investigated, heard at an administrative hearing, and ultimately resolved by the state EEO agency.

On a determination on the complaint by the state EEO agency, the EEOC typically will adopt the determination of the state EEO agency as its own decision. Only in rare cases involving persistent and persuasive complainants, or cases raising novel issues of law, will the complaining employee successfully convince the EEOC to take its own look at a complaint that was dismissed by the state EEO agency for lack of probable cause. Of course it is equally difficult for an employer to reverse a state EEO agency's determination at the EEOC. As a result of years of experience in a state EEO agency, and from numerous conversations with the EEO liaison officer with that state EEO agency, this author has concluded that the EEOC is not set up to handle the enormous caseload that would result from independently examining each EEOC complaint. Moreover, the EEOC personnel feel that instead of investigating complaints themselves, they are paying state EEO agencies to do that, and there is little inclination to engage in what would be perceived as duplicative efforts.

The investigation and resolution of EEO complaints by state EEO agencies is critical for two reasons. First, the complaining employee may have filed a complaint under the state's EEO law. And second, in all likelihood, the state-based and federal-based EEO actions will both be determined on an administrative level by the state EEO agency.

In addition to Title VII, we must also take note of ADEA, which was enacted in 1967. As its name indicates, the ADEA makes unlawful discrimination in employment on the basis of one's age, where the age of the complaining party is between 40 and 70. Initially the ADEA was administered by the Department of Labor, but in 1978 jurisdiction over ADEA complaints was transferred to the EEOC. Like Title VII-based complaints, ADEA-based complaints typically are deferred to state EEO agencies where state EEO agencies exist, and are handled administratively in a similar fashion as are Title VII complaints.

Of the 50 states, 42 have state EEO agencies. In those 42 states, a complaint filed with the EEOC must first be filed with the particular state's EEO agency. Also in those 42 states, complaints filed with the EEOC will be sent or "deferred" to the particular state's EEO agency.

The 42 states that have EEO agencies additionally administer their own state EEO statutes. Thus in those 42 states, the state EEO agencies act on complaints filed pursuant to that state's EEO statute and simlutaneously act on complaints filed under the federal law, namely the ADEA and Title VII.

Thirty-nine of the 42 state EEO agencies are organized and operate procedurally in a similar manner. For our purposes, we will refer to this common procedure as the "investigation and administrative hearing procedure." Under the investigation and administrative hearing procedure, the state EEO statute establishes the state EEO agency. Any person who believes he or she has been the victim of discrimination made unlawful under the state EEO statute, may file a complaint with the state EEO agency. The filing of the complaint is relatively informal and does not require the assistance of an attorney. Typically, the state EEO agency has various offices located throughout the state, where persons may speak to agency staff members. These agency staff members will listen to the person's story and then will write a complaint for the person to sign. When the complaint is signed, the complaining employee becomes a "complainant," the employee becomes a "respondent," and an investigation is begun.

After a complaint has been filed with the state EEO agency, the agency will commence an investigation by assigning the complaint to be investigated by a particular "investigator" on that agency's staff. In addition, the agency will send a copy of the complaint to the employer. After notice of the complaint, the employer will also receive a questionnaire. Typically this questionnnaire, also known as the "investigatory questionnaire," will require the employer to explain his or her reasons for the termination (or other challenged employer action). The employer's response is required by a certain time which is specified in the questionnaire. When completed, the employer's response to the complaint is sent to the state EEO agency, and the employer awaits further agency action. The employer's response to the complaint is also known as the employer's "position statement."

On receipt of the employer's response, the state EEO agency will determine whether further information is required from the employer, and whether a reply by the employee to the position statement is advisable. In some rare cases, the state EEO agency will dismiss the complaint at this point; this possibility will be discussed in greater detail later in the chapter.

If the agency decides to proceed further with the investigation, the next step is the conference before the agency's investigator. This conference has different names among the 39 state EEO agencies that use this investigation and administrative hearing procedure. The conference may be called an "investigatory conference," "regional conference," "confrontational conference," "fact-finding conference," or a similar name. In each case the conference is the first opportunity for the employee and the employer to confront each other in the presence of the investigator.

In most cases, the conference effectively concludes the investigation. Occasionally the employer's response or statements made in the course of the conference will cause the investigator to request more information from the employer.

At the conclusion of the investigation, the chief administrative officer on the investigatory level will issue an order in the matter. This person may be known as a "Regional Director," "Investigating Commissioner," or by a similar title. The order issued by this person will decide either that there is no merit to the complaint, or that there is some merit and further agency action is required. In the first situation, the order will decide that there is "no probable cause," "no reasonable cause," or that, using a similar phrase, there is no reason to believe that the employer has discriminated unlawfully against the employee. The complaint will thereupon be dismissed. With the narrow exception of certain appeals by the employee within the agency or to a court, the order of dismissal effectively will end the matter as far as the employer is concerned.

There may be cases where the agency will decide that there is some merit to the complaint. In such cases, the agency will issue an order finding "reasonable cause" or "probable cause," or that, using a similar phrase, there is reason to believe that the employer discriminated unlawfully against the employee. In such cases the agency will require the matter to be decided at an administrative hearing.

The administrative hearing will be held before an "administrative law judge," "hearing officer," "hearing commissioner," or before a person with a similar title who is regularly employed by that agency. Such a person will have had no involvement with the investigation of the complaint. Although substantially less formal than a court proceeding, the administrative hearing will be similar to a trial in that there will be examination and cross-examination of witnesses. Both sides will also have the opportunity to introduce documentary evidence, such as personnel files, employment applications, and so forth. At the conclusion of the administrative hearing, the person hearing the case will issue an order on the matter. In many states he or she will issue a proposed order to be sent to the chief officer of the agency. Also in many states both sides will be forwarded copies of the proposed order, and will be given the opportunity to object in writing to the proposed order.

The conclusion of the agency action with respect to the complaint will be the final order issued by the chief officer of the agency. The order will either dimiss or sustain the complaint. The complaint will be dismissed if the agency determines that the employer did not discriminate unlawfully against the employee. The complaint will be sustained if the agency determines that the employer did discriminate unlawfully against the employee. If the complaint is sustained, the agency will order legal relief to the employee, including but not limited to, back pay and reinstatement.

The agency's final order completes the investigation and administrative hearing procedure. An employer who is charged with unlawful discrimination in employment will be required to comply with this procedure in 39 out of the 50 states. Table 1 lists the 50 states and the District of Columbia, indicating the 42 states with EEO agencies, and the 39 that use the investigation and administrative hearing procedure.

TABLE 1 State EEO Agencies and Statutes of Limitations Under State EEO Laws

State and State EEO Law	State EEO Law Y/N	Provides for Investigation and Public Hearing Procedure—Y/N	Statute of Limitations Under State EEO Law
Alabama	N	—	—
Alaska			
Alaska State Laws Against Discrimination	Y	Y	300 days
Arizona			
Arizona Civil Rights Act	Y	Y	180 days
Arkansas	N	—	—
California			
California Fair Employment Practices and Housing Act	Y	Y	1 year
Colorado			
Colorado Antidiscrimination Act	Y	Y	6 months
Connecticut			
Connecticut Fair Employment Practices Act	Y	Y	180 days
Delaware			
Delaware Fair Employment Practices Act	Y	Y	90 days
Florida			
Florida Human Rights Act	Y	Y	180 days
Georgia			
No comprehensive statute	Y	Y	180 days
Hawaii			
Hawaii Fair Employment Practices Act	Y	Y	30 days
Idaho			
Idaho Fair Employment Practices Act	Y	N	1 year
Illinois			
Illinois Human Rights Act	Y	Y	180 days
Indiana			
Indiana Civil Rights Law	Y	Y	90 days
Iowa			
Iowa Civil Rights Law	Y	Y	180 days
Kansas			
Kansas Act Against Discrimination	Y	Y	6 months
Kentucky			
Kentucky Fair Employment Practices Act	Y	Y	180 days
Louisiana	N	—	—

TABLE 1 *(Continued)*

State and State EEO Law	State EEO Law Y/N	Provides for Investigation and Public Hearing Procedure—Y/N	Statute of Limitations Under State EEO Law
Maine			
Maine Human Rights Act	Y	N	6 months
Maryland			
Maryland Fair Employment Practices Act	Y	Y	6 months
Massachusetts			
Massachusetts Fair Employment Practices Law	Y	Y	6 months
Michigan			
Michigan Civil Rights Act	Y	Y	180 days
Minnesota			
Minnesota Human Rights Act	Y	Y	300 days
Mississippi	N	—	—
Missouri			
Missouri Fair Employment Practices Act	Y	Y	180 days
Montana			
Montana Human Rights Act	Y	Y	180
Nebraska			
Nebraska Fair Employment Practices Act	Y	Y	180 days
Nevada			
Nevada Fair Employment Practices Act	Y	Y	180 days
New Hampshire			
New Hampshire Law Against Discrimination	Y	Y	180 days
New Jersey			
New Jersey Law Against Discrimination	Y	Y	180 days
New Mexico			
New Mexico Human Rights Act	Y	Y	1 year
New York			
New York Human Rights Law	Y	Y	1 year
North Carolina	N	—	—
North Dakota	N	—	—
Ohio			
Ohio Fair Employment Practices Law	Y	Y	6 months
Oklahoma			
Oklahoma Civil Rights Act	Y	Y	180 days

TABLE 1 *(Continued)*

State and State EEO Law	State EEO Law Y/N	Provides for Investigation and Public Hearing Procedure—Y/N	Statute of Limitations Under State EEO Law
Oregon Oregon Fair Employment Practices Act	Y	Y	1 year
Pennsylvania Pennsylvania Human Relations Act	Y	Y	90 days
Rhode Island Rhode Island Fair Employment Practices Act	Y	Y	1 year
South Carolina South Carolina Human Affairs Law	Y	Y	180 days
South Dakota South Dakota Human Relations Act	Y	Y	180 days
Tennessee Tennessee Fair Employment Practices Law	Y	Y	180 days
Texas Texas Commission on Human Rights Act	Y	N	180 days
Utah Utah Antidiscriminatory Act	Y	Y	180 days
Vermont	N	—	—
Virginia	N	—	—
Washington Washington Law Against Discrimination	Y	Y	6 months
West Virginia West Virginia Human Rights Act	Y	Y	90 days
Wisconsin Wisconsin Fair Employment Act	Y	Y	300 days
Wyoming Wyoming Fair Employment Practices Act	Y	Y	90 days
District of Columbia District of Columbia Human Rights Law	Y	Y	1 year

As was stated previously, this chapter will be devoted to assisting the employer in responding to the complaint at the "investigation" stage of the procedure. The following chapter will be devoted to assisting the employer to respond to the complaint at the "administrative hearing" stage of the procedure.

We will examine both the investigation and administrative hearing stages of the procedure by using a hypothetical complaint based upon an assumed set of facts. Given our hypothetical complaint, we will then discuss and offer examples of each option available to the employer at each succeeding stage of the foregoing procedure. Our hypothetical complaint and assumed set of facts follows:

ABC Co. is a nationally known company producing widgets and employing 50 or more employees in each of the 50 states. John Doe is employed by ABC at one of its widget factories in New York State. He is 60 years of age and is a black male. Doe has been employed by ABC for 30 years on a widget assembly line. He has never been promoted, demoted, or reprimanded.

ABC routinely conducts annual performance appraisals of all employees by way of "personnel evaluation forms." These forms are completed by the immediate supervisor of the employee being rated and signed by the employee. The employee may not formally challenge or contest the rating he or she receives, but the form contains space at the end of the form where the employee may insert his or her objections or comments. The evaluation forms contain an overall employee numerical rating as follows: 1-Excellent, 2-Good, 3-Satisfactory, 4-Unsatisfactory. Doe always received a "2" (Good) until his most recent evaluation, when he received a "3" (Satisfactory). On that evaluation form, in the space reserved for employee comments, Doe had written as follows: "I am doing the same job I have always done for the last 30 years. The only reason for this rating is that my new supervisor is aware that I know more about this job than she does and that I should now be in her position."

On May 4, 1986, Doe had been passed over for promotion to Widget foreman. Formal applications for the position had neither been solicited by management nor received from any employee. However, Doe is certain that he was passed over because the departing Widget foreman, Rip Van Winkle, had asked Doe if he was interested in the promotion shortly before he left. When Doe responded in the affirmative, Van Winkle said he would recommend Doe as his replacement. Van Winkle has subsequently forgotten that conversation.

The promotion was given to Suzy Que. Que is a white female and is 30 years of age. She had worked alongside Doe for 10 years until her promotion. On each annual performance evaluation form Que has always received a "3" (Satisfactory). On May 4, 1986 she had been promoted instead of Doe on the recommendation of ABC's EEO Officer, who had written as follows:

Although Doe has received 2's (Good) and Que has received only 3's (Satisfactory), there truly is not much difference between the two ratings. At best, one might say that Doe is slightly more qualified for the position than is Que.

On the other hand, we already have black Widget Foremen in our New Jersey and Connecticut factories, and we have no female Widget Foremen (Forepersons?) at all. In addition, we should remember that Doe is getting on in years. His attitude that things should be done the same way they were done 30 years ago has caused us problems on certain occasions. As Jack has said, we need young blood to help get us out of our financial problems.

Jack Clark, referred to in the EEO Officer's memo, is ABCs president and chairman of the board. Within the past year he has organized a task force to consider responses to ABCs financial problems resulting from an influx of cheap widgets from Japan. One recommendation made by the task force was to reduce the payroll by discharging nonessential employees whose current personnel evaluation form ratings have declined from their prior ratings.

The task force has also recommended that a private investigative agency be hired to investigate the costly problem of employee pilferage. This recommendation is adopted. In the course of examining employee backgrounds, the investigative agency discovers that both Doe and Que had lied on their initial employment applications. Both employees had stated that they were graduates of Coolidge High School, but had attended only three years at Coolidge High at the time of their initial applications for employment. ABC Co. has an established rule of long standing that any intentional misrepresentation on an employment application constitutes grounds for immediate dismissal.

On March 1, 1987, Doe and Que are both summoned by the ABC personnel director. Doe admits to the misrepresentation with the explanation that "30 years ago, three years of high school was all that was expected of a black person who was not going to college." Que asserts that she attended night school after starting with ABC Co. and received a diploma from Coolidge High School two years after commencing employment. The personnel director says to both Doe and Que that he will have to discuss the matter with Clark before making a final decision.

The next day Doe is told that he has been terminated, effective immediately. He subsequently learns that Que was not terminated.

NOTICE OF CHARGE

Soon after the charge is filed, notice will be mailed to the employer. At a minimum, the notice should contain the charge itself, the name, address, and telephone number of the complaining employee, the name, address, and telephone number of all parties being charged, and the factual allegations allegedly giving rise to the charge including dates of alleged actions or statements. The complaint should be dated and should state which state and/or federal statutes are being relied on by the employee.

If you are located in a deferral state, examine the charge to determine whether the employee has filed charges under both federal and state law. Often an employee will file charges under *either* federal or state law and will improperly assume that he or she has filed charges under *both* federal and state laws. An employee's failure to file under both federal and state law when he or she can do so is significant to you as the employer because similar federal and state laws may have different statutes of limitation, and may cover different defined groups of employees. Also the remedies available to an employee may be different under similar state and federal laws.

Therefore, it is not uncommon for an employee in a deferral state to assume that his or her complaint is filed under state law because he or she is aware that the complaint he or she has filed with the EEOC under federal law will be, or has been, deferred to the state EEO agency. This assumption by the employee, however, is erroneous and may have negative consequences to the employee and fortunate consequences to you as will be seen later.

If, in a deferral state, a complaint is first filed with the EEOC, the complaint will be forwarded or "deferred" to the state EEO agency for investigation and will be deemed timely filed with the EEOC 61 days later. However, this deferral does not necessarily constitute a filing of a charge with the state EEO agency under state law. This is important because some state and federal laws covering the same type of discrimination may have different statutes of limitation within which an employee can sue his or her employer. The consequence to an employee who mistakenly assumes that he or she has also filed under state law, is that the statute of limitations under which he or she can sue the employer under state law may expire, and the employee may be barred from bringing such suit. Thus, it is possible—and sometimes occurs—that the statute of limitations will expire on a state cause of action at the same time that the state EEO agency is in the process of investigating a deferred federal complaint.

The significance of an employee's inability to file a complaint under state law may be especially great where the state statute gives broader remedies than the analogous federal statute. Thus, for example, age discrimination under federal law is prohibited only where the employee is between the ages of 40 and 70, whereas at least one state statute protects employees against age discrimination from the age of 18 years and up, without limit.[1]

Also examine the charge to determine which federal statute is relied on by the complainant. As we have seen, the EEOC processes complaints based upon Title VII as well as upon the ADEA. This is important because ADEA actions, if they are brought into federal court, must be commenced in federal court within two years after the accrual of the cause of action (extended to three years in cases of "willful" age discrimination), regardless of whether the proceedings before the EEOC have been terminated. By contrast, Title VII-based actions may be brought into federal court within 90 days of the EEOC's issuance of a right-to-sue letter, no matter how long after the alleged discriminatory act that time limit might be. The right-to-sue letter will be more fully discussed and explained later in this chapter. For now, it is sufficient to think of the letter as a plaintiff's entitlement to start a Title VII suit in federal court.

Most employees assume that they are within the time limit for bringing

---

[1] New York State Human Rights Law (New York Executive Law §§ 290 et. seq.)

TABLE 2 Summary of ADEA and Title VII Procedures

ADEA	Title VII
1. 300 days to file complaint with EEOC; 180 days to file complaint if nondeferral state	1. 300 days to file complaint with EEOC; 180 days to file complaint if nondeferral state
2. May commence lawsuit in federal court 61 days after filing EEOC complaint	2. May obtain right-to-sue letter on request 181 days after filing EEOC complaint
3. No right-to-sue letter required	3. If no request, EEOC will issue right-to-sue letter after finding of no probable cause or of probable cause
4. Lawsuit in federal court must be filed within two years after alleged discriminatory practice; within three years if "wilful"	4. Must commence lawsuit in Federal Court within 90 days after receiving right-to-sue letter

a federal court action at least as long as the EEOC is considering the complaint. This can prove to be a costly error for an employee who waits beyond the ADEA limitations period of two (or three) years. Therefore, an employer faced with an ADEA complaint before the EEOC should endeavor to keep the complaint at the administrative level for as long as possible, and thereby hopefully avoid later being brought into federal court. Table 2 summarizes the complex procedure for Title VII and ADEA complaints.

In our hypothetical case, John Doe has decided to file a complaint of unlawful discrimination against ABC Company. Doe lives and works in New York, which has at least one EEO agency. Doe can file his complaint with either the New York City Commission on Human Rights, or with the New York State Division of Human Rights. Doe decides to file a complaint with the New York State Division of Human Rights (NYSDHR). On March 3, 1987, Doe goes to the NYSDHR and is interviewed by an intake officer. After telling his story to the officer, Doe is given a copy of the proposed complaint, which he signs without making any changes. (The complaint is included as Table 3.) On March 4, 1987, Doe goes to the EEOC and is interviewed by an intake officer. A copy of Doe's EEOC complaint is included as Table 4.

Doe's complaints allege unlawful termination on the basis of his age and race, in violation of Title VII, ADEA, and the New York State Human Rights Law. Doe's EEOC complaint also alleges unlawful failure to promote, on the basis of his age and race, in violation of Title VII and ADEA. Soon thereafter, a copy of the complaint is sent to you as the employer and named respondent.

On examination of the complaint you note that the allegation of age discrimination regarding the failure to promote, has not been included in the charges filed under the New York State Human Rights Law. You also note that the allegation of age discrimination does not include a specific assertion that the age discrimination was "willful." This means that the age discrimination allegation can be taken into a federal court only if it is commenced in federal court on or before March 2, 1988, two years

TABLE 3 Complaint Filed with New York State Division of Human Rights

STATE OF NEW YORK : EXECUTIVE DEPARTMENT
STATE DIVISION OF HUMAN RIGHTS

State Division of Human Rights on the Complaint of	Complaint No.

JOHN DOE,
    Complainant,
    -against-

ABC CO.,
    Respondent.

I, John Doe, residing at 1 Any Street, New York, Tel. No. 123-4567, charge the above named respondent whose address is 1 Any Other Street, New York, New York, with an unlawful discriminatory practice relating to employment in violation of Article 15 of the Executive Law of the State of New York on or about March 2, 1987, because of AGE(X) RACE(X) COLOR(X) CREED( ) NATIONAL ORIGIN( ) SEX( ) DISABILITY( ) MARITAL STATUS( ) RETALIATION( )

The particulars are:

1. I am black and 60 years of age. I was employed by respondent for approximately thirty years up to and including March 2, 1987.
2. On March 2, 1987 I was terminated from employment by the respondent. On Information and Belief, I was terminated because I allegedly lied on my initial application for employment.
3. On Information and Belief, a younger, white, employee was also allegedly found to have lied on her initial application for employment. This other employee was not terminated or otherwise disciplined.
4. Based on the foregoing, I charge the ABC Co. with terminating me because of my age, race, and color in violation of the New York State Human Rights Law.

I have not commenced any other civil, criminal or administrative action or proceeding in any court or administrative agency based upon the same grievance.
_____ I also charge the above-named respondent with violating Title VII Civil Rights Act of 1964, as amended (covers race, color, religion, sex, national origin relating to employment) and hereby authorize SDHR to accept this verified complaint on behalf of EEOC subject to the statutory limitations contained in Title VII

_____

STATE OF NEW YORK)
COUNTY OF NEW YORK) s.s.:
JOHN DOE, being duly sworn, deposes and says: that he is the Complainant herein; that he has read the foregoing complaint and knows the content thereof; that the same is true of his own knowledge except as to the matter herein stated on information and belief; and that as to those matters, he believes the same to be true.

                                          s/ John Doe
                             _____

Subscribed and sworn to before me
this 3rd day of March, 1987

s/Notary Public
_____

TABLE 4 Complaint Filed with EEOC

CHARGE OF DISCRIMINATION	Charge Number ___ FEPA _x_ EEOC

_____ and EEOC
State or Local Agency if any

Mr. John Doe	(212) 123-4567

NAMED IS THE EMPLOYER, LABOR ORGANIZATION, EMPLOYMENT AGENCY, APPRENTICESHIP COMMITTEE, STATE OR LOCAL GOVERNMENT AGENCY WHO DISCRIMINATED AGAINST ME

ABC CO.

1 Any Other Street, New York, New York

Cause of Discrimination Based On: x Race x Color _ Sex _ Religion _ National Origin x Age _ Retaliation _ Other	Date Most Recent or Continuing Discrimination Took Place March 2, 1987

The Particulars Are:
1. I am black and 60 years of age. I was employed by ABC Co. for approximately thirty years up to and including March 2, 1987.
2. On March 2, 1987 I was terminated from employment by ABC Co. On Information and Belief, I was terminated because I allegedly lied on my initial application for employment.
3. On Information and Belief, a younger, white, employee was also allegedly found to have lied on her initial application for employment. This other employee was not terminated or otherwise disciplined.
4. On or about May 4, 1986 I was passed over for promotion, and a younger, white employee was promoted instead of me.
5. Based on the foregoing, I charge the ABC Co. with violation of Title VII of the 1964 Civil Rights Act and violation of the Age Discrimination in Employment Act.

s/ John Doe March 4, 1987	Notary

from the alleged unlawful termination on the basis of age. The failure to charge age discrimination regarding the promotion under the New York State Human Rights Law can have even more drastic consequences, as we shall see shortly. In addition, you note that Doe has neglected to charge discrimination on the basis of his sex in either the SDHR or the EEOC complaint.

STATUTE OF LIMITATIONS

When an employer receives notice of a charge filed with an EEO agency, the initial consideration should be whether that agency has jurisdiction or control over the matter. Whether or not an agency has jurisdiction, or the legal ability to consider and dispose of the matter, is a function of several statutory factors. Among the typical statutory requisites are those requiring employers to have in their employ a specified minimum number of employees, and requiring the employee to file his or her complaint within a specified period of time. This period of time is called the "statute of limitations" period.

Employment discrimination statutes do not cover every employer. Rather, the different employment discrimination statutes cover only those employers meeting the minimum number of employees requirement. If a particular employer does not employ the minimum number of employees, the employment discrimination statute is inapplicable to that employer, and an employee may not bring a charge of discrimination against that employer. For example, you must employ at least 15 people before you can be sued under Title VII, and 20 persons before you can be sued under the ADEA. In addition, state EEO laws may require a greater or lesser number of employees than is required under either Title VII or ADEA. Depending on the number of employees and the statutes involved, it is possible for an employer to be subject to the state EEO statute and not subject to the Title VII or ADEA, or vice versa.

Since the number of employees is rarely a matter of controversy, it should not be surprising to discover that questions of jurisdiction often do not involve the size of the employer in terms of the number of persons employed. In most cases where a question as to jurisdiction is raised, the issue is whether or not the complaint is timely. As noted previously, state and federal EEO laws require that complaints be filed within a specified period of time, known as the statute of limitations period. Any complaint filed under a particular statute after the statute of limitations period for that statute has elapsed, is said to be time-barred. This means that the EEO agency may not consider that particular alleged statutory violation even if it is otherwise meritorious. As will be seen, because time limitations under federal and state discrimination laws are unusually short, "statute of limitations" is an especially common defense available to employers.

In a deferral state, a charge must be filed with the EEOC no later than 300 days after the alleged unlawful discriminatory practice. In states without EEO agencies, the charge must be filed with the EEOC within 180 days of the alleged unlawful discriminatory practice. In legal jargon, this means that Title VII and ADEA actions have a 300-day statute of limitations in deferral states, and a 180-day statute of limitations in non-deferral states. These time limitations are rather short in comparison to time limitations for other legal actions. For example, a typical negligence action may be started up to three years after the alleged negligence in some states, and a typical fraud or contract action may be started up to six years after the alleged fraud or breach of contract in certain states.

The uncommon brevity of statutes of limitations in Title VII and ADEA actions is responsible for dismissals in many of those actions. An employer charged with violation of Title VII or ADEA has a perfect defense if he or she can take advantage of the statute of limitations. An untimely charge must be dismissed no matter how strong the employee's case, nor how weak the employer's position.

The statute of limitations defense assumes added importance in EEO actions since in these actions there is not just one, but two, and sometimes three, different statutes of limitation. These multiple statutes of limitation are the result of the intricate interplay of state and federal laws and the involvement of state and federal agencies. Each of these statutes of limitations must be met for the plaintiff/employee to continue his or her action.

The first of these statutes of limitations has already been discussed. If the employee is filing his or her charge in a deferral state, the Title VII or ADEA plaintiff must file the charge with the EEOC within 300 days after the alleged unlawful discriminatory practice. In a nondeferral state, the Title VII or ADEA plaintiff has only 180 days within which to file the charge with the EEOC.

The second statute of limitations arises in connection with a complainant's receipt of a "right-to-sue" letter from the EEOC. The right-to-sue letter is required for Title VII plaintiffs who wish to bring suit in federal court, and entitles the Title VII plaintiff to start a federal court action; hence the name "right-to-sue" letter. A right-to-sue letter may be issued by the EEOC in two ways; either on its own initiative, or on request by a complainant. The EEOC will issue a right-to-sue letter on its own initiative after a finding of either "no probable cause" or of "probable cause" following attempted conciliation. In addition, the complainant may obtain on request a right-to-sue letter from the EEOC, but will only be able to do so 180 days after the charge has been filed with the EEOC. Therefore, the Title VII plaintiff may make his or her request for a right-to-sue letter on the 181st day.

The third statute of limitations period concerns the time period within which the Title VII plaintiff must act following receipt of the right-to-sue letter. The employee must begin his or her Title VII action in federal court within 90 days of receipt of the right-to-sue letter. This means that the employee must start the federal complaint within 90 days. It is important to bear in mind that when an employee has filed a complaint with the EEOC, he or she is not considered to have also started a suit in federal court. All he or she has done is to file a charge with a federal agency, and the charge is not automatically transformed into a complaint in federal court. If the employee should fail to file the federal court complaint within 90 days of receipt of the right-to-sue letter, the case is over. Therefore, the Title VII plaintiff who waits more than 90 days to start his or her federal court Title VII action will be barred from doing so, irrespective of the fact that he or she had timely filed the charge with the EEOC.

Although the ADEA plaintiff, like the Title VII plaintiff, must first file the charge with the EEOC, the similarity of ADEA with Title VII procedures stops at that point. Unlike a Title VII plaintiff, the ADEA plaintiff does not require a right-to-sue letter before he or she can start an action in federal court. The ADEA plaintiff may file a federal court action at any time after 60 days following filing of the charge with the EEOC. However, the ADEA plaintiff has two different statutes of limitations to keep in mind. First, the federal suit must be commenced within two years of the alleged unlawful discrimination. Second, in cases where the ADEA plaintiff can show a case of willful, or intentional, violation of ADEA, the plaintiff will have up to three years instead of two, to commence the action in federal court. Since the cases of willful violations of ADEA are rare, the second statute of limitations for the typical ADEA plaintiff is that he or she must start an action in federal court within two years after the alleged age discrimination.

As with Title VII complaints, it is equally true in ADEA actions that if the ADEA plaintiff misses the statute of limitations within which to commence a federal court action, his or her federal ADEA action is over. In the ADEA case, as in the Title VII case, missing the second statute of limitations cannot be cured by having timely filed a charge with the EEOC. Thus, no matter how timely the filing with the EEOC, the ADEA plaintiff will have forfeited the federal court action unless it is commenced within two years after the alleged age discrimination. As was noted previously, it is not uncommon for an ADEA plaintiff to assume that, having timely filed the EEOC complaint, he or she can afford to wait until that agency has completed its investigation and conciliation of the complaint before bringing suit in federal court. While this may be perfectly logical, it is not the law, and the ADEA plaintiff as well as the employer must be alert to the possibility that the employee will lose the right to bring an ADEA action into federal court if he or she allows it to remain before the EEOC for too long a period of time. Accordingly, an employer faced with an ADEA complaint filed with the EEOC, should be aware of the potential benefit to the employer that could result from lengthy procedures before the EEOC regarding that complaint. Table 2 sets out in summary form the relevant limitations periods associated with Title VII and the ADEA.

So far, we have been talking only of statutes of limitations for discrimination actions brought under federal law. However, it is important to remember that there are also different statutes of limitations for EEO actions brought under state laws. As noted previously, often a complaint will be "double filed," or filed under both a state and federal EEO statute. The interplay between state and federal statutes of limitations remains unclear and will vary from state to state. Pending clarification of this procedural law, we must limit ourselves to stating that it is likely that the different statutes of limitations applicable to each statute must be met by the complainant. This becomes more complex when one considers that the statute of limitations under state EEO laws are often different from those described previously under Title VII or ADEA.

As was stated previously, 42 out of 50 states have state EEO agencies as well as state statutes making employment discrimination unlawful if based on certain considerations such as race, color, sex, age, religion, national origin, and so forth. Each of the state fair employment statutes has its own statute of limitations period within which an employee must file his or her complaint. These state statutes of limitations vary according to the state, and range from a minimum of 30 days to a maximum period of one year. Table 1 lists the various states and the District of Columbia, and the respective statute of limitations under the applicable state fair employment law.

In New York the statute of limitations under the New York State Human Rights Law is one year. While Doe's complaint is timely under the Human Rights Law, we should note that he has neglected to allege age discrimination under the Human Rights Law regarding the failure to promote him. Since the promotion occurred on May 4, 1986, Doe has until May 4, 1987—two more months—to amend his complaint under the Human Rights Law to allege age discrimination regarding the failure to promote. This is especially important since, in New York, age discrimination in employment is unlawful where the employee is 18 years of age or older. Unlike the ADEA, there is no maximum age at which age discrimination becomes lawful. The New York Human Rights Law makes it equally unlawful to discriminate against employees who are 19 and 99 years of age. By contrast, the ADEA protects employees from age discrimination only if they are between the ages of 40 and 70.

In addition to the expanded coverage under the Human Rights Law, we should also note that Doe's ADEA-based action is time-barred insofar as it seeks to challenge failure to promote. Since New York is a deferral state, Doe's complaint should have been filed within 300 days after the alleged unlawful discriminatory practice. If Doe was challenging the failure to promote, which promotion occurred May 4, 1986, he should have filed his ADEA-based complaint no later than February 28, 1987. Similarly, his Title VII-based complaint, as regards the failure to promote, is equally time-barred for the same reason.

Even though Doe's Title VII and ADEA actions are time-barred insofar as he challenges the promotion of Que in 1986, the respondent would be well advised to keep this information to itself for a while. The employer should wait until after May 4, 1987 to raise this defense. At that time Mr. Doe will also have lost his right to challenge the promotion under the New York State Human Rights Law, which has a longer statute of limitations period, of one year.

PRIVATE SETTLEMENT WITH THE COMPLAINANT

An employer's reaching a private settlement with an employee who has filed a charge of discrimination is encouraged by the EEO agencies and, depending on the circumstances of the case, may be in the employer's interest in the long run. From the standpoint of the federal and state EEO agencies, early settlement between employer and employee is welcomed and indeed encouraged in the face of an enormous caseload. Also from the employer's perspective, early settlement may be the wisest course of action depending upon the circumstances of the case. As a result of having dealt with hundreds of discrimination claims, it is this author's experience that on a proper set of facts, early settlement usually favors the employer. Therefore while the initial response of the employer to a discrimination complaint is understandably one of indignation, the employer faced with an EEO complaint should seriously consider whether a settlement is possible, and candidly consider agreeing to a settlement for several reasons.

First, as previously noted, early settlement tends to favor the employer at a time when the former employee continues to identify with the employer and the employer's company. It is this author's experience that within the first 90 days after a complaint of unlawful termination is filed, the employee nevertheless continues his or her psychological attachment to the former employer and to the employer's business. Also during this period of time, the terminated employee is still experiencing the immediate trauma that accompanies termination, especially at a time before the employee has become adjusted to living without his or her former income. As a result of these factors the terminated employee often makes initial demands that are relatively modest, making possible easy settlement and withdrawal of the complaint at an early stage. Often a promise of the next available opening, or merely of a full in-house investigation, may induce the employee to withdraw the charge. Also at this early stage, back pay liability is minimal, so that back pay may be waived by the employee, or compromised for a token amount.

Second, an employer's own analysis of the circumstances of the particular case may lead the employer to conclude that, on balance, settlement is more attractive than would be spending substantial time and money, and exposing the company to state and federal probes. The employer should not automatically reject reinstatement as part of a settlement. In many cases where there has been a reduction in force or similar mass layoff, it may make no real difference to the employer which of several employees are terminated.

In a related context, the employer should candidly investigate the circumstances of a case where an employee is terminated because of problems with a supervisor. In large companies with more than one department, it is not uncommon that a challenged termination is the result of a personality conflict between a supervisor and subordinate employee. In such a case the employer should draw its own conclusions about the underlying source of the conflict, and may conclude that an expensive discrimination law suit is too high a price to pay for a supervisor on a "power trip." Where the conflict between a supervisor and employee is a result of different and conflicting philosophies toward the work, the employer, and/or the employee's attitude, then it is appropriate to bar reinstatement. However, if the conflict between supervisor and the terminated employee reflects differing philosophies about life in general, or reflects different lifestyles, then the employer should seriously question whether he or she wants to spend time and money reflexively defending another employee who happens to be a supervisor.

Settlement prior to agency investigation avoids agency involvement in the employer's business; and it avoids any agency determination. Although settlement is always possible, it is only at this early stage that the settlement can be negotiated in the context of no agency finding or determination. As we shall see later, a settlement after the investigation has been completed is framed in the context of a conciliation agreement, or similarly worded document, which recites the fact that the investigation disclosed probable cause to support the allegation of unlawful discrimination. Similarly, a settlement prior to, during, or subsequent to an administrative hearing, will also note that the notice of hearing was the result of a finding of probable cause. The EEO agencies and the EEOC routinely maintain an index of respondents, including prior findings of probable cause in earlier cases against the same respondent, so that it is desirable to eliminate this possibility if it can be accomplished.

Settlement prior to the investigation is effected by the employer communicating directly with the complainant. There is no requirement that the agency be contacted or otherwise involved in this early settlement process. If successful, the settlement is reduced to writing, and the complainant is obligated to withdraw the complaint. Typically, complainants may not simply withdraw the complaints on their own volition, as would a plaintiff in a private action. Rather, EEO agencies and the EEOC, require that the complainant formally request to withdraw the complaint. In practice this is little more than a formality, since the EEO agency or

TABLE 5 Settlement Form

STATE OF NEW YORK : EXECUTIVE DEPARTMENT
STATE DIVISION OF HUMAN RIGHTS

State Division of Human Rights
   on the Complaint of   STIPULATION OF SETTLEMENT

JOHN DOE,
    Complainant,   Case No.
    -against-

ABC CO.,
    Respondent.

IT IS HEREBY STIPULATED AND AGREED, by and between the parties herein, that this matter be settled upon the following terms and conditions:

1. Complainant John Doe shall request to withdraw with prejudice his complaints currently pending before the New York State Division of Human Rights and the Equal Employment Opportunity Commission. John Doe shall not commence or file any other complaints against ABC Co. before any State, City or Federal agency, in any State or Federal Court or with any union under any collective bargaining agreement.

2. Upon notification of such withdrawals of said complaints, ABC Co. will reinstate John Doe to his previous position with ABC Co., without back pay. In addition, ABC Co. shall consider John Doe for the next available position as a Foreman in any ABC Co. factory located in New York State.

3. By entering into this stipulation of settlement, ABC Co. does not admit violation of any State or Federal statute, and specifically denies any violation of Title VII of the 1964 Civil Rights Act, of the Age Discrimination in Employment Act, or of the New York State Human Rights Law. This settlement is not to be construed as an admission by ABC Co. of violation of any State or Federal statute, nor of any of the aforesaid statutes.

Dated: New York, New York
     March 27, 1987

JOHN DOE
ABC CO.

By _____
TOM SMITH

TABLE 6 Letter to SDHR after Private Settlement

March 28, 1987
John Doe
1 Any Street
New York, New York

State Division of Human Rights
270 Broadway
New York, New York

RE: John Doe v. ABC Co.
    Case No.

Dear Investigator:

I am hereby requesting that my above complaint be withdrawn with prejudice upon the basis of a Stipulation of Settlement between the parties, a copy of which is annexed hereto.

Yours truly,

_____
JOHN DOE

EEOC routinely grant such requests, except for unique test cases of highly politicized complaints.

Let us assume for the moment in our hypothetical case, that a settlement has been concluded with Doe as a result of conversations had between Doe and ABC Company's EEO officer. The settlement terms are that

TABLE 7 Letter to EEOC after Private Settlement

March 28, 1987
John Doe
1 Any Street
New York, New York

Equal Employment Opportunity
  Commission
26 Federal Plaza
New York, New York

RE: John Doe v. ABC Co.
    Case No.

Dear Investigator:

I am hereby requesting that my above complaint filed under Title VII of the 1964 Civil Rights Act and under the Age Discrimination in Employment Act, be withdrawn with prejudice upon the basis of a Stipulation of Settlement between the parties, a copy of which is annexed hereto.

Yours truly,

_____
JOHN DOE

TABLE 8 SDHR Order of Withdrawal

STATE OF NEW YORK : EXECUTIVE DEPARTMENT
STATE DIVISION OF HUMAN RIGHTS

State Division of Human Rights
  on the complaint of

JOHN DOE,
    Complainant,

    Case No.

  -against-

ABC CO.,
    Respondent.

ORDER OF WITHDRAWAL

On March 3, 1987, John Doe, who is black, filed a verified complaint with the State Division of Human Rights charging the above-named respondent with an unlawful discriminatory practice relating to employment because of his race, color and age in violation of the Human Rights Law of the State of New York.

Thereafter, the complainant notified the Division of the withdrawal of the complaint in a written communication dated March 28, 1987.

Pursuant to the Human Rights Law and the Rules of Practice of the Division, the complaint is ordered withdrawn and the file is closed.

DATED AND MAILED: April 1, 1987

STATE DIVISION OF HUMAN RIGHTS

s/
REGIONAL DIRECTOR

TO: John Doe
    1 Any Street   COMPLAINANT
    New York, New York

    ABC Co.
    1 Any Other Street   RESPONDENT
    New York, New York

Doe will be reinstated with back pay and will be considered for the next available position as a foreman in any ABC Co. factory located in New York. In return Doe has agreed to withdraw both his federal and state complaints, and not to bring any other complaints regarding the termination or alleged failure to promote him in March 1986. Table 5 contains a form for the written settlement agreement between ABC Co. and Doe; Table 6 is a copy of a proposed "request to withdraw" from Doe to the NYSDHR; Table 7 is the "request to withdraw" addressed to the EEOC; Table 8 is the order of withdrawal from the NYSDHR; and Table 9 is the order of withdrawal from the EEOC (remember that the employer must conclude both the state-based and federal-based complaints).

TABLE 9 EEOC Order of Withdrawal

EQUAL EMPLOYMENT OPPORTUNITY COMMISSION
NEW YORK DISTRICT OFFICE
90 CHURCH STREET, ROOM 1501
NEW YORK, NEW YORK 10007

264-7161

John Doe
1 Any Street
New York, New York

RE: Charge No.

Dear Mr. Doe:

Your charge of employment discrimination has been withdrawn in accordance with your request.

On behalf of the Commission:

April 1, 1987	s/
Date	District Director

THE INVESTIGATORY QUESTIONNAIRE

Either simultaneous with notice of the charge or sometime thereafter, the employer will receive an investigatory questionnaire from the EEO agency investigating the complaint. This will not always be the same EEO agency with which the complaint was filed since, as we have seen, charges filed with the EEOC ordinarily are deferred to the appropriate state EEO agency. The questionnaire may come within a few weeks or a few months of notice of filing of the charge. The delay will vary depending on the backlog of the particular EEO agency.

The investigatory questionnaire should be taken seriously for several reasons. Any response to the questionnaire will require the employer to take a position with regard to the allegations contained in the charge. Clearly the employer will find it difficult if not impossible to change his or her position once it is adopted. In other words, the employer effectively will be unable to claim that the employee was dismissed because of a reduction in staff, if he or she has already said that the employee was dismissed because of poor work performance. Thus, the employer's response to the investigatory questionnaire must be carefully planned, so as to take full advantage of the best available defense, or defenses.

Another reason for taking the investigatory questionnaire seriously is that it may possibly eliminate the need for a sit-down conference. EEO agencies would prefer to dispose of EEO complaints without taking the time for a conference, and will do so in those cases where the complaint is clearly without merit or is susceptible to a documentary defense. While successful defense of an EEO complaint resulting in dismissal prior to an investigatory conference is not common, it does occur in limited situations and the possibility of such a resolution should not be overlooked.

A documentary defense would be available where simple reference to employee records and/or employer rules and regulations establishes conclusively that the complaint is without merit. As an example of a hypothetical documentary defense, let us assume that an employee has been terminated for violation of a written company regulation. Let us assume further that the employee has admitted in writing to having committed such violation. In such a situation, mere transmittal of a copy of the regulation together with a copy of the written admission, should suffice to successfully dispose of the complaint without further agency involvement.

It is unlikely that such a clear case of a documentary defense will present itself. More often, a documentary defense will be attempted where the employee has denied any violation of a company regulation, but has been unsuccessful in a grievance filed with a union. It is not uncommon for the employee/grievant to lose his or her grievance at the first or second level, and then discover that the union is not inclined to pursue the matter any further. While the disposition of a grievance filed under a collective bargaining agreement does not control automatically the outcome of the EEO complaint, it is clear that the EEO agency inevitably will suspect that a complaint may be without merit if it has already been tried and lost in a different forum.

Other examples of possible documentary defenses are where the complainant has failed to attain certain objectives that had been required as a condition of employment. Thus, a foreign-trained nurse or physician may have failed to qualify to practice in the United States within a specified period of time, or a recent graduate of a professional school may have failed to obtain his or her professional license within the requisite amount of time.

If the employer's position is that the termination was the result of a reduction in force, a documentary defense may be available by reference to the employee's personnel file. Thus, for example, the employer may be able to document that all employees with less than a certain number of years of employment were laid off, and that the complainant's personnel file demonstrates that he or she had less than the minimum number of years of employment necessary to avoid the layoff.

As has been previously stated, the investigatory questionnaire should be carefully considered even where it is not possible to avoid a conference by way of a documentary defense. The questionnaire will commit the employer to adopt a specific defense, which necessarily must be maintained throughout the case. The questionnaire should not be completed in haste. Accordingly, the first step that the employer should take is to request additional time to respond to the questionnaire. Such a request will routinely be granted.

The employer will require ample time to respond to the questionnaire because he or she first will conduct his or her own investigation into the complaint. The employer should not automatically dismiss the allegations in the complaint without having investigated such allegations personally.

While it is understandable that an employer would prefer to believe that his or her supervisors and other employees acted in accordance with the law, it is clear that the employer should uncover any illegal acts by his or her employees and agents before such acts are uncovered by the EEO agency.

At a minimum, any supervisors, agents, or employees should be required to present their positions to a neutral body within the company. An *ad hoc* task force recruited from various departments, or an ongoing EEO department within the company, are the best approaches because they offer greater guarantee of an objective result. In addition, existing documentation and memoranda relating to the complaint should be examined to ascertain whether they corroborate or undermine the position taken by supervisors or similar employees in response to the complaint.

If the employer's in-house investigation results in a finding that the complaint has merit, careful consideration should be given to a settlement. The employer should avoid the reflexive position that will merely saddle him or her with the consequences of an unauthorized and illegal act of an employee. Simply stated, a personal grudge or racially discriminatory bias of one employee should not become elevated to the status of a company problem. Early settlement is almost always less expensive than a later settlement, and it is certainly less expensive than losing an EEO lawsuit. Most if not all EEO agencies encourage settlement at any stage of the process, and this should be explored if the in-house investigation discloses significant weaknesses in the employer's position.

Properly conducted, the in-house investigation will uncover critical strengths and weaknesses in the employer's position, and will assist him or her in preparing a specific response to the questionnaire. Table 10 is a sample investigatory questionnaire from the New York State Division of Human Rights. Table 11 is a proposed response to the questionnaire, and Table 12 is a proposed affidavit to be included with the response.

In our hypothetical case, the respondent has already conducted an internal investigation of the charges in the complaint and we shall see that this information is used in preparing the employer's response. Initially, we note that the complainant is never referred to by his name. This is intentional, and is designed to de-personalize the complaint. In addition, in as many answers as possible, a direct answer has been avoided by referring the investigator to the annexed affidavit of the employer's EEO officer. This allows the employer to frame the responses in a context favorable to the employer, and to avoid one-dimensional responses so as to facilitate a multidimensional defense.

For example, the answer to question C.1.b does not commit the employer to a defense that the complainant was terminated for lying on his initial application for employment. Rather, where the question asks the reason for the "treatment received by the complainant," the division is referred to the affidavit of the employer's EEO officer. The affidavit notes that the complainant lied on his initial employment application, and that such conduct warrants immediate dismissal under established company policy. However, rather than rely on this alone, the affidavit also attests to the complainant's poor work performance, and does so in a manner that anticipates a rebuttal that the complainant received a "good"

TABLE 10 Investigatory Questionnaire

STATE DIVISION OF HUMAN RIGHTS	DOCUMENT AND INFORMATION REQUESTED (INVESTIGATION OR DENIAL OF EQUAL TERMS, CONDITIONS, AND PRIVILEGES OF EMPLOYMENT COMPLAINT) CASE No(s)
On the complaint(s) of JOHN DOE, COMPLAINANT(S) vs. ABC CO., RESPONDENT	

TO:

Please take notice that you are to supply one original and one copy of the following to the New York State Division of Human Rights on or before

_____ 198 _____

A. A written narrative reply to each numbered paragraph of the complaint.

B. *Document Request* (If the request has an "a" section and a "b" section, answer "a" for denial of promotion complaints and "b" for difference in treatment complaints)

_____ 1. Provide a copy of all documents contained in the entire personnel folder of the complainant or such other file maintained for personnel purposes as you may keep.

_____ 2a. Provide a copy of any job posting and a job description for the position which the complainant wanted promotion to. If there is no written description describe in detail the duties of and the requirements for the position.

_____ 2b. Provide a copy of respondent's policy and procedure manual which is applicable to the matter complained of (i.e., shop rules, disciplinary procedures, etc.). In none exists, describe in detail.

_____ 3a. Provide copies of all documents contained in the entire personnel folders of the people considered for the promotion or such files maintained for personnel purpose as you may keep.

_____ 3b. Provide copies of all documents contained in the entire personnel folders of employees who have been treated similarly to the complainant or such other files maintained for personnel purposes as you may keep.

_____ 4. Submit the EEO-1 Report form for the following year(s):

_____ 5. Submit all forms used in: (a) requesting references for prospective employees and (b) preparing reference replies for past or current employees.

C. *Information Request* (If the request has an "a" section and a "b" section, answer "a" for denial of promotion complaints and "b" for difference in treatment complaints.)

_____ 1a. State the specific reason(s) why the complainant was not promoted (attach additional sheets if necessary).

_____ 1b. State the specific reason(s) for the treatment received by the complainant.

TABLE 10 *(Continued)*

_____ 2a. State the (i) name, (ii) address, (iii) telephone number, (iv) race, (v) age, (vi) job title, and (vii) length of service of each person who participated in the decision to not promote the complainant and to promote the successful candidate. Indicate the role that each person played in the decision.

_____ 2b. State the (i) name, (ii) address, (iii) telephone number, (iv) race, (v) age, (vi) job title and (vii) length of service of each person who participated in the treatment received by the complainant. Indicate the role that each person played.

_____ 3. Were any warnings made to the complainant? If so, state the date(s), person(s) present, and the circumstances under which such warnings were made. Attach copies of all records of such warnings and specify respondent's policy with respect to them.

_____ 4a. State the (i) name, (ii) address, (iii) telephone number, (iv) date of hire, and (v) race, creed, color, national origin, age, and sex of all employees holding the job which the complainant wanted promotion to.

_____ 4b. State the (i) name, (ii) address, (iii) telephone number, (iv) date of hire and race, creed, color, national origin, age and sex of all employees holding the same job as the complainant.

_____ 5a. How many employees have been given a same or similar promotion to the one that the complainant was interested in? State the (i) name, (ii) date of hire, (iii) original title, (iv) date of promotion and (v) new job title. Limit to the last 24 months.

_____ 5b. How many employees have been given warnings or penalties or the type of treatment which gave rise to this complaint? State the (i) name, (ii) date of hire, (iii) job title, (iv) penalty, and (v) circumstances. Limit to the last 24 months.

_____ 6. What performance standards was complainant expected to meet? What standards did complainant fail to meet?

_____ 7. Did the complainant ever complain about receiving discriminatory treatment on the job? If so, specify the nature of the complaint(s), date(s) of complaint(s), the person(s) involved, and explain what was done pursuant to the complaint(s).

_____ 8. Name the person with authority to make settlement decision(s) for the respondent:

Name and Title of Person Completing Inquiry

I HEREBY CERTIFY THAT I HAVE AUTHORITY TO ANSWER THE INQUIRY ON BEHALF OF RESPONDENT.

_____
Signature

_____
(Area Code)   Telephone Number

_____
Date completed

TABLE 11 Response to Investigatory Questionnaire

STATE OF NEW YORK : EXECUTIVE DEPARTMENT
STATE DIVISION OF HUMAN RIGHTS

State Division of Human Rights
on the Complaint of

JOHN DOE,
    Complainant,
-against-

ABC CO.,
    Respondent.

RESPONSE TO INVESTIGATORY
QUESTIONNAIRE
Case No.

A. *As to particular No. 1:* The complainant had been employed at ABC Co.'s New York factory since 1955. The respondent does not dispute the complainant's allegations regarding his age and his race.

As to particular No. 2: The complainant was terminated on or about March 2, 1987. On March 1, 1987 the complainant admitted to ABC Co.'s Personnel Director that he had lied on his initial application for employment. *See,* Affidavit of Tom Smith, annexed hereto. This was one contributing factor in the decision to terminate the complainant. *See,* Affidavit of Tom Smith, and part C(1)(a), following.

As to particular No. 3: Insofar as the complaint fails to identify the "younger, white, employee," to which the complainant is referring, the respondent is currently unable to respond to this numbered paragraph. In this respect it should be noted that the respondent has at least one factory and fifty employees in each of the fifty states.

As to particular No. 4: ABC Co. strenuously denies any violation of any State or Federal laws, and specifically denies any violation of the New York State Human Rights Law, of Title VII of the 1964 Civil Rights act, or of the Age Discrimination in Employment Act.

B.1–Included herewith is a copy of the complainant's complete personnel file.

B.2a–Not Applicable

B.2b–See annexed Affidavit of Tom Smith.

B.3a–Not Applicable

B.3b–The respondent employs thousands of employees throughout the fifty states. There is an ongoing process of employees being terminated and hired. It would be unduly burdensome to the respondent and of no investigatory value to the Division, for the respondent to produce the complete personnel file of every employee it has ever terminated. The respondent would be prepared to comply with a more narrowly tailored request appropriate to the issues presented by the within complaint.

B.4–Included herewith are the EEO-1 forms for the year 1986.

B.5–ABC Co. does not have any form for such purposes.

C.1a–Not Applicable

C.1b–See, annexed Affidavit of Tom Smith.

C.2a–Not Applicable

TABLE 11 *(Continued)*

C.2b–See, annexed Affidavit of Tom Smith.

C.3–No specific warnings were given to the complainant for two reasons. First, the respondent was unaware that the complainant had lied on his original application for employment until the complainant admitted it on March 1, 1987. Second, the complainant routinely received copies of his Annual Performance Evaluations, and thus was aware of his deteriorating performance. See, also, Affidavit of Tom Smith.

C.4a–Not Applicable

C.4b–See, response to b.3b.

5.a–Not Applicable

5.b–Not Applicable

6. See, Affidavit of Tom Smith.

7. The complainant worked amicably for the respondent from 1955 to 1987 without ever registering a complaint of discriminatory treatment. See, Affidavit of Tom Smith.

8. Insofar as it is the respondent's position that the complaint is without any merit, the respondent is not prepared to enter into a settlement of this matter.

TABLE 12 Affidavit Included with Response to Investigatory Questionnaire

STATE OF NEW YORK : EXECUTIVE DEPARTMENT
STATE DIVISION OF HUMAN RIGHTS

State Division of Human Rights on the Complaint of	AFFIDAVIT
JOHN DOE, Complainant, -against-	Case No.
ABC CO., Respondent.	

STATE OF NEW YORK)
COUNTY OF NEW YORK) s.s.:

TOM SMITH, being duly sworn, deposes and says:

1. I am the Equal Employment Opportunity (EEO) Officer of ABC Co. I submit this Affidavit in response to the investigatory questionnaire in this matter.

2. The complainant in this matter was employed by ABC Co. from April 1, 1955 up to and including March 2, 1987. The complainant was employed at ABC Co.'s widget factory in New York.

3. Commencing in or about 1985, the complainant's job performance began deteriorating. The complainant began to display a hostile attitude towards his fellow workers, and especially towards his supervisor. Although the complainant's attitude was hostile in general, at no time did he ever complain to anybody re-

TABLE 12 *(Continued)*

garding any alleged discriminatory treatment. In addition, the complainant's attitude that things should still be done as they were done thirty years ago when he commenced employment, caused the respondent significant problems on certain occasions.

4. Although the above problems with the complainant started to become obvious in 1985, it was decided that he should be given a chance to improve, in consideration of his thirty years of employment with the respondent. Accordingly, the complainant was given the same rating that he had received for the prior year, with a verbal warning that the rating would be lowered the following year in the absence of improvement. Therefore, the rating of "Good" that the complainant received in 1984 was repeated for 1985, although it was clear to all parties concerned that the rating was in fact too high and subject to correction in the absence of improvement by the complainant.

5. Unfortunately, the complainant's work performance continued to deteriorate. By 1986, the complainant's supervisor could no longer keep these problems from being reflected in the written record. Accordingly, the complainant's performance evaluation for 1986 was lowered to "Satisfactory", this time with a verbal warning that he would face termination if his work performance did not improve.

6. For the past five years, the ABC Co. has been experiencing severe financial problems resulting from an influx of cheap widgets from Japan. A Task Force established to consider this problem recommended in January 1987 that respondent reduce its payroll expense by discharging all nonessential employees whose current Annual Performance Evaluation rating had declined from the prior year's rating. The complainant was one of the employees in this category.

7. In addition, in or about February 1987, respondent discovered that complainant had lied on his original application for employment. When confronted with this information on March 1, 1987, the complainant admitted to having lied on the employment application. Although it has never been reduced to writing, the respondent has an established rule of long standing that any intentional misrepresentation on an employment application mandates immediate dismissal.

8. Based upon all of the foregoing, the decision was made by the undersigned to terminate the services of the complainant as of March 2, 1987.

_____

TOM SMITH

Sworn to before me
this 5th day of May 1987

s/ Notary Public
_____

rating less than two years prior. Thus, the affidavit notes that the complainant's work performance had been deteriorating for some time, but that he had been given a "good" rating in 1985 essentially as a favor for his long tenure with the employer.

Certain questions have been answered with an explanation as to why the question is unduly burdensome, and some questions have not been answered at all, on the basis that they are not relevant to the complaint.

Thus, question B.3.b, requesting complete personnel files of other terminated employees, has met with the employer response that is as irrelevant and unduly burdensome to forward such files for all terminated employees, especially considering the employer's substantial labor force. Presumably, the personnel files of all employees terminated for lying on their applications for employment, or for poor work performance, could be supplied at a later date in response to a more limited request.

All questions dealing with failure to promote have been answered with the response that the questions are "not applicable." This preserves the employer's defense to any enlargement or amendment of the SDHR complaint to include failure to promote in May 1986. As we have seen, the allegation has been made in the federal complaints but not in the state complaint. However, having occurred more than 300 days prior to the date of filing—May 4, 1986 to March 3, 1987—such allegations are time-barred under the federal statutes. Such allegation is still timely under the state statute, since the time limit there is a full year. Thus, the employer's response avoids raising the issue while it is still timely under the state statute, in the hope that the missing allegation in the state complaint will not be noticed until it is too late. As an alternative, the employer might well consider the advisability of deferring any response at all, for another two months, so that the state time limit will have already expired when the employer's response is received. This then, is another good reason for requesting additional time to respond to the questionnaire.

Finally we note that the employer has refused to consider settlement at this point. Whether or not a settlement is ultimately reached, it is probably good practice to adopt a stated policy of no settlement at least until the employer has had a chance to explain his or her position. This preserves the employer's options and gives additional credibility to the employer's position.

DEALING WITH REQUESTS FOR INFORMATION AND DOCUMENTS

It is axiomatic that an employer does not have to reveal information that is not in his or her possession. With this in mind, employers should re-evaluate the records that they are preserving, some of which will never be useful to any one except a Title VII or ADEA plaintiff. If employees undergo written performance evaluations every year, the employer should carefully consider whether he or she wishes to retain evaluations that are more than three years old. There is nothing more defeating to an employer's defense of an ADEA claim, than 10 years of "excellent" performance evaluations. Personnel departments have an understandable desire to maintain a "complete" file on each employee, but employers must be wary least the "complete" file be used against them.

It is worth noting at this point that employers should be aware that performance evaluations may one day be the object of an EEO agency's investigation. Given this understanding, supervisors and personnel managers should be instructed that the evaluations are to be completed candidly. Many organizations have employees who are neither the best nor the worst in the company. In many cases these employees may fairly be characterized as mediocre. These mediocre employees tend to remain in their positions for long periods of time without either a promotion or a demotion.

When the company's financial picture is bright, there is often a tendency to retain these employees. In addition, they may periodically receive minimal pay increases to keep pace with inflation. Since these employees are not targeted for imminent termination, they typically will receive "satisfactory" ratings on annual performance evaluations. This all and often does occur in the context that truly good performers receive "excellent" ratings on their annual performance evaluations, and receive periodic pay increases well in excess of that needed to keep pace with inflation.

In times of financial difficulty, the "mediocre" employees are the logical choices for termination should there be a reduction in force. The problem occurs when this "mediocre" employee files his or her age discrimination complaint. Because this "mediocre" employee has neither been promoted nor demoted, he or she typically has substantially greater seniority than those in his or her level who were retained. It is also predictable that those who were retained are substantially younger and have been earning more money than this "mediocre" employee. The final blow for the employer occurs when this "mediocre" employee exhibits in front of the EEO agency (or jury) year-after-year of "satisfactory" performance evaluations. The EEO agency, or jury, will then pose the inescapable question of why a long-time satisfactory employee, who was never demoted, and who periodically received salary increases, has been terminated in place of younger similarly situated employees with less seniority and who were nevertheless earning more money.

An employer can avoid this problem by requiring candid completion of annual performance evaluations. Thus, for example, a "mediocre" employee should receive an "unsatisfactory" or "poor" rating, or the equivalent, on the performance report. In the alternative, the supervisor should include a comment to the effect that, "Mr. X is a poor performer, but I recommend that he be retained in his present position in order to give him a chance to improve." If this poor performer receives a salary increase, a note should be made that the increase is intended solely to keep pace with inflation, and is not to be interpreted as a merit-based salary increase. In this fashion, employers may safely retain employees, and without sparing them possible blunt criticism, may avoid possible legal liability in the event it becomes necessary to terminate them.

Our hypothetical case presents us with the classic scenario. Here, the complainant received a "good" rating in 1985 even though his work performance was deteriorating. As is established in the affidavit of the respondent employer's EEO officer, the complainant's work had deteriorated but, in view of his long tenure, the complainant was given only a verbal warning. Two years later, this comes back to haunt the employer, who must explain to a skeptical investigator why a "good" employee was terminated on the basis of "poor" work performance. This also detracts credibility from the "satisfactory" rating Doe received just the prior year. Clearly, the employer would be in a more favorable position had it given

Doe "unsatisfactory" ratings in 1985 and 1986, or at least included written statements documenting Doe's poor work performance.

Potential EEO plaintiffs may wish to compare their job applications with the applications of other employees who were retained, in an attempt to demonstrate that they had superior qualifications and educational background to similarly situated employees who were not terminated. It is evident that such a showing would be difficult, if not impossible, in the event that the old job applications were not available.

Employers should not rush to discard all personnel information now maintained, because certain employee records are necessary for arriving at informed employment decisions. In addition, some state and federal regulations require employers to maintain records for varying periods of time. At a minimum, however, employers should take inventory as to the types of employee records they are keeping, and whether maintenance of such records is truly beneficial to the company. If any of the records are neither necessary for business purposes, nor required by state or federal regulations, then serious consideration should be given to discarding them.

Those employee records that are maintained may someday be the object of an administrative request for production or examination. In the course of an investigation, the employer should be aware that a flat refusal to produce requested information will almost guarantee a finding of probably cause by an overworked investigator looking for any reason to "close" a file. On the other hand, producing too much information runs the risk of unforseen problems surfacing beyond any possible redemption.

In our hypothetical case, for example, the employer should be aware of the 1986 letter written by the EEO officer and of its potential for causing legal problems. The respondent's defense of poor work performance is seriously compromised by the statement in the letter that "there . . . is not much difference between the ["good" and "satisfactory"] ratings." In addition, the tone of the letter indicates that Que was promoted instead of Doe on the basis of her sex. Keeping all this in mind, the respondent should be alert to the dangers posed by the letter, and should refrain from producing it.

On balance it would seem that the best idea is to appear forthcoming while relying on the investigator to forgo a full examination. Thus, for example, requests for information might be met with prompt agreement to produce the materials if they are available and if they are not unduly burdensome. This gives the employer time to "conduct the search" and avoids making the investigator adamant. In fact, the investigator, who has many other cases to investigate, will usually agree to a delay of several weeks or a month, without any objection.

If the material requested is voluminous, its production should not automatically be denied. Instead, an employer might wish to advise the investigator that, due to the amount of information requested, only a "representative sample" of the material being requested will physically be produced at the offices of the EEOC or of the state EEO agency. At the same time, the investigator could be invited to inspect the remainder of the records at the employer's office. Often, an investigator will decide that he or she has better things to do than to spend a day poring through files at somebody else's office. If the investigator does show up, he or she will psychologically feel impelled to finish his or her examination by the close of the business day. If the records being examined have been collected from various offices or locations, the investigator should be made aware of this fact. In addition, the records should be redistributed to their original locations as soon as is practicable after the investigator leaves the premises. Once having made the trip to the employer's offices, it is unlikely that the investigator will want to return. At that point, when and if the complainant asserts that further examination is necessary, the investigator will run interference for the employer in justifying why further disclosure is unnecessary or irrelevant.

SUBPOENAS

Sometimes the EEO agency will not request information but will demand it. An official demand for production of evidence comes in the form of a subpoena calling for the production of documents. Compliance with an administrative subpoena is mandatory so long as the items required by the subpoena are reasonably within the scope of the agency's investigation, and production of the items would not be unduly burdensome on the employer. Administrative agencies do not have what is known as the "contempt power," or in lay terms, the power to put someone in jail. Since they lack the contempt power, they must ask a court to order compliance with a subpeona, in the event of noncompliance by the employer.

While courts will usually order compliance with an administrative subpoena, this will require a good deal of time and effort on the part of the agency. Given what has just been discussed, an employer served with an administrative subpoena should be aware that the agency will usually be responsive to a request to compromise, or "modify," the subpoena in return for voluntary complaince. On the other hand, the employer should also be aware that in the event of a blanket refusal to comply with the subpoena, the agency ordinarily will ultimately be successful in securing full compliance by way of a court order, requiring production of all items listed in the subpoena.

An employer should examine the subpoena to determine which arguments may reasonably be advanced in favor of modifying it. The first consideration should be the types of records and information demanded in the subpoena. Except where the employer is defending the termination on grounds of an economic slowdown or retraction, the employer may resist requests for financial records on the grounds that such records are not relevant. Thus, ordinarily, the subpoena will be limited to documents reflecting personnel decisions, such as employee evaluations, job applications, salary history, and so forth. Employee records may be further limited with respect to the employees included. Records regarding employees not in the complainant's unit or department may reasonably be considered irrelevant. Similarly, records regarding employees on a level higher or lower than that of the complainant may arguably be irrelevant.

Another consideration is time. Even where the records demanded in the subpoena are undeniably within the scope of the complaint under investigation, the subpoena may sometimes call for the production of records that are too old to be of any consequence. Production of records going back more than three to five years may often be resisted on the combined grounds that the records are too old to be relevant, that they are legally irrelevant since they go back beyond the applicable statute of limitations, or that their production would be unduly burdensome since they are no longer being stored in a readily accessible form or geographic area.

In addition, employers should not forget that the other employees whose records are being requested may arguably enjoy overriding rights of privacy. This is especially true where the employer is in a business or profession normally associated with recognized rights of confidentiality, such as hospitals and law firms.

The chances for voluntary modification of an administrative subpoena are good at least insofar as the initial subpoena is often overbroad in the first place. The majority of administrative subpoenas issued during an investigation are not drawn with great care, nor are they drawn by attorneys. Administrative subpoenas on the investigatory level are drawn by investigators using forms. Thus, in a termination case the investigator will routinely require all records of the complainant, plus all records of the other employees in the complainant's unit or department. Also it is common for the investigator to require a company-wide breakdown of all employees by age, race, sex, and national origin, despite the fact that these records are sent to the EEOC each year anyway, and often without regard to the actual basis of the complaint. Thus, for example, if the complaint alleges age discrimination only, records and information regarding sex, race, and national origin are irrelevant and their production should be resisted.

Even though production of information required by an administrative subpoena may successfully be resisted, the employer should also consider whether the resistance is really worth the effort. If a complaint is demonstrably spurious, the EEO agency may well be disposed to dismiss the complaint quickly. In such a situation, the employer will not want to give the EEO agency any reason to be suspicious. Thus, the production of even irrelevant information might be in the employer's best interest, so long as he or she is alert to the possible existence of any unforseen "bombshells" in the records being produced.

THE INVESTIGATORY CONFERENCE

The EEO agency will examine the employer's response to the questionnaire to determine whether an investigatory conference should be scheduled. The decision will be made by the investigator assigned to the complaint. The investigatory conference—also known in several states as the fact-finding conference—will be the first opportunity for the respondent and complainant to confront each other in the presence of the investigator. In most cases, the investigatory conference will also be the last step in the investigation, resulting in a subsequent determination by the EEO agency of either probable cause, or of no probable cause.

An investigatory conference is not scheduled in all cases, and it is not mandatory. Rather, it is an optional procedure that is within the discretion of the EEO agency. If, for example, a respondent has been successful in establishing a documentary defense, the EEO agency would issue a finding of no probable cause without an investigatory conference. However, it is also true that in most cases an investigatory conference will be scheduled some time after receipt of the employer's response to the investigatory questionnaire.

There is no reason for an employer to accelerate scheduling of an investigatory conference. Most investigators are working under substantial case loads, so that there ordinarily will be a hiatus of several months between the receipt of the employer's response to the questionnaire, and the scheduling of the investigatory conference. Requests for adjournment of an investigatory conference are routinely granted, so long as the investigator is given a reasonable basis for the request and does not suspect that the employer is engaging in dilatory tactics.

The employer should give careful preparation to the conference, since it will be his or her last real opportunity to avoid a finding of probable cause and the ensuing administrative hearing. The employer should be aware that the investigator usually will be receptive to a well-prepared defense that gives due deference to the EEO agency. Contrary to what many employers might assume, the investigator is usually not as interested in proving a complaint as he or she is in arriving at a supportable decision.

Many state EEO agencies have contracts with the EEOC providing for payment to the state agency for each EEOC-deferred complaint, on a per-case basis. Seen in this light, it becomes clear that a dismissal of a deferred complaint at the investigatory level for lack of probable cause, will result in earlier payment to the state EEO agency than would a finding of probable cause, requiring a full hearing. While the EEOC accordingly carefully monitors the statistical results of investigations to guard against unwarranted findings of no probable cause, employers should be aware that the investigator is often prepared to dismiss a complaint if given an appropriate showing.

If a complaint is groundless, a well-organized defense at the investigatory conference, accompanied by supporting documentary evidence conclusively showing the meritless nature of the complaint, will enable the investigator to quickly arrive at a decision that can be justified to the EEOC liaison officer. Moreover, the performance of investigators is often judged in part by the number of outstanding complaints they are able to resolve, either by settlement, determination of probable cause, or determination of no probable cause. Often the investigator is made aware that the disposition of a certain number of complaints per month is anticipated, or at least, that the greater the number of complaints resolved, the better the EEO agency will feel about that investigator's performance.

The effect of all this is to induce the investigator to arrive at a decision early during the investigation, and thereafter to concentrate on obtaining the minimum amount of evidence necessary to support such a decision.

One should also be aware that, while the investigator has seen a large number of cases of unlawful employment discrimination, he or she has also seen a large number of groundless complaints.

Counsel for the employer are permitted to attend the investigatory conference, although they are not allowed to cross-examine the complainant or the witnesses. There is no "testimony" nor any stenographic transcript of the investigatory conference. Counsel do not function as interrogators; rather, their function is hopefully to channel or direct the scope of the questions asked by the investigator, and to present the employer's defense in an organized fashion.

As a rule it is not recommended that the employer's major witnesses appear at the investigatory conference. In most cases, the employer will be represented by an attorney and EEO or personnel officer. The counsel should have appropriate affidavits from witnesses, or other necessary documentation, such as a personnel file.

Where actual presence of the employer's witnesses might be judged necessary, such as to determine questions of credibility or demeanor, the employer should carefully examine the options available. It is often established policy in the EEO agency that questions of demeanor and credibility are best left for an administrative hearing, in effect requiring a finding of probable cause. In such situation, the presence of the employer's witness may be unavailing and serve only to provide the complainant with the opportunity to question the witness. Unanticipated or spontaneous statements made by the witness may cause substantial injury to the employer's defense with no corresponding benefit to the employer.

In our hypothetical situation, the employer will be represented at the investigatory conference by its attorney and Tom Smith, the EEO officer. Smith will bring with him a copy of his affidavit and Doe's personnel file. The personnel file will include the initial application for employment and the annual performance evaluations for 1985 and 1986.

The counsel for ABC Co. will begin the employer's defense by eliciting from the complainant an admission that he lied on his initial application for employment. Predictably, the complainant will respond that Que also lied on her initial employment application. The respondent's EEO officer then attests to the fact that the complainant's work performance was deteriorating, and shows the investigator the 1986 performance evaluation.

At this point the investigator asks the respondent's counsel to set forth the specific reason for the termination. The respondent's EEO officer answers that the termination was the result of several factors including the combination of the breach of company policy and the poor work performance. Hopefully this establishes a basis for the termination while avoiding the question of Que, who also allegedly lied on her employment application. Thus, the respondent's position will be that Que was not terminated because her work performance was good, whereas Doe's work performance was poor, and that the discovery of the misrepresentation by Doe was just the culmination of employer dissatisfaction with Doe that had been increasing for a long period of time.

For purposes of our hypothetical problem, let us assume that the investigatory conference takes place after May 4, 1987, and that the SDHR complaint has not been amended since its filing. In such situation, the respondent should decline to answer any questions regarding the 1986 promotion of Que. That promotion is not part of the SDHR complaint, and the one-year statute of limitations under the New York Human Rights Law, will have expired. Furthermore, although the alleged failure to promote was included in the complaints under Title VII and the ADEA, such allegation was time-barred at the time it was made, since it was beyond the 300-day limit.

Should the investigator persist in raising questions regarding the alleged failure to promote, the respondent should seriously consider making a formal request for a legal opinion. Most state EEO agencies either formally or informally provide for such requests. The logic behind such a request springs from the fact that the complaint intake and investigation typically is conducted without any attorney being present on the part of the EEO agency. In our hypothetical, such a request will be made after the conference, in writing, and addressed to the EEO agency's General Counsel or analagous officer. The written request need not take any particular form and can be on regular letterhead stationery. The request should identify the specific complaint and the precise legal issue sought to be resolved by the General Counsel. Some EEO agencies maintain a collection of formal legal opinions that can be consulted by interested parties. The request for a legal opinion will be given serious attention and will hold up resolution of the investigation until the legal issue has been decided.

In most instances, the investigatory conference will be the final step in the investigation. Often some additional materials may be requested by the investigator, but this will rarely require a second conference. Thus, for example, in our hypothetical, the investigator might request copies of the personnel files of other employees who have been terminated. Assuming that the request is more narrowly tailored to the facts of the complaint than had been the investigatory questionnaire, the respondent would be well advised to comply with the request, since a failure to comply will almost guarantee a finding of probable cause.

If all has gone well our hypothetical investigator will subsequently cause to be issued, a determination of no probable cause, which will dismiss the complaint. However, it sometimes occurs that the EEO agency will issue a finding of probable cause. This will require the respondent to appear before an administrative law judge at an administrative hearing. The steps leading up to and including the hearing are the subject of Chapter 8.

After a finding of probable cause, the EEO agency will attempt to settle the matter. The process is now called "conciliation" and, if successful, culminates in a conciliation agreement. The major difference between a settlement coupled with a complainant's request to withdraw the complaint, and the conciliation agreement, is that only the latter form recites the fact that a finding of probable cause had been made. This is understandably upsetting to an employer, but it is still preferable to a full hearing if the parties can reach a settlement. In our hypothetical, let us assume that the parties can arrive at a conciliation agreement whereby the complainant is reinstated with back pay, is considered for the next available

TABLE 13 Conciliation Agreement

STATE OF NEW YORK : EXECUTIVE DEPARTMENT
STATE DIVISION OF HUMAN RIGHTS

State Division of Human Rights
  on the Complaint of

JOHN DOE,
    Complainant,   Case No.
  -against-

ABC CO.,
    Respondent.

Order After Conciliation

On March 3, 1987, John Doe, who is Black, filed a verified complaint with the State Division of Human Rights charging the above-named respondent with an unlawful discriminatory practice relating to employment because of his race, color, and age in violation of the Human Rights Law of the State of New York.

After investigation, the Division determined that it had jurisdiction over the complaint and that there was Probable Cause to believe that the respondent had discriminated unlawfully against the complainant on the basis of his race, color, and age in violation of the Human Rights Law of the State of New York.

Thereafter, the parties entered into a Conciliation Agreement upon the following terms and conditions:

1. Respondent shall adhere to the Human Rights Law.
2. Respondent shall reinstate complainant to his former position with the respondent, with back pay.
3. Respondent shall consider the complainant for the next available position as a Foreman at respondent's New York factory.
4. Respondent shall pay the complainant $500 damages for mental anguish.

Pursuant to the Human Rights Law and the Rules of Practice of the Division, the complaint is ordered conciliated upon the foregoing terms and conditions and the file is closed.

DATE AND MAILED: August 1, 1987

STATE DIVISION OF HUMAN RIGHTS

_____
REGIONAL DIRECTOR

TO: John Doe   COMPLAINANT
    1 Any Street
    New York, New York

    ABC Co.   RESPONDENT
    1 Any Other Street
    New York, New York

promotion to foreman at respondent's New York factory, and is given a payment for mental anguish in the amount of $500. Table 13 is the resulting conciliation agreement. However, in the event that the parties do not arrive at a conciliation agreement, Chapter 8 will describe the appropriate steps that the employer may take leading up to and including the administrative hearing.

DEFENDING EMPLOYMENT DISCRIMINATION CHARGES
THE HEARING

Robert N. Marx, J.D.

A finding of probable cause will ordinarily result in either conciliation or a subsequent administrative hearing. Conciliation is synonymous with settlement except that the resulting conciliation agreement will recite the fact that there had been a determination of probable cause. Conciliation, or attempted conciliation, takes place at the investigatory level, and has been discussed in Chapter 7. If the attempt at conciliation is unsuccessful the matter will be referred for an administrative hearing.

In most Equal Employment Opportunity Commission (EEOC)-deferred complaints, the finding by the state Equal Employment Opportunity (EEO) agency will be given substantial weight by the EEOC in arriving at its own decision. In fact in almost all cases, the EEOC will render the same decision as was rendered by the state EEO agency. Thus, for all practical purposes, the finding at the investigatory level by the state EEO agency will effectively end the investigation of the complaint on both the state and federal levels.

The EEOC elects to commence suit in federal court on only a small number of complaints. Typically such complaints represent large numbers of plaintiffs, or involve important issues of law. For the rest of the complaints, the EEOC determination of probable cause or of no probable cause, marks the end of the agency's involvement with the complaint. In either case, with respect to a finding of probable cause or no probable cause, the complainant will receive a notification from the EEOC advising the complainant that he or she has only 90 days within which to start a lawsuit in federal court. This notification, specifically required by Title VII, is known as a right to sue letter.

In contrast to this procedure, state EEO agencies which follow the investigation and public hearing described in Chapter 7, conduct further administrative proceedings after issuance of a determination of probable cause. Typically, a finding of probable cause will result in an administrative hearing on the complaint, which hearing will be before an administrative law judge of the state EEO agency. The administrative law judge is known by different titles in the various state EEO agencies. In some states he or she is known as a "hearing officer," "hearing examiner," or "hearing commissioner." We will refer to the "administrative law judge," which is functionally synonymous with the previous titles.

This chapter will discuss the steps leading up to the administrative hearing, the administrative hearing itself, and the posthearing procedure within the state EEO agency. The administrative hearing, also known as the public hearing, is the second major component of the investigation and public hearing procedure that was outlined in Chapter 7. The administrative hearing is similar to a court trial, except that some of the formalities of a trial are omitted.

During the investigation of the complaint (which was discussed in Chapter 7), employers sometimes appear before the EEO agency without an attorney. Although it is rare for employers to go unrepresented by counsel during the investigation, it can be done successfully in certain cases of marginal merit.

Once the complaint has proceeded beyond a finding of probable cause, it should be clear that professional legal assistance will be necessary. An employer charged with unlawful discrimination by a complainant has already lost the first round when a finding of probable cause has been made. Clearly then, an employer faced with a probable cause finding must seek out reinforcements in the form of an attorney experienced in EEO law.

One of the first steps the EEO attorney can take on behalf of the employer is to attempt to avoid the public hearing. It is not inevitable that an employer who receives a probable cause finding will have to appear at an administrative hearing. While it is generally true that a complaint will be noticed for a public hearing after a probable cause finding and failing conciliation, there are two possible approaches for avoiding the public hearing. Occasionally, one of these two approaches will be successful. The first approach is a formal request to reconsider the case, the second approach is engaging in prehearing settlement discussions.

APPLICATION TO REOPEN

The formal request to reconsider the case is known by different names in different states. In some states it is known as an "application to reopen," in others it is called a "request for redetermination," and in still others it is known by similar names. In New York this formal request is known as an "application to reopen," and since our hypothetical takes place in New York, we will refer to this procedure as an application to reopen.

Although known by different names in different states, application to reopen is functionally the same in the various states, and its use is based on a shared logic. When we referred in Chapter 7 to a formal request for a legal opinion, we noted that underlying that request was the fact that the EEO agency's attorneys ordinarily do not get involved in the EEO agency investigation. Thus, there is a recognition that on occasion, the EEO agency's investigator will improperly apply or interpret the EEO statute under consideration.

Similarly, in providing for applications to reopen, there is a recognition by the EEO agency that the investigators occasionally render incorrect and unsupportable decisions. By providing for applications to reopen, the EEO agency is attempting to weed out those probable cause determinations that are unjustifiable and which would prove wasteful from the EEO agency's perspective. Few applications to reopen are granted, but some are successful and, in any event, all applications to reopen are considered seriously by the EEO agency.

The form for an application to reopen is straightforward; it may be written on the employer's letterhead stationery. Of course, this may vary from state to state, and the employer or his or her EEO attorney should consult the rules of the particular EEO agency. The time within which an application to reopen may be made depends on the EEO agency's rules, but it is fair to state that the rules typically require the application to be made within a reasonable time after the employer's receipt of the determination of probable cause. Also, the issuance of a notice of hearing (to be discussed later in this chapter), will typically cut off any further possibility of an application to reopen.

The application should be addressed to the general counsel of the EEO agency, unless that agency's rules provide otherwise. The agency's rules should also be checked to see whether a copy of the application must be sent to the complainant or to his or her attorney. It may be helpful to send the application to reopen to the EEO agency by certified mail so as to record the date of receipt by the agency.

The application to reopen should explain to the EEO agency why the determination of probable cause was incorrect. The application will consist of factual and legal arguments together with any supporting affidavits or exhibits. Bearing in mind the function of the application to reopen, the employer should not attempt to use the application as a form of second investigation. Rather, it should be keyed or directed to specific errors of factual and legal conclusions made by the investigator during or as a result of the investigation. It has been noted, while the EEO agency recognizes that mistakes are made occasionally, the beginning presumption is that the determination made by the investigator was correct and it is up to the employer to convince the agency otherwise. Clearly, no EEO agency could ever resolve any complaints if each employer effectively were to be permitted two investigations.

The application to reopen should demonstrate why a particular factual or legal conclusion, specifically relied on by the investigator, was incorrect. Thus, the first step in preparing the application to reopen is to examine the file maintained by the EEO agency. Usually the file will contain an internal memo from the investigator to the administrative head of that particular investigating unit. This memo will set forth the investigator's reasons for making the determination of probable cause. If one of the stated bases for the probable cause finding can be challenged successfully, the application to reopen will have a realistic possiblity of being granted.

When the application is received, it will be referred to one of the staff attorneys of the EEO agency. The attorney to whom the application is assigned will advise the complainant of the application and afford him or her the opportunity to submit a written response to the application. When the complainant's response has been received, or when the complainant has failed to respond within the time alotted, the EEO agency attorney will consider the application to reopen on the basis of the papers. He or she will then make a written recommendation to the general counsel. The application to reopen is not argued in person.

The EEO agency will separately consider the legal and factual arguments raised by the employer in the application. Generally a factual argument will not succeed because the intent on the part of the EEO agency is not to second guess every probable cause finding. Factual arguments raised in an application to reopen will succeed only in rare cases, where, for example, the investigator clearly misunderstood or failed to consider a significant fact that was integral to the rendering of the probable cause finding.

The application to reopen will have greater chance for success where the employer is able to raise legal arguments. Legal arguments have a greater chance of succeeding because the investigator is not presumed to be as knowledgeable regarding the law as is the EEO agency attorney. When considering a legal argument made in an application to reopen, the EEO agency attorney will not have the feeling that he or she is redoing work that has already been done by the investigator and that it is the investigator's job to do. Rather, legally based arguments elicit the superior expertise of the EEO agency attorney, and induce him or her to consider the arguments seriously so as to avoid perpetuating a possible legal error, made in the course of the investigation.

For this reason a factual argument is best framed in the form of a legal argument involving agency procedure. Thus, for example, instead of arguing that the investigator misconstrued a particular set of facts, it would be more effective if an argument could be made that the investigator failed to afford the employer the opportunity to explain the facts relied on by the investigator. Of course it will not always be possible to frame the factual arguments in a legal context, but, where possible, the attempt should be made.

In our hypothetical example, let us assume that the EEO attorney for ABC Co. examines the file on the complaint maintained at the offices of the Division of Human Rights. On looking through the file, he finds a memo from the investigator setting forth the reasons for the recommended determination of probable cause. Among the reasons set forth for the recommendation of probable cause are the refusal of the ABC Co. to comply with the request for production of personnel files of all terminated employees, and the fact that the company policy regarding misrepresentations on employment applications had not been reduced to writing. The memo concludes that ABC Co. "failed to document its defense that the complainant was terminated because he lied on his application for employment." Table 14[1] is a copy of the "recommendation for finding of probable cause" contained in the file maintained by the Division of Human Rights.

Table 15 is a suggested "application to reopen." Rather than attempt to reargue the case, the employer has limited the application to three arguments, each one keyed to the memo recommending the determination of probable cause.

The first argument raised in the application is one of legal procedure. The attorney for ABC Co. has argued that the investigator was incorrect in refusing to modify the request for information contained in the investigatory questionnaire. The questionnaire had requested production of the personnel files of all employees terminated by ABC Co. (Table 10). The employer had not complied with the request on the basis of its explanation that production of all such files would be unduly burdensome and irrelevant. (Table 11). However, the employer had simultaneously offered to comply with a modified request that would be more narrowly tailored to the facts of the case. In its first argument the employer is asserting that it was unreasonable for the investigator to refuse to modify the request, and in addition, to use the employer's refusal to produce information as a basis for the probable cause finding.

The second argument raised by the employer in the application to reopen is also a legal argument although it does not involve a question of procedure. The employer's second argument in the application is that the employer's policy regarding misrepresentations on employment applications did not have to be reduced to writing. By inference, the investigator's memo recommending probable cause, requires employers to put all personnel policies in writing. The employer is arguing that there is no requirement in the New York Human Rights Law, or in the Rules of Practice of the Division of Human Rights, that all corporate personnel policies must be reduced to writing.

The employer's third argument is also a result of the investigator's statements in the memo recommending probable cause. This third argument is a straightforward factual argument. The third argument is that the investigator discounted the employer's defense largely because he did not understand the thrust of the defense. The employer's response to the investigatory questionnaire (Tables 11 and 12) did not set forth the misrepresentation as the only reason for the termination. To the contrary, as noted, the employer took great care to include both the complainant's deteriorating job performance together with the misrepresentation as combined reasons for the termination. By stating that ABC Co. "failed to document its defense that the complainant was terminated because he lied on his application for employment," it is clear that the investigator did not understand and thus did not consider the second reason advanced by the employer, that of the complainant's poor performance.

One side effect of an application to reopen is the increased period of time between the determination of probable cause and issuance of a notice

---

[1]Tables 1–13 are contained in Chapter 7, which discussed our hypothetical case during the investigatory stage of the EEO agency proceedings.

TABLE 14 Memo Recommending Finding of Probable Cause

To: George Jackson, Regional Director
From: Dick Tracy, Investigator
Subject: Doe v. ABC Co.
Date: June 5, 1987

Basis for Recommendation of Probable Cause

The above complaint was filed with this division on March 3, 1987, charging the above-named respondent with unlawful discrimination regarding employment, in violation of the Human Rights Law. More particularly, the complaint alleges unlawful discrimination on the basis of the complainant's race, color, and age, with respect to his termination by the respondent on March 3, 1987.

An investigatory conference was held in the matter on May 5, 1987. Present at the conference were the complainant, Tom Smith, respondent's EEO Officer, and respondent's counsel. The investigator opened the conference by requesting the respondent to set forth its response to the particulars of the complaint. The counsel for the respondent referred to the employer's response to the investigatory questionnaire, and stated that respondent's position, indicated in section A of the response, had not changed.

The complainant conceded that he had lied on his initial application for employment when he had stated that he was a high school graduate. Counsel for the respondent and respondent's EEO officer asserted that such misrepresentation constituted a clear violation of established company policy, and was a sufficient basis for the termination. In response, the complainant asserted that one Suzy Que, another employee of respondent, had also lied on her initial employment application, but had not been terminated.

When asked to produce documentation of the "established company policy" to which they referred, respondent's representatives were unable to do so. Respondent's representatives produced the complainant's personnel file but did not produce any of the personnel files of other terminated employees, which files had been requested in the investigatory questionnaire.

On the basis of the foregoing, it is recommended that a finding of probable cause be made in this matter, for the following reasons:

1. Respondent failed to produce the personnel files of employees who had been terminated, other than the complainant. Such failure suggests a presumption that the materials, if produced, would have supported the complainant.
2. The respondent failed to document the existence of its alleged personnel policy, that misrepresentation on an employment application constitutes basis for dismissal.
3. Even if the above documentation were produced, the evidence indicates that a younger, Caucasian employee of respondent, who also lied on her employment application, was not terminated.
4. Given the above, the respondent has failed to document its defense that the complainant was terminated because he had lied on his application for employment.

TABLE 15 Application To Reopen

August 5, 1987

John Johnson, Esq.
General Counsel
State Division of Human Rights
55 West 125th Street
New York, New York 10027

RE: John Doe v. ABC Co.

Dear Mr. Johnson:

Pursuant to section 465.18 of the Rules of Practice of the State Division of Human Rights (9 N.Y.C.R.R. section 465.18), ABC Co., the above-named respondent, makes this application to reopen the finding of probable cause issued in this matter on July 5, 1987.

The basis for this application is as follows:

1. The investigator recommended a finding of probable cause in part because the respondent had not complied with an irrelevant and unduly burdensome request that had been included in the investigatory questionnaire issued in this matter. More particularly, the investigatory questionnaire had required the production of all personnel files of all employees "treated similarly to the complainant."

   In its response, the respondent noted that it employs thousands of employees throughout the 50 states, and that there is an ongoing process of employees being terminated and hired. In view of the large number of employees, the respondent indicated that it would be both unduly burdensome and irrelevant, to produce the personnel file of every employee who had been terminated. In this respect it should be noted that the information requested was not limited as to geographical scope, job level, or to a specific period of time. While declining to produce all of the requested information, the respondent did state that it would be prepared to comply with a more narrowly tailored request that might be appropriate to the issues presented by the within complaint.

   It was legal error for the investigator to have based his recommendation upon the respondent's above action, without in any way replying to the respondent's clear request for modification, and without having advised the respondent that a failure to produce the materials would be interpreted as an admission of guilt. As such, the investigator's action deprived the respondent of due process of law, since it was effectively denied notice or opportunity to be heard regarding the division's use of the investigatory questionnaire, or to be heard regarding the division's response to the request for modification of the investigatory questionnaire. In addition, the finding of probable cause must be considered to be without basis in fact, since such finding admittedly is based not on facts but upon unwarranted presumptions.

2. The investigator improperly refused to consider the employer's defense regarding employee misrepresentations on employment applications. Such refusal was grounded upon the fact that the respondent's personnel policy regarding such misrepresentations, was not in writing. There is no provision under the Human Rights Law, or contained within the division's rules of practice, that would require employer personnel policies to be in writing. To be sure, such policies must be proven by the employer, but such proof

Table 15 *(Continued)*

need not always be in written form. Here, it is clear that the in-person testimony of respondent's EEO officer attesting to the existence of the personnel policy in issue, was flatly disregarded by the investigator, upon the sole basis that the policy was not reduced to written form. At the very least, this matter should be remanded for further investigation, and the investigator should be instructed to consider all of the evidence, both written and oral.

3. It is clear from the investigator's memorandum explaining the basis for the probable cause finding, that the investigator did not understand the employer's defense. Respondent specifically stated in its response to the investigatory questionnaire, and in person at the investigatory conference, that the complainant's misrepresentation on his employment application, was only one of several reasons for the challenged termination. Another reason for the termination was the complainant's poor work performance in the context of the respondent's financial difficulties. By focusing upon only one of several defenses, the investigator failed to accord proper weight to the employer's position.

It is therefore respectfully requested that an order be issued pursuant to the rules of practice of this Division, vacating the finding of probable cause issued in this matter on July 5, 1987. Please be assured that the respondent is prepared to comply fully with any requests for additional information that might be necessary for resolution of this application.

Your truly,

Tom Jones, Esq.
Attorney for Respondent

---

of hearing. Although it is possible that a state EEO agency will have staff attorneys whose sole function is to review applications to reopen, this is not usually the case. The reason for this is apparent in that the application to reopen is not one of the routine procedures in the processing of an EEO complaint. Many employers are not aware of the possibility of submitting an application to reopen, and thus do not make the application. In addition, not all complaints will provide a realistic basis for making the application.

Typically the application to reopen will be assigned to one of the staff attorneys who is also assigned to administrative hearings. The result of this is that the application to reopen is given to someone who has other, more pressing, things to do. Therefore, the application is not processed on a priority basis, and it may take weeks or even months before a decision is rendered.

If the application is granted, the state EEO agency has two options. In some rare cases involving questions of statutes of limitations or jurisdiction, the state EEO agency may dismiss the complaint in its entirety. More often, the complaint will be sent back for further investigation. In the latter case, the file will usually contain an explanatory memo to the investigator indicating in what ways the investigation was considered deficient. This explanatory memo will be of great assistance to the employer in preparing a defense in the ensuing second investigation.

The employer should examine the explanatory memo to ascertain the tone of the memo. Sometimes the memo will advise the investigator as to what additional information is needed to establish a case of unlawful discrimination. In these cases, the employer can anticipate a second finding of probable cause unless he or she can keep the investigator from obtaining the additional required information.

In instances where the application to reopen had been granted on the basis of procedural objections, the explanatory memo will advise the investigator as to what additional procedures must be afforded the employer in order to eliminate any procedural defects in the original determination of probable cause. In these cases as well as in the first type of case, the employer can anticipate a second determination of probable cause.

However, in yet other cases, the tone of the explanatory memo will suggest that the case is weak and that it probably ought to be dismissed. In such situations, the memo will advise the investigator that the case appears to be without merit, or that the investigator apparently misjudged a certain fact or set of facts. In these cases the employer can anticipate an ultimate finding of no probable cause.

SETTLEMENT PRIOR TO NOTICE OF HEARING

As was mentioned in Chapter 7, settlement is encouraged by the state and federal EEO agencies at all stages of the processing of the complaint. After an application to reopen has been denied, or where no such application has been made, unconciliated complaints which have received a determination of probable cause will be referred for a public hearing which is also known as an administrative hearing.

There is usually some time lag between the referral for a public hearing and the actual issuance of a notice of hearing. Depending on the state EEO agency involved, this time lag can be several weeks or even months. During this period of time the employer may wish to communicate to the EEO agency that he or she is interested in settling the matter. The reasons in favor of the employer's entering into a settlement have been discussed in Chapter 6 and will not be repeated here, except to note that the arguments in favor of settling the matter can be considered to be more compelling after a finding of probable cause has been issued.

The employer should once again consider settlement even if it was not possible to settle the complaint during the investigation. In addition, by communicating to the EEO agency a willingness to consider settlement, the employer may extend the time period before issuance of a notice of hearing. If the employer is realistically talking about settling the case, the EEO agency usually will not schedule the case for the public hearing until the settlement discussions have proven unsuccessful. In some cases the complaint will be scheduled for a public hearing with a notation being made that the employer is interested in discussing settlement. This possibility will be discussed in connection with the notice of hearing.

ISSUANCE OF A NOTICE OF HEARING

In the state EEO agencies which follow the investigation and public hearing procedure outline in Chapter 7, the complaint eventually will be scheduled for a public hearing. The employer's first official notice to this effect will be his or her receipt of a notice of hearing. The notice of hearing will advise the employer to appear and present a defense to the complaint at a public hearing at a specified place on a specified date. This will usually be at one of the offices of the state EEO agency, two to four weeks from the issuance of the notice of hearing.

Prior to issuance of the notice of hearing a staff attorney of the state EEO agency will have been assigned to that particular complaint. The EEO agency attorney will be required to present the case in support of the complaint at the public hearing. Although most of the time assigning a particular complaint to a staff attorney has the same effect as assigning free counsel to the complainant, there are differences between assigning counsel to present the case in support of the complaint, and assigning counsel for the complainant. No duty of loyalty or of attorney–client relationship exists between the EEO agency staff attorney and the complainant. This makes it an open question as to whether any attorney–client privilege exists. In addition, the EEO agency attorney's services are limited to the parameters of the complaint and the scope of the public hearing; such services do not extend to any other lawsuit in any other courts or before any other administrative agencies.

Typically, the state EEO agency attorney will receive the file to which he or she has been assigned six to eight weeks prior to the scheduled hearing date. This is not a lot of time considering the fact that the agency attorney is usually working under a heavy caseload and in light of the fact that he or she has had no prior connection with that complaint. Given these factors, the EEO agency attorney can understandably be less than anxious to prepare for and try any particular case at a public hearing.

We have seen previously that in some cases the file will be assigned to the EEO agency staff attorney with a notation that the employer is interested in discussing settlement. In such cases, the agency attorney will contact the employer or his or her representative shortly after receiving the file.

Settlement discussions between the EEO agency attorney and the employer or his or her representative, will not necessarily postpone issuance of a notice of hearing. However, such discussions may facilitate an adjournment of the public hearing after the notice of hearing has been issued. Of course in some cases the EEO agency will assert that a settlement can always be concluded at the time and place of the public hearing, and therefore that settlement discussions do not constitute sufficient reason to adjourn a hearing date. However, it is also true that the EEO agency may not want to schedule for hearing a case that ultimately settles, where such scheduling would prevent the public hearing of another case that is to be tried. State EEO agencies have a limited number of hearing locations and a limited number of administrative law judges. In most situations the objective is to save the space and the administrative law judge for the case that will be tried. Thus, many state EEO agencies will welcome the opportunity to adjourn a hearing that may be settled, and schedule in its place for public hearing a case that appears more likely to be tried. Depending on the particular emphasis within the agency at any particular time, this point of view may or may not result in adjournment of a scheduled hearing where the parties are actively involved in settlement discussions.

MOTION FOR MORE DEFINITE STATEMENT

Most, if not all, state EEO agencies provide in their rules (or in their practice) for a procedure whereby the employer may interpose what is known as a motion for a more definite statement. The employer who makes such a motion is asserting that the complaint as it exists is so vague in certain respects that it is impossible for the employer to answer the complaint intelligently. The motion is submitted by mail to the general counsel of the state EEO agency.

The motion for a more definite statement should be made either prior to or shortly after issuance of the notice of hearing. The notice of hearing will usually require the employer to submit an answer to the complaint within a specified period of time or risk a default. Although it is actually unlikely that a default will be taken in the absence of an answer, nevertheless it is not good practice to run the risk. For this reason, the motion for a more definite statement should be made, if it is made at all, within the specified period of time for the employer's answer. By making the motion, the employer effectively postpones the submission of an answer until the motion has been decided.

Even where the motion for a more definite statement is provided for in the rules and regulations of the state EEO agency, it is rare for any such motion to be made. First, most employers are not aware of their opportunity to make the motion. Second, it must be acknowledged that state EEO agencies are usually hostile to the motion, and this hostility derives from the recognition that the complaints are not written by attorneys. As a result of this factor, complaints are not expected to comply with the more formal pleading requirements of a lawsuit in a court. Third, the motion means added work for the already overworked agency attorney. For these reasons, it is unlikely that the motion for a more definite statement will be granted.

Nevertheless the motion should be made where the employer reasonably believes that the complaint is too vague in certain respects to allow that employer to submit an answer. In the unlikely event that the motion is granted, the complaint will be amended so as to provide the added information that is deemed lacking. The amendment may be made by the complainant, or by the state EEO agency itself, depending on the particular practice of the agency.

In our hypothetical, the ABC Co. has made a motion for a more definite statement, which appears as Table 16. The reader will note that the authority for the motion comes from a different New York State statute, the New York State Administrative Procedure Act. This Act specifies general rules of procedure that are applicable to all New York State agencies, including the New York State Division of Human Rights. The New York State Administrative Procedure Act is patterned after the federal Administrative Procedure Act, which applies to all federal agencies, including the EEOC. The federal Administrative Procedure Act also provides for a motion for a more definite statement, which may be made in the course of a proceeding before the EEOC. Many states have similar provision in their own statutes, or in the rules of practice of the agencies themselves.

Table 16 indicates that the ABC Co. has requested more definite statements regarding two particulars of the complaint. With respect to particular number 1 of the NYSDHR complaint, the employer is asking for a more definite statement as to when the complainant began working for ABC Co. With respect to particular number 3, the employer is requesting a statement as to the name of the other employee who allegedly had also lied on her employment application but who was not terminated or otherwise disciplined.

Since both of these requests ask for information that is arguably within the employer's possession, it is unlikely that the motion will be granted in either respect. A motion for a more definite statement would have a better chance of being granted where the employer could realistically demonstrate that the complaint is vague as to what specific employer actions are being challenged, or where the basis of the alleged unlawful discrimination is unclear. For purposes of our hypothetical, we will assume that, after somewhat cursory consideration, the motion for a more definite statement is denied.

THE EMPLOYER'S ANSWER

Denial of the motion will now require the ABC Co. to submit its answer to the complaint. The answer is not a long or complicated document; it is necessary merely to answer the particulars of the complaint. It will also preserve or protect the employer's defenses, including legal defenses. A sample answer is included as Table 17.

The answer of ABC Co. includes what is known as a general denial. This means that the ABC Co. is denying all of the assertions made by John Doe in his complaint. It is not necessary for ABC Co. to include in the answer, the reasons for denying the statements made in the complaint. It is sufficient to deny the statements in the answer, and to save the reasons and proof for the hearing. Our sample answer also includes certain standard defenses. Although none of these defenses appear applicable to our

TABLE 16 Motion for a More Definite Statement

STATE OF NEW YORK: EXECUTIVE DEPARTMENT
STATE DIVISION OF HUMAN RIGHTS

State Division of Human Rights,
on the Complaint of,
JOHN DOE,
Complainant,

-against-

ABC CO.,
Respondent.

MOTION
FOR A MORE
DEFINITE
STATEMENT
Complaint No.

SIRS:

PLEASE TAKE NOTICE THAT, pursuant to section 465.3 of the Rules of Practice of the State Division of Human Rights (9 N.Y.C.R.R. section 465.3) and section 301 of the Administrative Procedure Act, the above-named respondent requests that the division issue an order providing for a more definite statement of the particulars of the above complaint, on the grounds that the complaint as it now exists is too vague to permit the respondent to answer said complaint. In particular, the respondent requests that the complaint be made more definite as to the following items:

1. With respect to the first numbered particular of the complaint, a statement as to when the complainant commenced employment with the respondent;

2. With respect to the third numbered particular of the complaint, a statement as to the name of the other employee who allegedly had also lied on her employment application, but who was not terminated or otherwise disciplined; and

3. With respect to the complaint in its entirety, such other and further statements as the Division may deem necessary and proper.

Dated: New York, New York
November 1, 1987

Yours, etc.

TOM JONES, ESQ.
Attorney for Respondent
1 Any Other Street
New York, New York
(212) 123-1234

TO: JOHN JOHNSON, ESQ.
General Counsel
State Division of Human Rights
55 West 125th Street
New York, New York

TABLE 17 Answer of Respondent

STATE OF NEW YORK: EXECUTIVE DEPARTMENT
STATE DIVISION OF HUMAN RIGHTS

State Division of Human Rights
on the Complaint of
JOHN DOE,
                Complainant,
    -against-
ABC CO.,
              Respondent.

ANSWER
Complaint No.

ABC CO., the above-named respondent, as and for its Answer to the complaint, alleges as follows:

1. General Denial.

First Affirmative Defense

2. The complaint is time-barred under the applicable statute of limitations.

Second Affirmative Defense

3. The Division does not have personal or subject-matter jurisdiction over the respondent or this complaint.

Third Affirmative Defense

4. The complaint fails to state a claim upon which relief can be granted.

WHEREFORE, the respondent demands that the complaint be dismissed, and that the respondent be awarded the costs and disbursements of this action, together with reasonable attorney's fees.

Yours, etc.

TOM JONES, ESQ.
Attorney for Respondent
1 Any Other Street
New York, New York
(212) 123-1234

STATE OF NEW YORK)
COUNTY OF NEW YORK) s.s.:

TOM SMITH, being duly sworn deposes and says that he is the EEO Officer for ABC CO., a domestic corporation and the within named respondent, that he has read the foregoing Answer and that all of the allegations therein are true of his own knowledge, except as to the matters therein stated to be alleged on information and belief, and as to those matters, he believes it to be true.

_____
                        TOM SMITH

Sworn to before me this
20th day of February 1988
s/_____
      Notary Public

hypothetical, it is usual practice to include such defenses as a matter of routine.

PREPARATION FOR THE PUBLIC HEARING

It is now necessary for ABC Co. to prepare for a public hearing on Doe's complaint. As noted previously the public hearing, also known as the administrative hearing, is similar to a court trial but is less formal. Similarly, the preparation for the public hearing is in some respects similar to preparation for a court trial, but it too is less formal.

Preparation for a court trial ordinarily involves each side taking pretrial testimony of the other party's witnesses, in the presence of a stenographer. In addition, preparation for a court trial typically involves procedures whereby each party has the chance to examine pertinent documents and materials held by the other party. All of these procedures—pretrial examination of witnesses and inspection of documents—collectively are referred to as "discovery." Discovery constitutes a major part of the preparation for a court trial, and its completion is considered essential before an attorney is prepared to take a case to trial.

Discovery as such is not generally permitted in administrative hearings, and public hearings before EEO agencies are no exception to the practice. None of the state EEO agencies permit discovery without specific permission of the agency. Typically the rules of practice of the state EEO agency will provide for a procedure whereby the employer makes an application to the agency to allow discovery. The experience of this author is that discovery is rarely, if ever permitted.

The absence of discovery prior to the public hearing is in part the result of the limited time for preparation. In contrast to a court trial, where trial preparation can consume months or even years, the employer will ordinarily have only a few weeks to prepare for the public hearing. The employer receives the notice of hearing shortly before the scheduled hearing date, which is usually only two to four weeks later. Requests for adjournment of the hearing, even if granted, cannot be expected to delay the hearing for more than a month or two. When the employer receives the notice of hearing, preparation for the public hearing must commence immediately.

The employer will begin his or her preparation for the hearing by consulting the records of the previously conducted internal investigation of the complaint, and of his or her position statement that has been submitted to the investigator. (See Chapter 7.) In addition, it is recommended that the employer or his or her representative examine the file in the possession of the state EEO agency. This should be done even if it was formerly done in connection with the preparation of an application to reopen.

The employer should prepare his or her witnesses for testimony at the hearing, and should assemble the documentation and other materials that might be necessary. In our hypothetical example, ABC Co. will likely want to produce Doe's personnel file, and as witnesses, Que, who is Doe's superior, and Tom Smith, ABC Co.'s EEO officer.

Smith will produce the personnel file and introduce Doe's initial employment application. Smith will then testify that Doe admitted lying on the application, and will further testify to the long-standing personnel policy regarding misrepresentations on employment applications. Smith will also testify to Doe's poor performance, as will Que so testify.

At the same time that ABC Co. will be preparing for the public hearing, the EEO agency attorney will also be preparing for the hearing, and may issue a subpoena in connection with that hearing. We have discussed subpoenas previously in Chapter 7, and most of what was said there is similarly applicable here. The one major difference is that since the employer has already received a finding of probable cause, there is no need on the employer's part to still be concerned that a failure to produce information will precipitate a finding of probable cause; such finding has already been made.

Most subpoenas issued by the EEO agency in preparation for the hearing will call for the production of specified records at the hearing itself. Sometimes, however, the subpoena will call for production of the identified documents to be produced in advance of the hearing at the offices of the EEO agency. The validity of such procedure varies from state to state, and the employer should check the applicable procedural law or rules of practice in effect in his or her particular state.

Production of subpoenaed documents in advance of the public hearing should be resisted where possible since such advance production gives added advantage to the EEO agency attorney. Where the employer must collect documents from various locations or sources to comply with the subpoena, the employer may delay production of such documents with the explanation that added time is required to obtain all the documents. This is especially true if the documents are old, or have been transferred to a different medium, such as microfilm.

Production of subpoenaed documents at the public hearing itself is not as disadvantageous to the employer as production of documents in advance of the hearing. Typically the documents produced at the public hearing will be examined cursorily by the harried EEO agency attorney. Often the administrative law judge will give the EEO agency attorney 10 or 15 minutes to look over the documents during a recess in the hearing. This tends to discourage careful scrutiny of the materials produced. It is not necessary for the employer to organize the materials nor is it recommended that the employer organize such materials for the EEO agency attorney's benefit. The employer is required only to comply with the subpoena; not to help the EEO attorney do his or her job.

Aside from documents, the EEO agency usually has the power to subpoena witnesses. This is rarely done on the theory that the employer's witnesses will tend to support the employer's position. If the employer's employees are subpoenaed and called to testify by the EEO agency's attorney, then that attorney may not cross-examine that witness absent a showing that the witness is a hostile witness. Thus, absent a showing of hostility, the EEO agency attorney may only examine such a witness via direct, and not, cross-examination.

Even if a showing of hostility is made and cross-examination is permitted, the effectiveness of such cross-examination will be limited, since the EEO attorney has not had the benefit of prior discovery. As noted before, discovery is a procedure followed in cases that go to court whereby both sides will be able to examine the other side's witnesses before the actual trial, and where the examination and answers given by all examined witnesses will be recorded in a transcript. Accordingly, when such court cases go to trial, attorneys on both sides will be able to refer to prior examination of witnesses and may be guided by the answers that had been given previously.

As mentioned previously, discovery is rare in preparation for public hearings. The result is that the EEO agency attorney will not have a prior transcript to which he or she can refer, and accordingly, when he or she attempts to cross-examine the employer's witnesses he or she does not know and cannot be sure in advance what those witnesses' testimony will be. This difficulty facing an EEO agency staff attorney in cross-examining adverse witnesses without a prior transcript is a collateral benefit redounding to the employer as a result of the agency's denial of discovery. The existence of this collateral benefit is the basis for my earlier statement in Chapter 7 that it is generally not recommended that the employer's witnesses appear at the investigatory conference.

In preparing for the hearing the employer should give consideration to using charts and graphs. Such evidence is welcomed by the agency and generally has a strong persuasive effect where adequately supported by the underlying documentation. In our hypothetical, ABC Co. may wish to compare Doe's salary increases with the salary increases received by other employees, so as to demonstrate that the relatively small raises Doe received were keyed to inflation and should not be interpreted as being merit-based.

Additionally ABC Co. may wish to use graphs or charts to illustrate its "financial difficulties" defense. One of the defenses asserted by ABC Co. is that financial difficulties in the company have constrained the company to terminate its marginal employees. ABCs position is that one indicator of marginal employee status is where an employee's rating on the annual performance evaluation has been lowered from the previous year. Thus, ABC maintains that Doe, who received a "good" rating in 1985 but only a "satisfactory" rating in 1986, was a marginal employee whose termination was caused in part by financial difficulties. Given this defense, the employer might wish to provide the administrative law judge with a chart or graph demonstrating such financial difficulties so as to give credibility to the employer's defense. While many employers might be reluctant to reveal such information, if the employer is a public corporation, the information may have already been disclosed.

To summarize briefly, the employer's preparation for the public hearing should consist of consulting the records of the previous internal investigation of the complaint; preparing his or her witnesses; preparing charts, graphs and other documentary evidence; and responding to possible subpoenas from the EEO agency. This preparation must be completed in a relatively short period of time, usually within only two to four weeks from the employer's receipt of the notice of hearing.

It is sometimes possible to adjourn the hearing. The date specified in the notice of hearing may be impossible for the employer to meet for a variety of reasons, including vacations of key witnesses. Also, given such relatively short notice, counsel for the employer may be otherwise engaged on the date specified in the notice of hearing. Requests for adjournment are a matter of discretion and the agency response will vary from agency to agency and from time to time.

THE ADMINISTRATIVE HEARING

If there has been a finding of probable cause, absent successful conciliation, settlement, or reopening, the day will eventually come when the employer must defend his or her actions at a public hearing. The public hearing is the second critical juncture in the investigation and public hearing procedure that has been outlined previously.

It is only at the investigation stage or at a public hearing that the employer will receive the full attention of the EEO agency and a realistic opportunity to successfully defend himself or herself against the complaint. It is only at these two points that the employer can anticipate true neutrality and total objectivity on the part of the EEO agency.

We have seen that the presumption on the part of the EEO agency is that most applications to reopen will be denied, in part because of the policy view that questions of credibility are best left to the investigator and to the public hearing. Similarly we have noted that the motion for a more definite statement is usually unsuccessful, and encounters not simple partiality, but outright hostility.

These presumptions and such hostility is not present at the public hearing. Contrary to what many employers might think, the state EEO agency does not presume that the employer appearing before the agency at a public hearing is automatically guilty of unlawful discrimination. In fact some administrative law judges, uncomfortable with their image as being pro-complainant, consciously adopt a solicitous attitude towards employers appearing before them in an attempt to be viewed as unbiased. Thus, the public hearing is the employer's second realistic opportunity to walk away from the state EEO agency with a determination in his or her favor.

The public hearing is best viewed as a mini-trial. It is less formal than a trial, but it also retains some of the fundamental legal procedures and modes of examination, as are used in court trials. It is more formal than the investigatory conference, and is less formal than a court trial. While there is no transcript of the proceedings at the investigatory conference, the public hearing will either be recorded and transcribed by a court reporter, or taped by a recording machine without transcription. In either case, the important point is that the parties to the public hearing are making a record that may one day be reviewed by the commissioner or head of the EEO agency, or by a reviewing court.

The documents and other materials produced by the parties at the public hearing, will be formally marked as exhibits and retained together with the transcript. The procedure under which the exhibits are accepted in the public hearing is carefully controlled, although it too is less formal than the procedure in a court. Again, this is clearly different from the procedure at the investigatory conference. There either party was free to submit documentary and other materials without any formal procedure. Indeed, we have noted that evidence may be accepted by the investigator after the investigatory conference has been concluded. This is not done in administrative hearings, except under extraordinary circumstances and in accordance with strict procedural requirements. In fact, this author, who has tried well over a hundred administrative hearings, cannot recall a single case where evidence was accepted after the public hearing had been concluded.

The administrative or public hearing is controlled by the administrative law judge. The administrative law judge makes all the decisions with respect to the testimony and questioning of witnesses, the introduction of nontestimony evidence, such as documentary evidence, the conduct of all persons in the room where the public hearing is being conducted, and the scheduling and rescheduling of the public hearing after the initial hearing date. The administrative law judge is best thought of as a judge, but is unlike a judge in two major respects.

The administrative law judge, unlike a judge, does not have contempt power, or more colloquially, the power to put somebody in jail. The contempt power is held only by a judge. We noted this previously when we pointed out that the EEO agency must go to a court in order to force compliance with a subpoena issued by that agency. Lacking the contempt power, the administrative law judge has no enforcement powers of his or her own. As with subpoenas, orders of the administrative law judge are not enforceable except by resort to a court. Thus, for example, if the administrative law judge orders the employer to produce a certain document, and if the employer refuses, the employer cannot be fined or put in jail unless an administrative law judge so orders.

However, it should also be borne in mind that the administrative law judge will be deciding the case, at least in the first instance. This is a power in itself, and is the true power behind the administrative law judge's authority. The employer, as well as the complaining employee, is seeking a favorable decision from the administrative law judge. It will clearly be disadvantageous to the employer's position and to his or her credibility, if he or she refuses to produce materials that are specifically requested by the administrative law judge. Of course some materials may be so damaging to the employer's case that it is the lesser of the two evils to arouse the ire of the administrative law judge by refusing to produce the materials. This is a strategic decision that must be made by the employer, and is similar to the decision discussed earlier, when the investigator requests potentially damaging documents.

Lacking the contempt power, the administrative law judge may be viewed as less powerful than a judge. However, in another respect, the administrative law judge may also be seen as more powerful. The administrative law judge has greater power to participate in the public hearing, than does a judge to participate in a court trial. The administrative law judge is not restricted, as is a judge, to simply making decisions on procedural questions. To the contrary, the administrative law judge, if he or she feels so inclined, may actively engage in examination of witnesses and order the production of evidence. The administrative law judge may take over the examination of a witness and is not restricted to merely amplifying the testimony already given. The administrative law judge may question the witness as to matters beyond the scope of the subjects covered in the examination and cross-examination by the attorneys.

Of course the administrative law judge may not participate in the public hearing with the interest of proving either the employer's or the employee's positions. By participating in the public hearing, the administrative law judge must not abandon a neutral role; he or she may be a participant but not an advocate. Rather, the administrative law judge must be solely interested in discovering the full story, and thus is empowered to examine witnesses and to order the production of evidence, where the parties have given the administrative law judge only part of the full story.

Thus, the administrative law judge is in some respects less powerful than a judge, but may be more able to participate in the public hearing, than is a judge to participate in a court trial. In addition, the lack of contempt or enforcement power is compensated to some extent by the fact that it is the administrative law judge who will make the initial decision regarding the complaint. As we shall see, this initial, or "recommended," decision, is almost always the same as the final decision reached by the EEO agency. It should be noted that there is no jury in the administrative hearing.

Aside from the administrative law judge, the persons present at the public hearing will be the parties, their attorneys, and any witnesses. If the proceedings are being recorded and transcribed by a stenographer, or court reporter, then that person will also be present. In other cases, the parties will find themselves testifying into a recording machine.

There may also be members of the public present, although this is rare. The public hearing, as the term provides, is open to the public. However, it is not publicized nor does it take place in a court. Except in cases of unusual public interest, or where public interest groups are involved, it is rare to find a member of the general public at a public hearing.

The public hearing is not held in a court, but usually is in one of the offices of the state EEO agency. Sometimes, it is held in a state-owned building used for general administrative and executive purposes. The furnishings are not as formal as in a court, and in many cases consists of a simple arrangement of tables and chairs in an unadorned setting.

In the same way that the complaint has been assigned to the EEO agency staff attorney, the public hearing has been assigned to a particular administrative law judge. Prior to the public hearing, the administrative law judge will typically know nothing about the case except for the complaint and the answer. The administrative law judge is handed a bare file containing only the notice of hearing with the complaint annexed.

Although procedures vary from state to state, it should be stressed that in most states the public hearing is conducted without any reference to the investigation. Thus, the administrative law judge does not see or become aware of any aspect of the investigation. Nor does the administrative law judge see or become aware of any other prehearing activity regarding the complaint, such as an application to reopen or its disposition. None of the material contained in the file is given to the administrative law judge except for the complaint and sometimes the answer. No exhibits, documents, or materials produced for the investigator during the course of the investigation are made available to the administrative law judge. He or she will become aware of them only if and when they are produced at the public hearing. This procedure is known as a hearing *de novo*, which is Latin for a hearing "from the beginning."

At the public hearing the parties will present their positions according to the less-formal procedure of an administrative hearing. In most cases the parties will appear with an attorney. It is rare for an employer to come to a public hearing without an attorney. For this reason, we will not burden the reader with a detailed description of the exact procedure used in a public hearing. It will be sufficient to note that the procedure is similar to, although less formal than, that used in a court trial.

As in a court trial, the parties attempt to prove their respective positions by having witnesses testify on their behalf, by cross-examining the adverse party's witnesses, and by introducing documents, which are marked as exhibits.

In our hypothetical, let us assume that both ABC Co. and Doe are represented by attorneys. Although Doe could legally retain his own private attorney, let us assume that he has decided to accept the EEO agency attorney that has been assigned to his complaint. Let us also assume that the first hearing date is March 4, 1988.

Doe, as the complaining party, is the first person to testify. Doe testifies to his 30 years of employment, to the meeting where both he and Que acknowledged that they had lied on their initial applications for employment, and to his subsequent termination. He also testifies to the fact that Que is still employed by ABC Co., that he is black, and that she is Caucasian.

In response to questions from the EEO agency attorney, Doe also testifies to his having been passed over for promotion to foreman in 1986. At this point the attorney for ABC Co. objects to the last testimony on the ground that the failure to promote was not included in the NYSDHR complaint, and that the public hearing is thus limited to the issue of termination only.

In response, the NYSDHR attorney requests that the administrative law judge formally amend the complaint to include allegations of unlawful failure to promote, and in addition, to charge unlawful sex discrimination as a basis for the failure to promote as well as the termination. The power of the administrative law judge to amend complaints is routinely provided in the rules of practice of EEO agencies, and specifically is included in the rules of practice of the New York State Division of Human Rights. Those rules provide that the amendment of the complaint is at the discretion of the administrative law judge.

The two components of the amendment raise the issue of the statute of limitations from two different perspectives. The proposed amendment to include the question of the promotion in 1986 raises the issue of the statute of limitations where the specific alleged unlawful discriminatory practice was not mentioned in the complaint. The proposed amendment to charge sex discrimination raised the issue of the statute of limitations as well. It is clear that is would be too late to file either amendment as an original complaint since both the termination and the promotion oc-curred more than one year prior to the hearing date of March 4, 1988. It will be recalled that the statute of limitations for filing a complaint under the New York State Human Rights Law is one year from the date of the alleged unlawful discriminatory act.

For purposes of our hypothetical, let us assume that the administrative law judge decides to grant the motion to amend the complaint in both respects. Since ABC Co. could not have been prepared to defend the al-leged failure to promote, and therefore has been deprived of adequate notice, the administrative law judge adjourns the hearing for a date two months subsequent.

Adjournment to nonconsecutive hearing dates is a feature of admin-istrative hearings that is often disturbing to attorneys and employers who are accustomed to court trials. In a court trial, the trial usually is conducted on consecutive days until the trial is completed. In administrative hearings, it is rare for the hearing to be continued on consecutive days. A public hearing that requires three days to complete, may be, and often is, heard on three different days that are weeks or even months apart.

In our hypothetical example, the public hearing is continued and con-cluded on the second hearing date, May 5, 1988. At the second hearing date Que testifies for ABC Co. She testifies to Doe's poor performance. On cross-examination she acknowledges that she, too, lied on her initial employment application, and that she had received only "satisfactory" ratings at the time when she was promoted. The NYSDHR attorney then produces portions of Doe's personnel file which indicate that he had re-ceived "good" ratings when Que was promoted. On further examination by ABC Co.'s attorney, Que testifies that shortly after her employment with ABC Co. started, she received her diploma from Coolidge High School.

ABC Co.'s second and final witness is Smith, the EEO officer. Smith testifies to the fact that while both Que and Doe lied about having grad-uated high school, Que had in fact graduated by the time the misrepre-sentation had been discovered. In contrast, Doe never corrected the mis-statement of fact.

Smith also testifies to the fact that, in view of both Doe's misrepresen-tation and his poor work performance, the decision was made to terminate Doe and not to terminate Que. In addition, he testifies that Que suffered disciplinary action for falsely stating on her employment application that she had graduated high school. Smith testifies that Que's job seniority had been recalculated so as to commence only from the time that she in fact had received her high school diploma. Smith produces documentation from Que's personnel file indicating that she had agreed to this procedure as an alternative to termination. On cross-examination, Smith concedes that the decision to recalculate Que's seniority had been made on April 10, 1987, after ABC Co. had notice of Doe's complaint.

This completes the public hearing on Doe's complaint. At this point the administrative law judge asks the parties whether they intend to file posthearing briefs or memoranda. The NYSDHR attorney states that he will not be filing a brief, and the employer's attorney states that he will be filing a brief. The administrative law judge specifies a date for submission of briefs, and closes the public hearing. Included as Table 18 is a sample posthearing brief in our hypothetical case. The brief is abbreviated, and is intended simply to demonstrate the format and general approach the employer would take in writing the posthearing brief.

TABLE 18 Posthearing Brief

STATE OF NEW YORK: EXECUTIVE DEPARTMENT
STATE DIVISION OF HUMAN RIGHTS

State Division of Human Rights
on the Complaint of
JOHN DOE,
                    Complainant,
       -against-
ABC CO.,
                    Respondent.

Introduction

On March 3, 1987, John Doe filed a verified complaint with the State Division of Human Rights charging ABC Co. with unlawful discrimination regarding employment on the basis of his age, race and color, in violation of the Human Rights Law (Article 15, Executive Law).

After investigation, the division, by order dated July 5, 1987, found that it had jurisdiction over the complaint, and that there was Probable Cause to believe that the respondent had engaged in unlawful discriminatory practices regarding employment, in violation of the Human Rights Law. The matter was thereupon referred for a public hearing before an administrative law judge of the division of human rights.

The matter came on for public hearing on March 4, 1988, before Norman Clarkson, an administrative law judge of the division of human rights. The respondent appeared by counsel and the case in support of the complaint was presented by an attorney on the staff of the Division.

Subsequent to commencement of the public hearing in the matter, the complaint was amended pursuant to the rules of practice of the division, to additionally charge the respondent with unlawful discrimination regarding employment on the basis of complainant's sex, in violation of the Human Rights Law. Said amendment was granted over the timely objection of respondent's counsel. The matter was thereupon adjourned and continued and concluded on May 5, 1988. This brief is submitted by the respondent in support of respondent and in opposition to the complaint.

Statement of the Facts

In or about 1955, John Doe, the complainant herein, was hired by the respondent to work in its New York widget factory (Tr.   ).[a] Each year, the employees of the respondent would receive a rating on an Annual Performance

---

[a] References are to the transcript of the proceedings at the public hearing.

TABLE 18 *(Continued)*

Evaluation (Tr.   ). The Evaluation would be completed by the employee's supervisor, and would reflect the supervisor's appraisal of the employee's job performance (Tr.   ). The employees are rated according to a scale which is as follows: 1-Excellent, 2-Good, 3-Satisfactory, 4-Unsatisfactory (Tr.   ).

In 30 years of employment, the complainant never received an excellent rating, nor a promotion. (Exh. H[the complainant's personnel file], Tr.   ). The complainant routinely received "Good" ratings, and was considered to be an average, unexceptional employee (Exh. X, Tr.   ).

Commencing in or about 1984, the respondent began experiencing problems with the complainant. (Tr.   ). The complainant exhibited a brittle attitude towards his work, and a hostile attitude towards his supervisors. (Tr.   ). In completing the complainant's 1985 evaluation, his supervisor initially considered giving the complainant a "satisfactory" rating. (Tr.   ). However, after some discussion, it was decided to give him another "good" rating with a verbal warning. (Tr.   ). This was done in consideration of the complainant's thirty years of employment. (Tr.   ). Thus, the rating that the complainant received in his 1985 evaluation did not reflect his true performance as judged at the time by his supervisors.

Unfortunately, the complainant's job performance continued to deteriorate. (Tr.   ). Sometime subsequent to the 1985 evaluation, complainant's supervisor resigned, and replacements for that supervisor were considered. (Tr.   ). Based on numerous criteria, including career potential, work attitude, and furtherance of respondent's affirmative action program (Exh. Y), the decision was made to offer the promotion to Suzy Que. (Tr.   ). Ms. Que accepted, and accordingly was promoted on May 4, 1986. (Tr. Exh. Z [Que's personnel file]).

The complainant was never considered for the promotion in view of his deteriorating work performance. (Tr.   ). In fact, given such deterioration, it was decided that the 1985 verbal warning had been insufficient. Accordingly, on the 1986 Evaluation, the complainant's rating was lowered one level, to "Satisfactory". (Tr.   , Exh. X). However, it should be noted that as in 1985, the 1986 Evaluation did not reflect the respondent's actual appraisal of the complainant's job performance. Even though the complainant's performance was still considered to be unsatisfactory, the decision had been made to lower the rating by only one level. (Tr.   ). As before, this was done in consideration of the complainant's thirty years of employment and in the hope that he could still improve. (Tr.   ).

Starting in the mid-1980s the respondent began experiencing severe financial problems. (Tr.   ). These problems resulted in large part from an influx of cheap widgets from Japan. (Tr.   ). In early 1987 the respondent set up an internal task force to examine this problem and to recommend responses to it. (Tr.   ). The first report of the task force was issued in February 1987. (Exh. T). One of the recommendations included in the report was to reduce payroll expenses by dismissing all nonessential employees who had received a lower rating in 1986 than in 1985. (Exh. T).

Pursuant to such recommendation, respondent's personnel office commenced an exhaustive review of all nonessential employee files. (Tr.   ). In the course of this review two items of information were discovered that are relevant to this proceeding. First, by virtue of his 1985 "good" rating and his 1986 "satisfactory," the complainant was included within the category of employees to be dismissed. (Tr.   ). Second, it was discovered that both Suzy Que and the complainant had stated in their initial employment applications that they were graduates of Coolidge High School, whereas neither were graduates of any high school at the time of their applications. (Tr.   , Exh. X, Exh. Z).

TABLE 18 *(Continued)*

Respondent has maintained a firm policy of longstanding that misrepresentations by an employee on an employment application constitute grounds for immediate dismissal. (Tr.   ). Accordingly, on or about March 1, 1987, both Suzy Que and the complainant were summoned to the personnel office. (Tr.   ). At the meeting both employees admitted the misrepresentations. (Tr.   ). However, Ms. Que submitted proof that, subsequent to commencement of her employment, she attended night school, and in fact, received a diploma from Coolidge High School in 1978. (Tr.   ).

Given the facts of the complainant's poor job performance and his inclusion within the category of employees to be dismissed, the complainant's admission to the misrepresentation merely accelerated the decision that had already been made to terminate his employment. (Tr.   ). Accordingly, the complainant's employment was terminated the following day, March 2, 1987. (Tr.   ).

In contrast, Ms. Que had a promising employment history and demonstrated a positive attitude. (Tr.   ). Since her ratings had remained level, she was not targeted for dismissal. (Exhs. T, Z). In addition it was decided that there was no lasting effect to the respondent from her misrepresentation, since she had in fact graduated from high school shortly after commencement of employment. (Tr.   , Exh. Z). Accordingly, the decision was made not to terminate Ms. Que, but to reduce her seniority so that it would run only from the time that she had in fact graduated high school. (Tr. m Exh. Z). Thus, both Ms. Que and the complainant suffered adverse employer action as a result of their violations of respondent's policy. However, the employer action in each case was appropriate to the complete employment picture presented by each employee.

Point I:

The Amendments to the Complaint Were Barred by the Statute of Limitations

Although the rules of practice of the division provide for the administrative law judge to amend the complaint at the public hearing, such amendment must be made in accordance with the Human Rights Law. That statute requires any complaint that is filed thereunder to be filed within one year of the date of the alleged unlawful discriminatory practice. Section 297.5 Human Rights Law.

The amendments to the complaint were both untimely. The amendment to charge unlawful sex discrimination, was made on March 4, 1988. The last employer action occurred on March 2, 1987, when the complainant's employment was terminated. Any complaint challenging such action was required to be filed no later than one year subsequent, or by March 2, 1988. There is no authority to support the implied assumption of the administrative law judge, that the amendment could "relate back" to the date of the original complaint. Lacking such authority, it is clear that the amendment charging unlawful sex discrimination was time-barred.

The amendment to the complaint to challenge the promotion of Suzy Que on May 4, 1986, is similarly time-barred. In that situation, the amendment of the complaint occurred on March 4, 1988, clearly well in excess of the one-year limitations period.

Point II:

The Complainant Failed to Establish a Case of Unlawful Discrimination

The standard of proof in an action under the Human Rights Law is the same as that articulated by the U.S. Supreme Court in Title VII or ADEA actions.

TABLE 18 *(Continued)*

The relevant case law provides that, after the employer has articulated a legitimate, nondiscriminatory reason for the challenged employer action, then the complainant has the burden of proving that the articulated reason was pretextual. *Texas Department of Community Affairs v. Burdine*, 450 U.S. 248 (1981). Moreover, the ultimate burden of persuasion always remains with the complainant. *Id.*

Here the respondent demonstrated that the complainant was not promoted in 1986 because of poor work performance. This was established at the public hearing by the testimony of complainant's supervisor, by the testimony of respondent's EEO officer, and by the complainant's personnel file.

The respondent also demonstrated that the decision to terminate the complainant's employment was made in early February 1987, on the basis of objective company-wide recommendations made by a task force. This decision was precipitated by the subsequent discovery that the complainant had lied on his employment application, a long-standing basis for immediate termination.

Suzy Que was not treated similarly to the complainant precisely because the position was not similar. Ms. Que was not targeted for termination, her work performance was satisfactory, and the effect of the misrepresentation had been mitigated by the time of the discovery. Thus, there was no unlawful discriminatory action by the employer with respect to either the promotion of Ms. Que in 1986, or the termination of the complainant's employment in 1987.

In addition, insofar as there was no evidence introduced in the record as to the respective ages of the complainant and Ms. Que, there is no basis for any finding of unlawful discrimination on the basis of the complainant's age.

Conclusion

The complaint should be dismissed.

Dated: New York, New York
June 5, 1988

Respectfully submitted,

_____

TOM JONES, ESQ.
Attorney for Respondent
1 Any Other Street
New York, New York
(212) 123-1234

RECOMMENDED DECISION AND OBJECTIONS

After submission of the posthearing briefs, the administrative law judge will issue a recommended decision. The provision for issuance of a recommended decision is contained in the rules of the NYSDHR, and is typical of most state EEO agencies. There is usually a very large time lag between the conclusion of the public hearing and issuance of the recommended decision, with six months or more being common.

The recommended decision is sent to the parties or their attorneys, with notification that they can submit written objections to the recommended decision within a specified period of time. Typically, the issuance of a recommended decision is the last involvement of the administrative law judge in the matter. After the recommended decision, the case file is assigned to a unit in the commissioner's office, or in the office of the administrative head of the state EEO agency.

In the New York State Division of Human Rights, this office is known as the order preparation unit. It is staffed by attorneys employed by the NYSDHR, but who do not participate in either investigations or in public hearings. The job of the members of the order preparation unit, or of similarly named units in other state EEO agencies, is to review the recommended decision from a strictly legal perspective. By that we mean that the attorneys in the order preparation unit check only that the legal findings and conclusions are in conformance with the law, and that the legal relief recommended may properly be awarded by the agency. The members of the order preparation unit do not get involved in the question of whether the recommended decision is factually correct; they do not retry the case. Questions as to the credibility of various witnesses or of the proper weight to be assigned to different items of evidence, are left to the discretion of the administrative law judge. It is the administrative law judge who physically saw and heard the witnesses, and is in the best position to judge their demeanor or credibility.

This is not to say that the factually based findings of the administrative law judge are accepted without question. Such findings remain subject to the ultimate decision of the commissioner, or, in other state EEO agencies, to the decision of the administrative chief of that agency. By statute, in each state, it is the commissioner, or similarly named agency head, who is empowered to render the final decision on the complaint. This power to decide the case may not be delegated to subordinates. Although the power to hear the case may be delegated, the power to decide the case may not be similarly delegated. The commissioner may be assisted in the trial of the case and in the preparation of a recommended decision, but such assistance must stop at the point where the case is decided.

Accordingly, the commissioner, or similarly named agency chief, will independently review the file to resolve the factual issues and to decide the case. In his or her review of the file, the commissioner will examine the transcript of the proceedings and exhibits, the recommended decision, and any objections submitted by the parties. We hasten to add that in approximately 90 percent of the cases, the commissioner's decision will be substantially the same as the administrative law judge's recommended decision, but this is not always true. The point to remember is that, on occasion, an effectively prepared set of employer's objections to a recommended decision can convince the commissioner to issue a final decision that is different from the recommended one.

In our hypothetical we have included as Table 19 a sample recommended decision and order. Table 20 is a sample of objections to the recommended decision and order, and Table 21 is a sample final decision and order. As was the case with our sample posthearing brief, these forms

TABLE 19 Recommended Decision and Order

STATE OF NEW YORK: EXECUTIVE DEPARTMENT
STATE DIVISION OF HUMAN RIGHTS

State Division of Human Rights
on the Complaint of
JOHN DOE,

                        Complainant,

    -against-
ABC CO.,

                   Respondent.

RECOMMENDED
DECISION
AND ORDER
Complaint No.

TO THE PARTIES LISTED BELOW:

Enclosed herewith is the recommended decision and order; pursuant to the Rules of Practice of the Division of Human Rights, the parties may submit written objections to the recommended decision and order provided that such objections are submitted within 21 days of the date of this order. Objections should be in writing and should be sent to the Order Preparation Unit, State Division of Human Rights, 55 West 125th Street, New York, New York 10027. Parties should limit their objections to concise statements of disputed issues of law or of the facts, and should not attempt to reargue the case or refer to materials that are not included in the record.

Procedure in the Case

On March 3, 1987, John Doe filed a verified complaint with the State Division of Human Rights charging ABC Co. with unlawful discrimination regarding employment on the basis of his age, race and color, in violation of the Human Rights Law (Article 15, Executive Law).

After investigation, the division, by order dated July 5, 1987, found that it had jurisdiction over the complaint, and that there was probable cause to believe that the respondent had engaged in unlawful discriminatory practices regarding employment, in violation of the Human Rights Law. The matter was thereupon referred for a public hearing before an administrative law judge of the Division of Human Rights.

The matter came on for public hearing on March 4, 1988, before Norman Clarkson, an administrative law judge of the division. The respondent appeared by counsel and the case in support of the complaint was presented by an attorney on the staff of the division.

Subsequent to commencement of the public hearing in the matter, the complaint was amended pursuant to the Rules of Practice of the Division, to additionally charge the respondent with unlawful discrimination regarding employment on the basis of complainant's sex, in violation of the Human Rights Law. The matter was thereupon adjourned and continued and concluded on May 5, 1988. A posthearing brief was submitted on behalf of the respondent on June 5, 1988.

Findings of Facts

1. ABC Co. is a domestic corporation that at all relevant times employed four or more employees in the State of New York.
2. The complainant is a black male.

TABLE 19 *(Continued)*

3. The complainant was hired to work in respondent's New York widget factory in or about 1955.

4. From 1955 up to and including 1985, complainant received "good" ratings on his annual performance evaluations. In 1986, the complainant received a "satisfactory" rating.

5. Suzy Que is a Caucasian female.

6. Suzy Que was hired to work in respondent's New York widget factory in or about 1976.

7. From 1976 to the present time, Suzy Que received "satisfactory" ratings on her annual performance evaluations.

8. On respondent's annual performance evaluations, a "good" rating is superior to a "satisfactory" rating.

9. On or about May 4, 1986, Suzy Que was promoted to the position of foreman, instead of the complainant, who had indicated his interest in the position.

10. On March 1, 1987, both Doe and Que admitted that they had incorrectly stated in their respective employment applications that they were high school graduates. Respondent has a long-standing personnel policy that provides for immediate dismissal in the event of misrepresentation by an employee on his employment application.

11. On March 2, 1987 the complainant's employment was terminated by the respondent. Que's employment was not similarly terminated.

Decision

The evidence indicates that Suzy Que was promoted instead of the complainant even though she had consistently received lower ratings on her annual performance evaluations. Respondent's assertion that the complainant's performance was "deteriorating" is not credible in light of the fact that he was rated "good" in 1985, the last rating for either employee at the time of the promotion. Since Que had less seniority and lower performance ratings than the complainant, her promotion in 1986 instead of the complainant is explainable only by unlawful discrimination on the basis of his race, color, and sex.

Respondent has similarly failed to justify its termination of the complainant on March 2, 1987. Assuming that both Suzy Que and the complainant had lied on their initial applications for employment, and assuming further that such misrepresentation constituted grounds for dismissal, respondent could not explain why only the complainant was terminated. It is clear that similarly situated employees must be treated similarly, and that violation of a company regulation may not be used as a pretext for unlawful discrimination. Accordingly, it is obvious that the termination of the complainant constituted discrimination on the basis of his race, color, and sex, in violation of the Human Rights Law.

The record is barren as to the age of either the complainant or of Suzy Que. Thus, there is no basis for a finding of age discrimination.

Order

Based on the foregoing, and pursuant to section 297.4 of the Human Rights Law, it is hereby

ORDERED, that the complaint be dismissed insofar as it alleges any age discrimination in violation of the Human Rights Law, and that the respondent take

TABLE 19 *(Continued)*

the following steps which are deemed necessary to effectuate the purposes of the Human Rights Law:

1. Respondent shall offer to reinstate complainant to his former position, with back pay; and with seniority and other benefits to be calculated retroactive to the date of complainant's original date of hire;

2. Respondent shall pay $1000 to the complainant as damages for mental anguish;

3. Respondent shall promote the complainant to the next available position as foreman in its New York factory;

4. Respondent shall cooperate with the Division's representatives in any compliance investigation in this matter.

5. Respondent shall adhere to the Human Rights Law.

Dated: New York, New York
      August 1, 1988

_____
Norman Clarkson
Administrative Law Judge

To: John Doe
    1 Any Street
    New York, New York

    ABC Co.
    1 Any Other Street
    New York, New York
    Attn. Tom Jones, Esq.

    State Division of Human Rights
    55 W. 125th Street
    New York, New York
    Attn: Ralph Jenkins, Senior Atty.

TABLE 20 Objections to Recommended Order

August 5, 1988

Order Preparation Unit
State Division of Human Rights
55 West 125th Street
New York, New York 10027

RE: John Doe v. ABC Co.

Dear Sirs:

Pursuant to the rules of practice of the division, and in compliance with the notice of recommended decision and order in this matter, the respondent herewith submits the following specific objections:

1. The administrative law judge improperly granted the motion to amend the complaint at the public hearing. The Human Rights Law provides that any complaints filed under that law must be filed within one year of the alleged unlawful discriminatory practice. Section 297.5 Human Rights Law.

TABLE 20 *(Continued)*

The amendment at the public hearing on March 4, 1988, was clearly more than one year from March 2, 1987, the last date of complainant's employment. Moreover, there is no authority for "relation back" of the amendment to the date of the original complaint. Accordingly, the proposed amendments were time-barred and should not have been granted by the administrative law judge.

2. As to the second sentence of the Recommended Decision, the administrative law judge improperly refused to consider the in-person testimony of complainant's supervisor and the respondent's EEO Officer, that the complainant's job performance was unsatisfactory. As a result of such improper refusal, the administrative law judge incorrectly found that the complainant had a better performance record in March 1986. In fact, the testimony at the public hearing was clear, that the complainant's job performance had been considered unsatisfactory since 1984. Therefore, the recommended conclusion that the promotion of Suzy Que in 1986 was motivated by unlawful discrimination, must be rejected as a matter of law.

3. As to the second paragraph of the recommended decision, the administrative law judge improperly considered Ms. Que and the complainant to have been similarly situated in March 1987. In fact the record is clear that the complainant was already targeted for termination at that point, and Ms. Que was not similarly targeted. The inclusion of the complainant in the category of employees to be terminated was made according to objective criteria implemented on a company-wide basis. In addition, the record is clear that the respondent was satisfied with Ms. Que's job performance, but was unsatisfied with the complainant's job performance. Since the complainant and Ms. Que were not similarly situated, it was erroneous as a matter of law, for the administrative law judge to conclude that dissimilar treatment could be explainable only by unlawful discrimination.

4. In fact, the record is clear that the decision to terminate the complainant's employment was the combined result of the misrepresentation, the complainant's poor work performance, and implementation of the task force recommendation.

Based on the foregoing, it is clear that the recommended findings of unlawful discrimination should be rejected, and that the complaint should be dismissed.

Respectfully submitted,

TOM JONES, ESQ.
Attorney for Respondent
1 Any Other Street
New York, New York
(212) 123-1234

---

are abbreviated and are intended simply to demonstrate the format and the approach taken in each situation.

The recommended decision is a finding of unlawful discrimination on the basis of race and sex. The recommended decision finds unlawful termination as well as unlawful failure to promote. The recommended decision does not find unlawful age discrimination because Doe failed to

TABLE 21 Final Order

STATE OF NEW YORK: EXECUTIVE DEPARTMENT
STATE DIVISION OF HUMAN RIGHTS

State Division of Human Rights
on the Complaint of
JOHN DOE,
                                 Complainant,

          -against-
ABC CO.,
                                 Respondent.

ORDER AFTER
HEARING
Complaint No.

Procedure in the Case

On March 3, 1987, John Doe filed a verified complaint with the State Division of Human Rights charging ABC Co. with unlawful discrimination regarding employment on the basis of his age, race, and color, in violation of the Human Rights Law (Article 15, Executive Law).

After investigation, the division, by order dated July 5, 1987, found that it had jurisdiction over the complaint, and that there was probable cause to believe that the respondent had engaged in unlawful discriminatory practices regarding employment, in violation of the Human Rights Law. The matter was thereupon referred for a public hearing before an administrative law judge of the Division of Human Rights.

The matter came on for public hearing on March 4, 1988, before Norman Clarkson, an administrative law judge of the Division of Human Rights. The respondent appeared by counsel and the case in support of the complaint was presented by an attorney on the staff of the division.

Subsequent to commencement of the public hearing in the matter, the complaint was amended pursuant to the Rules of Practice of the Division, to additionally charge the respondent with unlawful discrimination regarding employment on the basis of complainant's sex, in violation of the Human Rights Law. The matter was thereupon adjourned and continued and concluded on May 5, 1988. A posthearing brief was submitted on behalf of the respondent on June 5, 1988.

On August 1, 1988, notice of a recommended decision and order was given to the parties. Objections to the recommended decision and order were received from the respondent on or about August 15, 1988.

Findings of the Facts

1. ABC Co. is a domestic corporation that at all relevant times employed four or more persons in the State of New York.

2. The complainant is a black male.

3. The complainant was hired to work in respondent's New York widget factory in or about 1955.

4. From 1955 up to and including 1985, complainant received "good" ratings on his annual performance evaluations. In 1986 the complainant received a "satisfactory" rating.

5. Tom Smith, respondent's EEO officer, testified that the complainant's performance had begun to deteriorate prior to 1986, and was subsequently documented by the 1986 annual performance evaluation. This was corroborated at the public hearing by Suzy Que, complainant's supervisor.

TABLE 21 *(Continued)*

6. Tom Smith also testified to respondent's difficult financial position, and to the recommendation by respondent's task force that all nonessential employees whose annual performance evaluations had been lowered from the previous year, should be terminated. The record is clear that the complainant, by virtue of his 1985 "good" rating and his 1986 "satisfactory" rating, was included within the category of employees to be terminated.

7. Suzy Que is a Caucasian female.

8. Suzy Que was hired to work in respondent's New York widget factory in or about 1976.

9. From 1976 to the present time, Suzy Que received "satisfactory" ratings on her annual performance evaluations.

10. On respondent's annual performance evaluations, a "good" rating is superior to a "satisfactory" rating.

11. On or about May 4, 1986, Suzy Que was promoted to the position of foreman, instead of the complainant, who had indicated his interest in the position.

12. On March 1, 1987, both Doe and Que admitted that they had incorrectly stated on their respective employment applications that they were high school graduates. Respondent has a longstanding personnel policy that provides for immediate dismissal in the event of misrepresentation by an employee on his or her employment application.

13. In or about 1978, Suzy Que in fact received a diploma from Coolidge High School. The complainant never received a diploma from any high school.

14. On March 2, 1987, the complainant's employment was terminated by the respondent. Que's employment was not similarly terminated.

Decision

The complaint is time-barred insofar as it seeks to challenge the promotion of Suzy Que instead of the complainant in 1986. Said promotion occurred on May 4, 1986. Under the Human Rights Law, the complainant could have filed a complaint challenging such promotion, up to and including March 4, 1987. Section 297.5 Human Rights Law. Although the complaint was filed within one year from the date of the promotion, the initial complaint did not challenge or refer to the promotion. The initial complaint challenged only the termination. The complaint may not subsequently be amended to challenge an employer's action, when at the time of such amendment, the employer's action is more than one year prior to the date of the amendment.

Insofar as the complaint charges unlawful sex discrimination, it is similarly time-barred. The proposed amendment to charge sex discrimination, was granted on March 4, 1988, which was more than one year subsequent to both the promotion and the termination. Accordingly, the amendment was prohibited by the Human Rights Law's statute of limitations. Section 297.5 Human Rights Law.

The respondent successfully articulated a legitimate nondiscriminatory reason for the complainant's termination. As noted, the complainant was already targeted for termination as a result of the recommendation of respondent's task force. The complainant's work performance was also considered to be deteriorating. His violation of the corporate policy against misrepresentation on employment applications was apparently the final precipitating factor in the decision to terminate his employment.

The complainant's reference to one Suzy Que is unavailing, since Que was not similarly situated with the complainant. Although Que had also lied on her

TABLE 21 *(Continued)*

employment application, she had corrected any effect of such misrepresentation prior to its discovery by the employer. This was not the case with the complainant, who never graduated high school. The employer's decision to impose a different penalty for her violation, in view of her earlier mitigation of the effects of such violation, was a rational business decision and does not raise an inference of unlawful discrimination. In addition, Que was not in the category of employees targeted for termination, since her performance ratings remained at the same level. Finally, there was no showing that there was any employer dissatisfaction with Que's work performance.

There is accordingly no basis for a finding of race or color discrimination as to the termination of the complainant. The record is barren as to the age of either the complainant or of Suzy Que. Thus, there is no basis for a finding of age discrimination.

Order

Based on the foregoing, and pursuant to Section 297 of the Human Rights Law, it is thereby,

ORDERED, that the complaint be and the same hereby is dismissed.

Dated: New York, New York
November 1, 1988

WINSLOW THOMPSON
Commissioner

TO: John Doe
    1 Any Street
    New York, New York

    ABC Co.   State Division of Human Rights
    1 Any Other Street   55 West 125th Street
    New York, New York   New York, New York 10027
    Att: Tom Jones, Esq.   Att: Ralph Jenkins
                                                     Senior Attorney

testify either as to his own age or to Que's age. Since there is no proof of either person's age in the record, there cannot be any finding based on that factor.

The recommended decision finds that Doe was unlawfully passed over for promotion on the basis of his race and sex, since the record shows that he had greater objective qualifications at the time of the promotion. The recommended decision notes that the personnel files of Doe and Que indicate that Doe was rated "good" whereas Que was rated only "satisfactory." The administrative law judge had discounted the testimony of ABC Co.'s EEO officer as to the verbal warning given to Doe in 1985, on the basis that the annual performance reports should be taken at face value, and there is no reflection on Doe's 1985 report of any employer dissatisfaction. The administrative law judge finds that, given Doe's superior record at the time, the promotion of Que, who also had less seniority than Doe, is explainable only by unlawful race and sex discrimination.

The recommended decision also finds unlawful termination since both Que and Doe had lied on their employment applications, but only Doe had been terminated. The administrative law judge finds that, as similarly situated employees, they should have been treated similarly, and that the employer's failure to so treat them is explainable only by unlawful discrimination on the basis of race and sex.

The employer's objections assert that the administrative law judge was incorrect in granting amendment of the complaint at the public hearing. ABC Co. asserts that such amendment was prohibited by the one-year statute of limitations. Even if the 1986 promotion is to be considered, ABC Co. argues that the testimony of its EEO officer should have been credited to amplify the annual performance reports. ABC Co. asserts that on the basis of such testimony the administrative law judge should have found that the employer's dissatisfaction with Doe constituted a legitimate business reason for not promoting him in 1986.

As to the termination, ABC Co. argues that Doe and Que in fact were not similarly situated. Although they both were guilty of the same violation of ABC Co.'s personnel policy, Que had received her high school diploma by the time the violation was discovered. Doe, by contrast, was still without a diploma. In addition, the employer's objection argues that the misrepresentation constituted only part of the reason to terminate Doe. ABC Co. asserts that the company's financial condition together with Doe's deteriorating work performance were contributing factors in the decision to terminate Doe and should have been considered by the administrative law judge.

The commissioner's order after hearing (Table 21) indicates that the employer's objections have prevailed. The commissioner finds that the amendments charging sex discrimination, and challenging the failure to promote, were both time-barred under the statute of limitations. In addition, the commissioner finds that ABC Co. has proven a legitimate nondiscriminatory reason for the termination. The commissioner finds that the violation by both Doe and Que of the company policy regarding misrepresentations, did not cause them to be considered similarly situated since Que ultimately graduated and Doe did not. In addition, although undocumented in 1985, the subsequent annual performance report did demonstrate employer dissatisfaction as a contributing cause for the termination. The commissioner finds that there was no proof of unlawful discrimination, and accordingly orders the complaint dismissed.

CONCLUSION

We have now followed our hypothetical set of facts and complaint from the initial filing to the ultimate Order After Hearing. The reader is no doubt aware that we have constructed the scenario so that the employer would keep losing at each stage of the procedure until the very end. The purpose has been to allow the reader to follow a complaint through a complete procedure, without its being truncated by an early dismissal. If there is one lesson to be gleaned from all this, it is probably that there is no such thing as too much documentation. We have seen the trouble caused our hypothetical employer by his or her failure to record dissatisfaction with the employee from the moment that such dissatisfaction commenced. In the same vein, a written statement as to the reasons for the termination might have produced a no probable cause finding after the investigation, and might even have convinced Doe not to file a complaint. We hope that the reader has gained some insight into how to avoid being sued for alleged unlawful employment discrimination, or if he or she is sued, how to prevail in such a proceeding before a state EEO agency.

Chapter 9

TERMINATION WITHOUT TREPIDATION
A FAIL-SAFE APPROACH

Robert L. Wenzel, J.D.

Many of the preceding chapters of this book have dealt with the erosion of an employer's unfettered freedom to hire, promote, and terminate at will. Today an employer finds his or her human resources decision challenged in many different arenas. It is not uncommon for the employer community to find a termination challenged in federal and state administrative agencies, as well as the civil court system under the theory of wrongful termination.

Employer liability for wrongful termination springs from bad decisions, poor documentation, and faulty procedures in the evaluation and termination process. In an effort to limit liability not only must we address the substantive reasons for termination, but we must also examine the procedure that is utilized in arriving at the conclusion of termination.

Certainly most employers hope that newly hired employees will become successful and productive. Termination should only be contemplated as a last resort for those employees who cannot or will not exhibit appropriate behavior. The following chapter is designed to provide a practical guide for handling those employee behavior problems which may lead to termination as well as the termination itself.

PROGRESSIVE DISCIPLINE

For many years employers have utilized the principles of progressive steps of discipline in order to mold, shape, control, and correct the behavior of their employees. Most managers are aware that the job of a manager is getting results through the efforts of others, as opposed to getting results through their own efforts. In order to bring their employees into a mode of behavior which will accomplish the supervisor's needs, managers have adopted various forms of the progressive steps of discipline.

Progressive discipline is a system in which discipline is imposed in graduated levels of severity against an employee who does not meet the standards of his or her employer.

Generally speaking, the progressive steps of discipline fall into the following levels: *oral notice, written notice, suspension,* and *termination.* The oral step should be taken first in most cases in order to correct a behavior pattern, followed by the successive steps of progressive discipline in the event that the anticipated behavior did not occur.

An enlightened employer will oftentimes have a written discipline policy contained within their procedures and policies manual. For those employers who have such a policy, a word of caution is given. Should you have such a written policy in either your policy and procedure manual or your employee handbook, you may be forming an obligation to conduct yourself in a prescribed manner. Therefore, while I recommend a written progressive steps of discipline policy, I do caution not to implement such a policy unless you really mean it. State and federal agencies will check to see if you have followed your own policies and consistently applied them.

I have included a suggested policy of discipline and counseling which can be adopted easily by most organizations. This policy is one of three that have been included for your use by Cathleen Jordan, President of Jordan/Keene Consultants, Mission Viejo, California.

The foundation of the progressive steps of discipline is notice. If an employer is to achieve a certain method of behavior, the only way this achievement can be accomplished is by notifying the employee of the expected level of performance and any deficiency that may exist. Consequently, the concept of notice is essential in all that we do in the discipline process which begins with the oral step of notifying the employee that a deficiency in performance exists.

ORAL STEP

The oral step of notification should occur between the immediate supervisor and the employee. It is helpful if the immediate supervisor has established a job description which outlines the duties and responsibilities of the job. When the employee's performance becomes deficient, the supervisor need only then review the job description with the employee and point out the deficiencies of performance. It's a good idea for the supervisor to make a note of the oral discussion and place the note memorializing the oral discussion in the employee's personnel file. At a later date it may be important to know the first notice which the employee had of the deficiency. I do not recommend any specific written form for the oral step in the progressive steps of discipline since the goal of the oral step is informal notice of the deficiency.

The oral step should be conducted in a rather informal environment wherein the supervisor utilizes the best counseling and coaching techniques in order to persuade the employee into an acceptable behavior pattern.

The basic conclusion of the oral step of the progressive steps of discipline should be a clear understanding between the supervisor and the employee of the following: (1) the deficiency, (2) the expected level of performance, and (3) the expectation that performance must be immediate and sustained.

WRITTEN STEP

In the event that the employee should not exhibit the correct behavior and overcome the deficiency, the supervisor must, within a reasonable period of time, contemplate the second step of the progressive steps of discipline. Traditionally the second step of the progressive steps of discipline is the written step. Many employers will utilize a specific form for the written step in the disciplinary process. I have included a suggested form entitled "Employee Warning Report" (Figure 9.1).

Some employers recommend the yearly performance appraisal form for use during the second step of the progressive steps of discipline. The format is not important, but the form utilized should be used consistently for all employees.

I personally prefer the use of the performance appraisal for the second step of discipline. The performance appraisal is the official company document which is used to notify an employee of those aspects of the employee's behavior which are unsatisfactory or superior and those aspects of the employee's behavior which are unsatisfactory and need improvement. Therefore, it would make good sense to utilize this performance appraisal form during the second step of the progressive steps of discipline, even though it might not be time for the employee's normal review. As with the first level of discipline, notice is the key factor in the application of the second written step. The employee is receiving notice that he or she has failed to achieve the expected level of performance and that if the deficiency is not improved and sustained on an immediate basis, it may be cause for termination.

While the objective of improving employee behavior remains the same, the difference between the first and the second step of discipline is merely one of degree of severity. The written step is designed as a more serious approach to the disciplinary problem. In the written step of discipline, we are memorializing our discussion with the employee and most generally giving the employee a copy of the written step of discipline. Even though the second step is more severe, the story is the same. We are informing the employee that his or her behavior is deficient in a specific area; we are informing the employee of the expected level of behavior; and we are informing the employee that immediate and sustained improvement is necessary. The language should be clear and unambiguous and the employee should sign the written step. Great care should be taken so that there is no mistaking that the employee is aware of the deficiency.

Much discussion has been held regarding whether or not to inform

EMPLOYEE WARNING REPORT

Employee's Name: _____

Position: _____ Department: _____

Reason for Warning: ___ Attendance   ___ Carelessness   ___ Safety

                        ___ Disobedience   ___ Work Quality   ___ Tardiness

                        ___ Other: _____

Date of Occurrence: _____ Time of Occurrence: _____

Company Statement	Employee Statement
THE ABOVE-MENTIONED DEFICIENCY IF NOT IMPROVED ON AN IMMEDIATE AND SUSTAINED BASIS WILL BE CAUSE FOR TERMINATION.	

Required Action

_____

Employee's Signature: _____ Date: _____

SIGNATURE DOES NOT INDICATE AGREEMENT WITH THIS WARNING, BUT SERVES TO ACKNOWLEDGE THAT A COPY OF THE DOCUMENT HAS BEEN RECEIVED.

Supervisor's Signature: _____ Date: _____

Figure 9.1. Employee warning report.

the employee that the failure to correct the deficiency of performance will result in termination. It is my personal belief that if the progressive steps of discipline are designed with the objective of improving behavior and the objective of notice to the employee, we need not hold any surprises from the employee. If I were the employee receiving the written step, I would want to know that failure to correct the deficiency could result in termination. Therefore, in order to accomplish our objectives, I recommend that at the second step of discipline that the following language be included: "Immediate and sustained improvement in the area of deficiency is necessary or termination will result." A clear, concise statement to this effect with a copy to the employee certainly will defeat any argument by the employee that he or she did not know their job was in jeopardy.

Many employers utilize a disciplinary probation period during this written step of discipline. The employer will document the second step of discipline and may give the employees 30, 60, or 90 days to improve on their deficiency of performance. It is my recommendation that no such disciplinary probation period be utilized. There are two reasons why a specific probationary period is inadvisable: (1) *A new contract of employment may be formed.* There are many who would argue that an employee placed on a written probationary period of 30, 60, or 90 days in order to correct a deficiency of performance is thereby subject to and part of an employment contract. This argument has successfully been made at times ensuring the employee 30, 60, or 90 days of continued employment at which time the employee is given the opportunity to correct the deficiency. I believe that many employers would not wish to enter into such a contractual arrangement in that, should the employee not exhibit any improved performance, the employer would wish to retain complete and full authority to terminate at any point in time. (2) *The disciplinary probation period does not resolve the problem.* A formal disciplinary probation period of 30, 60, or 90 days will oftentimes bring a limited time focus on the employee's performance. This disciplinary probation period has been likened to an amusement park roller coaster wherein the employee enters the roller coaster on the first day of the probationary period and slowly climbs his or her way to the anticipated level of performance which is the top of the hill. Having all been on a roller coaster, we know that following the climb is the plummet down the other side. Many supervisors have expressed their concern regarding the effect of this stipulated disciplinary probation period by stating that the employee's performance magically improves on the last day of probation only to be followed by a deterioration of performance, and some months later being faced with a reoccurrence of the same deficiency. Consequently, I recommend the elimination of a structured 30, 60, 90 day period of probation. After all, what the employer is looking for is immediate and sustained improvement and that is what should be said.

Much has been said regarding an employee's refusal to sign a performance appraisal or refusal to sign on any document which memorializes a deficiency. Oftentimes the employee will refuse to sign such a document indicating that he or she feels that such a signature would imply agreement with the evaluation. Contained within your document which you will utilize for the second step of the disciplinary process should be the statement underneath the employee's signature line that: Signature does not indicate agreement with the statements contained herein, but only serves as an acknowledgment that a copy of the document has been received.

Should an employee refuse to sign, I would suggest explaining that the signature does not impute agreement, but rather only acknowledges receipt of a copy of the written document. Nevertheless, some employees may continue to refuse signature. In the event such refusal continues, it is wise for the supervisor to call in a witness at the conclusion of the interview when a copy of the document is given to the employee. It should be noted as an aside that in many states employers are required by Labor Code to give employees copies of any documents which they sign. Again, if we are being true to the essential element of the progressive steps of discipline which is notice, a copy of the written step of discipline is a logical and beneficial step.

For those supervisors who have great difficulty in reducing their thoughts to clear concise writing, I recommend an excellent publication entitled "Supervisors Guide to Documentation and File Building for Employee Discipline." This easy to read guide has been authored by Ronald C. Ruud, Esquire and Joseph J. Woodford. With their permission, Chapter Three of this publication is included for your review.

BASIC WRITING SKILLS FOR DOCUMENTATION

The examples in the following chapters are from actual disciplinary cases. They have been selected to illustrate a variety in style and format and yet contain all the essential elements of a good disciplinary document. These samples are designed to be used as guides or models. But there is no perfect disciplinary document that will fit all circumstances. Thus, it is critical that modifications are made to adapt the examples to unique circumstances and requirements.

Any supervisor can learn to write good disciplinary documents. Like most skills, it takes time and practice to master. With experience, quality should improve along with a decrease in the time needed to prepare documentation. The basic concepts that must be mastered relate to the most common mistakes made by supervisors in writing disciplinary documents.

Mistakes commonly made in the writing of disciplinary materials are:

(1) Lack of clear, direct, relevant communication from the supervisor to the subordinate;
(2) Reliance on general statements instead of specific factual detail; and
(3) Reliance on conclusions without laying a factual foundation.

Tactful, Indirect Communication v. Clear, Direct, Relevant Communication

When the famous 18th century French writer Voltaire said, "Words were given to man to enable him to conceal his true feelings," he was describing a common human behavior that is far too often manifested in disciplinary documents. Instead of expressing the true facts and dealing with the problem head-on, supervisors have a tendency to pussyfoot and equivocate. This is usually rationalized as a need to be tactful and build human relations.

The mollycoddling supervisor only causes a breakdown in communications. Open, direct and frank transmissions of information to a subordinate is critical in every disciplinary document. In simple terms, the employee must know specifically what is wrong and what he must do about it and what will happen if he fails to follow the supervisor's directions. There can be no room for the employee to apply his own interpretation to any written disciplinary communication from management.

This is not to say that tact and human relations don't have a place in documenting employee discipline. It is possible to be factual and direct in communicating with workers without engaging in a personal attack. When communicating dissatisfaction to a subordinate, focus on the specific facts rather than on the person. An analysis of the specific shortcomings in the employee's job performance must be communicated, not just the assessment that the person is a lousy employee. This should be followed with a sincere offer to help the employee to improve his job conduct or skills.

General v. Specific

The "Golden Rule" in writing any documentation is "ALWAYS BE SPECIFIC AND FACTUAL." One major purpose of documentation is to record specific detail such as times, dates, names, places, events, etc. Unfortunately for management, disciplinary reports often only contain general statements about the problem and omit the critical detail needed if a disciplinary case goes to a hearing before an arbitrator or hearing officer.

A good illustration of this problem is a situation where an employee receives a memorandum for habitual tardiness. A poorly drafted memo would say, "John Doe is frequently late for work." A well written document would be specific. For example: "During the months of January and February, 1981, John Doe was late to work as follows:

Date	Minutes Late
January 3	11
January 6	17
January 22	22
January 30	12
February 4	33
February 9	19
February 13	12″

The good example tells the reader how many times John Doe was late, on which dates he was late, and the number of minutes he was late.

General statements are difficult to substantiate if challenged in a disciplinary hearing. Specific factual statements can be substantiated if preserved in written documentation of the event or events. The chart at the end of this chapter which compares general terms versus specific terms illustrates this point.

Conclusion v. Fact

The skillful supervisor writes narrative that describes the employee's faults in a factual manner. If conclusions are used, they should be supported by a specific factual foundation. For example, to say, "John Doe was found sleeping on duty," is a conclusionary statement. Facts in support of that conclusion might be, "Upon entering the print shop, John Doe was observed sitting at the desk, his head was lowered and eyes closed, he did not acknowledge my presence for a full five minutes, he responded after his name was repeated three times." Another example would be, "John Doe made an offensive vulgar remark in public." The factual foundation for that conclusion might be, "John Doe, while on duty, announced to the Friends of the Library meeting on March 3, 1980, that the Library Director is a damn, no-good son of a bitch."

It is essential that the disciplinary writer be able to distinguish specific from general statements and fact from conclusions. Once these concepts are understood, the supervisor is well on the way to becoming a competent writer. The specific, factual document not only proves up management's case, but it also assists the supervisor in meeting the test of cross-examination if the matter goes to hearing. The following chart is a training aid used in workshops to develop these critical basic writing skills.

General Conclusion	Specific Fact
Numerous, frequently, often	Seven times within past two months.
Violates provision of master contract	Took a morning break in excess of ten minutes allowed in Article X, Section 3 of the contract on June 6, 8, 10, 11, 12, 13 and 17, 1980.
Used a dirty, offensive word on a customer	On April 1, 1981, told Maria Garcia to "Shove your water bill up your ass."
Is frequently tardy	Was more than ten minutes late to work on August 3, 6, 22, 30 and 31, 1979.
Work station is dirty	John Doe's work station located at the number 3 service rack on June 3, August 1 and August 6, 1980, was found to have oil standing on the floor, used rags were on the floor and work bench instead of the metal trash can, tools were on the floor, . . .
Inaccurate mathematics discussion	Teacher explained that one number of a binomial may be divided by a monomial to simplify an algebraic fraction.
John Doe was intoxicated	After he returned from lunch at 1:15 p.m. on August 28, 1979, John Doe's speech was slurred, he staggered when he walked, he fell against the file cabinets two times, and there was a strong smell of alcohol, . . .
John Doe does not follow instructions	On October 1, 1981 at 8:15 a.m., John Doe was directed by his supervisor to help in the jail. At 9:25 a.m. it was necessary to direct him once again to report to the jail. At 10:00 a.m. John Doe still had not followed the directive of a superior officer.

SUSPENSION

Many employers will utilize suspension as the third step of discipline. Some employers are contractually obligated to such a suspension based on the collective bargaining agreement. Suspension in a disciplinary sense is designed to be a more severe step than the written step of discipline. In other words an employee's attention should certainly be gained if he is suspended from work for any given period of time. The disciplinary suspension which is designed to punish the employee for his lack of correct behavior oftentimes has quite the opposite effect. I have heard many employers state that they have eliminated the disciplinary suspension period since the employees tend to think of these absences from work as merely extended vacations without pay.

Another reason to utilize the suspension step in the progressive steps of discipline is for investigatory purposes. Many employers find themselves in a situation where they are trying to investigate the facts surrounding a potential termination in order to make their ultimate decision.

Unless contractually obligated, the latter reason for a suspension seems to be the more defensible. Certainly time should be taken to investigate all terminations in order to ensure the facts and that the course of action is not only a fair course of action but consistent with prior conduct.

Consequently, an employer without contractual obligations would be well advised to institute a suspension period as part of the progressive steps of discipline but to utilize that suspension period for investigatory purposes only.

TERMINATION

Finally, the ultimate step in the progressive step of discipline process is the termination itself. Termination is viewed at times as an independent act. Oftentimes employers forget that the termination itself is actually part of the progressive discipline approach. Again, going back to the essential element of the progressive steps of discipline being that of notice, it is imperative that notice be properly executed in the termination interview itself.

An old saying is that if a termination takes more than five minutes, something has gone wrong or the preparation for that termination has been inadequate. The termination interview is no time for a debate. If the employer has correctly done his or her homework, it should merely be an informative step whereby the employee is notified that their uncorrected deficiency of performance is resulting in termination. The employer should review with the employee the fact that the oral notice was given, that written notice was given, that full investigation was conducted and that the deficiency had not been corrected and thereby termination is resulting. A sample termination policy has been included for your review.

I recommend that any supervisor conducting a termination interview have a witness. Following the conclusion of the termination interview it's a good idea for both the witness and the supervisor to reduce to writing the conversation which took place during the termination interview.

Procedurally then the steps in the progressive notice to the employee of deficient behavior include the oral step, the written step, investigatory suspension, and finally, termination.

The steps of progressive discipline is not a process, however, which must be mechanically followed in all cases. Employers must retain discretion to deviate from their written policy when circumstances dictate. Many serious offenses, such as insubordination, may be handled at the second step, completely eliminating the oral step altogether. Even more serious offenses, such as theft, might require investigatory suspension and termination.

Documentation must occur on the oral, written, suspension, and termination steps. The trier of fact will want to know when the problem began and how the employee received notice. The trier of fact will want to know whether or not the employee was aware that the employer expected improved performance and what that level of expectation was. The trier of fact will want to know whether or not the employee was aware that failure to improve performance would result in termination. Consequently, the documentation of the four steps of progressive discipline must be present in order to show notice to the employee and thereby meet the challenge of defending a termination if necessary.

RIGHT TO UNION REPRESENTATION

The issue of the right of an employee to union representation during meetings with management is a troubling area for most supervisors. This question was addressed by the U.S. Supreme Court in 1975 when it handed down the leading case in the field, *NLRB v. Weingarten*, 420 U.S. 251 (1975). The *Weingarten* case was a case from the private sector involving the rights of employees under the National Labor Relations Act. Under *Weingarten* and related cases, the standards of employee rights to union representation are always subject to change and therefore you should consult an attorney if you have a question. At this time it appears that:

1. An employee has the right to the presence of a union representative during an employer conducted investigatory interview which the employee reasonably believes might result in disciplinary action or a significant purpose of the interview is to investigate facts to support disciplinary action. The employee's "reasonable belief" must be based on an objective consideration in the light of all the circumstances involved in the particular meeting. If an employee is told that the meeting is not for the purpose of taking disciplinary action and no punitive action will result, then the employee cannot reasonably believe that discipline will result.

2. Employees do not have the legal right to have a union representative present at meetings where discipline is to be announced. In other words, management has already investigated and determined the disciplinary action to be taken. Under such circumstances, there is no right to have a union representative present when management gives the employee the predetermined discipline.

3. The obligation is on the employee to request that a union representative be present at the meeting. Management does not have to inform the employee of this right.

4. Management is not required to postpone an interview because a particular union representative requested by the employee is not available when other representatives of the union are available.

5. The role of the union representative is that of an observer on behalf of the employee. The union representative ensures that the rights of the

employee are not abridged. But the employer cannot refuse to allow the union representative to speak at an employee interview. In listening to the employee's version of the incident under investigation, the supervisor is required to allow the union representative to help the employee in presenting the facts. This does not give the union representative the right to interfere with the investigation being conducted by the employer. The employee, even with a union representative present, may be required to personally respond to the employer's job-related questions.

6. The right of representation at meetings with management does not apply to normal employer–employee conversations; such as the giving of instructions, training, or needed correction of work technique. Unless the collective bargaining agreement requires otherwise, a union representative does not have to be present when a supervisor is discussing an evaluation or evaluation observation of the employee's normal work. Such meetings are a regular event involving an employee's work performance which is of a direct concern to the employer, and, in most situations, is not disciplinary in nature. But once an employee has been notified that his or her performance needs improvement, any subsequent evaluation conferences, based on the employee's work, may be reasonably considered as possibly leading to a disciplinary action. In such cases it may be wise to allow a union representative to be present.

STANDARDS OF PERFORMANCE

Rules and regulations are a standard part of almost every employer's policy and procedure manual. The obvious design of including such rules and regulations is to increase the efficiency and the administration of the company. Such rules of conduct also serve as a standard by which the employee can determine what the company considers to be terminable conduct.

Many employers overburden their policy and procedure manual by trying to list every conceivable violation of company policy and procedure that could result in a disciplinary action. Certainly such an exhaustive list is not only cumbersome but will never be all-inclusive. Open language should be used when listing terminable offenses so that that list may be amended or expanded at the sole discretion of the employer. I have included a sample "Standards of Conduct" policy for your review.

DOCUMENTATION

Implementing and documenting the progressive steps of discipline will only serve to prove up that the employee received adequate notice. Only half the job of documentation has been completed at this point. The employer must also be able to prove up the substantive reason for the termination. The employer must be able to prove that the reason for termination is substantial, a violation of company policies and procedures consistent with being fair and morally just.

Before examining the way that we can document the substantive reason for performance, we should take a moment and discuss the potential period of time between the time of termination and the time of producing the evidence. In the administrative forum the time frame fluctuates greatly depending on the work load of the administrative agency. Generally speaking, the Equal Employment Opportunity Commission (EEOC) requires that all complaints be filed within 300 days from the cause of action. State administrative agencies have different time frames and should be checked. Investigation, however, may occur at varying intervals following the filing of the complaint. Investigation may be immediate or may be at some considerable period of time later.

In the event that an employee pursues his or her course of action in the civil court arena, the time frame may substantially lengthen. For example, in California the statute of limitations for an oral contract is two years and the statute of limitations is four years for a written contract. The discovery period will vary in length, but most generally will last approximately one year. The employer and the employee during this period of discovery may be required to answer interrogatories, requests for production of documents, and respond to depositions. Following the conclusion of discovery, a trial date will be given based on the work load of the particular court. Therefore, it is not unusual nor outside of the realm of possibility to consider that an employee's cause of action may not get to the trier of fact for as much as three to six years. This time delay has serious implications regarding our discussion of evidence as it relates to the substantive reasons for termination. All evidence should be compiled with an eye towards the preservation of this evidence for a considerable period of time.

The following discussion contains recommendations for those tools which you can use to document the substantive reason for the termination:

1. *Business Records.* The court may recognize those records which are regularly kept by the employer in the conduct and ordinary course and scope of its business. The court will not accept those records which are prepared for litigation purposes. In order to enter business records into evidence, you must enter those records through the custodian of records. Each state and the federal court has specific rules as to qualification for the custodian of records and these qualifications should be reviewed. Generally speaking, business records can support many different kinds of termination. For example, a termination for excessive tardiness can be supported by the actual timecards or timesheets themselves. These timecards or timesheets may be considered to be business records since they are kept in the ordinary course and scope of business and, therefore, could be entered into the record as business records which support the fact that the employee was tardy.

Other business records may pertain to performance as an example. Many manufacturing facilities will keep performance records based on individual and departmental performance. These written records should be considered as business records which support an individual's deficient performance. An employer should be thoughtful in gathering up those business records which support the underlying reason for termination, as these business records can be admitted into evidence at a later point in time.

2. *Written Customer Complaints.* Many service organizations and organizations with public contact require a high level of customer relations skills. Should an employee's performance be deficient in this area, many employers will be tempted to terminate employees based on oral customer complaint. I caution that oral customer complaints are not sufficient documentation for termination that may be challenged several years in the future. Years from now you may be required to produce the witness customer who claimed that your service representative was rude and abusive. You may be unable to locate that customer or the customer may not have a full recollection of the complaint. Further, individuals become nervous when placed in the position of a witness in a formal proceeding and may have less than a full recollection of the details.

Consequently, I recommend that termination action not be taken merely on the basis of oral customer complaints. Customer complaints need be written complaints in the customer's own handwriting and signed by the customer. In order to attempt to enter these documents into evidence at a future point in time when the witness is no longer available, the document should contain the language, "I declare under penalty of perjury that the above is true and correct" preceding the signature of the customer.

Practically speaking, I recognize the difficulty in reducing a customer complaint to writing in the format as described above. Nevertheless, if you are to avoid liability for a termination, you must have the proper documentation. Should an employee be deficient in customer service, you must be able to prove that the employee received complaints from customers.

3. *Witness Statements.* Much of the discussion discussed regarding written customer complaints applies to witness statements. Employee witness statements are often critical to the documentation of the substantive reason for termination. Relying on oral testimony and hoping that this testimony will be the same some years later is a dangerous business. Consequently, I make the same recommendations for employee witness statements as I did for customer complaints. Witness statements should be taken at the time of the incident and should be in the employee's own handwriting. The employee should declare under penalty of perjury that the statement is true and correct, and there should be a signature by the employee. In the event that the employee's language is other than English, the statement should be drafted in the employee's proficient language and then translated at a later date by a court certified translator.

4. *Dated and Signed Photographs.* Often employers overlook the value of the camera. The cameras can be an invaluable tool to an employer and serve as documentation in an employee termination. Recently an employer in the Los Angeles area used a photograph to substantiate employee theft. The subject employee was employed on the graveyard shift and covertly placed scrap metal in the trunk of his car for future sale on the black market. The employee's car while exiting the parking lot became "hung up" on the crown of the street due to the heavy load of scrap metal

in the trunk of the car. The employee was asked to open the trunk and a picture was taken of the employee opening the trunk full of scrap metal, including the license plate on the automobile. There was no question that the employee had been terminated rightfully for theft.

In order for a photograph to be entered into the record, it must be dated and signed by the processor.

Other ways of preserving evidence include preserving examples of poor work, correspondence, and company communications with employees.

THE PERSONNEL FILE

Assuming that the employer has properly documented the progressive steps of discipline and applied those steps consistently, as well as properly documented the substantive and underlying reasons for termination, we should give some discussion to the repository of all this information. The personnel file should be the all and end all. All information concerning the employee's performance with the company, including the deficiencies of performance and the causes for termination, as well as the supporting evidentiary material, should be included within the personnel file. There are many good reasons why the personnel file should be the final and only repository of this information.

If a decision of termination should be made based on the facts available, we must be confident that we have all the facts before us. Many times supervisors, department heads, and managers will keep a "secret file" on their employees. I am not confident what the motivation for keeping a secret file is; however, I do know that in the past I have maintained such secret files. The problem with the secret file is that information which is discoverable is not considered during the termination evaluation process, since the secret files may reside in the bottom desk drawer of the immediate supervisor or be at remote locations. Therefore, I recommend that employers keep one personnel file and that all documentation, including the documentation of the progressive steps of discipline as well as the substantive reasons for termination, are included within the one personnel file.

INDEPENDENT REVIEW

In order to limit the liability for a wrongful termination charge or an adverse finding from an administrative agency, it is recommended that the personnel file be reviewed by an independent third party before the ultimate decision for termination is made. If secret files have been eliminated and the gathering of evidence documenting both procedure and substantive reasons for termination has been adequate, then the independent third party can review the file and serve as the trier of fact before the issue ever gets to an administrative agency or to the trial court. I recommend that the in-house trier of fact be the human resources individual in the company, since that person likely has some experience with administrative and civil court challenges to terminations. Below are listed five questions that should be asked by the in-house trier of fact when the personnel file is being reviewed. If these five questions can be answered in the affirmative, it is my feeling that there is a substantial limitation to any liability that might be incurred by the employer. The five questions are as follows:

1. Was the employee informed in writing of his or her deficiencies, the expected improved behavior, and that the lack of immediate sustained improvement would result in termination?
2. Has all evidence and documentation regarding the deficiency, both before and after the warning, been placed in the personnel file?
3. Did the employee have reasonable time to eliminate the deficiency?
4. Were there any circumstances beyond the employee's control which prevented elimination of the deficiency?
5. Is the application of the discipline consistent with others?

A thoughtful review of the previously mentioned questions will substantially reduce the liability that the employer faces for a termination.

In conclusion, if the termination process is both fair and equitable, provides notice to the employee and is well documented, it stands a good chance of surviving a challenge. In the final analysis legislation and case law dictate that the employer plan and implement terminations with great care.

Appendix A

SUGGESTED POLICY

SECTION: Employee Relations (700)	PAGE: 700.4 1
EFFECTIVE: 3/1/82 REVISED: 7/1/84	APPROVED BY:

Subject:	COUNSELING AND DISCIPLINE
Philosophy:	The counseling and discipline process outlined in this policy is designed to ensure fair and equitable treatment of all employees. Routine disciplinary procedures begin with an informal verbal counseling session, then move on to a formal documentation in writing, to possible suspension, and ultimate termination of employment unless a prior step has resulted in a corrective action.
Policy:	All instances where disciplinary action is required are to be thoroughly examined. Consistent corrective action will be applied in all cases where similar circumstances exist.
Responsibility:	Supervisors are responsible for ensuring uniformity in the application of disciplinary procedures. The specific circumstances, overall work record and length of service should be considered in each situation.
Procedure:	As a guideline to corrective action, the Company has established a sequence of usual steps in the disciplinary process:

1. Verbal Counseling (Informal)

2. Written Warning (Formal)

3. Possible Suspension

4. Termination of Employment

Verbal Counseling:	If an employee is experiencing difficulty in work performance, in relationships with the supervisor or fellow employees, or is failing to perform at an acceptable level, or if established work rules are not being adhered to, the supervisor should attempt to correct the problem with verbal counseling through the normal course of work activities.

Though informal, this is the first step in the corrective procedure. All verbal efforts to correct a problem are to be recorded on the Employee Warning Report. The date, the topic of the verbal counseling and a brief description of the discussion should be provided. The supervisor should sign the form and forward to Personnel for retention in the employee's personnel file.

It is not necessary at this point to have the employee sign the form, or to supply the employee with a copy.

SECTION: Employee Relations (700)	PAGE: 700.4 2

Such counseling memos will be removed from the employee's file annually, provided there are no further warnings for the same offense.

Written Warning:

If this informal process is not effective, then it will be necessary for the supervisor to initiate formal action to resolve the problem.

There are circumstances, however, when the following procedure would be used as the initial corrective action. These would include very serious performance problems, or very serious difficulties in interpersonal relationships, serious breaches of company policy, etc. In other words, problems that although not considered misconduct or insubordination would, if repeated, be cause for termination.

The following is a formal, two-step process which stresses identification and discussion of work-related problems with the employee.

1. The supervisor should meet with the employee to discuss the specific problem, clarify misunderstandings, and define what must be done to eliminate the problem:
   a. Explain specifically what change in performance or behavior is necessary and ensure the employee understands what must be corrected.

b. An Employee Warning Report is to be completed by the supervisor and reviewed with the employee. The employee is to be given an opportunity to sign the form.

c. If the employee refuses to sign the form, the supervisor should note, "Refused to Sign" on the form and have it witnessed. There is a section available on the form for the employee to give a written rebuttal of the Employee Warning. On occasion it will be advantageous to have another member of management present during the meeting. This witness should also sign the form.

d. The supervisor specifies that immediate and sustained improvement is necessary by the employee. Timely follow-up is essential. Set a follow-up date at this point and advise the employee you will meet again on that date to discuss the progress made.

SECTION: Employee Relations (700)	PAGE: 700.4 3

e. After the discussion is completed, the written Employee Warning Form is to be reviewed by the supervisor's manager. The initiating supervisor retains the form for completion at the time follow-up action is taken, and sends a copy to Personnel for review and retention.

2. The follow-up meeting should take place on the date specified. Continued counseling should have taken place between the first meeting and the follow-up meeting. The follow-up approach is as follows:

a. If satisfactory improvement has occurred, the employee is to be complimented and encouraged to continue his or her progress. This is to be noted on the Employee Warning Form and forwarded to the personnel department for review and retention for one year.

b. If the problem is not resolved, the process may be repeated, or if the circumstances warrant, move into one of the next phases of the disciplinary process.

Suspension Without Pay:

Suspension of an employee may be used either as the third step in progressive discipline, or as a separate disciplinary action resulting from a serious violation, or may be eliminated altogether.

A supervisor must carefully consider the decision to suspend an employee. It should be stressed that suspension deprives an employee of income and should only be used as an additional step in progressive disciplinary action or in place of termination for a serious offense when there are mitigating circumstances, (i.e., long-term employee, no previous disciplinary history, employee under personal stress, etc.).

If, after serious consideration, the supervisor feels that suspension is appropriate, the employee should be placed on an investigatory suspension, not to exceed three days. Approval for such action shall be obtained from the supervisor's manager. It is highly desirable that the Executive Vice President and/or the Director of Operations be involved in such decisions.

A thorough investigation of the circumstances surrounding the suspension as well as a review of previous disciplinary record(s) will be conducted. Documentation on the suspension and investigation must be forwarded to the personnel department and will be retained in the employee's personnel file.

SECTION: Employee Relations (700)	PAGE: 700.4 4

If, after investigation, a decision is made that the suspension is appropriate, the supervisor and the supervisor's manager will discuss and reach an agreement concerning the duration of the suspension. The maximum duration of any suspension will not exceed two weeks.

If, after investigation, a decision is made that the suspension is not appropriate, the employee will be reinstated with no loss in pay.

Termination:

If an employee is to be terminated due to unacceptable performance or lack of adherence to work rules, specific and documented communication between the supervisor and the employee, (as outlined in this policy), must have occurred. If the employee action involves a serious breach of Company rules, (refer to Standards of Conduct Policy), and immediate discharge is warranted, full documentation of the circumstances, investigation, employee statement, etc. must be completed.

All terminations must be reviewed by the Personnel Manager, and have the approval of the Executive Vice President and/or the Director of Operations.

SECTION: Termination of Employment (800)	PAGE: 800.1 1
EFFECTIVE: 3/1/82 REVISED: 7/1/84	APPROVED BY:

Subject:

TERMINATION OF EMPLOYMENT

Philosophy:

It is the intent of _____ to ensure that the termination of employment is handled in a consistent and fair manner. All terminations, therefore, must be coordinated with the Personnel Department, and have the approval of the Executive Vice President and/or the Director of Operations. An exit interview may be conducted with an employee who resigns, whenever possible. This is to ensure that all aspects of the separation are understood by the employee, and to obtain information that may be useful in improving employee relations.

Policy:

All terminations are to be handled in a consistent manner in accordance with the provisions outlined in this policy. No employee is to be terminated, either voluntarily or involuntarily, without the direct involvement of the Personnel Department, approval of the Manager/Director responsible for the function, and the Executive Vice President and/or the Director of Operations.

There are two types of termination of employment: Voluntary Termination and Involuntary Termination.

Voluntary Termination:

When an employee initiates a resignation for personal or other reasons, the separation is considered voluntary. The supervisor is responsible for determining the true and specific reason for the resignation. When feasible, the supervisor should make an attempt to retain the employee.

When an employee has been absent for three consecutive days without notification, it will be assumed that the employee has resigned. The last day worked is the date of separation.

Failure to return from an approved leave of absence will also be considered as resignation. The date of the expiration of leave will be the separation date.

Notice of Resignation:

Employees who voluntarily resign are expected to give written notice of resignation to their immediate supervisor. Generally, two weeks notice is expected.

Pay In Lieu of Notice:

On occasion, the employee will be permitted to work up to the requested date of separation. This date will be the employee's last day worked and the actual date of separation. If it is determined to be in the best interest of the Company to release the employee immediately, the employee will be paid through the effective date of resignation, (a maximum of 20 working days). The actual date of separation is the employee's last day worked.

SECTION: Termination of Employment (800)	PAGE: 800.1 2

Involuntary
Termination:

An involuntary termination is one that is initiated by the Company. The process of involuntary termination places certain obligations on the Company in behalf of the employee. Managers should carefully consider their decision to terminate an employee. The employee has the right to be fully informed concerning the specific reason(s) for termination.

Before an involuntary termination is made, the counsel of the Executive Vice President and/or the Director of Operations, and the Personnel Department must be obtained. If, after such counsel, involuntary separation is decided upon, the immediate supervisor should so advise the employee in the presence of the Personnel Manager, or another member of management.

There are two basic categories of involuntary termination:

Layoff:

A layoff can occur and the employee's record will indicate an involuntary separation without cause resulting from layoff. The date of separation will be the employee's last day worked.

Employees on layoff status may be considered for future openings prior to consideration of new applicants.

Discharge for Cause:

Every reasonable effort should be made by the Supervisor to assist an employee in meeting the minimum job standards of performance. When an employee is not able to meet these standards or if the demands of the job exceed the employee's abilities, he or she must be given a formal written statement by his or her immediate supervisor. (Refer to Counseling and Discipline Policy.) This statement must outline the situation and include a reasonable period of time within which to correct deficiencies. A copy of the written statement must be sent to the personnel department for inclusion in the employee's personnel file.

If the employee's performance does not improve, then the employee should be told by the supervisor that he or she is being terminated and the reason(s) for termination. The date of separation is the employee's last day worked.

If the employee would rather resign, he or she would be granted this option. The employee's record will reflect a voluntary separation.

An employee may be terminated immediately for an offense of a grave nature or for violation of a Company rule or regulation. This type of separation will be considered involuntary and with cause.

SECTION: Termination of Employment (800)	PAGE: 800.1 3

No employee will be terminated without the prior approval of the Director of Operations and notification to the Personnel Manager.

Severance Pay:

The amount of severance pay, if any, is based upon a number of factors, (e.g., length of service, level of responsibility, reason for separation, etc.). Approval for severance pay must be obtained from the Executive Vice President and/or the Director of Operations. These approvals must be obtained prior to any commitment regarding severance pay to a terminating employee.

Severance pay is not granted to employees who are discharged for cause.

Exit Interview:

Whenever possible, an exit interview will be conducted with the employee who voluntarily terminates. This is to ensure that all aspects of the final arrangements are understood by the employee and that any outstanding obligations to the Company are satisfactorily settled prior to the employee's departure. It also provides an opportunity to obtain information which can be of assistance to management in improving employee relations.

The personnel department will schedule and conduct all Exit Interviews.

Responsibility:	The Personnel Department is responsible for administering this policy. Supervisors are responsible for ensuring that all terminations, whether voluntary or involuntary, are in compliance with the provisions of this policy.
Procedure:	In order to protect the interests of both the Company and the employee, all terminations must be coordinated with the personnel department as far in advance as possible of the proposed termination date. All corrective attempts to assist an employee's performance and any warnings should be documented and placed in the employee's personnel file.
	Supervisors must notify personnel by telephone immediately upon notice of voluntary termination, giving the last day to be worked. The written notice of intent to resign should be forwarded to Personnel immediately.
Company Property:	It is the supervisor's responsibility to notify personnel as to whether an employee has a cash advance or other Company property which must be reclaimed.

SECTION: Termination of Employment (800) | **PAGE: 800.1 4**

	A Personnel/Payroll Action Form, an Employee Exit Questionnaire, and a Termination Report are to be completed on each terminating employee.
Final Compensation:	All terminating employees must be paid in full in accordance with state labor law requirements.
Termination of Insurance Benefits:	Life insurance and medical/dental coverages will generally terminate, effective on the last day of the month in which the employee was terminated, unless otherwise provided by the actual policies or approved by the Executive Vice President. Personnel will handle the termination of insurance coverages and forward a Notice of Conversion Rights to the terminated employee.
Replacement Employees:	If a replacement employee is required, the Personnel Requisition should be completed, approved and submitted to the personnel department as soon as possible.

SECTION: Employee Relations (700)	PAGE: 700.2 1
EFFECTIVE: 3/1/82 REVISED: 7/1/84 APPROVED BY:	

Subject: STANDARDS OF CONDUCT

Philosophy: _____ expects all employees to observe certain standards of behavior while at work. These standards are not intended to restrict an employee's legitimate rights, but to apply the same standards to everyone.

Policy: While it is not company policy to discharge an employee for the first violation of rules and regulations, violations of certain rules and regulations are more serious than others. In those instances, the company has no alternative other than immediate discharge. We feel the following actions on the part of employees may be cause for disciplinary action, including discharge without prior warning.

All instances where disciplinary action is required are to be thoroughly examined. Consistent corrective action will be applied in all cases where similar circumstances exist. Supervisors are responsible for insuring uniformity in the application of disciplinary action. The circumstances involved, overall work record, and length of service of the employee involved are to be considered.

1. Insubordination.
2. Dishonesty.
3. Intoxication/influence of drugs.
4. Improper solicitation on company property without permission.
5. Negligence in the performance of duties.
6. Willful destruction or theft of company property.
7. Other major violation of the rules and regulations of the company.
8. Other grounds as deemed necessary from time to time.

Responsibility: Supervisors are responsible for taking appropriate action when Company standards of conduct are violated.

SECTION: Employee Relations (700)	PAGE: 700.2 2

Procedure: If an employee violates any of the above rules, or is failing to perform at an acceptable level, specific and documented communication between the supervisor and the employee normally must occur before termination will be considered.

When a serious violation of company rules occurs and immediate termination appears warranted, sufficient documentation of the circumstances, resulting investigation and the employee's statement must be documented.

All terminations must have the approval of the supervisor's manager and must be in consultation with the Personnel Manager.

Refer to the Counseling and Discipline Policy for information on handling disciplinary actions.

Chapter 10

TERMS OF TERMINATION
RESOLVING THE ISSUES

Bennett W. Root, Jr., J.D.

Tricky and difficult as making a valid decision to terminate employment may be, effecting that decision probably will be as challenging. Deciding in a vacuum that any hypothetical employee, say "Smith," should be terminated presents its own difficulties (*See* Chapter 3). Telling "Smith" correctly requires a refined balance of skill and commitment. An error in the communication of the separation decision may cause an unnecessary, but costly, lawsuit. Careful preparation and proper presentation are the keys to effective results.

Legal vs. Practical Determinants

Though statisticians would challenge the definitiveness of the results—a sample size that is too small and a control group which is ill-defined or nonexistent—a careful observer would conclude that wrongful termination lawsuits are not directly correlated with the existence of the facts and court cases justifying them; all too often such cases appear to correlate most directly with the degree of anger and/or surprise of the terminated employee. Stated differently, among those who litigate claiming wrongful termination, justification for the lawsuit is less likely to motivate such a suit than is uncontrolled negative emotion resulting from being terminated.

Were one to construct a profile of a "generally representative" wrongful termination plaintiff, it would be a surprised, wounded, middle-to-top-level manager. Rightfulness of the action aside, a feeling of mistreatment more than actual mistreatment itself appears to produce lawsuits. This is form over substance to be sure, but as "unreliable" or "unscientific" as the observations may be, they suggest desirable behavior patterns for employers to consider in addition to the concepts developed elsewhere. Such suggestions form the core of the discussion that follows: As a practical matter, how can your employer direct its conduct towards employees to be terminated to minimize the desire to retaliate or vindicate themselves by filing a lawsuit?

Preparation Is the Key

Many of the individuals who will end up terminating one or more employees really have very little experience in effecting a termination. More troublesome, those that can claim significant experience have usually gained that experience under a now changed set of laws and applicable court decisions. Thus, the experience that they have had, successful in the past, is very likely to be unsuccessful in the future. In fact, that prior experience may very well be training for disaster if it is not rechanneled in light of the extensive new developments affecting the limits of rightful termination.

Because *how* the termination is effected may itself create a cause of action, supplemental cause of action, or even a basis for punitive damages where none otherwise existed, careful and thorough preparation is the key to successful separations from employment. The termination may well be stressful for the employee being terminated, but is as likely to be equally stressful for the manager or supervisor effecting the termination. What if the employee demands a witness, or an advocate? What if the employee has, or claims he can present an air-tight alibi? What if the employee believably asserts retaliation or sexual harassment or asserts that he or she is a whistle blower? What if the assertion is that the prospective terminee is the new union organizer? Should you ignore these assertions and bull ahead with the termination? Should you negate the termination and run the risk of returning a problem employee to the work environment where an industrial injury might "happen" shortly thereafter? These and many other questions require careful preparation.

Wrongful termination suits are generally presumed to be jury trials if, when and as they actually get to trial. Rarely does a jury contain members who have had extensive experience (or really any relevant experience) in terminating employment. Any person with such experience would likely be removed by plaintiff's counsel, if possible, by a preemptory challenge. Thus, one can bank on the fact that any jury will usually have unrealistically high expectations of how delicately and intelligently the person effecting a termination of employment should have handled the situation. If he or she is nervous, and therefore unclear, or unprepared and thus is not able or willing to reiterate the reasons for discharge, there may be a perception of wrongfulness or unfairness. If the person handling the discharge is unclear or unable to explain the full severance benefit package or even debate the merits of the termination, this tentativeness will be exploited by a plaintiff's lawyer as evidence of an improperly thought out, bad faith decision. A future lawsuit may be almost over before it begins. Given these facts of business life, preparation for the termination conference is of the utmost importance. Although there will be unique matters to be considered by each employer in addition to those discussed in the following, the most common issues to be considered in preparation for the termination conference are discussed in the following pages.

REVIEW CASE AND CAUSE: DETERMINE DIRECTION

In the normal course of events, line personnel, with or without direction from the human resources staff, will have made a tentative decision to terminate hypothetical employee "Smith." It will then be up to the human resources department either to review the tentative termination decision and approve its implementation or, in many cases (and assumed in the discussion that follows), to implement that decision itself. This review is the last line of defense, and the time for careful preparation for the termination conference. Regardless of whether your approval or your implementation is sought, it is necessary to review both the specifics of the case and the conclusion of cause, and to finally determine which of several directions is best for the employer and the employee.

Confirming the Asserted Basis for Termination

As part of the last line of defense, it is crucial to review the asserted basis for the termination to assure that it is reasonable and justified under the actual known circumstances. Where the initial work has been done well, this will usually be rechecking to assure that appropriate steps have been taken, and that necessary records and documents have been gathered, all as is consistent with the company's procedures.

PROOF, NOT CONJECTURE. It is necessary that the human resource/personnel professional carefully sort out the subtleties between proof and assumption. In this regard, direct evidence from a first-hand source regarding violation or breach of a company rule or policy is certainly the most desirable proof. It is particularly important to assure the "first-hand" nature of the evidence gathered. Too often managers rely on supervisors' versions of what the supervisor had been told by one or more employees. Although there may often be no intended misrepresentation, it is almost a universal experience that in the retelling of a story, the story is changed somewhat. Most of us have had the experience of a story starting out with one person and being completely different by the time it has been retold several times. Similarly, what an employee says to a supervisor may be translated by the supervisor, unwittingly and unintentionally, into management "lingo" or supervisory shorthand. This can result in a variance of the facts within the conclusions which will be passed up the line. If the human resource/personnel professional is forced to rely on the conclusions, rather than being able to examine the underlying details, the risk of error in communication, and hence a wrongful termination, is increased materially. It is thus important that the person assigned to make the final review of the facts and factors supporting the termination be able to review the original facts, not simply the conclusions. First-hand evidence and/or statements from first-hand witnesses are essential.

In reviewing the facts, it is also essential that the human resource/personnel professional assure that all witnesses have been contacted and their statements considered in the process. All sides of the matter must have been thoroughly reviewed. Obviously, reasonable people can differ in their observations of what happened at a particular time and place and the context of the particular incident. It is precisely those differences, if uninvestigated, which may allow an erroneous termination decision to go unchallenged until litigation. Thus, it is critical that the final review of the tentative termination decision conclude that all perspectives have been reviewed and considered in making the final decision to terminate employment.

In assuring that all sides of the matter have been considered, it is also important that the employee's perspective, including any mitigating factors or excuses be thoroughly evaluated. While you may wish to disregard any particular factor suggested by an employee as a mitigating one, or one which would alleviate a proposed penalty, it is most important that the employee's perspective be ascertained. After all, if the case were ultimately to go to litigation, the jury will patiently, often eagerly, listen for the mitigating facts. If you fail to be sensitive to them at the point immediately prior to a final termination decision, the risk of a valid lawsuit increases significantly. Too often the circumstance presents itself where an employee has been repeatedly counseled and told that termination will necessarily result if he or she is tardy one more time. After the next tardiness, termination does in fact result, but it is not until the jury becomes a factor that the company is made aware that the tardiness was due to a serious accident involving the employee's child and necessary delays at the hospital. No company wants to hear this the first time in depositions or at trial.

In reviewing the evidence supporting the tentative termination decision, it is particularly important to assure that the various statements and perspectives are properly documented as is consistent with company policy. If not fully documented, you should seek such documentation. The nuances of a particular incident are often the difference between successfully presenting one's case or not. Yet time dulls all memories, and for better or worse under our system of jurisprudence, people who are accused of crimes and people who claim they were wrongfully terminated are generally given the benefit of the doubt when necessary facts and details cannot be remembered accurately. It is suggested, therefore, that detailed written statements be taken at the investigatory stage (but no later than the final approval stage) of any termination case.

It is generally good procedure to have such statements written out by the employee from whom they are given in his or her own handwriting, or at least dictated and transcribed in his or her own words. If the interviewer's statement is essentially what is taken because the interviewer has put words in the mouth of the employee or done so by writing the statement for the employee to sign, it is very likely to be given less weight should a credibility problem later arise or if there should be a need to use the statement because the witness if unavailable. In cases where employees do not have a good written and/or spoken command of the English language, it is generally preferable that statements be in the first language of the employee so that the detail and nuances can be preserved and relied on. For ease of use of the statement, whether it is handwritten in English or another language, the company may later have them transcribed and typewritten, but the original should be retained in all cases so the translation or transcription can be verified.

Finally, in collecting and reviewing the evidence, it is appropriate at this final review to assure that all physical evidence, including tests or medical reports, if any, are reviewed for accuracy and essential consistency. Test results or other data that becomes available after the final termination decision is made may well be excluded as a basis to support the termination. Thus, it will be important to assure that any professional reports, tests or other physical evidence is reviewed and is supportive of the termination decision. Although beyond the scope of this discussion, it should also be noted that issues like "chain of custody" for physical evidence must be assured. These matters should be reviewed with your own counsel as circumstances warrant.

CLEAR VIOLATION AND CONVINCING PROOF. After review of employee statements and other evidence supportive (and detractive) from the tentative termination decision, the reviewer should ask himself or herself whether the violation of rules or policies was clear and the proof of the violation was convincing. In this regard, it has been suggested, perhaps with tongue in cheek to some extent, that the employer apply the "red-faced test" and/or the "rule of 13." Simply put, if you could not explain why the company terminated this employee to your mother without getting red in the face, perhaps the termination is not a good one. Stated differently, if the 13 people behind you in the check-out stand at the grocery, after hearing a brief, credible synopsis of the case, would not agree with you, then perhaps the termination should be rethought. The author in no way means to minimize the subtlety of the process or the importance of nuance, detail and careful work in mentioning these kinds of broad-brushed "acid test" approaches, but as most trial lawyers will tell you, juries often are right in the decisions they make. Employers are often suspect in the decisions they make. The combination of the two means that a simple statement of the company's position and the employee's position should, in the vast majority of cases, be sufficient to justify the termination decision without hesitation or embarrassment. Should this not be the case, the author urges a thorough review of the policy matters leading to the termination.

Confirming Equal Treatment or Justification for Differential Treatment of Employees

It is generally the rule that employers must treat employees in similar situations similarly. Stated differently, the common, and appropriate, assumption is that employees should be treated equally. Some employers may respond more harshly than others to a particular fact situation, but within bounds of general reasonableness, consistency among an employer's employees is far more important than consistency of various different employers' practices. Thus, an employer need not be unreasonably lenient simply because the employer across the street or across the town is (although there may be some employee organization issues, not relevant here, that should be considered). Within the company, however, the employer will generally be held to equal treatment of employees.

EMPLOYEES NOT SIMILARLY SITUATED. It is obviously true that differences among employees abound in employment situations which are not similar. Some employees are hourly, others are salaried. Certain rules of conduct or dress may apply to some employees but not to others. These, and a multitude of other job-content differences are valid, and are recognized as being appropriate. Reasons for termination, however, seem to be much more generalized. At the time of writing, for example, only one significant court decision has recognized the validity of different measures of objective demonstration of performance required for those in different decision-making roles. Therefore, it is suggested that the employer be very hesitant about applying different rules or standards to those who are allegedly situated differently. It appears likely that the lenient employer's rules will be extended as far as reasonably possible within the company unless and until the employer makes absolutely clear the boundaries that apply to particular types of expected performance or conduct.

Although it is understandable why an employer would have different performance standards, rules of conduct and/or penalties for different kinds of employees in certain circumstances (e.g., absenteeism or sick leave as between hourly and salaried-exempt personnel), there are other rules or conduct regarding which it is more difficult to accept a variance. If one tolerates petty theft, for example, among one group of employees, it is likely to fall on deaf ears when an employer screams foul because an employee in another group contests being terminated although a proven petty thief. Like other job differences, differences in standards of conduct or penalties for violation of given standards should be job related: Hours and days of work may be appropriately different for nonexempt and exempt employees, but standards regarding theft and honesty generally should be universally applied.

Given these concepts, it is appropriate for the human resource/personnel professional to give great scrutiny to any suggested difference in treatment between groups of employees. If it is suggested that unequal treatment is appropriate because of dissimilar circumstances, it should be absolutely clear that those different expectations were either historically communicated and are fundamentally reasonable on the one hand, or are so clearly obvious under community standards that it would be difficult for any reasonable human being to differ in accepting differences in expectations.

OLD PRACTICES—NEW STANDARDS. It inevitably arises in an employer's experience that old policies become inappropriate. Sometimes there has been lack of enforcement of existing rules, other times the needs of the employer or the mores of the community change. In either event, it is almost universal that a situation will arise in which the historic penalty does not suit the "crime," and where the appropriate penalty has not been uniformly applied in the past. Thus, the employer is apparently on the horns of a dilemma: stuck with a policy which is either too lenient for its reasonable needs or consigned to unequal treatment of those who are similarly situated. Fortunately, this situation is not static, and, with proper employer action, can be remedied prospectively. Where an old standard or practice has become outdated, it is appropriate and necessary for the employer to give reasonable advance notice of its change in policy and expectation. There should similarly be time for compliance with the new procedure. Thus, in reviewing the appropriateness of the tentative discharge decision, the human resource/personnel professional must assure that any apparently unequal treatment in reasonably similar situations has been *preceded* by clear notice of a change in requirements, and that the evidence of violation of the changed procedure *postdates* the notice of changed expectations. Failure on either of these points would mean that an employee was being disciplined or discharged for conduct, which at the time it was done, had been tolerated by others similarly situated. A discharge in such circumstances may likely be found to be wrongful. Thus, it may be that there will be a short "time warp" when terminations or disciplinary actions supported by the facts occurring before the new standards are published will be risky. Such circumstances should be reviewed carefully with senior management and/or counsel before a tentative termination decision is implemented.

Confirming Compliance with All Employer Procedures

In part, because it hardly need be said, it should be said: The human resource/personnel professional last checking a tentative termination decision must assure that the employer is in full compliance with all of its own applicable procedures. Increasingly in this country, judges and juries are looking at jobs as close to property rights. It should not be surprising, then, that there is an increasing amount of importance placed on "due process" regarding any employee who is the subject of a tentative termination decision. While one could write a book on what does and does not constitute "due process," at the very least it requires the employer to comply with all of its own procedures and policies which may be applicable.

This admonition sounds almost like a tautology. Therein lies the difficulty: What procedures are "applicable" to which cases? As American Airlines found out when it attempted to terminate Mr. Cleary (as discussed in Chapter 3), general procedures not made specifically *inapplicable* may apply broadly to all situations. Although that particular case has been discussed previously, it may be worth reconsidering briefly here.

American Airlines had a review board procedure which was available to employees to use in various termination cases. Cleary was an "at-will" employee who was terminated for reasons that, in American Airlines' mind were clear, and there seemed no reason to proceed through the review board procedure. Thus, American Airlines went ahead and terminated Cleary's employment without permitting the review procedure. Cleary sued and won, *not* because he proved that the facts supporting his termination were wrong, but rather because he had long service and because he had been denied access to American Airlines' review board procedure. (The case had arisen on a procedure ground. The appellate court sent the case back for a trial. It was later settled, so the substantive issues were never publicly resolved.)

The result in *American Airlines* should not be so astonishing. It should, however, provide a guidepost to assure that all procedures which are not expressly, by their own terms, made inapplicable to a case, have been applied to the case or have been clearly waived (and documented) so they have been made inapplicable by the choice of those involved.

It may be that a particular procedure would, under these circumstances, be made applicable where it was not intended. As this is a problem in the drafting of the procedure and not the employee's fault, a court might well accord the current employee the protection of the procedure. It would be up to the employer to correct its mistake for the next case. Thus, at any time that the human resources/personnel professional finds that an applicable procedure has not been followed, it should be a warning sign which either causes the employer to confirm the express waiver of the procedure or to go through the procedure before finalizing the tentative termination decision. Failing to do either of these, the employer may well face reversal of its decision to terminate on a technical or procedural ground even before any of the real reasons for the termination come into play. Stated succinctly, ambiguous documents for procedures will most always be interpreted against the employer and the scope of protection extended to the employee. In reviewing any particular case, then, it is important to err on the side of inclusion, even at the risk of delaying implementation of the termination decision.

Deciding on the Next Step

The purpose in this section is to provide an outline for the human resource/personnel professional or other person designated within the organization to confirm that the tentative decision to terminate is proper. Of course, if everything has gone properly in making the tentative termination decision, the answer in all probability will be to implement the termination. Consideration of some techniques for implementation are discussed in the second section that follows and a discussion of issues to be included in preparing for the termination conference follows immediately. In some situations, however, the review of the tentative termination decision turns up a flaw in the process or a missing fact which would make the defensibility of a final decision to terminate, at this time, suspect. In such circumstance, it is the author's belief that it is appropriate for an employer to return to the investigative stage or the missed procedural stage to reprocess an incomplete (perhaps erroneous) tentative decision to terminate. In other cases, where the errors and omissions are minor, it may be appropriate to go ahead with the termination on a "what if" basis, expecting to establish the missing facts or waivers of procedures in the terminaton conference itself.

If the former option is selected (returning to the investigative or procedural processes), the decision customarily will be returned to the line management with the suggestion that certain matters be reviewed or certain omitted matters be completed. If the latter decision appears appropriate, the "what if" termination conference, the persons effecting the termination decision should go ahead and schedule the termination conference, but build into the preparation for that conference an early opportunity to establish the missing documentation, facts, waivers of procedure, or other missing essentials. Finally, the person handling the termination conference should be prepared to abort implementation of the termination should any of the required information not be forthcoming. In such a circumstance, it may be appropriate to suspend an employee pending completion of the required steps or, under some circumstances, return the employee to the work environment so the necessary procedures can be completed and an appropriate decision made.

ESTABLISH ACCEPTABLE OPTIONS AND APPLICABLE SEVERANCE BENEFITS

Establishing Acceptable Options

In preparation for the termination conference, discussed in the following, the author suggests that the person implementing the termination decision plan carefully for the conference, including for the various questions that may be raised. He or she should also prepare an outline or a checklist, both to assure that points are not omitted and to provide a document to refresh his or her recollection later in case the substance of the discussion in the conference is challenged. Obviously before such an outline or checklist can be finalized, it is important to consider what, if any, acceptable options exist either during or as a result of the conference, and what severance benefits and understandings will be part of this termination. In addition to any matters left open in the review of the tentative termination decision (the "what if" procedure discussed previously), there are a variety of issues which should be considered in advance of the termination conference. Although a number of these will depend on the particular employer, there are several which are relatively standard and are considered briefly below.

EMPLOYEE REPRESENTATION. Although there has been some current vacillation on what the rules are or should be, certain employees may have a right to have a co-worker or union representative as a witness and/or advocate in the termination conference, or part of it. Because the applicable rules change from time to time, it is appropriate to check with the employer's counsel to assure that proper rules are being followed.

It is currently the law that unionized employees, on request, have a right to have a co-worker or union representative in an investigatory conference where it is reasonably believed by the employee that the result of the conference could lead to discipline or discharge from employment. These rights are often referred to as *Weingarten* rights, after the case creating them. See *National Labor Relations Board v. J. Weingarten, Inc.,* 420 U.S. 251 (1975). At present, *Weingarten* rights do not extend to nonunion employees. Although many employers make it a policy to grant any employee a witness/advocate on request, it is worth considering in advance what the rules will be to assure that this particular employee option is not extended beyond that which the employer desires it to be, consistent with the law. In this regard, the following factors should be reviewed in forming or updating an employer policy regarding *Weingarten* options:

> Will an employee witness/advocate be allowed for all employees or only unionized employees?
>
> Will such a witness/advocate be allowed for all disciplinary conferences, those conferences which will result in termination or only those conferences which are truly investigatory in nature (the law does not require an employee witness/advocate be permitted in the type of conference which is limited to announcing a predetermined disciplinary or termination decision)?
>
> Will the witness/advocate be allowed to participate in the entire conference or only investigatory or predecision making portions?
>
> Will an employee be offered the opportunity to have a witness/advocate as opposed to being given that right only if he or she requests it?

Each employer should settle on its *Weingarten* policies well before any disciplinary or termination conference begins. The policy should be uniform, at least for those employees similarly situated. In this way, a disciplinary or termination conference can proceed as smoothly as it will without interruption for policy decisions or any variation from procedures that might make an otherwise proper conference objectionable.

RESIGNATION IN LIEU OF TERMINATION. Beyond questions of whether the employer may accept or encourage an employee witness/advocate, the employer will have to consider whether it will seek or accept the resignation of an employee in lieu of termination. To some extent, this question may be a tempest in the teapot because such a resignation perhaps means less than it appears to mean.

Once a decision to terminate has been made and communicated to an employee, there is at least some doubt about whether a "resignation" or a "release" given in consideration of allowing the employee to resign will be effective as what it appears to be. An employee who resigns in lieu of termination may be deemed to have been terminated for unemployment insurance purposes, union grievance procedures, state fair employment, and federal Equal Employment Opportunity Commission matters and, not surprisingly, wrongful termination suits. While an uncoerced, truly voluntary resignation and/or a specific release may be sufficient to protect the employer from one or all of these posttermination maladies, the circumstances under which the resignation or release was given may later be challenged and often upset. The factors weighed in determining whether a release is valid are discussed in greater detail later. Suffice it to say where offered as an alternative to termination, a resignation may not be what it appears to be, or have the value it would normally have.

On the other hand, allowing a resignation in lieu of termination may create some obligations on an employer that it might not otherwise have. If, for example, the agreement for the resignation involves purging the employees' file so it is "clean" and/or not disclosing the reasons for termination, an employer could subject itself to liability to the resigning employee should someone disclose, say, to a prospective employer the contents of the file or the work history of the employee. Such an agreement can get especially complicated and delicate should the employer have the employee's personnel file subpoenaed before the file has been purged. Yet if the file is actually purged, the employer may be defenseless if sued for wrongful termination.

Under these circumstances, one might appropriately question whether there is any real value to a resignation in lieu of termination. It is the author's view that this may be appropriate in certain situations, but not as often as it historically appeared. Many wrongful termination suits are driven by anger and embarrassment, an inability to explain sudden change of plans to family and friends, and so forth. Thus, a resignation in lieu of termination may serve to soften the retaliatory or vindictive actions of an employee who is to be separated, but who is not prepared to manage a "termination" in his or her working life without striking back at the former employer. Most employers do not (yet) have resident psychologists or psychiatrists on staff, and it may be difficult to sort out when such an option will be particularly effective. Nevertheless, the human resource/personnel professional must plan in advance of the conference whether to encourage or accept a resignation in lieu of termination.

One caution, finally, about accepting resignations in lieu of terminations. Too often it occurs when a resignation is accepted in lieu of termination that the employee seeks out a lawyer who prepares but does not serve a wrongful termination lawsuit, and then in support of the lawsuit, the lawyer directs one or more people to call the termination employer for a "reference check." The caller carefully notes all of the former employer's statements about what a "good employee" so-and-so was. Plaintiff's lawyer may then attempt to use such an "admission" to show that the termination decision itself was in bad faith or made on pretextual grounds. On the other hand, if the former employer gives the employee a bad recommendation, it has breached its agreement regarding the resignation and may have defamed or otherwise "reinjured" the former employee. It would appear, therefore, that the employer is caught on the horns of a dilemma. If it says things that are injurious to the former employer's reputation, even though true, it has breached the agreement, explicit or implicit in the resignation. If the employer says things that are good, but untrue, it has supported the claim of the separated employee that the decision to separate him or her was in bad faith because, after all, the employee was doing a good job.

This dilemma can be easily avoided by having the general rule that in reference situations, the employer only confirms the employee's dates of employment, position(s) or classification(s) held, and ending wage or salary, all with appropriate authorization. If this is the regular procedure, the risk has been reduced to someone complaining about the crypticness of your information. The author believes this is a healthy reference procedure even though it renders accepting a resignation in lieu of termination relatively less useful than it has been historically. Restricting incorrect references effectively limits use of in-lieu resignations to situations where it is reasonably believed that description of a permissive resignation can and will so soften the anger and frustration of termination that one stands a materially better position to avoid a wrongful termination suit.

TRANSFER AND DEMOTION. Many times termination is the only option considered by an employer when an employee is not satisfying reasonable expectations of quality and quantity of work output. Although it would rarely be true in a theft case or, say, a discharge for fighting, the employee who is subject to discharge for unsatisfactory work output may be appropriately evaluated for a transfer or even a nonpunitive demotion.

It is undeniably true that hiring and training people for your organization is expensive. To simply terminate someone, especially if they have a number of years of good service, because they are unsatisfactorily performing in a particular position, is wasteful and may subject the company to unnecessary litigation. When reviewing a tentative termination decision in such circumstances the human resources/personnel professional should consider transfer or demotion of the affected employee to an area where he or she can make a meaningful contribution to the company.

Transfer and voluntary demotion are often overlooked because it is thought bad to dump "problems" on someone else or unwise to permit a disgruntled and perhaps negatively motivated employee to remain within the organization. If the employee is, and after transfer will likely remain, disgruntled and negatively motivated, termination may well be the better course, both for the employee and the employer. It is suggested, however, that in certain circumstances an opportunity for transfer or working with different personalities or in a different environment may be something from which both the employee and the employer can benefit. A voluntary demotion or one concurred in by the employee may permit the employee to work at a comfortable and productive level. Even if costs of recruiting and retraining were not a factor, it is simply not true that most employers are able to go out in the marketplace and hire people who they know will do a better job; too often one problem is simply exchanged for another. To borrow an old saying, in some situations, the devil you know may be better than the devil you do not know. Thus, it is worthwhile to consider prior to implementation of a termination decision, whether the employer will offer the affected employee an opportunity to transfer or demote, or whether the company will accept that suggestion if requested by the employee.

In addition to considering whether there should be any transfer or demotion permitted, the person reviewing the case should consider whether or not any transfer or demotion would be only to a vacant position. Also, whether it would be permitted to a position that is presently held by someone with less company service or perhaps on probation, or whether it would be allowed to any position which is agreed on, perhaps based on the employee's entire work experience. Although "bumping" another employee from his or her position would be atypical, it may be particularly difficult for an employer to deny an employee an opportunity to transfer to a position which is vacant, unless it can be reasonably demonstrated that the employee has done some act or a series of acts which are so egregious that he or she should be removed from the organization altogether.

One final note on transfer and demotion is in order. Some employers have attempted to transfer or demote an employee in lieu of terminating him or her in order to avoid creating a termination, but select a job that is so beneath the affected employee's skills, abilities or employment "station," that they know the employee cannot accept the proper transfer and is likely to "quit." Most courts would find such a transfer a "constructive discharge" and treat the matter as a termination. However, it remains true that if an employer can find a job which the employee could reasonably do, it may mitigate the kind of damages that accrue in a subsequent lawsuit and allow any question of wrongfulness to be raised and resolved at a very low cost level, comparatively speaking.

PROBATION, SUSPENSION, AND ONE LAST CHANCE. Evaluating termination options regarding probation, suspension and/or, one last chance usually arise for one of two reasons: First, in the review of the tentative termination decision discussed previously, the human resources/personnel professional finds that the case is not as clear and convincing as one might have had it or that prior disciplinary handling of similar cases will not support outright termination. Second, the person affected may be a long-service and/or valuable employee and he or she requests such treatment or the employer desires to retain the employee's service, but must impose some discipline for some clearly established act or omission. In either of these situations probation, suspension, or one last chance alternatives may provide the options necessary to maintain morale and discipline among those people who make up the vast majority of the work force without necessarily losing a particular individual who has transgressed to a rule or policy.

Probation is a concept which has about as many variations as there are employers that use it. It is common for employers to have some sort of a "probationary period" at the beginning of employment. Usually this is a misnomer. Employers who believe that they engage employees as at-will employees but place them on probation so they can be terminated within the first 30 to 90 days without reason, may unwittingly imply that some reason is needed after the probationary period. Such a position undercuts the at-will nature of employment. Probation as a corrective tool after employment is underway may be both more realistic and more consistent with at-will employment. In the latter context probation connotes a time when the employee is on special notice to modify his or her behavior. If there is an occurrence or absence of any particular predefined set of facts or circumstances, termination will likely result without further rehabilitation efforts. Thus, in this author's view, probation should not be just a first look to see whether the employee can "make the team," but rather it should be a tool to redirect, reshape and re-enforce behavior consistent with employer needs and objectives. Other methods can be used for an effective "first look."

Probation should be used sparingly, and should be limited to those kinds of employee deficiencies which can reasonably be expected to be corrected by the employee on a long-term basis within the time frame set for the probation. If the employee is essentially incorrigible, probation is likely to be both frustrating and destructive of an employer's general ability to maintain morale among other employees. Probation is, after all, an attention getter. It can work when an employee can solve the problem, but needs to take solving the problem more seriously. However, if the employee is not able to learn from the experience and direct his or her own behavior in the future properly, it is likely that probation as a disciplinary tool will not avoid a termination at a later point and, therefore, will not save the employee.

Even so, probation may help save the employer. Much of wrongful termination litigation is really a question of an emotive judgment about whether or not the employer and the employee were in good faith. Therefore, it is possible that giving an opportunity to an employee to correct unsatisfactory performance through a probationary scheme may make the need for termination of those who cannot change that much more obvious. This is especially true in situations where the employee's conduct, though unacceptable, does not rise to a level of serious misconduct. In such situations the concept of progressive discipline, discussed in more detail elsewhere, is critically important. Should the human resources/personnel professional, on the tentative termination review, find that a progressive discipline has not been given or has not been effective, he or she may wish to consider probation as an alternative to termination.

The length of probation will depend on a number of factors, including the length of time necessary for the employee to meaningfully demonstrate that he or she has corrected the problem and can perform at a level or in a way that is acceptable to the employer. On the other hand, probation should not be interminable. Weeks or months, depending on the circumstances, may make sense but years probably do not. Moreover, for probation to be an effective option (beyond completing a progressive discipline requirement), it must be agreed on as desirable between the employee and the employer. For an employer to put a recalcitrant employee on probation is almost a sure disaster. Therefore, in the termination conference, if this option is a viable one, the human resources/personnel professional must work out in advance how the concept of the probation will be introduced, that is, at whose initiative, and what the outside boundaries or parameters of an acceptable probation may be. After having done this, it will be possible to line out a constructive program of probation to be agreed on by both parties. It is suggested that this be reduced to a brief written form and signed by both parties so that it is clear what the timing and terms of the probation are. Although this particular tool will not likely be one for common use, it can be uncommonly successful when used well.

The use of a disciplinary suspension in lieu of termination is one of the possible termination options which should be considered. Suspensions customarily are of short duration and are periods of unpaid, mandatory leave-of-absence, as opposed to the longer period of probation where the employee continues working but subject to particular directed work patterns. Disciplinary suspensions may be from one to five days in normal circumstances and may be up to 30 days or longer in rare cases. Longer disciplinary suspensions would more commonly occur when an employer reinstates an employee who was suspended pending investigation and then returned to work at the conclusion of that investigation.

Employers often are reluctant to suspend employees because like the old parental adage, it hurts me as much as it hurts you. Of course, there is truth in that criticism. It is the author's view, however, that such a criticism should not make suspension a tool unavailable as an option to termination. For an employer that has adopted a progressive discipline system, that is, one where discipline is increasingly severe in order to assure that the employee knows the seriousness of the matter in the employer's mind, the suspension is perhaps the most convenient bridge between warnings and termination. Similarly, because it affects the employee's paycheck at a time not chosen by him or her, it can even be effective in dealing with a chronic absenteeism problem.

In order for suspension to be most effective, the employer may wish to consider imposing the suspension at a time when it does not conveniently extend a weekend, a holiday or vacation day or days. Suspension should not be postponed a significant time into the future away from the event which has caused the suspension, but it need not follow exactly on an absence or a weekend, thus making it less effective as a marker of unacceptable conduct in the employee's mind.

The suspension should be clearly established as a disciplinary suspension by the employer with fixed dates to start and end. The employee should be directed to report to work at a particular time and to a particular person at the conclusion of the suspension. And, under a progressive discipline system the employee should be advised, both in the disciplinary conference and in the documentation of the suspension that further conduct of the same type or unrelated misconduct will lead to his or her termination from employment.

Finally, an employee may seek, or under certain circumstances an employer may be willing to give, a disciplinary circumstance the characterization of "one last chance." This termination option would normally be developed at the termination conference either because the facts known to the employer do not, on the review discussed earlier, support the termination or because there is some mitigating fact which was not known earlier which would make it apparent that the tentative decision to terminate should be aborted and a lesser disciplinary penalty imposed. This particular kind of warning should be written, or at least a written memorialization of its terms be made, generally with a copy to the employee so that it is clear in his or her mind, as well as in the employer's, that this is to be regarded as one last chance. The writing should clearly state that repetition of the conduct or other misconduct will lead to further, more serious discipline, perhaps suspension if there is an orderly chain of progressive discipline, or simply up to and including termination of employment if there is no ladder of disciplinary response established at the employer.

One last chance warnings can be an effective tool for behavior patterns that can be corrected. Too often, however, an employer ends up repeatedly using one last chance warnings because it cannot face the prospect of having the employee off due to suspension, it cannot be attentive enough to enforce a probation, or it cannot face the prospect of rehiring in the open market. Each of these employer conditions courts disaster. When an employee's file contains half a dozen, or even more, one last chance warnings, the credibility of the employer has been effectively destroyed. How can an employee who has received so many one last chance warnings be expected to know when his or her last chance arrives? In these kinds of circumstances, a termination, even though backed up by a number of warnings, may in fact be less defensible than a termination where the employer has followed a clear path and has acted in a predictable way. If the one last chance warning is to be effective for a period of time and then expires, it is important to note such, so that both the employer and the employee know where they stand. Essentially, a one last chance warning of three or perhaps even six months duration is another form of probation and probably should be handled analogously. In any event, it is worth exploring as a serious level of discipline, but one with minimal immediate impact on either the employer or the employee. It will generally be appropriate for relatively minor offenses and inappropriate for major, clear violations of policies or procedures.

OTHER OPTIONS AND EQUAL TREATMENT. There are other forms of employer responses to employee misconduct, many of which would be considered disciplinary (and some of which would not). For example, some employers have attempted to take away seniority or service credits and reinstate an employee as a new hire. It is suggested that these kinds of options have serious defects: They remove the employer reaction so far away in time from the misconduct incident that they become merely punitive and not corrective. There is little good to say for such a system legally or otherwise. Moreover, the more "options" an employer entertains, the more difficult it is to have equal treatment for employees similarly situated. Because that is a prime consideration in any effective disciplinary program, it is suggested that it will be easier for the employer and more effective in constructive discipline if a relatively small number of options to terminations are made part of the employer's disciplinary tools and such options are then used in circumstances and for employees who are essentially similarly situated. Failure to take this approach may create such a plethora of circumstances that they can neither be fairly administered by the employer nor be meaningfully understood by an employee, or worse, a court or jury.

Establishing Acceptable Severance Benefits

For both the employee and for the employer, consideration and discussion of normal and special severance benefits can be the critical part of the termination conference. In some cases such discussions can even make the difference between whether there is subsequent agency action or court litigation or not. Strangely enough, however, it is usually not the existence of severance benefits, even lavish severance benefits, that correlates with the absence of wrongful termination litigation, but rather how the severance benefits are provided and sometimes what form they take. Where the company simply provides a lump sum severance benefit, there may be apparent peace and harmony following termination, but if the company has done nothing in its severance program to alleviate the psychological concern about why the employee was severed and reenforce the need to get on with his or her working life, even large and generous severance programs may simply be a bromide that defers the pain until the benefits wear out.

FORMAL SEVERANCE PLAN. Many employers have a formal severance plan and, therefore, the extent to which the human resources/personnel professional needs to establish applicable options will be to apply the plan to the facts. This may be more complex than it sounds. Many severance plans have various levels of benefits depending on the reasons for severance, the years of service or other variables. On separation there may be some legitimate difference of opinion about what a particular employee is entitled to under a formal severance plan or, viewed differently, there may be some leeway about how the facts are characterized to permit a particular individual benefits in more than one area. This may provide a skilled person with an opportunity in the termination conference to reduce materially the risk of wrongful termination litigation, postdecision.

Obviously, before the conference begins, the plans should be reviewed to the extent necessary to assure that the employer has made a proper decision about where the employee should be classified, what his or her benefits are, what the requirements are for attaining such benefits, and what the timetable will be for payment of benefits. Each of these questions is likely to come up in the termination conference or shortly thereafter. Indecision or vacillation concerning them may well be perceived by a jury as bad faith, even though it merely reflects some flaws in the employer's processes. Because of the importance of severance benefits and the presumption that employers should know what their own plans are and how they work, it is particularly important that time be spent in this area so that the proper answers are readily available and can be appropriately documented.

It should be noted that formal severance plans may well be covered by the Employment Retirement Income Security Act ("ERISA"), and the statutory and case law that followed, so that one way to review the plan with an employee may be to work through the summary plan description and point out the applicable features of the plan. It is the author's belief that it is worthwhile to encourage an employee being terminated to call the person who has discussed the severance benefits directly should questions later develop. This will help eliminate the potential confusion that similar questions might be answered different ways by the plan administrator, or others, who may not know the detailed facts and circumstances revolving around a particular employee's case.

OTHER SEVERANCE PRACTICES. In certain parts of the country, it may be that an informal practice of granting severance benefits may rise to the level of a "plan," all of which may have certain ERISA overtones beyond the scope of this chapter. Nevertheless it is clear that where an employer has a practice or often-repeated history of providing some severance benefits (although not a formal plan), it is important to ascertain precisely what will be applicable when the termination conference occurs. The person conducting the conference must be prepared to answer the same kinds of questions that would occur concerning a formal plan. It is even more important, however, where there is a practice or custom that careful notes be made and perhaps a copy given to the employee so that any future misunderstandings can be resolved quickly and efficiently rather than allowed to fester and support or cause a wrongful termination action or other proceeding.

The employer should be aware that it is doubtful that severance arrangements which are customary or part of an informal policy will be the independent consideration necessary to support an effective release of the employer against any posttermination claims or suits by an employee. Aside from whether and how an employee can release statutory rights, for example, to sue about age discrimination or violation of a whistle blower statute, it is the normal rule that a general release of claims that an employee may have against an employer, including those for wrongful termination, will not be effective unless it is supported by consideration independent of and additional to the employee's "entitlements" at the time of separation. Prior consideration, or amounts that were already due an employee though not actually paid, will usually not support a release of claims; moreover, any release attained under these circumstances may be avoided by an employee who later decides he or she wants to litigate various claims. Releases are the subject of a more detailed discussion in the following, but suffice it to say for the present that payment of or agreement to pay those kinds of benefits provided under a preexisting severance plan, whether formal or informal, will not likely make a release valid, and the employer should not rely on any such release.

NEGOTIATION OF SUPPLEMENTAL BENEFITS. With increasing regularity, employers are debating whether it is better to pay and switch employees rather than switch and fight with former employees. Many employers, fearful of becoming a "soft touch" have decided not to negotiate supplemental benefits to avoid litigation. Others, however, are finding it effective to negotiate a supplemental or special separation package at least for middle and top management employees. Such supplemental benefit packages vary greatly in content, but most include both the payment of some money (perhaps with certain posttermination assistance with location of new employment), and an agreement that there will be no litigation. Additionally, there may be agreements regarding consulting, confidentiality, statements of reasons, time and terms for separation from employment, tax-planning, and so forth.

Supplemental benefits or packages of the type discussed previously have gone under various names, including golden parachutes, or depending on design, golden handcuffs. In the proper circumstances, they present an effective means for an employer and employee to plan their separation and divorce. Such opportunities should certainly be considered thoroughly, both as a policy matter for the employer, and in specific factual contexts. They may be especially important where the need for termination is clear but the facts, circumstances or surrounding context indicates that it would be preferable to have a negotiated departure rather than run the risk of a litigated departure.

Although the use of the terminology is substantially less than precise, to the extent there is a difference between a golden parachute and golden handcuffs, it is usually whether the employee can simply take the money and bail out, or whether the employee must satisfy certain conditions subsequent or perhaps even perform certain consulting functions for the employer during the time over which the negotiated severance benefits are paid out. Neither is necessarily more effective from a legal point of view. The question is how the company wants to order or conduct itself with respect to separated employees. The golden parachute allows severance of relationships at a particular point in time and obviates the need for the employer and the employee to interact in the future. Golden handcuffs often contemplate continuing interaction, which though desirable in certain situations, may be largely undesirable in many others. These are precisely the kinds of issues which defy rigid ordering and must be considered and discussed on a case-by-case basis by each employer.

Any contemplated supplemental benefits should be reviewed in advance with your counsel. Within the same company, variations in applicable state law may make a prior solution to an apparently similar problem unworkable. For example, in many states on the east coast, certain types of covenants restricting future competition may be supported by independent, contemporaneous consideration; in certain western states, it is much more difficult to legally restrict the future employment options of an employee severing his or her employment. Moreover, the effectiveness of negotiated agreements of the type described herein are increasingly being attacked at one level or another and the effectiveness of covenants not to sue, covenants not to compete, covenants not to disclose confidential information, and so on, may not continue to be effective to the same extent they are currently.

Because the substance of the terms of the golden parachute or golden handcuffs will vary so substantially from one employer to another, and even with the same employer from one court jurisdiction to another, it is impossible to give a general outline of an appropriate agreement. It is this author's experience that each must be crafted with care and generally will be negotiated and probably amended one or more times before being finalized. This is not to imply that the process is a prolonged one; on the contrary, negotiations are generally quick and an agreement is reached (or not) quietly. However, there is often substantial give and take in the process. In fact, where there is not an openness to such give and take, that is, where the employer merely says take it or leave it, the effectiveness of the negotiated separation, at least to the extent that it is designed to protect the employer from postseparation litigation or comment, is likely reduced substantially. This can best be understood when viewing the general requisites of an effective covenant not to sue or general release, usually the thing without which no employer would likely enter into substantial supplemental benefit package.

EFFECTIVE COVENANT NOT TO SUE OR RELEASE. There are some niceties that the purist would cite to distinguish a covenant not to sue from a general release. Broadly speaking, however, they are of similar impact on the employee and the employer: They eliminate entirely, or restrict substantially, the ability of the employee to litigate various claims against the employer. A general release is normally designed to be omnibus in character, that is, eliminate all claims of whatever sort, whether arising out of the employment relationship, the separation from employment, or otherwise; a covenant not to sue may be more restricted, and more likely to deliver what it advertises.

At least in an employment context, there are several foundational underpinnings which are generally required for most courts to give weight to a release or covenant not to sue. First among these underpinnings is that the release or covenant be voluntarily given. Other factors which affect the validity of a release, not necessarily in order of importance, include (1) whether or not the employee is represented by counsel, (2) whether the employee understands the effect of the release or the covenant, (3) whether the employee has the business sophistication to understand the value of what is being released, (4) whether there is adequate consideration for the release, (5) whether there is adequate time to consider the effect of the release and, (6) whether there is coercion or deception in obtaining the release or covenant. This list of factors is not exhaustive, and certain factors do not apply in certain jurisdictions; however, in general, it is increasingly the law that effective releases or covenants not to sue regarding employment matters need to be voluntary, willing, and supported by new and valuable consideration. Because the effectiveness of the release or covenant is of central importance to the employer, it should receive careful attention just as the rest of any severance package should.

SETTLING UPON OPTIONS AND SEVERANCE BENEFITS. As is apparent from the matters previously discussed, there are a wide range of options to be considered regarding termination of employment and applicable severance benefits. Each of these items must be considered in advance if the termination conference is to go smoothly. Of course, this is a prime employer objective. If the employer is unsure of which options are to apply, or is clumsy in presenting them, there is an increased risk of litigation.

Once the options have been settled on, it will be important to reduce to writing the decisions that have been made, both in planning for the termination conference and during or immediately subsequent to that conference. In this regard, it is important to keep things as simple and straightforward as possible. In a fairly recent case, an employer was admonished by the EEOC that documents in heavy "legalese" may not be effective; if they are not understandable to the person involved, their integrity becomes suspect. Thus, in the the final steps of preparation for the termination conference, after the options have been selected, you should assure that you have the necessary documents, tailored to the circumstances in such a way that it is clear and readily understandable what was agreed on and by whom.

THE TERMINATION CONFERENCE

It all comes down to this: Training and rehearsals make the play; practice and planning create good results. While a play may succeed or a game be won or lost for extraneous reasons, it is almost always the case that poor planning and insufficient practice produce poor results. This is no less true for the termination conference itself. This is the time that the careful planning and the appropriateness of your procedures can help you produce litigation-free results.

Preliminary Details

Initially, of course, the time and place of the termination conference must be set and the participants selected. Because the objective of effecting the termination decision is to do it as fairly, decently and quickly as a thorough presentation permits, it is suggested that a quiet, nonthreatening place be selected. Of course if one were simply announcing the decision to terminate employment, and the quality of the employee's participation in that discussion or attitude after termination were not important, location, and many of the other matters discussed herein are of reduced importance. In most cases, however, location and other details are important. Many employers have defeated their own objectives by not selecting a neutral, quiet place which will make it easier for an employee going through a difficult time to talk about choices he or she must make, vent understandable anger or concern, and start the transition to a new employment mind set.

Although there are many places that may be appropriate, there is one place to be particularly avoided. Do not attempt to try to conduct your termination conference in the employee's normal work space. Among other things, it may create unnecessary embarrassment and humiliation for the employee and create an independent cause of action separate and apart from the allegations that the termination itself was wrongful. The really significant damages that come from wrongful termination suits are, usually, because of embarrassment or humiliation or other related matters that could have been avoided by taking care to treat the employee with fairness and dignity.

The timing of a termination conference is also important, although perhaps not as critical. In most cases, an employee who has been terminated will not be asked to return to his or her work station, except to clean out personal belongings. Cleaning out is best done after others have gone to avoid unnecessary embarrassment and aggravation to the employee. It is not necessarily true that a termination at the end of the day on a Friday (or at the end of the work week) is done at the best time. It may be important for a successful conference follow-up and transitioning of the employee that there be some remaining time in the week either to use out placement options or to assist the terminated employee otherwise.

Because people and companies are different, it is virtually impossible to suggest a universally good time and place to effect termination decisions. It is important, however, given the planning about how you expect the conference to go and the needs of the employee and/or of the employer, that you select a time and place that will meet the requirements of the particular situation, not just the normal time, or one which seems convenient.

In addition to the time and place of the conference, the people you wish to be there must be selected and notified. It is customary, and the author believes advisable, for the employer to have two representatives in the termination conference. This allows one person to freely discuss matters that should be covered in the conference while the other takes notes as appropriate to document matters discussed and agreements reached. Of the two participants, usually one with line experience who knows the employee and one from human resources/personnel who knows the company's policies, procedures, and severance plans can best fill the needs. It is rarely advisable to have an immediate supervisor do the termination conference, although he or she may be an appropriate person to have at the conference. In normal circumstances someone more distant from the immediate situation can be more responsive to the needs of the employee and the employer, as well as more sensitive to the particularities of the situation, than can the immediate supervisor.

Finally, in terms of preliminary details, it is suggested that you practice, perhaps even role play, the termination conference if you have not recently and successfully done a number of such conferences. Successful termination conferences under the law today are difficult to do and are extremely stressful on both sides. Done poorly, they are also extremely dangerous to employers. Like any other serious presentation, quality practice makes for quality results. This is no exception; in fact, for most of us it would be highly advisable to actually go through the words you expect to use and perhaps even have some questions posed to you to respond to before the termination conference starts. This will increase your confidence in handling the conference and, though it may seem strange, is likely to make it easier for you, for the employee being terminated, and for any other people who are participating, silently or otherwise, in the conference.

Substantive Elements of the Termination Conference

Generally each termination conference will have some or all of the following substantive points:

State the purpose of the meeting and the decision to terminate

State the reasons for the decision to terminate and offer to explain the decision

State the severance benefits, and any available supplemental benefits and requirements

Review any policies that continue to be applicable and collect company property

Review the posture to other employees and prospective employer

Conclude the conference

The foregoing outline of the basic points of the termination conference will require supportive detail and perhaps custom tailoring, depending on the particular circumstances. Some of the possible details are considered in the following.

It is possible that you have not made a final decision about termination and/or lesser disciplinary action, but instead are holding a "what if" termination conference. If that is the case, it is important to say so at the beginning, emphasizing the possibility that termination or other disciplinary action may result. Because this is essentially an investigatory conference which may or may not lead to termination or other discipline, it is at this point that a union employee's request for a *Weingarten* representative *must* be honored. You need not advise the employee of the right to such representation, but you need to disclose accurately the purpose of the conference if you may need to use its results in any further discipline or discharge procedure, or litigation.

Except in an investigatory conference, it will normally be appropriate to have a brief statement of the reasons for the decision to terminate (or otherwise discipline the employee) immediately following your statement of the decision, although you need not go into a detailed explanation. In fact, sometimes a detailed explanation is destructive of moving an employee's attitude towards that of his or her future rather than his or her immediate past. Nevertheless, you certainly need to be prepared to state in some detail what the facts of the employer's investigation are and what the basis for the termination is. If the employee has or indicates a willingness to talk about the facts, especially if there may be facts which you have not heard, you should listen. This does not mean you need to, or should, argue with the employee about what the facts are. To the extent the employee indicates there are facts of which you have not been made aware or reasons why the termination should be inappropriate which you have not had an opportunity to consider, careful notes should be made so that all matters can be thoroughly reviewed. If there is a postdecision process for the employee to invoke, you should remind him or her of that policy.

After the discussion for the facts, including any facts that the employee has brought to your attention, you will have to decide whether to proceed with the conference as planned, suspend the conference to review certain facts which the prior investigation did not disclose, or abort the conference altogether. In either of the last two categories, the employee should be told what your decision is, and, particularly if the conference is being suspended, the employee should be advised about whether he or she is being suspended pending the continuing investigation or is to return to work as normal. If you suspend the conference for a few minutes, ask the employee to wait briefly while you investigate. The employee should not be forced, however, to stay if he or she insists on leaving; it is normally better to finish the conference as best you can under these circumstances and then complete the investigation. If necessary, you can make a revised decision if the subsequent investigation of the circumstances warrants.

Discussing the severance benefits will obviously depend in large part on the extensiveness of those benefits and the experience and sophistication of the employee. If you intend to extend optional benefits and/or seek a negotiated separation, that should be discussed at this point. (If the employer is seeking a mutual parting of the ways, that will become the purpose of the meeting and be discussed as the first item; if the employer is willing to accept an employee's suggestion that they have a mutual parting with some enhanced benefit, that will first surface within the termination conference.)

If you are using out placement or job counseling, it will behoove you to discuss your presentation with the out placement counselor and his or her company to assure that you are coordinating your efforts in the best possible way. Remember, however, that the out placement firm is very unlikely to be sued for wrongful termination, so despite its history or soothing words, assure that you have done that which you believe is necessary to maximize the protection of your employer.

Reviewing any applicable continuing policies or procedures would normally include reminding an employee if there is an internal dispute resolution program, either mandatory or voluntary, reaffirming confidentiality agreements, if any, establishing how and when any remaining vacation or other pay is to be paid, and a variety of other details dependent on the employer's benefit structure. It is also appropriate at this time to collect any property belonging to the employer, such as keys and credit cards, and make arrangements for return of company cars, samples, repayment of loans, and so on. You may prefer to handle some or all of these matters at a different time, perhaps to provide later contact point or see how the employee is managing the termination, but if so, the arrangements for such further meeting(s) should be covered in the termination conference.

As you near the end of the conference, you need to state clearly what the employer's posture will be to persons outside of the conference. This may be affected substantially by employee desires, but an agreement to give a good recommendation where you are terminating for misconduct may be an invitation to potential disaster for the reasons previously discussed. In any event, what is to be said concerning the employee's separation to fellow employees and prospective employers should be established and any reasonable corrections that the employee has to suggest should certainly be considered. In this connection, unless you are advised otherwise by your counsel, there generally is no duty to give a detailed explanation either to fellow employees or to prospective employers. Therefore, saying little or nothing is generally preferable to elaborate explanations. Such a policy will also help avoid charges of defamation or blacklisting, or other accusations which occasionally arise in posttermination litigation.

Finally, you should conclude the conference promptly, but not so hastily or abruptly that it gives the impression of lack of respect for the employee or the situation. Although acceptable to include a statement of personal regret (if sincerely felt) regarding the result, you should avoid, directly or indirectly, praising the discharged employee's work or job performance in order to bring the conference to a close on a more positive note. Tempting though it may be to inject your personal thoughts about the employee's work, even if sincerely felt, it is almost assuredly the way to make an institutional problem at a later date.

Although termination conferences are never easy, careful preparation and custom-tailoring of the basic outline presented will make a difficult job substantially easier, and the result better.

POSTTERMINATION EVENTS

The termination conference itself may be stormy or harrowingly quiet. It may be suspended, very substantially off-plan or run like a Swiss watch. The only generalization about termination conferences which is not patently false is they do not give an accurate guide to posttermination events. A stormy posttermination conference may be the last hurrah or the shot heard round the world. A quiet conference may portend a storm. While proper preparation and presentation will reduce posttermination litigation (certainly legitimate litigation), lawsuits are increasingly common. It therefore rarely makes sense to put away a file until certain posttermination events have occurred, or sufficient time has run to assure that there is no posttermination action.

Elusive Statute of Limitations

Because most wrongful termination concepts are state law concepts, there is no general statute of limitations. Moreover, because the umbrella of wrongful termination embodies both contract and tort claims and in many states public policy statutes as well, even in any particular jurisdiction it is often unclear which limitation applies. Is there a contract of employment? Is it written or oral? Does an employee handbook or other policies and procedures constitute a partially written contract of employment? In California, for example, it is easily arguable that a statute of limitations on various causes of action within the wrongful termination concept could be 180 days, one year, two years, three years, four years, or, with some twists and turns perhaps even longer. Moreover, in most jurisdictions, statutes of limitation only limit the time for the filing of an action and not necessarily serving the action or beginning the litigation in earnest.

The classified ads in several major cities openly solicit wrongful termination plaintiffs to bring their lawsuit to various attorneys. Too often, a boilerplate or a shotgun complaint is filed, that is, one which has very general allegations because plaintiff is fishing for a settlement or sometimes because the lawyer has not even taken the time to thoroughly understand the potential case. The complaint may sit for months or perhaps years before being served. Consequently, it is possible that a wrongful termination suit may come to life long after an employer has implemented the termination decision. It may be important, therefore, to make periodic checks of local court dockets and even to pay particular attention to employment reference checks that occur a long time after a period of quiet. While some employers might prefer not to know of pending suits, the potential departure of witness or erosion of evidence or other sorts of changes over time which make suits less easy to defend may require employers to check periodically so that they have some idea about the size, the shape, and the number of the icebergs, especially if there is a need to know about pending litigation or a condition subsequent for payment of money.

Use of Out Placement

An increasing number of employers are using services of so-called out placement agencies. For many, out placement is somewhat like the mirror image of recruitment firms. Out placement specialists do not, in most cases, actually find jobs for those who are separated from employment. More often they train employees in how to get jobs and assist them in their own efforts of placement. In this regard, an out placement firm can provide a valuable service for an employer.

Most of us have not had to look for a job recently, and are not sufficiently experienced at it to be on the cutting edge. An out placement firm can assist an employee in improving his or her skills so that finding the right job becomes easier. Depending on the nature of the out placement service, this may involve working with the employee to do relatively simple things, like physical preparation of a resume, or to do relatively complex things, like sophisticated employment counseling, and periodic encouragement for an employee to continue an effective job search.

A key here is "effective" job search. What some out placement agencies attempt to provide is a continuing impetus to the terminated employee to find a job. Most agencies keep statistics and will be delighted to tell you about their successes. Most contend their services reduce out-of-work time, including for employees difficult to place, a pool of potential plaintiffs. Moreover, because they are more knowledgeable about the job market than are most newly terminated employees, these agencies may very well help an employee find a job that is either more rewarding or for which he or she is better suited. Each of these services, if successful, reduce the litigation risk to the terminating employer.

Some out placement agencies can perform certain additional and valuable functions. It is the author's experience, and I believe that of others regularly working in this area, that anger, frustration, bewilderment and embarrassment are more often drivers of wrongful termination litigation than the legitimacy of the case itself. Out placement counselors can, and some of them do, effectively rechannel that negative energy into the search for a new job. Where that redirection takes place, the odds of wrongful termination litigation drop substantially. Out placement personnel counselors can be available at the time of a termination, or shortly thereafter, to help an employee through the emotional difficulties that are necessarily present in any termination. This is particularly helpful in situations where an employee knows that termination was, in fact, justified, but his spouse or friends or work-mates, consciously or subconsciously, force the employee into reacting against his or her former employer. An effective out placement program which does not leave the employee adrift may be able to reduce or eliminate an employee's external pressures to sue.

If these out placement services are so good, one might be tempted to ask why the employer's personnel department doesn't simply create an out placement division to handle its own terminations. Conceptually, of course, that would be a possibility where there is sufficient volume to warrant. But to the extent that an employee simply returns to his or her old employer or is in a position to fraternize with prior co-workers rather than go to a different office with a different group of faces, the problem of seeking a new job and emotionally leaving the former employer behind may be made more difficult. Although good out placement services are expensive, they may be worth considering in certain particular circumstances because that very expense may be a good investment if litigation can thus be avoided.

Alternatives to Conventional Litigation

As the volume of wrongful termination suits increases and the cost and debilitating effects of such lawsuits increasingly burden employers and the traditional courtroom processes, employers and society in general will seek alternative dispute resolution procedures. Although still in their infancy, several options are worth evaluating as possible alternatives to potential future litigation defense costs.

INTERNAL DISPUTE RESOLUTION. Some companies are experimenting with mandatory internal dispute resolution, ending with binding arbitration or one of the other forms of dispute resolution discussed in the following. Internal review, of course, has been around for decades. What is new, however, is that the end of the process is no longer dominated by persons who are employed and perhaps beholden to the employer itself. Increasingly third party neutrals or others specializing in dispute resolution are the final point of these internal procedures. At least in those areas where wrongful termination cases are beginning to grow like weeds, it is the author's view that a properly drawn and administered internal dispute resolution program is worth considering.

Although there are few proven models to date, some internal dispute resolution programs resemble, essentially, a union grievance procedure, although the program is applicable to nonunion employees. There is no accident in this. Just as a number of cases have found that wrongful termination actions do not lie where an employee had access to a binding grievance and arbitration procedure of the type found in many union contracts, employers are looking for nonunion procedures that can provide similar protection, both for the employer and the employees. It is too early to tell whether internal dispute resolution procedures modeled along these lines are simply a fad or the track to a more sane future, but they are showing promise and are worth consideration.

EXTERNAL MEDIATION. For years there has been a small handful of people that could accurately explain the difference between arbitration and mediation in an employment context. That number is expanding rapidly now, and is likely to grow. Mediation generally involves voluntary acceptance of a neutral third party who is expressly recognized by an employer and an employee as a resolution facilitator, but one who has no authority to make a binding judgment on either party. Instead, the mediator attempts to resolve disputes through the use of various exploratory techniques, such as separating issues from interests and using confidential agenda analysis to fashion a mutually acceptable arrangement adopted voluntarily by the disputants. Although this approach may appear to be witchcraft initially, there are specialists around the coutnry who use mediation effectively as an alternative to employers and employees beating on each other in the courtroom.

Again, it is too early to tell with certainty what the future is for these mediative processes regarding wrongful terminations. It would appear they are most effective in certain kinds of disputes where disciplinary action may be called for, but termination not required. Examples of appropriate areas where such services might be used would include issues of poor productivity, work jurisdiction, sexual harassment, and so on. In some cases, however, mediation services are also effective to resolve post-termination disputes.

MINI-TRIALS AND PRIVATE DISPUTE RESOLUTION. Another promising dot on the horizon for avoiding the costs, problems, and uncertainties of litigation is the possibility of private dispute resolution. Private dispute resolution embraces a variety of options including engaging retired jurists to handle private "litigation" by mutual consent. This may be particularly useful where speed and confidentiality are desirable for one or both parties. Although the forms and approach differ substantially among those offering these services, again, they provide an effective and oftentimes substantially more desirable alternative where all the other alternatives to dispute avoidance have failed. Because these processes are private, the parties have great flexibility in adjusting the requirements to fit their substantive needs. It is the author's guess that there will be increasing use of these kinds of private dispute resolution systems over the next several years including for wrongful termination cases.

It is possible, of course, that through legislation various states will mandate a public agency constructed like the National Labor Relations Board or perhaps like Great Britain's Employment Boards to take all wrongful termination matters out of the hands of private employers and their employees. If there were universal arbitration or legislatively adopted special employment courts, some of what has been discussed herein might well become unnecessary. The vast majority of issues considered in this chapter will remain, however. At a minimum, reasonableness will still be a requisite. Yet even with the current changes in the law and those still to come, employers can conduct their business and learn to discipline and terminate employees properly and with dignity. Those who do learn will not have to shoulder the costs of litigation, the burden of punitive damages or the prospect of excessive jury awards.

Chapter 11

THE EMPLOYER'S SURVIVAL KIT
BASIC STEPS TO DEVELOP AN EFFECTIVE AFFIRMATIVE ACTION PLAN

Cynthia Maduro Ryan, J.D.

Equal employment opportunity has evolved from a "social responsibility" program into a legal obligation that can have severe consequences for any employer that falls short of its requirements. An employer found guilty of discriminatory employment practices can face back-pay awards, punitive damages, negative publicity, and court-ordered changes in personnel practices.

Employment discrimination is prohibited principally by four federal laws: Title VII of the Civil Rights Act of 1964, as amended,[1] which forbids discrimination based on race, color, religion, sex, and national origin; the Civil Rights Act of 1866 and 1870;[2] the Age Discrimination in Employment Act of 1967;[3] and the Equal Pay Act of 1963,[4] which requires equal pay for equal work regardless of sex. In addition, Executive Orders 11246[5] and 11141[6] prohibit discrimination by government contractors and subcontractors. Also, state laws on equal employment opportunity have an impact on employers.[7]

An affirmative action plan's purpose is to further equal employment opportunity by assuring that current employment practices are nondiscriminatory and by eliminating the effects of past discrimination. While an affirmative action plan is a necessity for government contractors and

---

[1] 42 U.S.C. section 2000e *et seq.*
[2] 42 U.S.C. sections 1981, 1982.
[3] 29 U.S.C. section 621 *et seq.*
[4] 29 U.S.C. section 206(d).
[5] Exec. Order No. 11246, 3 C.F.R. section 339 (1965).
[6] Exec. Order No. 11141, 3 C.F.R. section 179 (1964).
[7] *E.g., Cal. Gov't Code* section 12940 *et seq.* (West Supp. 1985).

subcontractors,[8] if properly installed and implemented, it can generally help all employers to avoid costly litigation awards. Although employers have a responsibility to provide equal opportunity employment, accomplishing the objectives is not an easy task. Profits and equal opportunity are not mutually exclusive. Many companies have a hidden liability for discriminatory practices. Companies sacrificing equal opportunity in the name of profit may see those profits devoured by next year's back-pay award or settlement.

The difference between "affirmative action" and "equal employment opportunity" is as follows: Affirmative action relates to those *positive actions* employers take to see that all employees, including the protected classes, are affected equally by any employment practices. These practices include but are not limited to recruitment and screening of applicants, placement, salary administration, training programs, discipline, benefits, promotions, and terminations. The positive actions undertaken are designed to continue to keep the personnel practices objective, job-related, well-understood, and fairly administered.

Equal employment opportunity means *fairness* in hiring so that all people, regardless of race, color, religion, age, sex, national origin, or physical handicap, which are the protected class categories, have an equal chance of obtaining any job for which they are qualified.

The net result of affirmative action and equal opportunity will be a workforce in which all groups, including the "protected classes," are represented at all levels.

AFFIRMATIVE ACTION PLAN—GENERAL OUTLINE

The most important measure of an affirmative action plan is its *results*. Affirmative action plans are instituted in one of three ways:

1. *By Government Requirement.* The need for affirmative action was first recognized in Presidential Executive Orders from 1961 through 1967 requiring government contractors to take positive, continuing, results-oriented affirmative action to eliminate job discrimination. The present Executive Order 11246 (as amended by Executive Order 11375)[9] requires all major contractors and subcontractors to conduct their own self-analysis to determine if their employment system has discriminatory effects, and to take appropriate remedial affirmative action, without need of any legal proceedings. The Order requires large contractors (ones holding federal contracts of $50,000 and having 50 or more employees) to implement written Affirmative action plans.

2. *Voluntary Plans.* The most voluntary agreement possible is the one instituted by a company itself. Such approaches assist in ensuring full

[8] Exec. Order No. 11246, 3 C.F.R. section 339 (1965), as amended by Exec. Order No. 11375, 32 Fed. Reg. 14303 (1967); 41 C.F.R., Part 60-1 *et seq.* (1984).
[9] *Id.*

compliance with equal opportunity laws. Such voluntary compliance programs are positive expressions of "good faith" to both the courts and regulators.

3. *Court-Ordered Plans.* As might be expected, some of the most stringent provisions are to be found in court-ordered affirmative action agreements which are administered by the courts themselves, who sometimes appoint the Equal Employment Opportunity Commission (EEOC) to monitor the progress of an agreement and report back to the court. Such agreements carry provisions for court enforcement, should it be discovered that a company is in default.

Extensive efforts to develop procedures, analyses, data collection systems, report forms, and written policy statements are meaningless unless the end product will be measurable with yearly improvement in hiring, training, and promotion of the protected classes in all parts of an organization. However, in reaffirming a company's equal opportunity policy, the essence of an affirmative action plan should be: (1) to establish and maintain a strong company policy and commitment;[10] (2) to assign responsibility and authority for the affirmative action plan to appropriate company officers;[11] (3) to analyze the present work force in identifying jobs, departments, and units where protected classes are underutilized;[12] (4) to set specific, measurable, and attainable hiring and promotion goals, with target dates in each area of underutilization;[13] (5) to ensure that every executive, manager, and supervisor is responsible and accountable for helping to set the goals;[14] (6) to reevaluate job descriptions and hiring criteria to assure that they reflect actual job needs;[15] (7) to find protected classes who qualify or can become qualified to attain the goals;[16] (8) to review and revise all employment procedures to ensure that they do not have any discriminatory effect and that they help to attain the goals;[17] (9) to focus on getting protected classes into upward-mobility and relevant training pipelines;[18] and (10) to develop systems to monitor and measure progress regularly.[19]

---

[10] 41 C.F.R. section 60-2.21 (1984); *Parham v. Southwestern Bell Tel. Co.,* 433 F.2d 421, 429 (8th Cir. 1970).

[11] 41 C.F.R. section 60-2.22 (1984); *Parham,* 453 F.2d at 429.

[12] 41 C.F.R. sections 60-2.11, 60-2.23 (1984); *Palmer v. District Bd. of Trustees,* 748 F.2d 595, 596-97 n.5 (11th Cir. 1984).

[13] *Id.; see also* 41 C.F.R. section 60-2.12 (1984).

[14] 41 C.F.R. section 60-2.22 (1984).

[15] *Waters v. Olinkraft, Inc.,* 475 F. Supp. 743, 753 (W.D. Ark. 1979).

[16] 41 C.F.R. section 60-2.13(j) (1984); *Jones v. Cleland,* 466 F. Supp. 34, 37 (N.D. Ala. 1978).

[17] 41 C.F.R. section 60-2.13 (1984); *Smith v. Union Oil Co. of Cal.,* 17 F.E.P. Cases 960, 999 (N.D. Cal. 1977).

[18] 41 C.F.R. section 60-2.10 (1984); *Jones,* 46 F. Supp. at 37–38.

[19] 41 C.F.R. section 60-2.13(g) (1984).

DEVELOPMENT OF A WRITTEN EQUAL EMPLOYMENT OPPORTUNITY POLICY AND AFFIRMATIVE ACTION COMMITMENT

The chief executive should issue a written statement of personal commitment, legal obligations, and the importance of equal employment opportunity as a business goal to all employees.[20] Specific responsibility and accountability should be assigned throughout the employment structure to every executive, manager and supervisor. The statement should include at least the following elements.

1. *Company Policy.* Equal employment opportunity for all persons, regardless of race, creed, color, sex, national origin, handicap, or age is a fundamental company policy.

2. *Goal-Setting.* Goal-setting procedures are required with measurement and evaluation components, similar to other company programs based on defined business objectives.

3. *Affirmative Action.* Special positive actions throughout the company may be required to overcome effects of past discrimination.

4. *Program Responsibility.* Responsibility for the affirmative action plan needs to be assigned to a top company executive; however, all management personnel share this responsibility. Performance by all management personnel of this plan will be evaluated in the same fashion as is performance on other company goals.

5. *Benefits.* Achievement of affirmative action goals will provide positive benefits to the company through more complete utilization and development of previous underutilized personnel.

6. *Employment Practices.* Affirmative action will affect all employment practices, including but not limited to, recruiting, hiring, transfer, promotions, training, compensation, benefits, layoff, and terminations.

IMPLEMENTATION OF THE AFFIRMATIVE ACTION PLAN

The importance of the affirmative action plan is indicated from the start by the person charged with the authority and responsibility to implement the plan.[21]

1. *Affirmative Action Official.* Appoint a top management official as head of the affirmative action plan, directly responsible to the chief executive.

---

[20] *See generally* 41 C.F.R., Part 60-2 *et seq.* (1984); *Thomas v. Basic Magnesia, Inc.*, 22 F.E.P. Cases 1284, 1287 (N.D. Fla. 1980).
[21] See *supra* note 11.

2. *Time Commitment.* Managing the affirmative action plan requires a major time commitment and proper staff support is necessary.

3. *Responsibilities.* Responsibilities of the person managing the affirmative action plan should include the following:

    a. *Policy Development.* Developing a written policy statement, a written affirmative action plan, and internal and external communication procedures.

    b. *Company Liaison.* Serving as a liaison between company, government regulatory agencies, minority and women's organizations, and other community groups.

    c. *Technical Assistance.* Assisting line management in collecting and analyzing employment data, identifying problem areas, setting goals and timetables, and developing procedures to achieve the goals.

    d. *Program Monitoring.* Designing, implementing, and monitoring internal audit and reporting systems to measure program effectiveness.

    e. *Reporting.* Reporting periodically, to the chief executive on the progress of the affirmative action plan in relation to company goals.

    f. *Communications.* Assuring that current legal information affecting affirmative action is disseminated throughout the company.

4. *Company Officials.* All company officials should clearly understand their own responsibilities for ensuring compliance with the equal employment opportunity laws and carrying out the affirmative action plan as a basic part of their jobs.

PUBLICATION, INTERNALLY AND EXTERNALLY, OF THE AFFIRMATIVE ACTION PLAN

1. *Communications.* Company officials should be fully informed about the company's affirmative action plan by the following measures:[22]

    a. *Chief Executive.* Written communication and policy statement from the chief executive.

    b. *Procedural Manuals.* Inclusion of the affirmative action plan and policy in the company's handbooks and manuals.

    c. *Special Meetings.* Special meetings held periodically to discuss the affirmative action plan, summarizing individual responsibilities and progress.

2. *Performance Appraisal.* All executives, managers, and supervisors need to be advised that performance on affirmative action goals will

---

[22] 41 C.F.R. section 60-2.21 (1984); *See also Thomas,* 22 F.E.P. Cases at 1287; *Parham,* 433 F.2d at 421.

be rated along with other criteria in evaluation for promotions and merit increases, and that inadequate cooperation or obstruction of the affirmative action plan will incur penalties or disciplinary action.

3. *Training.* Educational materials and training sessions to communicate legal requirements for affirmative action should clarify specific responsibilities affecting the operations of each area of the company. "Awareness" training may be helpful in sensitizing executives, managers, and supervisors to the type of employment barriers and attitudinal stereotypes which often hinder equal employment opportunity and affirmative action plans.

4. *Employee Communications.* All employees should be informed of company policy through such measures as the following:

   a. *Bulletin Boards.* The company's equal employment opportunity and affirmative action statement and the federal equal employment opportunity poster should be posted on bulletin boards throughout the company facilities.

   b. *Employee Handbook.* The equal opportunity and affirmative action policy should be included in the employee handbook.

   c. *Newsletters.* Publicity on the subject should be presented in company newsletters.

   d. *Company Publications.* Articles and pictures, featuring minority and female employees in varied high-level and nontraditional jobs, should be included in company publications.

   e. *Training Programs.* Presentation and discussion of the affirmative action plan should be part of the employee orientation and all training programs.

   f. *Handouts.* Copies of the affirmative action policy statement and a summary of the affirmative action plan's key program elements should be provided to all employees.

   g. *Employee Meetings.* Special meetings should be conducted periodically with all employees to explain the affirmative action goals.

5. *Union Communications (if applicable).* Union officials should be invited to cooperate in developing and implementing the affirmative action plan from its inception.

6. *External Communications.* Publicize the affirmative action policy externally in the following fashion:

   a. *Recruitment Sources.* Notify regular recruitment sources annually that they must refer applicants on a nondiscriminatory basis.[23]

   b. *Advertising Media.* Advertising media should be informed that help wanted ads cannot be placed in columns segregated by sex. Include the statement that the company is an "Equal Opportunity Employer (Male/Female)" in all advertising.[24]

---

[23] 42 U.S.C. section 2000e-2(b); 29 C.F.R. section 1604.6 (1984); *see also Abron v. Black & Decker Mfg. Co.*, 439 F. Supp. 1095 (D. Md. 1977), *rev'd on other grounds*, 654 F.2d 951 (4th Cir. 1981).

[24] 29 C.F.R. section 1604.5 (1984); *Abron*, 439 F. Supp. at 1111.

c. *New Recruitment Sources.* Utilize new recruiting sources, including schools, colleges, community groups, and others who have special contacts with women, minority, and other protected class groups.[25]

WORKFORCE ASSESSMENT AND UTILIZATION

Analysis of the current employee group is the first step toward defining specific affirmative action goals.[26]

1. *Current Employment.* Identify present areas and levels of employment.

   a. *Assessment.* Identify the number and percentage of minority and female employees (and other protected classes, if applicable) currently employed in each division, office and major job classification. Include the following information:

      i. *Total Employees.* Total employees in each job classification.

      ii. *Salaries.* Current salary or pay range for each job classification.

      iii. *Males by Job Classification.* Number and percentage of males in each job classification.

      iv. *Females by Job Classification.* Number and percentage of females in each job classification.

      v. *Male Minorities by Job Classification.* Number and percentage of male minority persons in each job classification (using EEOC race classifications).

      vi. *Female Minorities by Job Classification.* Number and percentage of female minority persons in each job classification (using EEOC race classifications).

   b. *Job Classifications.* Use job classifications in payroll records rather than the broad job categories reported in EEOC forms.

   c. *Minority Group Assessment.* Include information for each minority group present in the work force: black, Hispanic, Asian, American Indian, other (using these EEOC race classifications). Information should be shown for each group which constitutes 2 percent or more of the population of the relevant labor area.

2. *Underutilization and Concentration.* Identify areas of underutilization and concentration.[27]

   a. *Underutilization.* Underutilization has been defined as having fewer minorities or women in a particular job category than would

---

[25] 41 C.F.R. section 60-2.24(e) (1984); *Commonwealth Oil Refining Co. v. EEOC*, 720 F.2d 1383, 1384 (5th Cir. 1983); *Waters*, 475 F. Supp. at 753; *Lo Re v. Chase Manhattan Corp.*, 19 F.E.P. Cases 1366, 1368 (S.D.N.Y. 1979); *United States v. Household Finance Corp.*, 4 E.P.D. ¶ 7680 (N.D. Ill. 1972).

[26] See *supra* note 12.

[27] See *supra* note 12; *Abron*, 439 F. Supp. at 1108–09; *Jones*, 466 F. Supp. at 37–38.

reasonably be expected by their presence in the relevant labor market. Underutilization also means employing persons in jobs where the company does not make adequate use of their skills and training.

b. *Concentration.* Concentration means more of a particular group (females, males, blacks, etc.) in a job category than would reasonably be expected by their presence in the work force.

c. *Interpretation.* Where statistics reveal significant underutilization or concentration, there is a strong possibility that discriminatory practices are operating in some aspects of the employment system, and that remedial action should be taken to eliminate such practices.

3. *Extent of Underutilization.* Determine the extent of underutilization of minorities and females.[28] Survey the Company's labor area (the area in which the Company can reasonably expect to recruit, usually the standard metropolitan statistical area) to determine the following:

a. *Minority Population.* The percentage of each minority group in the total population of the area.

b. *Workforce Composition.* The percentage of each minority group and of females in the workforce.

c. *Unemployment.* The extent of unemployment for minorities and females.

d. *Availability of Skills.* The availability of minorities and females with required skills.

e. *Company Workforce.* Availability of promotable and transferable females and minorities in the Company's workforce.

f. *Training Available.* Institutions in the community capable of training people in needed skills.

g. *Company Training.* The organization's capability for training to qualify minorities and women for all job classifications.

DEVELOPMENT OF GOALS AND TIMETABLES

Any serious business program requires setting measureable goals and reasonable timetables for achieving them. Some actions to comply with the law can and should be taken immediately, while others can require different timetables.[29]

---

[28] *Id.*
[29] See *supra* note 13; *see also Craik v. Minnesota State Univ. Bd.,* 731 F.2d 465, 472 (8th Cir. 1984).

1. *Immediate Action.* Immediate action should be taken to assure that salaries and benefits are the same for all employees who perform substantially similar work, and that sex, race, religion, age, handicap, or national origin is not a factor in placing employees in jobs with different pay levels or opportunities for advancement.

2. *Long-Range Goals.* Long-range goals and timetables may be needed to eliminate employment discrimination and effects of past discrimination.

   a. *Ultimate Goal.* The ultimate long-range goal of the affirmative action plan should be representation of each group identified as "underutilized" in each major job classification in reasonable relation to the overall labor force participation of such group.

   b. *Flexibility.* Long-range goals should not be rigid and unchangeable because they cannot be based on exact predictable statistics.

3. *Annual Targets.* Once long-range goals have been set for each underutilized group in each job category, specific, numerical annual targets should be developed for hiring, training, transferring, and promoting, to reach these goals within the targetted time frame.

   a. *Factors Affecting Targets.* Annual targets will depend on such factors as anticipated turnover, expansion or contraction, availability of persons with required skills, realistic appraisal of the extent of the skills necessary for particular jobs, time necessary to acquire such skills, the possibility of on-the-job or other training to acquire skills, and similar considerations.

   b. *Development.* Targets should be developed for the organization as a whole, for each unit, and each job category.

   c. *Participation.* Each organizational unit of the company should participate in setting annual targets and should be held responsible for meeting them.

   d. *Overall Responsibility.* Overall responsibility for goals should remain with the assigned affirmative action official.

   e. *Reporting.* A reporting, monitoring, and evaluation system should be established to assure that there is measurable yearly improvement in hiring, training, transfer, and promotion of each group in each area where underutilization has been identified.

DEVELOPMENT AND IMPLEMENTATION OF POSITIVE ACTION PROGRAMS

To achieve long-range goals and intermediate yearly targets, a company must first identify where discriminatory barriers may be operating in the employment system, and then take necessary steps to eliminate them, and to equalize opportunities for those suffering effects of past discrimination.

It is the *consequence* of employment practices, *not the intent,* which determines whether discrimination exists requiring remedial action.

1. *Recruitment.* Analyze and review recruitment procedures for each job category to identify and eliminate discriminatory barriers.[30]

    a. *Analysis.* Establish objective measures to analyze and monitor the recruitment process. It is impossible to eliminate subjective judgment, but applicant flow and other monitoring records will help identify potential sources of continuing discrimination.

        i. *Applicant Flow Records.* Develop an applicant flow record, indicating for each applicant: name, race, age, handicap, national origin, sex, referral source, date of application, whether a job offer was made and the job offered, or reason why a job offer was not made, and the name of the person(s) making the employment decision.[31]

        ii. *Periodic Reports.* Prepare periodic reports of applicants and interviews for each job opening and the percentage of total applicants and of total hires by job category.

        iii. *Records.* Retain records of protected classes not hired, who interviewed them, who made decisions not to hire, and the written reasons for not hiring.

    b. *Training.* Train persons involved in the employment process to use objective standards and to support affirmative action goals.[32]

    c. *Protected Class Staff.* Utilize protected classes in the entire personnel process, specifically: in policy-level positions; as interviewers; on recruitment visits to schools; in advertising material; and as referral sources. If a company really offers equal job advancement opportunities, and the company's "credibility" is good, present protected class employees will be an important recruitment source.

    d. *Affirmative Strategies.* Institute affirmative strategies to recruit for all jobs where underutilization has been identified.

        i. *Applicant Files.* Maintain an affirmative action file of protected class applicants not hired, who are potential candidates for future openings and contact these candidates first when there are openings.

        ii. *Advertising.* Adopt an affirmative approach to advertising.[33]

            A. *Media Selection.* Advertise regularly in media directed toward minorities, women, and other protected classes.

---

[30] See *supra* note 25.

[31] 41 C.F.R. section 60-3.15 (1984); *Craik,* 731 F.2d at 477; *United States v. County of Fairfax,* 25 F.E.P. Cases 662, 670-71 (E.D. Va. 1981); *United States v. U.S. Steel Corp.,* 5 E.P.D. ¶ 8619 (N.D. Ala. 1973); *United States v. Virginia Elec. & Power Co.,* 327 F. Supp. 1034, 1045 (E.D. Va. 1971).

[32] *Smith,* 17 F.E.P. Cases at 999.

[33] See *supra* note 25.

B. *Written Ads.* Place classified ads only under "Help Wanted" or "Help Wanted, Male–Female" listings. Be sure that the content of ads does not indicate any race, sex, or age preference.

C. *Male–Female Emphasis.* Where jobs traditionally have been typed as "male" or "female," emphasize interest in recruiting both sexes. All advertising should include the phrase "Equal Opportunity Employer, Male–Female."

iii. *Employment Agencies.* Explain company policies to employment agencies.

A. *Job Orders.* When placing job orders with employment agencies, emphasize the company's policy of hiring applicants based on merit, and its interest in referrals of qualified minorities, males and females for all jobs.

B. *Specialized Agencies.* Contact agencies that specialize in minority, female, and other protected class applicants.

C. *State Employment Service.* List jobs at all levels with the local employment development department.

iv. *Schools and Colleges.* Improve relationships with schools and colleges.

A. *Schools.* Establish and maintain personal contact with counselors and principals of schools in the relevant labor area, particularly schools with a large minority enrollment. Investigate possibilities for part-time workstudy programs and summer job programs which can provide new employees. Work with school personnel to develop curriculum and training to equip students for jobs leading to good careers in your company.

B. *Colleges.* Schedule recruiting visits and write to colleges with large minority and female enrollments.

v. *Community Organizations.* Develop and maintain contact with minority, women's and community organizations. Good informal referral sources include minority and female group leaders, ministers, doctors, and community improvement groups.

vi. *Additional Sources.* Develop additional sources of recruitment.

A. *Training Programs.* Existing training programs in the community may provide qualified applicants.

B. *Veterans.* Returning veterans include many minorities with skills and may be contacted through the local Veterans Administration Office.

2. *Selection Standards and Procedures.* The selection process, whether consciously or unconsciously, is a most sensitive area of a company's employment practice relative to ensuring full compliance with the equal employment laws and affirmative action goals. A careful review and evaluation of every step of this process is necessary to assure

that job requirements, hiring standards, and methods of selection and placement are nondiscriminatory, and that they contribute toward affirmative action goals.[34]

a. *Employee Selection Guidelines.* The EEOC's Employee Selection *Guidelines* prohibit job qualifications or selection standards which disproportionately screen out persons in groups protected by Title VII unless (1) they can be significantly related to job performance and (2) no alternative nondiscriminatory standards can be developed to meet requirements shown to be justified by "business necessity."

  i. *Procedures Subject to Guidelines.* Employee selection procedures subject to the EEOC's *Guidelines* include all tests and other requirements such as biographical information, background requirements, specific education or work experience requirements, interviews, application forms, and interviewer rating systems which result in a significantly different rate of rejection for groups protected by Title VII.

  ii. *Validation of Selection Procedures.* Validation is required only where existing selection procedures have a statistically significant adverse effect on groups protected by Title VII.[35] Validation is a very specific, technical and complex process, defined in detail in the EEOC Selection *Guidelines.* Validity studies must be conducted by professionally trained psychologists.

  iii. *Practical Effect.* The EEOC selection *Guidelines* require that a company identify, analyze, and monitor every step of the selection and assignment process including all procedures for initial hire, transfer, promotion, training, or any employment opportunity, to discover if any step has adverse impact on groups protected by Title VII.

  iv. *Analysis of Adverse Rejection Rates.* If a significantly different rejection rate is found in any step of a selection procedure, analyze the cause. It may be bias on the part of those applying the procedure, or the use of such a procedure only for certain groups, or the way in which a seemingly neutral procedure affects a protected group.

    A. *Job Analysis.* Conduct job analysis to identify actual tasks performed, their frequency, and importance of specific employee traits or skills needed for the job.

    B. *Standards.* Be sure that job descriptions and hiring standards reflect major job functions identified and do not require higher qualifications.

    C. *Alternatives.* If selection procedures still produce adverse rejection rates on protected groups, consider whether each

---

[34] 29 C.F.R., Part 1607 *et seq.* (1984); 41 C.F.R., Part 60-3 *et seq.* (1984); *Harrison v. Lewis*, 559 F. Supp. 943, 948 (D.C. 1983); *U.S. v. Virginia Elec.*, 327 F. Supp. at 1040.
[35] See *supra* note 34.

remaining standard or practice really is necessary for the safe and efficient operation of the business, and what other procedures might be used to achieve the same objective without discriminatory effect.

D. *Validation.* Undertake the extensive work and cost of professional validation only if such actions as stated above fail to eliminate the discriminatory impact of selection procedures.

b. *Application Forms and Preemployment Inquiries.* The EEOC and the courts have found that many common preemployment inquiries disproportionately reject minorities and females and usually are not job related.[36] Inquire only on the following basis: "Does this question tend to have a disproportionate effect in screening out minorities and females?" "Is this information necessary to judge this individual's competence for performance of this particular job?" "Are there alternative, nondiscriminatory means to secure the necessary information?" Major questions which should be eliminated from preemployment inquiries, or carefully reviewed to assure that their use is job-related and nondiscriminatory in effect, include the following:

i. *Race, National Origin, Religion.* Inquires about or records of information about race, national origin, or religion do not constitute per se violations of Title VII, but such inquiries and records will be examined very carefully if discrimination charges arise.[37]

ii. *Education.* The courts have found nonjob-related educational requirements, which have a disparate effect on protected class groups, a major area of illegal discrimination. Eliminate the requirements for a high school (or higher) diploma, if not needed for a specific job. Be sure that English language requirements do not bar employment of people with little or no English, if this is not an important job requirement.[38]

iii. *Arrest and Conviction Records.* An individual's arrest record has been ruled by the courts to be an unlawful basis for refusal to employ, unless a "business necessity" for such policy can be established.[39]

iv. *Credit Rating.* A negative employment decision based on an applicant's poor credit rating has also been found unlawful, where credit policies have a disproportionate negative effect

---

[36] 29 C.F.R. sections 1604.7, 1605.3, 1606.5 (1984).

[37] See *supra* note 36; *Sugarman v. Dougall*, 413 U.S. 634, 643 (1973).

[38] 29 C.F.R. section 1606.6(b)(1); *Griggs v. Duke Power Co.*, 401 U.S. 424, 431 (1971); *U.S. v. Virginia Elec.*, 327 F. Supp. at 1040.

[39] *Carter v. Gallagher*, 452 F.2d 315, 326 (8th Cir. 1971), *cert. denied*, 406 U.S. 950 (1972); *Gregory v. Litton Systems, Inc.*, 472 F.2d 631, 632 (9th Cir. 1972); *Green v. Missouri Pac. R.R.*, 523 F.2d 1290, 1298-99 (8th Cir. 1975).

on minorities and the employer cannot show "business necessity" for such rejection.[40]

v. *Sex, Marital, and Family Status.* Whether a candidate is male or female, married or single, and number and age of children are examples of questions frequently used to discriminate against women which relate to capacity for job performance.[41] Any such question which directly or indirectly suggests or results in limitation of a job opportunity in any way is unlawful discrimination.

vi. *Physical Requirements.* Application questions and hiring standards related to height, weight, and other physical requirements should be retained only where necessary for performance of a particular job.[42]

vii. *Age: Date of Birth.* Questions about age may be used to violate the Age Discrimination in Employment Act.[43]

viii. *Experience.* Experience requirements should be reviewed and reevaluated to assure necessity for specific jobs. Requirements should be eliminated where jobs can be quickly learned.[44]

ix. *Availability for Weekend or Holiday Work.* It may be necessary for an employer to have information about availability for Saturday, Sunday, or holiday work, but Title VII requires that employers make reasonable accommodation for "an employee's or prospective employee's religious observance or practice if it does not create undue hardship on the conduct of the employers' business."[45]

x. *Friends or Relatives Working for the Company.* Questions about friends or relatives working for the company may reflect a preference for friends and relatives of present employees, and would be unlawful if they have the effect of reducing employment opportunity for protected class groups.[46]

xi. *Appearance.* Employment decisions based on factors such as length or style of hair, dress, and other aspects of appearance have been found to violate the law, if they disproportionately

[40] *Johnson v. Pike Corp. of Am.,* 332 F. Supp. 490, 494 (C.D. Cal. 1971); CCH EEOC Decisions (1983) ¶ 6386; CCH EEOC Decisions (1973) ¶ 6312.

[41] 41 C.F.R. section 60-20.3 (1984); 29 C.F.R. sections 1604.2, 1604.4, 1604.10 (1984).

[42] *Dothard v. Rawlinson,* 433 U.S. 321, 328-33 (1977); *New York State Div. of Human Rights v. New York-Pennsylvania Professional Baseball League,* 3 E.P.D. ¶ 8208 (N.Y. 1971).

[43] 29 U.S.C. section 621 *et seq.; Hodgson v. First Fed. Sav. & Loan Ass'n of Broward County,* 455 F.2d 818 (5th Cir. 1972).

[44] *Rowe v. General Motors Corp.,* 457 F.2d 348, 358-59, 360-61 (5th Cir. 1972); *Waters,* 475 F. Supp. at 753.

[45] 29 C.F.R. sections 1605.2-1605.3 (1984).

[46] *Local 53 v. Vogler,* 407 F.2d 1047, 1053-54 (5th Cir. 1969); *Lea v. Cone Mills Corp.,* 301 F. Supp. 97, 100 (M.D.N.C. 1969), *aff'd,* 438 F.2d 86 (4th Cir. 1971); CCH EEOC Decisions (1983) ¶ 6492.

affect employment on the basis of race, national origin, or sex.[47]

   c. *Testing.* Any test which adversely affects the employment status of groups protected by Title VII must be professionally validated as an effective, significant predictor of effective job performance. Pending validation of tests, a company may decide, as some firms have, to eliminate those tests which screen out a disproportionate number of protected class applicants.[48]

      i. *Use of Test Scores.* Use test scores as only one of several criteria to evaluate for selection.

      ii. *Substitutes for Tests.* As substitutes for tests, or supplements to validated tests, consider more substantive interviews, and use of probationary periods to provide evaluation of ability based on performance.

   d. *Interviews.* Biased and subjective judgments in personnel interviews can be a major source of discrimination. Interviewers should be trained to evaluate each candidate's individual ability and potential, and to know actual job requirements based on realistic job descriptions.[49]

   e. *Rating of Selection Standards.* Review any system of rating or "weighting" certain items in application forms, tests, or interviews which may have a disparate effect on minorities or females.

   f. *Monitoring the Selection Process.* The following elements of the selection process should be monitored with records indicating the effect of each activity by race, national origin, and sex.

      i. Recruitment sources.

      ii. Application forms and preemployment inquiries.

      iii. Job descriptions (for job-relatedness).

      iv. Tests (for disparate effect).

      v. Interview procedures and results.

      vi. Physical examination.

      vii. Reference and security checks.

      viii. Job assignment.

3. *Upward Mobility System.* Assignment, job progression, promotions, transfer, seniority, and training are factors for upward mobility. To improve female, minority, and protected class employment in all jobs in which they are underrepresented, review all practices, both

[47] *Donahue v. Shoe Corp. of Am.,* 337 F. Supp. 1357, 1359 (C.D. Cal. 1972); CCH EEOC Decisions (1973) ¶ 6240.
[48] 41 C.F.R., Part 60-3 *et seq.* (1984); 29 C.F.R., Part 1607 *et seq.* (1984); *Griggs,* 401 U.S. at 430, 436; *United States v. Household Finance Corp.,* 4 E.P.D. ¶ 7680 (N.D. Ill. 1972); *Albermarle Paper Co. v. Moody,* 9 E.P.D. ¶10,230 (1975); *United States v. County of Fairfax,* 25 F.E.P. Cases 662, 670 (E.D. VA. 1981).
[49] *Bauer v. Bailar,* 647 F.2d 1037, 1042-43 (10th Cir. 1981).

formal and informal, affecting assignment, transfers, promotion, and training for jobs at all levels.[50]

a. *Identify the Barriers.* Identify barriers to upward mobility of minorities and females.

   i. *Present System.* Determine present systems or practices affecting transfer and promotion, both formal and informal.

   ii. *Requirements.* Identify requirements and procedures for transfer and promotion.

   iii. *Supervisor's Influence.* Determine the extent to which supervisors' evaluations and recommendations are a major factor in transfer and promotion.

   iv. *Effect on Minorities and Females.* Determine whether requirements for selecting apprentices and special bidding procedures for incumbent workers have a disparate effect on and/or tend to lock out members of a protected class.

b. *Establish Affirmative Action Records to Monitor Upward Mobility.* Records are needed to identify existing barriers and determine needed affirmative action for upward mobility.

   i. *Records.* The following records should be maintained.

      A. *Personnel Transactions.* Promotion, transfer, and termination rates for each minority group, for females and other protected class members by job category.

      B. *Training.* Number and percentage of each minority group, of females and other protected class members in apprenticeship and all training programs.

      C. *Progression.* Charts showing formal lines of progression.

   ii. *Analysis.* The following analyses should be made.

      A. *Upward Mobility.* Identify jobs held by minorities, females, and other protected class members in terms of job progression and opportunities for upward mobility compared to other employees.

      B. *Promotion Referrals.* Compare rate of minorities, females and other protected class members who are referred for promotion but not promoted to that of other employees.

      C. *Barriers.* Identify seniority and other factors that operate as barriers to upward mobility.

      D. *Experience and Other Requirements.* Determine if present requirements for work experience in entry jobs are necessary to perform the next job in formal lines of progression or

---

[50] *Robinson v. Lorillard Corp.*, 444 F.2d 791, 795-96, 799-800 (4th Cir. 1971); *United States v. St. Louis-San Francisco Ry. Co.*, 464 F.2d 301, 307-08 (8th Cir. 1972), *cert. denied*, 409 U.S. 1116 (1973); *Hicks v. Crown Zellerbach Corp.*, 319 F. Supp. 314, 322-25 (E.D. La. 1970), *modified*, 321 F. Supp. 1241 (E.D. La. 1971); *Rowe*, 457 F.2d at 358-9, 360-61; *Abron*, 439 F. Supp. at 1117; *Women's Comm. For EEO v National Broadcasting Co.*, 19 F.E.P. Cases 1703 (S.D.N.Y. 1977); *Copeland v. Usery*, 13 E.P.D. ¶ 11,434 (D.C. 1976).

merely convenient means of qualification for promotion. Determine how much time is really needed to gain work experience for promotion.

c. *Develop Affirmative Programs to Overcome Identified Barriers.* Take remedial affirmative action to eliminate barriers and overcome the effects of past discrimination.

i. *Selection Guidelines.* Be sure that all selection standards and procedures for promotion, transfer, and training conform to the EEOC's Selection *Guidelines.*

ii. *Employee Ability.* Be sure that procedures for selecting candidates for promotion, transfer, and training are based on fair assessment of an employee's ability and work record.

iii. *Merit System.* Adopt a company wide merit promotion plan; post and otherwise publicize all job promotional opportunities and encourage employees to bid on them, particularly employees who traditionally have not had access to better jobs.

iv. *Employee Evaluation.* Develop a formal employee evaluation program, based on objective measurable factors.

v. *Supervisory Responsibility.* Require supervisors to include a specified percentage of protected class members among those promoted, consistent with annual affirmative action goals. Require supervisors to submit a written justification when apparently qualified employees are passed over for upgrading or promotion.

vi. *Promotion Eligibility.* Make clear to employees and supervisors that protected classes are eligible for promotion to any job, on the basis of individual qualifications, regardless of whether some jobs have traditionally been held by one sex or race.

vii. *Remedial Action.* Target members of any identified "affected class" for priority remedial action in transfer, promotion and relevant compensatory benefits, and pay. Identify protected class members qualified for upward mobility.

A. *Qualifications Comparison.* Review records of all employees and analyze comparative qualifications.

B. *Potential Assessment.* Interview employees to further assess their potential and get additional information on their background and career interests.

C. *Employee Comparison.* Compare job performance, length of service and other factors affecting salaries and promotion rates of minority and female employees with qualifications of other employees who have been promoted.

D. *Remedial Action Files.* Set up a remedial action file of protected class employees qualified for promotion and use this file first when openings occur in job classifications.

viii. *Career Counseling.* Establish a career counseling program, to encourage employees in dead-end jobs to qualify for better jobs.

ix. *Cooperative Programs.* Provide training at the job site through cooperation with local training and education institutions.

x. *Training and Education.* Set specific numerical or percentage goals for participation of protected class members in all company sponsored training.

A. *Management Training.* Management training should be a high priority in view of the small number of protected class managers.

B. *New Programs.* Develop new training programs to help those who have not had opportunity to acquire on-the-job experience to qualify and compete for promotions.

C. *Tuition Aid.* Encourage protected class members to participate in company tuition aid programs.

xi. *Job Restructuring.* Consider restructuring jobs to reduce the gap and increase the steps between present low-skill and higher-skill jobs.

4. *Wage and Salary Structure.* Compare job descriptions and actual functions of jobs held by protected class groups, length of service and other factors affecting pay rates. Title VII requires equal pay regardless of race, age, national origin, religion, or sex. Equal pay is required for jobs of equal skill, effort, and responsibility.[51]

5. *Benefits and Conditions of Employment.* Review all benefits and conditions of employment to see that they are equally available without discrimination to all employees.

a. *Employee Benefits*

i. *Retirement Plans.* Assure that males and females are eligible for retirement and pensions of the same basis, including equal retirement age and equal benefits.

ii. *Conditional Benefits.* Assure that benefits are not conditioned on the basis that the employee is "head of the household" or "principal wage earner" (such a condition is not job related and tends to discriminate unduly against females).

iii. *Family Benefits.* Assure that benefits for husbands and families of female employees are the same as those available to wives and families of male employees.

iv. *Female Employees.* Assure that benefits available to wives of male employees are available to female employees.

b. *State "Protective Laws."* Many states have laws or regulations developed under an earlier concept of "protecting" women from hard and dangerous work, or providing special working conditions for them. The EEOC's *Guidelines,* court decisions, and opin-

---

[51] 29 U.S.C. section 206(d); *Craik,* 731 F.2d at 478–79; *Melanson v. Rantoul,* 536 F. Supp. 271, 286-87 (D.R.I. 1982).

ions of state attorney general's have generally established (if the laws have not yet been repealed) that equal employment requirements of Title VII supersede such state "protective" laws.

    i. *Hiring.* Do not refuse to hire, transfer, or promote women because of state laws prohibiting female employment in certain occupations (i.e., in jobs requiring lifting of specified weights, requirements that women can work only specified hours, or for specified numbers of hours per day or week).

    ii. *Minimum Wages.* Minimum wage or premium pay requirements for women under state laws should be equally applicable to men.

    iii. *Minors.* State laws which discriminate on the basis of sex with regard to employment of minors are superseded by Title VII.

  c. *Pregnancy and Maternity.* Any written or unwritten policy which excludes applicants or employees from jobs because of pregnancy, or requires them to stop work at a specified time period violates Title VII and should be rescinded.[52]

6. *Layoff, Recall, Discharge, Demotion, and Disciplinary Action.* The standards for deciding when a person shall be terminated, demoted disciplined, laid off, or recalled should be the same for all employees, not applied differently for protected classes.[53] The following records should be kept to monitor this area.

  a. *Terminations.* Records of all terminations should be kept indicating total, name, date, number of protected class group by job category, and reason for termination.

  b. *Layoffs and Demotions.* Records of layoffs and demotions should be kept indicating total, name, date, number of protected class group by job category, reason for action, and recall rights.

  c. *Exit Interviews.* Exit interviews should be conducted with all employees who quit to determine to what extent lack of training and actual or perceived discriminatory treatment are causes of turnover.

7. *Revisions of Union Contract.* Both employers and unions are responsible for nondiscrimination under Title VII. An employer may not blame failure to take affirmative action on barriers in a union contract or threat of a suit if such action is taken. Legally, a union is obligated to revise any contract provisions that have a discriminatory effect, regardless of membership preference. If a union is unwilling to negotiate such changes, they should be made unilaterally. Such unilateral action to comply with Title VII does not violate the "good faith bargaining" provisions of the National Labor Relations Act.

---

[52] 29 C.F.R. section 1604.10 (1984); *La Fleur v. Cleveland Bd. of Educ.*, 465 F.2d 1184 (6th Cir. 1972), *aff'd*, 414 U.S. 632 (1974); *Bravo v. Board of Educ. of Chicago*, 4 F.E.P. Cases 994 (N.D. Ill. 1972).

[53] *McDonnell-Douglas Corp. v. Green*, 411 U.S. 792, 804 (1973); *Perryman v. Johnson Products Co.*, 580 F. Supp. 1015 (N.D. Ga. 1983); *Smith v. Western Elec. Co.*, 35 E.P.D. ¶ 34,656 (N.D. Tex. 1984).

a. *Union Membership.* Membership in unions must be open without discrimination.

b. *Union Referrals.* Referrals by unions must likewise be made without discrimination for all jobs.

c. *Seniority Systems.* Seniority systems which perpetuate a discriminatory effect on formerly excluded or segregated classes must be changed.

ESTABLISHMENT OF AN INTERNAL AUDIT AND REPORTING SYSTEM TO MONITOR AND EVALUATE PROGRESS

For over 20 years, equal employment opportunity laws have had an increasingly strong impact on the way employers conduct the personnel part of their business, their policies and practices. Unfortunately employers that are acting in good faith can also be accused of discrimination. The fact is, even practices that are nondiscriminatory on their face, and that are not intended to be discriminatory, can be in violation of the law. In determining a violation of the law, the courts and regulatory authorities consider the *result* of the practices and not the *intent*. Thus, any employment practice or policy, even if neutral in intent, which has a "disparate effect" on members of a "protected class" (those groups specific in the law) or which perpetuates the effect of past discriminatory practices, constitutes unlawful discrimination.

Pitfalls of this kind abound. Therefore, in order to avoid costly violations and lawsuits, employers should engage in "self-help programs" to anticipate problems and undertake corrective measures prior to governmental intervention and/or civil actions. The "EEO audit" is designed to assist employers in conducting a thorough analysis and review of employment policies, procedures, and practices in order to ensure equal employment opportunity compliance with the ever-increasing complex federal and state laws and regulations.

What is not generally appreciated by employers is that the phrase "discrimination in employment" is broadly construed by the courts and regulators. Under the broad interpretative regulations, "employment" includes compensation, promotion, termination, benefits, career progression, and virtually any company activity affecting the status, income, advancement, or work environment of any individual employee or class of employees. Therefore, an employer's policies, procedures, and practices must be periodically reviewed and appropriately documented in order to ensure that no inadvertent action could be treated as suspect by the regulatory authorities or the courts. An internal reporting system to continually audit, monitor, and evaluate progress is essential for a successful affirmative action plan. Designing and implementing this EEO audit system is a key responsibility of the affirmative action officer.

1. *EEO Audit Elements.* A properly conducted EEO audit, complete with a summary report, includes but is not limited to:

   a. Analysis of company's written policy statements pertaining to equal opportunity and other related personnel matters

   b. Review of application forms and preemployment inquiries

   c. Review of recruitment materials

   d. Review of employment manuals, employee brochures, and bulletins

   e. Review of testing materials

   f. Review of training programs

   g. Review of employment benefits and compensation practices

   h. Discussions with personnel department's management about the utilization of written job descriptions and qualifications

   i. Review of the most recent EEO-1 report (and the previous three years)

   j. Determination by "protected-class" categories of statistical compliance with existing work force statistics

   k. Review of the number of applications for each major job grouping and hires by "protected class" for the last 12 months

   l. Review of the list of promotions and transfers relative to "protected-class" categories and the compensation variables

   m. Determination of whether statistical disparities are justified and are the result of proper criteria

   n. Review of the affirmative action plan

   o. Review, if any, of compliance charges and legal actions for a three-year period

   p. Examination of systems established to deal with regulatory investigations and on-site inspections

2. *Reports.* The following specific reports should be prepared periodically. All records should indicate the person responsible, and basis and reason for action taken.

   a. *Employee Survey.* Survey of current employment by race, national origin, sex, job classification, salary, or wage level.

   b. *Work Force Analysis.* Analysis of internal and external work force availability by race, national origin, and sex.

   c. *Goals and Timetables.* Identification of areas of underutilization and concentration, and establishment of hiring and promotion goals and timetables.

   d. *Selection Process.* Records on applicant flow and each step of the selection process: hires, placements, promotions, requests for transfers, transfers, and training program participation by race, national origin, and sex.

   e. *Referral Sources.* Source of referrals and hires, by race, national origin, and sex.

   f. *Progress.* Progress of the company and subunits toward goals.

3. *Race and Sex Identification for Affirmative Action Purposes.* Caution is required by those making personnel decisions to ensure nondiscriminatory treatment. It is advisable to keep such racial and sex identification information separate from individual personnel files. However, if the commitment to affirmative action has been communicated effectively to all those making personnel decisions, and race, sex, and national origin identification in personnel files clearly is being used for the purpose of implementing identifiable goals, such use is not unlawful.

4. *Review of Periodic Reports.* Periodic reports should be reviewed and evaluated by the affirmative action officer and discussed with department managers, with recommendations for improvement, where needed, to meet annual goals. Top management should be informed of the progress and of recommendations to improve unsatisfactory performance in any area where needed.

DEVELOPMENT OF SUPPORTIVE COMPANY AND COMMUNITY PROGRAMS

The following is a list of company and community programs that should be considered in support of the affirmative action plan.

1. *Training for Supervisors.* Training is an important means of reaching and involving every supervisor in the plan. Well-developed training can provide positive responses to potential hostility, misunderstanding and resentment. Training sessions also should communicate legal rulings, individual responsibility, detailed requirements of the plan and provide specific help to meet problems that will arise.

2. *Personnel Counseling.* Personnel counseling can help meet employee needs and provide information about advancement opportunities and training needed to qualify for promotion. Counseling may significantly affect work performance, employee stability, retention, and attendance.

3. *Transportation.* If lack of public transportation makes it difficult for some minority and female employees to reach the work-site, consider providing assistance or working with transit authorities to improve transportation.

4. *Child Care.* Consider providing, or sharing in the cost to provide, child care services during work hours in order to help attract and retain female employees.

5. *Affordable Housing.* Employment opportunities often are in areas where racial or economic restrictions prevent minorities and lower-paid employees from living within a reasonable distance. Consider working to get more housing in the labor area that is racially open and within the financial means of lower-paid employees.

6. *Job-Related Education.* Work with educational institutions to improve the relevance of school curriculum to job opportunities, to strengthen career guidance and to prepare minorities and females for better job opportunities. Employ students on a part-time, work-study, or internship basis.

7. *Cooperation with Job-Related Community Programs.* Key members of management should participate in programs of the local Urban Coalition, Community Relations Board, Employment Councils, and similar organizations working on jobs, education, training, and housing opportunities.

CURRENT STATUS OF AFFIRMATIVE ACTION PLANS

The Reagan Administration, moving dramatically to advance its view of the proper means to remedy past discrimination, has notified a variety of governmental jurisdictions that they must modify existing decrees that settled employment discrimination charges.

The Justice Department has indicated that the existing decrees covering 51 governmental bodies require modification to comply with the U. S. Supreme Court's affirmative action ruling in *Firefighters Local Union 1784 v. Stotts.*[54]

But civil rights lawyers and some state and local officials, strongly disagree with the Administration's interpretation of that case. Some officials have stated flatly they will not join the Administration in legal moves to modify decrees, a process that could reactivate emotional controversies which many have considered settled.

In a 6–3 ruling, the Supreme Court held in *Stotts* that federal court orders could not interfere with a bona fide seniority system, so as to protect blacks from being laid off. The Administration contends that the ruling effectively bars courts from ordering preferential treatment on the basis of race or sex, except to compensate actual victims of discrimination. But since *Stotts* was decided, many federal judges have construed the ruling narrowly and have allowed use of numerical goals under various circumstances. In fact every federal district court and court of appeals that has interpreted *Stotts* has rejected the Justice Department's interpretation as overly broad.[55]

Nevertheless, the Justice Department has been reviewing dozens of closed employment discrimination cases after *Stotts* was decided by the Supreme Court. Lawyers in the Department's Civil Rights Division have been notifying cities and states that their affirmative action plans, which stem from lawsuits filed by the Justice Department under earlier administrations, were invalidated by the *Stotts* ruling.

---

[54] *Firefighters Local Union 1784 v. Stotts,* U.S., 81 L.Ed.2d 483, 104 S.Ct. 2576 (1984), in press.
[55] *See generally* "Title VII of the Civil Rights Act of 1964—Court Authority to Modify Consent Decrees," 98 *Harv. L. Rev.* 267 (1984).

The Justice Department states that the best and simplest way of bringing decrees in line with the *Stotts* ruling is to eliminate any mandated numerical goals and instead establish a recruitment program.

Other lawyers and law enforcement officials disagree with the Justice Department's interpretation. Many believe the *Stotts* decision was a firm statement as to protecting good-faith seniority systems and did not extend to all affirmative action plans.

The U. S. Court of Appeals for the Ninth Circuit has read the *Stotts* decision very narrowly. The Ninth Circuit has limited the *Stotts* holding to the effects of judicially modified consent decrees on bona fide seniority systems.[56] Despite the Justice Department's urgings, the Ninth Circuit has refused to extend *Stotts* to all affirmative action plans.

Numerous other decisions echo the Ninth Circuit's holding.

1. The Sixth Circuit Court of Appeals held that *Stotts* had "no effect" on a case involving a consent decree establishing a race-conscious affirmative action plan for the Cleveland Fire Department.[57]

2. A separate panel of the Sixth Circuit upheld the Detroit Fire Department's affirmative action plan against a *Stotts* challenge.[58] The Sixth Circuit decided that contrary to the facts of *Stotts*, no employees with vested seniority rights were deprived of them in the case of the Detroit Fire Department's affirmative action plan.

3. Yet another separate Six Circuit panel upheld a voluntary affirmative action plan against a *Stotts* challenge.[59] According to the Sixth Circuit, *Stotts* is not applicable in such a case because the affirmative action plan involved was not the product of any court order. Instead it resulted from voluntary decisions in the collective bargaining process between the school board and the bargaining agent for the teachers.

4. The Third Circuit Court of Appeals decided that *Stotts* had no effect on the "unanimous" holdings of all federal courts of appeal that Title VII, like the equal protection clause, does not forbid race conscious remedial action.[60] The Third Circuit upheld an affirmative action plan against a *Stotts* challenge because there was no override of a bona fide seniority plan, and no requirement of race-concious layoffs.

5. The Second Circuit Court of Appeals has also explicitly rejected the Justice Department's broad interpretation of *Stotts*.[61] The Second Circuit limited the holding in *Stotts* to affirmative action plans that affect bona fide seniority systems.

6. The Ninth Circuit also upheld an affirmative action plan implemented by a public employer to remedy a long-standing male–female imbalance in the workforce.[62] Further, the Ninth Circuit Court of Appeals has consistently relied on the U. S. Supreme Court's pronouncement that Title VII does not forbid private employers and unions from agreeing

[56] *Diaz v. American Tel. & Tel.*, 725 F.2d 1356 (9th Cir. 1985).

[57] *Vanguards of Cleveland v. Cleveland*, No. 83-3091, slip op. (6th Cir. Jan. 23, 1985).

[58] *Van Aken v. Young*, 750 F.2d 43 (6th Cir. 1985).

[59] *Wygant v. Jackson Bd. of Educ.*, 746 F.2d 1152 (6th Cir. 1984).

[60] *Kromnick v. School Dist. of Philadelphia*, 739 F.2d 894 (3d Cir. 1984).

[61] *EEOC v. Local 638*, No. 1106, slip op. (2d Cir. April 13, 1984).

[62] *La Riviera v. EEOC*, 682 F.2d 1275 (9th Cir. 1982).

to the voluntary adoption of a bona fide affirmative action plan aimed at eliminating racial imbalance in traditionally segregated job categories.[63]

7. The federal district court for the District of Massachusetts has explicitly rejected the Justice Department's interpretation of *Stotts*.[64] The court found that had the U. S. Supreme Court intended to radically change its interpretation of Title VII law, so as to require a finding of actual discrimination in any affirmative action case, it would have said so. Thus, this court concluded that in the absence of clearer authority, *Stotts* was limited to a discussion of layoffs made in violation of a bona fide seniority system.

8. Yet another federal district court refused to read *Stotts* to require direct findings of discrimination in a voluntary affirmative action plan.[65] This court approved an affirmative action consent decree.

Contrary to the Justice Department's interpretation, many jurists and lawyers believe that the Supreme Court in *Stotts* strongly implied that the underlying affirmative action consent decree was permissible under Title VII. The implication of this decision is that the actual remedy provided by the initial consent decree in *Stotts* was valid and did not exceed the bounds of Title VII, although the subsequent displacement of white employees was invalid.

Moreover, the City of Memphis vigorously protested the district court's modification of the consent decree in *Stotts*. The Supreme Court mentioned the City's objections on numerous occasions and referred three times to the power of a district court to order modifications over the objections of one of the parties. The logical inference is that the Supreme Court would treat differently a modification to which both parties agreed. Since the decree was essentially coercive in *Stotts*, the Supreme Court did not address the case as involving voluntary action. In sum, *Stotts* does not appear to restrict the ability of employers to adopt voluntary affirmative action plans.

The Supreme Court in *Stotts* relied principally on two provisions of Title VII: Sections 703(h) and 706(g). Both of these provisions limit a court's power to award certain relief. Neither provision addresses what action an employer may take voluntarily.

At most, then, the *Stotts* holding applies to court-ordered remedial action and only to affirmative action plans that affect bona fide seniority systems. Moreover, the *Stotts* holding is limited to mandatory (not voluntary) affirmative action plans ordered by a court order over the objection of a party. The *Stotts* holding does not appear to apply to voluntary actions such as consent decrees.

On April 15, 1985, the Supreme Court granted certiorari in the case of *Wygant v. Jackson Board of Education*.[66] The case involved a voluntary affirmative action plan contained in a collective bargaining agreement between the school board and the teachers' union. The collective bar-

---

[63] *United Steelworkers of Am. v. Weber*, 443 U.S. 1983 (1979).
[64] *Deveraux v. Geary*, 596 F. Supp. 1481 (D. Mass. 1984).
[65] *Britton v. South Bend Community School Corp.*, 593 F. Supp. 1223 (N.D. Ind. 1984).
[66] *Wygant, supra* note 59.

gaining agreement provided that, under some circumstances, teachers with seniority could be laid off to advance the goals of the affirmative action plan. The Sixth Circuit Court of Appeals upheld the validity of the collective bargaining affirmative action plan.

The Supreme Court's decision to hear the *Wygant* case means that the Court is prepared to consider the validity of a public employer's voluntary affirmative action plan that impinges on bona fide seniority systems. Implicit in the Court's decision to grant certiorari is the fact that, in the Court's opinion, *Stotts* did not decide the issue.

The Supreme Court will not hear arguments in *Wygant* until the fall 1985. A decision probably cannot be expected until the spring 1986. Thus, to some extent, private employers will continue to be faced with uncertainty, although the *Wygant* case appears to only be addressing for public employers the issue of a bona fide seniority system and not all types of affirmative actions.

Employers with work force statistics reflecting underutilization in the protected class categories still have no alternative but to engage in affirmative action or be subjected to regulatory and legal complaints utilizing those damaging statistics against the employer. Since the lack of discriminatory intent is irrelevant in such cases, because the courts and regulators look to the consequences of the employment practices, unfavorable workforce statistics showing underutilization of protected classes can be very harmful to the defense of an employer's case.

However, the statistical data and analyses developed in conjunction with the affirmative action plan, should be well-guarded and maintained by a select few within the company. If such precious data is not protected to the extent possible, almost as if it were a trade secret, it might be used against the employer in a regulatory and/or court action. Therefore, the acknowledgment of the existence of an affected class could be used against the contractor or employer as an admission that past discrimination currently exists in the workforce. Contractors and employers should be careful in using the words "underutilization" and "problem areas" pursuant to Revised Order No. 4 and in their affirmative action plans. Instead, the contractor or employer should define such terms and indicate that their use has been required in the context of the affirmative action plan and in no way suggests any independent significance nor constitutes an admission of guilt. To the extent possible, all affirmative action data should be carefully protected by a select few within the company. This is because only in rare instances in a court or regulatory action will disclosure of goals and timetables be exempt, and only if such disclosure does not further the public interest and is in fact confidential proprietary information. Moreover, protection and limited distribution of the data to the extent possible is essential, because there exists a memorandum of understanding between the Office of Federal Contract Compliance Programs (OFCCP) and the EEOC regarding the sharing and exchanging of the employer's data. Therefore, such statistical workforce data and other affirmative action memoranda can be viewed as liability documentation. On the other hand, improving the workforce with affirmative action is, on a long-term basis, the best way to ultimately avoid discrimination complaints and lawsuits.

Reverse discrimination liability is also another area of potential vulnerability for employers, if the affirmative action plan is not properly implemented and administered.[67] However, in evaluating the whole person for employment, the elimination of unlawful considerations coupled with the acknowledgment that protected classes have overcome certain barriers and giving full consideration for such achievement, can avoid the contention that the person was solely preferred as a protected class member, especially in situations where there is an identifiable victim of the preference.[68] Moreover, it is permissible for an employer to consider a person's ability to relate and communicate to a particular social, ethnic, or sex group based on a person's total life experiences (e.g., educational, cultural, etc.), where such abilities are required as essential ingredients for successful performance of the job position. However, it is also axiomatic that the affirmative action plan must be administered in a manner legally consistent with the nondiscriminatory tenets of Title VII of the Civil Rights Act of 1964.

Over the years, affirmative action has repeatedly survived litigation challenging its compatibility with civil rights law.[69] Affirmative action plans are not attempts to create a self-perpetuating system of superiority for protected classes, because affirmative action plans terminate when nondiscriminatory processes replace discriminatory ones.

Affirmative action plans are systematic efforts to implement equal employment opportunity policies by identifying and remedying discrimination. Affirmative action was designed to clarify, by use of a "management by objectives" system, a concrete, positive way for companies to be in full compliance with the equal opportunity laws.

Properly designed and administered affirmative action plans can create a climate of equality and equanimity throughout a company's workforce, while complying with the national policy of equal employment opportunity.

[67] The Equal Employment Opportunity Commission has issued comprehensive guidelines on voluntary affirmative action that embody the principles articulated in *United Steelworkers of Am. v. Weber,* 443 U.S. 193 (1979). Affirmative Action Guidelines 29 C.F.R. section 1608 (1984). These guidelines encourage those covered by Title VII (public and private employers, unions, and employment agencies) to engage in a three-step process (section 1608.4) in implementing an affirmative action plan: (1) to undertake a "reasonable self-analysis" (section 1608.4(a)) to identify discriminatory practices; (2) to determine if a "reasonable basis for concluding action is appropriate" exists (sections 1608.3 and 1608.4(a)); and, if such a basis is found; then (3) to take "reasonable action," including the adoption of practices that recognize the race, sex, or national origin of applicants or employees (section 1608.4(c)). If such procedures are followed and the plan is challenged as violating Title VII, the EEOC pursuant to special regulatory powers (section 1608.10) can certify the lawfulness of the plan. Such certification effectively insulates the plan from "reverse discrimination" claims.

[68] *De Funis v. Odegaard,* 82 Wash. 2d 11, 507 P.2d 1169 (1973), *vacated as moot,* 416 U.S. 312 (1974).

[69] *Southern Ill. Builders Ass'n v. Ogilvie,* 471 F.2d 680 (7th Cir. 1972); *Associated Gen. Contractors of Mass., Inc. v. Altshular,* 490 F.2d 9 (1st Cir. 1973), *cert. denied,* 416 U.S. 957 (1974); *Contractors Ass'n of E. Penn. v. Secretary of Labor,* 442 F.2d 159 (3d Cir.), *cert. denied,* 404 U.S. 854 (1971).

Appendix **A**

APPLICABLE EQUAL EMPLOYMENT LAWS

1. Federal Equal Employment Laws
    a. Title VII of the Civil Rights Act of 1964 (29 U.S.C. Section 2000(e); 29 C.F.R. Sections 1601 et seq.).
        i. Covers employers with 15 or more employees.
        ii. Enforced by Equal Employment Opportunity Commission (EEOC).
        iii. Prohibits discrimination in employment based on race, color, national origin, religion, and sex.
    b. Age discrimination in Employment Act of 1967 (29 U.S.C. Section 621; 29 C.F.R. Section 850 et seq.).
        i. Covers employers with 20 or more employees.
        ii. Enforced by EEOC.
        iii. Prohibits discrimination on the basis of age between 40 and 70.
    c. Equal Pay Act of 1963 (29 U.S.C. Section 206; 29 C.F.R. Sections 800 et seq.).
        i. Applies to *all* employers (including public employers) under the Fair Labor Standards Act.
        ii. Enforced by EEOC.
        iii. Mandates equal pay for equal work, without regard to sex.
    d. Executive Order No. 11246 (as amended by E.O. Nos. 11375 and 12086).
        i. Prohibits discrimination by federal contractors on the basis of race, color, national origin, religion, and sex.
        ii. Requires employers having 50 or more employees and federal contracts exceeding $50,000 to have a written affirmative action program which establishes "result-oriented procedures, goals, and timetables for increased hiring and upgrading of minorities and women."
        iii. Enforced by Department of Labor's OFCCP.
        iv. E.O. No. 11141 declares it to be the policy of the federal government that federal contractors not discriminate on the basis of age.
    e. Veterans Re-employment Act of 1974 (38 U.S.C. Sections 2021 et seq.).
        i. Applies to all public and private employers.
        ii. Protects the rights of an employee who serves in the military to be reinstated to employment without loss of status or benefits and not to be discharged without cause for one year following such reinstatement.

  iii. Also protects right of employees in Military Reserves and National Guard to leaves of absence.

  iv. Is a private right of action.

f. Vietnam-Era Veterans Readjustment Assistance Act of 1974 (38 U.S.C. Section 2011 et seq.; 41 C.F.R. Section 60-250).

  i. Applies to employers having contracts with the federal government of $10,000 or more.

  ii. Requires affirmative action to employ disabled Vietnam Era veterans.

  iii. Enforced by the Department of Labor.

g. Rehabilitation Act of 1973 (29 U.S.C. Section 701 et seq.; 41 C.F.R. Section 60-741).

  i. Sections 503 (29 U.S.C. Section 793) and 504 (29 U.S.C. Section 794) require affirmative action to employ the physically and mentally handicapped.

    A. Section 503 applies to employers having contracts with the federal government in excess of $2500; Section 504 applies to employers receiving federal financial assistance in any amount.

    B. Defined broadly; anyone who has physical or mental impairment which substantially limits ability to work.

    C. Must make "reasonable accommodation."

  ii. Enforced by the Department of Labor.

Appendix *B*

GLOSSARY

ACCOMMODATION TO HANDICAPS. May mean changing a job slightly, doing it in a different order, modifying the equipment, moving supplies nearer to a workbench, and so on. If the accommodation clearly affects the safe and efficient running of the organization or substantially affects costs, the employer may not be obligated to make the accommodation.

AFFECTED CLASS. A group of people with a common characteristic (race, sex, religion, national origin) who have been denied equal opportunity in violation of Title VII (this denial may occur at any step of the employment process, for example, recruitment, placement, promotion, compensation, shift assignment, etc.).

AFFIRMATIVE ACTION PLAN. A document required under the Office of Federal Contract Compliance Programs (OFCCP) regulations for government contractors. The employer is obliged to compare the internal distribution of minorities and females to their incidence in the external labor market and determine whether or not it is at "parity" (see parity) with the external labor market. The affirmative action plan is a statement of goals, timetables, and programs indicating how the employer plans to move from its current status to parity.

AVAILABILITY. A technical term that refers to the percentage of women and minorities in a company's geographic hiring area and internal percentages. A government agency investigating a discrimination charge or reviewing the results of an affirmative action plan may compare the availability of minorities and women in the hiring area to their percentage representation in the company in specific employment categories to see if they are being "underutilized" (see underutilization).

BONA FIDE OCCUPATIONAL QUALIFICATION (BFOQ). If you want to hire a man, someone under 40, or an applicant who speaks English without an accent, then be prepared to prove that the qualification you want is legitimate (bona fide). In order to prove that a sex, age, language requirement, and so on, is necessary to perform the job, you have to prove that no woman, no person over 40, or no person with a foreign accent could do the work satisfactorily. The only BFOQs that have made it through the courts are requirements for women to model women's clothes or play women's roles in plays and movies, or for men to do similar work. You may also specify children (age requirement) for modeling children's clothes, and so forth.

BUSINESS NECESSITY. Discrimination may be lawful if you can prove that it is "essential" to the safe and efficient running of your operation, and that no other less discriminatory practice would work. Virtually air-tight proof is required. While exceptional financial hardship sometimes qualifies as a business necessity, this too is limited. Financial losses due to real or imagined customer or employee preference never qualify as a business necessity (see Customer Preference, Co-Worker Preference).

CHARGING PARTY. The person who files a discrimination charge with the Equal Employment Opportunity Commission (EEOC).

CLASS ACTION SUIT. A lawsuit filed by a government agency or private individual for all the women (or blacks, Hispanics, etc.) in an organization rather than for just an individual. When the plaintiff wins a class action suit, the company usually has to give back pay to members of the group(s) that were discriminated against, guarantee that more will be hired, promoted, and so on, and install an affirmative action plan to ensure short- and long-term results.

COMPLIANCE. The degree to which an organization achieves results with its affirmative action plan and adherence to federal regulations and guidelines in this area.

CO-WORKER PREFERENCE. If the current employees, no matter how capable, do not want to work with a woman, black, Hispanic, and so forth, it is not a legal excuse for not hiring, promoting, or assigning minorities or women to any job or task.

CUSTOMER PREFERENCE. This is never an acceptable reason or "business necessity" for not observing the law. Even if all your business is done with one customer and that customer threatens to terminate the relationship if you hire minorities or women, it is still illegal to give in to the threat and discriminate. It is not lawful to defer to a customer preference which forces ignorance of the law (Title VII, the Age Discrimination Act, etc.).

HANDICAPPED PERSON. Anyone who has a physical or mental problem which "substantially limits" activities that may affect his or her employment. The definition also covers people who once had a physical or mental problem and have recovered, as well as those who only appear or are regarded as having a limitation but do not. Since these individuals are discriminated against just as much as those who have current and real handicaps, they are covered by the law as well.

PARITY. The quality or state of being equal. In this context the term "parity" is used to describe a condition in which the percentage of protected classes employed by an organization is equal to the percentage of those protected classes in the organization external labor market.

PROBABLE (OR REASONABLE) CAUSE. In contrast to the "proof beyond a reasonable doubt" required in criminal cases, the EEOC and other government civil rights agencies need only find probable (or reasonable) cause to conclude that discrimination exists in an organization's employment practices. If the case goes to court, the court will apply a "preponderance of the evidence" standard.

RETALIATION. To take any adverse action against an employee for accusing the organization of discrimination, is a violation of Title VII. This also covers people who testify against the company or in any way help others to file charges. It does not matter how accurate the charges are. Even people who make up shocking lies are protected. Retaliation may be anything from the cold shoulder to a change in job assignments to discharge or other discipline.

RESPONDENT. The company or organization named in a discrimination charge.

SELECTION (OR HIRING) PROCESS. The steps involved in employment (or nonemployment). Includes: initial screening interview; filling out application; tests for employment; background and/or reference checks; actual interview for employment, and decision whether or not to hire the individual.

706 AGENCY. When a discrimination charge is filed with the EEOC, it is required by law to hand the charge over to an approved state or local government agency for investigation, which then has a minimum of 60 days to investigate. The agencies are nicknamed "706 Agencies" because it is Section 706 of Title VII that requires the EEOC to defer charges to them.

UNDERUTILIZATION. Having a lower percentage of minorities or women in a particular "job category" than there is in the company's hiring area. This concept also includes the availability of minorities and women in the organization.

UNLAWFUL EMPLOYMENT PRACTICE. Any policy or practice that discriminates and therefore violates one of the equal employment opportunity laws. The *result* of the practice is what counts—not its *intent*.

Appendix **C**

AFFIRMATIVE ACTION CHECKLIST

	Yes	No

1. Do I understand and am I familiar with the Company's overall affirmative action plan? (This will give a "big picture" background to the situation in your own unit.) _____ _____

2. Did I attend the last meeting held on affirmative action? _____ _____

3. Did I read the last written materials I received on equal employment opportunity and affirmative action? _____ _____

4. Do I know the affirmative action administration? (Learn what support programs and specialized resources are available—use their expertise: that know-how can save you time and trouble. Remember they are there to provide you staff service and assistance.) _____ _____

5. Do I know my department/section/unit's goals and timetables? (Discuss with your superior.) _____ _____

6. Do I have an analysis of my work force by qualification and distribution by level, by minority group? (See sample Problem/Deficiency Questionnaire and Worksheet.) _____ _____

7. Do I have a plan to place these individuals in jobs where their skills are fully utilized? (Discuss with your superior—if you can't upgrade them in the unit, consult with Personnel staff about other possible organizational vacancies.) _____ _____

8. Do I plan ahead to meet my goals? (Extra time may be needed to recruit a minority member or woman if one is to be hired. Prepare and forward job requisitions as early as possible. A greater selection of candidates can be recruited if ample time is allowed. Ample time is also needed if a current employee is to be reassigned, promoted, or transferred.) _____ _____

9. Do I maintain the "single standard" principle in my unit so that all employees are evaluated, recognized, developed, and rewarded on a fair and equitable basis? _____ _____

10. Have I ever communicated equal employment policy and affirmative action goals to employees under my supervision? (Maintain open, two-way communications in your work group. Make sure that all employee concerns are fairly heard and employees feel free to express themselves. Handle all complaints and grievances with professional care.) _____ _____

11. Do I ensure that all work unit facilities are made available on a nondiscriminatory basis? _____ _____

12. Do I take responsibility for preventing harassment or other unfair treatment of employees placed through affirmative action efforts? _____ _____

13. Do I provide any necessary help to assist minority members and women to succeed on the job, just as you would assist any new employee? (If special or unusual adjustment problems occur with an individual employee, consult the personnel staff.) _____ _____

Appendix D

PROBLEM AREA AND DEFICIENCY QUESTIONNAIRE

1. Where do problem areas and deficiencies exist in your area (job category/job group)
   a. Underutilization
   b. Overutilization
2. Are there focus job titles in your department (i.e., specific jobs that have underutilizations of minorities and females)?
3. Review the total selection process, taking into account the referral ratio of minorities and females to the hiring supervisor.
4. Where are there heavy concentrations of females and minority group members?
5. What is the turnover rate in your area?
   a. Are you expecting expansion and/or contraction within the year?
   b. How do these factors affect specific goals and timetables for the hiring and promotion of minorities and females?
6. What 1975 affirmative action goals have been achieved?
7. On reviewing the problem areas and deficiencies for your department, what can you do to ensure the upgrading of your minority and female employees?
   Consider the following:
   a. Job posting
   b. Counseling
   c. Coaching when interviewing for other jobs
   d. Training and development
   e. Tuition reimbursement
   f. Monitoring affirmative action growth
   g. Community involvement and activity

Appendix *E*

ADDITIONAL DOCUMENTATION

TABLE 1 Affirmative Action Goals Worksheet

1. Labor Force Parity

	% of Staff	No. of Employees
Hispanic		
Black		
Other Minorities (Orient., Am. Ind.)		
Total Minority		
Caucasian		
Total Staff		
Females		

2. EEO Job Categories

	Number of Employees			% of Staff		
	Male	Female	Min.	Male	Female	Min.
Officials and Managers						
Office and Clerical						

TABLE 1 *Continued*

3. Underutilization Analysis

    a. Total Staff

	Underutilized? (Yes/No)	No. of Additional Employees Needed for Parity
Hispanic		
Black		
Other Minorities (Orient, Am. Ind.)		
Females		
Total Minorities		

4. Goals for 1985

	Office & Clerical	Officials & Managers
Anticipated No. of Openings		

Affirmative Action Goals _____

_____

TABLE 2 Quarterly EEO Status Report

To Be Completed By Each Location

Company	Location		Quarter Ending (Mo./Day/Yr.)

1. PERSONNEL ACTIVITY
(Complete the table for personnel actions that occurred during the quarter.)

JOB CATEGORY PERS. ACTION	TOTAL	ALL EMPLOYEES		MINORITY EMPLOYEES							
				MALE				FEMALE			
		Male (Min. & Non-Min.)	Female (Min. & Non-Min.)	Blk.	Hisp.	Asian or Pac. Is.	Am.In. or Alas. Nat.	Blk.	Hisp.	Asian or Pac. Is.	Am.In. or Alas. Nat.
Offs.& Mgrs.											
Hired											
Terminated											
Promoted											
Professionals											
Hired											
Terminated											
Promoted											
Technicians											
Hired											
Terminated											
Promoted											
Sales Workers											
Hired											
Terminated											
Promoted											
Off. & Cler.											
Hired											
Terminated											
Promoted											
Craft Workers											
Hired											
Terminated											
Promoted											
Operatives											
Hired											
Terminated											
Promoted											
Laborers											
Hired											
Terminated											
Promoted											
Serv. Workers											
Hired											
Terminated											
Promoted											
Total											
Hired											
Terminated											
Promoted											

TABLE 3 Audit Analysis

LOCATION _____   TIME PERIOD _____

JOB GROUPING	TOTAL	TOTAL MALE	TOTAL FEMALE	% FEMALE	TOTAL MIN.	% MIN		MALE					FEMALE		
							B	H	AA	AI		B	H	AA	AI

JOB GROUPING _____

APPLICANTS															
OFFERS															
HIRES															
PROMOTIONS															
TRAINEES															
TERMINATIONS															

JOB GROUPING _____

APPLICANTS															
OFFERS															
HIRES															
PROMOTIONS															
TRAINEES															
TERMINATIONS															

JOB GROUPING _____

APPLICANTS															
OFFERS															
HIRES															
PROMOTIONS															
TRAINEES															
TERMINATIONS															

xvii

TABLE 4 Availability Analysis by Job Group

FEMALES

Facility_____   Selected Labor Area_____

Job Category	Job Group							
	Total		Black		Hispanic		Other	
	#	%	#	%	#	%	#	%
1. Unemployment								
2. Seeking Employment								
3. Labor Force Participation								
4. Requisite Skills In Immediate Labor Area (If Available)								
5. Requisite Skills In Selected Labor Area								

6. Availability Of Promotable Females Into This Job Group_____

_____

7. External Training_____

_____

8. Internal Training_____

	Total	Black	Hispanic	Other
9. Analysis and Conclusion Availability %___				

Rationale_____

_____

_____

TABLE 5 EEO Monthly Recruiting Activity Log

Month Ending _____

PLANT OR OFFICE:		DATE	
COMPILED BY:		TITLE	

INSTRUCTIONS: This log is to be maintained on a day to day basis each month and the information re-capped on HWF Form 1935 (E.E.O. Quarterly Report)

(1) DATE	(2) POSITION FOR WHICH INTERVIEWED	(3) JOB CATEGORY	(4) JOB GROUPING	(5) GROUP					(6) SEX		(7) HANDICAPPED	(8) DISABLED VETERAN Vietnam Era Vet	(9) WAS APPLICANT HIRED			(10) SOURCE
				CAUCASIAN	BLACK	HISPANIC	ASIAN AMERICAN	AMERICAN INDIAN	MALE	FEMALE			YES	NO	UNKNOWN	DESCRIBE REFERRAL SOURCE

PLEASE USE SEPARATE LINE FOR EACH APPLICANT

Appendix *F*

STATISTICAL INFORMATION

Current reliable data on the availability of minority and women workers within a certain geographic area is frequently difficult to obtain. However, the EEOC maintains that "excessive data collection" is unnecessary and urges employers, instead, to concentrate on affirmative efforts to locate and/or train female and minorities in jobs where they are underrepresented rather than making an "intensive effort to locate data justifying their underutilization."

Following are data sources for utilization analysis and developing affirmative action goals.

Sources of Data

1. *Workforce Data Packages*
   Assists employers in preparing utilization analysis and affirmative action plans are being prepared by State Employment Services to meet Federal contract compliance requirements. Request information for specific labor areas from appropriate Research Director of State Employment Security Agencies.

2. *Census Bureau*
   U.S. Department of Commerce
   Washington, D.C. 20233
   Basic data on population, education, employment, and occupational status may be obtained from the following publications:

   a. *1970 Census of Population: General Social and Economic Characteristics PC (1) –C Series.* Separate reports for each state, with data on age, race, sex, Spanish heritage, mother tongue, years of school completed, vocational training, employment status, occupation, industry and other factors. Order from Superintendent of Documents, U.S. Government Printing Office, Washington, D.C. 20402, or U.S. Commerce Department Field Offices.

   b. *1970 Census of Population, Detailed Characteristics PC (1) –D Series.* More detailed breakdowns. For details write: Publications Distribution Section, Bureau of Census, U.S. Department of Commerce, Washington, D.C. 20233, or Superintendent of Documents.

   c. *U.S. Census of Population Final Report.* Available from Superintendent of Documents.

3. *Women's Bureau*
   Employment Standards Administration
   U.S. Department of Labor
   Washington, D.C. 20210
   A Guide to Sources of Data on Women and Women Workers for the United States and for Regions, States, and Local Areas.

4. *Office of Research*
   Equal Employment Opportunity Commission
   Washington, D.C. 20506
   Job Patterns for Minorities and Women in Private Industry, 1971. 10 Volumes (U.S. Summary and 9 Census Regions).

5. *Bureau of Labor Statistics*
   U.S. Department of Labor
   Washington, D.C. 20210

   a. *Geographic Profile of Employment and Unemployment* (annual).

   b. *Industry Wage Surveys.* Write Bureau of Labor Statistics.

6. *Educational Data Sources*

   a. *Equal Employment Opportunity for Minority Group College Graduates: Locating, Recruiting, Employing* (1972).

   b. *Women's Rights Almanac* (1974).

7. *State and Local Data Sources*

   a. State and local employment services. Basic data and special studies on employment and unemployment.

   b. State and city department of human resources, and departments of industry, labor, or commerce also prepare employment, unemployment, and skill surveys.

   c. Regional offices, Equal Employment Opportunity Commission.

   d. Regional Offices, Manpower Administration, U.S. Department of Labor.

Appendix **G**

SELECT SOURCES OF REFERENCE

Affirmative Action in the 1980s: Dismantling the Process of Discrimination. Washington, D.C.; U.S. Commission on Civil Rights Jan. 1981.

Calvert, Robert, Jr. *Affirmative Action: A Comprehensive Recruitment Manual.* Garrett Park, MD: Garrett Park Press, 1979.

Cannon, Joan B., and Ed. Smith. *Resources for Affirmative Action: An Annotated Directory of Books, Periodicals, Films, Training Aids, & Consultants on Equal Opportunity.* Garrett Park, MD: Garrett Park Press, 1982.

Directory of Special Programs for Minority Group Members: Career Information Services, Employment Skills Banks, Financial Aid Sources. Willis L. Johnson (ed.), 3rd ed. Garrett Park, MD: Garrett Park Press, 1980.

Fullinwider, Robert K. *The Reverse Discrimination Controversy: A Moral and Legal Analysis.* Totowa, NJ: Rowman & Littlefield, 1980.

Greenwalt, R. Kent. *Discrimination & Reverse Discrimination.* New York, Random House, 1983.

Johnson, Ronald D. "Voluntary Affirmative Action in the Post-Weber Era: Issues and Answers." *Labor Law Journal,* Vol. 32, Sept. 1981, pp. 609, 620.

McConnell, Michael W. "Affirmative Action After Teal: A New Twist or a Turn of the Screw?", *Regulation,* Mar./Apr. 1983, pp. 38–44.

Minority Organizations: A National Directory. 2nd ed. Garrett Park, MD: Garrett Park Press, 1982.

Minority Vendor Business Directory. Pittsburgh: Gulf Oil, 1973 (updated periodically).

Swanson, Stephen C. "Affirmative Action Goals: Acknowledging the Employer's Interest," *Personnel Journal,* Mar. 1983, pp. 216–220.

Appendix H

SAMPLE POLICY: ANNOUNCEMENT OF AFFIRMATIVE ACTION PLAN

To: All Employees and Applicants for Employment

The company firmly supports the national policy, contained in the Presidential Executive Order #11246 and the regulations and Orders flowing therefrom, which require government contractors to take affirmative action to employ, promote, and carry out other personnel actions of all qualified individuals without regard to race, color, creed, religion, sex, age, ancestry, and physical or mental handicap.

This national policy is reaffirmed in the company's policy, "Equal Employment Opportunity." This policy extends to all employees and all aspects of the employment relationship, including recruitment and hiring, placement, training, education, transfer, promotion, layoff, recall, termination, disciplinary action, social and recreational programs, employee benefits, and compensation policy.

I personally endorse the policy of equal employment opportunity and have directed the establishment and maintenance of an affirmative action plan designed to ensure such policy is carried out in a meaningful way. The full cooperation and assistance of all employees is expected to carry out the meaning and intent of this policy and program.

The affirmative action officer of the company has been designated to coordinate with managers to ensure results producing implementation of our affirmative action program. This officer will also direct periodic audits to assure strict adherence to our policy and program of equal employment opportunity and status reports will be made to me on a periodic basis.

I am confident that all of you will provide your total support to implement this program successfully. Any employee who has questions regarding our equal opportunity policies or our Affirmative Action Plan should feel free to discuss them directly with the affirmative action officer of the company. I am also available to anyone who wishes to further discuss this subject.

By: _____
Chief Executive Officer

Appendix I

SAMPLE POLICY:
EQUAL EMPLOYMENT OPPORTUNITY POLICY

The company, through responsible managers, shall recruit, hire, upgrade, train, and promote in all job titles without regard to race, color, religion, sex, national origin, age, handicap, or status as a disabled veteran or a veteran of the Vietnam Era.

Managers shall ensure that all other personnel actions such as compensation, benefits, layoffs, returns from layoffs, company-sponsored training, educational tuition assistance, social and recreational programs, shall be administered without regard to race, color, religion, national origin, sex, age, handicap, or status as a disabled veteran or a veteran of the Vietnam Era.

Managers shall base employment decisions on the principles of equal employment opportunity and with the intent to further the company's commitment.

Managers shall take affirmative action to ensure that minority group individuals, females, veterans of the Vietnam Era, and qualified handicapped persons and disabled veterans are introduced into the work force and that these employees are encouraged to aspire for promotion and are considered as promotional opportunities arise.

Appendix J

SAMPLE LETTER TO OUTSIDE SOURCES

To: (Employment services, agencies, unions, and so forth)

The company, because of its contractual relationship with the federal government, is subject to the provisions of Executive Order 11246 of September 24, 1965, Executive Order 11375 of October 13, 1967, Executive Order 11758 of January 15, 1974, and Section 402 of the Vietnam Era Veterans Readjustment Act of 1974. By virtue of the provisions of these Executive Orders and this aforementioned Act, this company is obliged not to discriminate against any employee or applicant for employment because of race, color, religion, sex, national origin, age, handicap, or status as a disabled veteran or a veteran of the Vietnam Era. This obligation not to discriminate in employment includes, but is not limited to, the following:

1. Hire, placement, promotion, transfer, and demotion
2. Recruitment, advertisement, and solicitation for employment
3. Training during employment
4. Selection for training, including apprenticeship
5. Rates of pay or other forms of compensation
6. Layoff and termination

This notice is furnished to you pursuant to the provisions of Executive Order 11246, Executive Order 11758, and the Vietnam Era Veterans Readjustment Act of 1974.

THE COMPANY

By: _____
(Name)

_____
(Title)

Appendix **K**

SAMPLE AFFIRMATIVE ACTION PLAN

AFFIRMATIVE ACTION PLAN

The information contained herein is proprietary and confidential. This plan is deemed to contain information which concerns or relates to confidential statistical data and other pertinent information which is subject to the provisions of 18 U.S.C. Section 1905 and as such is not to be released without prior written authorization of the Company. Such information is considered to be exempt from disclosure under the Freedom of Information Act.

Chief Executive Officer

Affirmative Action Officer

Table of Contents

Introduction

Equal Opportunity Policy   Section 1

Dissemination of Policy and Plan   Section 2

Implementation of Policy and Program   Section 3

Goal Setting   Section 4

Definitions   Section 5

Summary   Section 6

Introduction

To: The company employees

The company is committed to equal employment opportunity. Utilizing our affirmative action plan as a sound base, we actively support and encourage participation in the solving of critical national social problems.

This brochure summarizes the company's affirmative action plan. We feel it is a sound, positive program which requires your understanding and agreement. Demonstrated performance and the recognition of individual merit are prime criteria in our decisions relative to employment and promotion. For although this plan formally details the relationship between the company and its employees, the plan's nucleus is the relationship between people.

Our affirmative action plan requires your continuing support and cooperation to guarantee its effectiveness. The company's greatest asset is its people, and through each of us this program will gain momentum in demonstrating the company's commitment to equal employment opportunity.

Chief Executive Officer

SECTION 1

Equal Opportunity Policy

The company recognizes its obligation to its shareholders and to the public to be a good corporate citizen. To this end, we have through employment and through the sale of our products, offered the personal security which enables individuals to better exercise their rights and responsibilities.

In every phase of the conduct of our business, be it with our employees, agents, borrowers, shareholders, lessors, lessees, vendors, or others, we will continue to be guided by the highest principles which best serve the interests of our shareholders and the general public. In all such pursuits, we will continue to look to the integrity of this corporation and to the integrity of the individual without regard for race, age, religion, sex, marital status, physical handicap, color, national origin or ancestry.

The company's equal employment policy is to recruit and select applicants for employment solely on the basis of their qualifications. The company's policies regarding salary administration, transfer and promotion are based on demonstrated performance and potential. As part of the company's general program of employee relations, all personnel practices, including those relating to fringe benefit administration, selection for training, retention and termination are not influenced by an employee's race, age, religion, sex, marital status, physical handicap, color, national origin, or ancestry.

The company takes affirmative action to ensure that this policy is followed in spirit as well as in letter to make certain that equal opportunities in the company are available to all.

SECTION 2

Dissemination of Policy and Plan

INTERNAL COMMUNICATION. The company intends that its equal opportunity policy and affirmative action plan be known and understood within the company. Various media will be used to accomplish this communication. In particular, discussion of the plan will occur at new employee orientation meetings. The required governmental equal employment opportunity posters, and the company's policy will be displayed on company bulletin boards.

EXTERNAL COMMUNICATION. Various community groups, organizations, colleges and universities, and the company's employment sources, suppliers, group policyholders, other outside business institutions, and any other channels of entry as may be developed and prove beneficial in furtherance of our objectives, will be made aware of the company's affirmative action plan.

SECTION 3

Implementation of Policy and Program

AFFIRMATIVE ACTION COMPLIANCE OFFICER—EQUAL EMPLOYMENT OPPORTUNITY COORDINATOR. The chief executive officer has designated the affirmative action compliance officer with primary responsibility for development and execution of the company's affirmative action plan. The equal employment opportunity coordinator will administer the plan on a day-to-day basis in conjunction with the affirmative action compliance officer and the personnel department. The general responsibilities include:

To keep abreast of equal employment opportunity developments and regulations.

To make an annual review of the company's affirmative action plan in light of new regulations, and to recommend annually to the company revisions to strengthen the plan.

To work in conjunction with senior officers and members of management in establishing realistic goals and timetables designed to assure the success of the plan and further the principles of equal employment opportunity.

To devise, initiate, and monitor systems and procedures to measure the effectiveness of the affirmative action plan, identifying the areas requiring remedial action and reporting semiannually to the company progress being made in achieving goals and objectives. Senior officers and management members will be consulted in conducting this review.

To investigate all equal opportunity complaints from government compliance agencies; to report such matters to the appropriate officers with recommendations as may be necessary; and to keep the affirmative action committee generally informed.

To review through the job evaluation and salary policy committee, exempt job classifications to ensure that all positions are accurately and equitably assigned to grade levels within the management job structure. Through the personnel department, to review all nonexempt job classifications in the same manner.

To review through the job evaluation and salary policy committee, the salary policy of the company to ensure that compensation practices are in compliance with the philosophy of the equal opportunity policy and the affirmative action plan.

To inform all employees of their opportunity to participate in company sponsored educational, training, recreational and social activities.

PERSONNEL DEPARTMENT EMPLOYMENT. Continuing review will be made of all selection process, including employment forms, to avoid inadvertent discrimination because of race, age, religion, sex, marital status, physical handicap, color, national origin, or ancestry.

The company seeks to promote from within when possible, in filling job vacancies. The job posting program gives home office employees an effective channel through which to learn about job vacancies and to request consideration for a particular position.

Tests will be administered to applicants to determine qualifications required by the job. The only tests which will be used in connection with employment will be those which are job-related.

Recruiting procedures include contacts with sources to assist in the referral of female and minority applicants.

Employment advertisements and recruiting materials will continue to state that the company is an "equal opportunity employer through affirmative action."

TRAINING. As part of management training and development programs, information will be communicated to inform participants of governmental rules and regulations covering equal employment opportunity, and of its affirmative action plan. Emphasis will be placed on providing training and education programs for all personnel. Training opportunities will be provided through on-the-job training; tuition refund programs; education programs; managerial and technical training programs designed to improve present job performance with career potential; and special training opportunities to help employees improve their performance.

SALARY ADMINISTRATION. The company's promotion policies will seek out the best qualified employee when an opening occurs regardless of race, age, religion, sex, marital status, physical handicap, color, national origin, or ancestry.

Salary administration policies and practices, including those relating to job descriptions, job evaluations, establishing of salary ranges and grade levels, performance appraisals and recommendation and approval of salary increases, will be reviewed to avoid inadvertent discrimination.

A library of job descriptions will be maintained to ensure that those descriptions lend themselves to the specification of job duties and functions, and that experience, education and basic qualifications are realistically expressed in each job description. Job specifications will be available to recruiting sources in connection with the hiring of new employees.

BENEFITS. The company's fringe benefits policies and practices will be reviewed to avoid inadvertent discrimination.

MANAGEMENT. The chief executive officer has stipulated that officers, managers, and supervisors are responsible for the affirmative action plan in their respective areas of responsibility and are accountable for the expected results. Management at all levels must provide a work environment for employees so that they are afforded an equal opportunity to perform up to their full potential and capability.

AFFIRMATIVE ACTION COMMITTEE. A standing committee has been appointed, composed of individuals from the law department, the personnel department, and other operating areas of the company. The responsibilities of this committee are:

To advise the Company with respect to all phases of the Plan

To assist in the implementation of the Plan

To suggest approaches for communicating the Plan

To review overall progress of the Plan

To assist and advise in the review of information relative to alleged or identified discriminatory practices and complaints

To encourage employees of the company to serve on minority employment councils, community relations boards, and other similar organizations

SECTION 4

Goal Setting

A goal, although a numerical objective, is fixed realistically in terms of the number of vacancies expected, and the number of qualified applicants in the relevant job market. In establishing goals under the affirmative action plan, the company will aggressively recruit, place, and increase utilization of minorities and women in all areas of the company's operation, consistent with availability and qualifications.

SECTION 5

Definitions

"Equal employment opportunity" is just that: fairness in hiring so that all people, regardless of race, color, religion, age, sex, national origin, physical handicap, or marital status, have an equal chance of obtaining any job for which they are qualified.

"Affirmative action" relates to those positive actions that the Company takes to see that *all* employees are affected equally by any employment practices. These practices include recruitment and screening of applicants, placement, salary administration, training programs, discipline, benefits, promotions, and terminations. The positive actions we undertake are designed to make our personnel practices objective, job-related, well understood, and fairly administered. The net result of equal opportunity and affirmative action will be a work force in which all groups are represented at all levels.

SECTION 6

Summary

The commitment of the company to the principles of equal employment opportunity is clear. Through employment practices which make fullest use of an individual's ability, without regard to race, age, religion, sex, marital status, physical handicap, color, national origin, or ancestry, the company will demonstrate this commitment. Management at all levels will make a good-faith effort to ensure the success of the affirmative action plan.

Chapter 12

WRONGFUL HIRING?

Steven M. Schneider, J.D.

The creation of employer liability at the time of hiring is the focus of this chapter. This topic is the opposite side of statutory or judicial protection granted long-term employees, or employees who allege that their terminations violate a specific statutory prohibition. Instead this chapter concentrates on the identification of factors present in the hiring process that can generate wrongful termination claims, regardless of how short the period of employment.

A watershed development in this "wrongful hiring" area occurred on May 22, 1984, the date of the U. S. Supreme Court's decision in *Hishon v. King & Spaulding*, 467 U. S. 69, (1984). This decision extended application of Title VII of the 1964 Civil Rights Act to the associate attorney hiring process of law firms. However, statements about the nature of employment commitments in that unanimous decision create concern about "wrongful hiring" concepts.

Hishon was a female attorney employed in 1972 as an "associate" with King & Spaulding, a large Atlanta law firm. Like most law firms King & Spaulding organized itself as a general partnership. Hishon was terminated in 1979 after the firm decided not to admit her to the partnership.

Hishon alleged in her complaint that the prospect of partnership was an important factor in her decision to accept employment. She contended that King & Spaulding used the possibility of becoming a partner as a recruiting device to induce Hishon, and other young lawyers, to become associate attorneys. Hishon alleged that King & Spaulding represented that advancement to partnership after five or six years was "a matter of course" for those associates "who received[d] satisfactory evaluations," and that associates were promoted to partnership "on a fair and equal basis." She contended that the firm's promise to consider her for partnership on an alleged "fair and equal basis" created a binding employment contract, on which she had relied in accepting employment.

King & Spaulding, like many large law firms, had an "up or out" system in considering associates for partnership. As the Supreme Court noted: "Once an associate is passed over for partnership at respondent's firm, the associate is notified to begin seeking employment elsewhere." 467 U.S. at 65.

Hishon's claim under Title VII involved the law firm's alleged sex discrimination in rejecting her for partnership. The Title VII aspects of this case are of critical importance to all business entities organized as partnerships. Of universal importance to this chapter, and to all employers regardless of their entity status or formation, are Chief Justice Burger's statements for a unanimous Court (Justice Powell concurred in the decision separately) regarding creation of contractual commitments in the hiring process.

As Chief Justice Burger stated in *Hishon v. King & Spaulding* about the contractual relationship created when hiring an employee:

Once a contractual relationship of employment is established, the provisions of Title VII attach and govern certain aspects of that relationship. In the context of Title VII, the contract of employment may be written or oral, formal or informal; an informal contract of employment arises by the simple act of handing a job applicant a shovel and providing a workplace. The contractual relationship of employment triggers the provision of Title VII governing "terms, conditions, or privileges of employment." Title VII in turn forbids discrimination on the basis of "race, color, religion, sex, or national origin."

Because the underlying employment relationship is contractual, it follows that the "terms, conditions or privileges of employment" clearly include benefits that are part of an employment contract. Here petitioner in essence alleges that respondent made a contract to consider for partnership. Indeed, this promise was allegedly a key contractual provision which induced her to accept employment. If the evidence at trial establishes that the parties contracted to have petitioner considered for partnership, that promise clearly was a term, condition or privilege of her employment. Title VII would then bind respondents to consider petitioner for partnership as the statute provides, *i.e.,* without regard to petitioner's sex. The contract she alleges would lead to the same result." 467 U. S., 104 S.Ct. at 2233–2234; 81 L. Ed.2d at 66, in press.

By these words, the Supreme Court in its unanimous opinion in *Hishon* recognized that employment is a contractual relationship, and, as with any contract, many of its terms and commitments are established at its creation.

The *Hishon* case can be called the first Supreme Court "wrongful hiring" decision. By finding that employer liability can exist due to alleged employer statements made in the applicant interview process, the Supreme Court probably created a new exposure area for employers.

After *Hishon*, employment managers can no longer breathe a sigh of relief if a terminated employee had neither a lengthy number of years on the job, nor was discharged for refusal to perform an act that could violate a statute. Indeed, *Hishon* may impact especially employees terminated within their first few years of employment, particularly during their first year of work.

It is not overly imaginative to be concerned about the impact of this decision. While a few states have some degree of statutory protection against alleged employer misrepresentations in the hiring process, many states leave such claims for judicial resolution under common law. *Hishon* stands as a beacon illuminating for plaintiff's counsel how to draft a "wrongful hiring" complaint. The common law recognizes civil actions for wrongfully or negligently inducing significant changes of another's status or position to his or her detriment; wrongful hiring cases may come to be phrased under such common law theories of recovery as breach of contract, promissory estoppel, and fraud and deceit.

The remainder of this chapter reviews the principal factors which, especially in combination, seem likely to attract a litigated claim in this "wrongful hiring" area. Before discussing such factors, a review of statutory protection in this area is necessary to ascertain the focus and concerns of such protection, which may later springboard into judicial extension of these statutory concepts even in states that lack such legislation.

STATE STATUTORY PROTECTION

Hidden away in the statutes of several states are laws prohibiting certain "misrepresentations" in the hiring process. Some of those statutes are Depression-era vintage or earlier, originally enacted to limit exploitation of agricultural or other workers (such as strikebreakers). Such statutes currently appear to have primary applicability to white collar employees, especially those in sales, technical, professional, and managerial positions who allege misrepresentation in their hiring.

For example, California Labor Code sections 970–972 essentially provide a civil action, with double damages, for any person who has been induced to move to California, or from one location to another within California, by means of certain false representations "for the purpose of working in any branch of labor." Misrepresentations concerning either (1) the kind, character, or existence of such work; or (2) the length of time such work will last, or its compensation are sufficient to trigger these statutory provisions.

These protective provisions recently have been revived in California, despite the reviving court's admission that the statute was passed "in contemplation of problems more prevalent in the Great Depression than more recent times." *Sheriff v. Revell, Inc.*, 165 Cal. App. 3d 297, 310, 211 Cal. Rptr. 465 (2d Dist. Ct. App., Mar. 6, 1985, *as modified* Mar. 21, 1985), *rev. den. with order not to publish opinion* (Cal. Sup. Ct., July 1, 1985); see also *Munoz v. Kaiser Steel Corp:* 156 Cal. App. 3d 965, 979-81, 203 Cal. Rptr. 345, 354-55 (4th Dist. Ct. App., 1984).

Alaska has a similar statute, section 23.10.015, H.B. 273, Ch. 59, L. 1971 (allowing for actual damages and attorney's fees). *Minnesota* has a similar statute, providing for recovery of actual damages plus attorney's fees. (Section 181.65.) *Montana's* similar statute, in pertinent part, requires the misrepresentation to concern the kind or character of the work involved. (Section 39-2-303.)

Nevada's statute is similar to California's, but provides for recovery of actual damages plus attorney's fees. (Section 613.030.) *Oklahoma* has a similar statute, providing for recovery of actual damages and attorney's fees (Title 40, chapter 5, sections 167–170), as does *Oregon* (sections 659.210 and .220).

Washington makes employer misrepresentations a misdemeanor (section 49.44.050, L. 1909), as does *Colorado* (chapter 97) and *Idaho* (section 18-3101). In *Massachusetts* a fraudulent or false job advertisement or notice is also a criminal act (chapter 149, section 21, L. 1908, as amended). *West Virginia* also prohibits false statements by employers in the hiring process (section 21-2-6).

At least 11 states thus appear to have some legislation prohibiting employer misrepresentations in the hiring process. State judicial decisions may have limited, at least for the time being, some of these statutes either to agricultural labor or to importation of strikebreakers, the genesis for many of these laws. However, as with so many other things, from alfalfa sprouts to skateboards, California's recent revival of its own decades-old statutory provisions in this area may presage judicial activism in other states in the "wrongful hiring" area. At least in the states that appear to have some kind of legislation prohibiting employer misrepresentations in the hiring process, "wrongful hiring" litigation may soon begin to surface.

Of course judicial activism is itself a phrase of relative value. Successful plaintiffs who convince their state courts to accept a civil claim emanating from a half-century or older statute prohibiting misrepresentation in hiring will happily note that court's contribution to the progress of the common law. The unhappy employer who has been on the receiving end of such a surprise judicial development undoubtedly will bemoan the sudden and unexpected activism of his or her state's judiciary.

Our own review of the judicial decisions to date touching the "wrongful hiring" area suggest the repetition of factual patterns which eventually may invite such judicial activism, even in the 39 states that may not have statutes prohibiting misrepresentation in the hiring process. After all, judges are human beings dedicated to the pursuit of justice. "Conservative" judges prefer that major leaps forward in legal protection be propelled by legislatures, which (at least in theory) can weigh and consider numerous competing issues, arguments and factions. "Liberal" judges, on occasion, feel compelled to make such leaps of legal rights by the factual circumstances of the particular case before them. While this is a gross over-simplification of the numerous and complex factors of judicial motivation, it does seem prudent for employers to avoid those factual circumstances in the "wrongful hiring" area that cry out for a remedy. Most human resources professionals are well aware of at least one "wrongful hiring" situation in their own experience could well engender from the public the feeling that "There ought to be a law against that!" The following attempts to describe such factors in the hiring process which, particularly in combination, may give rise to such an outcry.

Stated differently, this chapter is concerned with human resources professionals trying to make sure that their company is not involuntarily placed in the role of a legal pioneer in the "wrongful hiring" area. The author informs his own clients that it is easy to recognize a legal pioneer, especially in contested cases dealing with wrongful termination issues, because the legal pioneer's backside quickly becomes full of arrows.

With a salute then to past legal pioneers in this area, the following factors require enhanced scrutiny by human resources professionals when they appear in the hiring process, especially in combination. As will be seen, these factors without careful attention and risk management may create employer liability.

One's In Before the Other's Out

One factor which should be of concern to human resources professionals is when a replacement is hired before the person to be replaced is terminated. This occasionally happens deliberately or through inadvertence, especially when the members of management involved in the replacement hiring decision are not the same individuals involved in the termination situation.

This is a potential risk factor, of course, because the timing sequence raises the possibility of pretext for the termination. Pretext is especially likely to generate claims if the person being terminated is in a protected statutory category (i.e., because of minority group status, age, sex, physical handicap, etc.). The pretext issue gets raised when the reason given the terminated employee for separation is weak or contrived, and that employee later learns that the replacement was already hired before he or she was informed of the termination. Such a feeling of being ill-treated or lied to generates hostility, which quickly focuses on the validity or invalidity of the reasons given for the termination.

Employer problems in dealing with this situation often result when management finds it difficult to articulate a "smoking gun" incident that finally led to the decision to replace the employee in question. However, legally appropriate reasons for such an action usually exist, although their documentation can become difficult, and indeed suspect, because of the timing of the termination and resulting pretext issues.

This particular factor—one's in before the other's out—by itself does not usually suffice to create employer liability. But it is a dangerous factor in combination with others, especially other factors suggesting employer misrepresentation in the terminated employee's hiring situation. Indeed, a hostile employee whose replacement was hired before the employee was informed of separation can present an emotionally compelling case of alleged employer wrongdoing if the claim also concerns alleged employer misrepresentations in the hiring process, as well as alleged pretextual reasons for the termination. It can be especially emotionally compelling if the employee terminated, in fact, was hired by the employer for the wrong reasons.

Hiring for the Wrong Reasons

This factor occurs when management locates a very attractive job applicant, especially one unlikely to be found in the near future. The tendency is to find or create a position for such an attractive candidate, despite the fact that dispassionate analysis may suggest that no such position exists which needs to be filled by this particular individual at the particular time.

Indeed, the cases indicate that the following factors often lead to the employment of such an individual irrespective of an objective lack of immediate need for his or her presence:

1. The individual may be hired not because the hiring organization has a need, but to keep the competition from hiring that individual. This has occurred with individuals leaving decades of government service when the private employer deals with that individual's agency in contract bidding. This has also occurred with scientists and other technical experts who are well known, and highly skilled in research or application techniques critical to the hiring organization. The usual articulated justification for the engagement of such an individual is: "If we don't get him (or her), our competition will!"

2. A second, and perhaps more common example of hiring someone not needed is when a perceived key individual in a competitor's organization suddenly becomes available. The perception is that that individual carries within his or her head the keys to the competitor's future acts, product development, or marketing strategies. Human resources professionals should be alert when management appears to be saying "Get this guy so we can find out what he knows!" rather than focusing on what available position within the organization could be served by the employment of that individual *after* his or her knowledge of the competitor has been divulged.

Precisely because the employment of an individual in this category may be very short term, it seems critical that a real job exist for him or her within the hiring organization to avoid potential "wrongful hiring" liability.

The decision of *Rabago-Alvarez v. Dart Industries, Inc.*, 55 Cal. App. 3d 91, 127 Cal. Rptr. 222 (1976) is instructive on this point. This decision predates the wrongful termination decisions of the 1980s. In *Rabago-Alvarez v. Dart Industries*, the plaintiff had worked for one employer for 16 years and had extensive experience in using a "party plan" sales technique demonstrating products in people's homes. One of defendant's personnel was assigned to research this selling technique, and observed plaintiff at one of her presentations. Defendant then hired the plaintiff. During her interviews, the plaintiff expressed a fear that defendant might be hiring her for the purpose of learning her special selling techniques and then terminating her after she had disclosed what she knew about them to defendant's personnel. Needless to say, the plaintiff allegedly was assured that the position being offered her was "a permanent position as long as her work efforts were satisfactory."

Indeed, the personnel director for defendant allegedly told plaintiff that if her job performance was as represented to him by the first interviewer, she would be employed by the defendant "as long as the company remained in existence." Plaintiff allegedly was also assured that she would never be terminated arbitrarily, but only if there was good cause, such as failing to perform her work functions and assignments. Plaintiff's total employment period lasted only 13 months, until she was terminated by a new sales manager.

After a trial, apparently to the court and not to a jury, judgment was entered in plaintiff's favor for in excess of $16,000, presumably only on contractual theories of relief.

It is not difficult to believe that were such a case presented to a jury in the 1980s, when tort theories are often usable as grounds for recovery in wrongful termination cases, a judgment for plaintiff would have far exceeded that amount.

3. Other examples of hiring someone for the wrong reason include a company that survives on government contracts hiring one of its former government contracts officers. There are some obvious conflict of interest problems inherent in any such employment, and government regulations may limit what such an individual can do, or at least when he or she can do it, for the hiring organization. In any event, public or media perception of the unfairness of such an employment is one factor often leading to its brevity.

4. Similarly, hiring a well known industry consultant as an employee, when the principal motivation is to keep his or her knowledge of your company away from the competition, is another potential creator of "wrongful hiring" liability. Again, what the individual hired knows in this circumstance is often much more critical to the hiring organization than what that person actually can do for the organization.

Finally, it has never seemed overly logical to hire an industry consultant, rather than let one's competition do so, as a solution to that individual's knowledge about your organization. Employment, as opposed to consultancy, is seldom a sterilizer of a consultant's knowledge of your company. Indeed, a dissatisfied employment experience with your company may create a hostile former consultant and former employee, instead of merely a neutral former consultant.

5. One of the frequent generators of potential wrongful hiring liability is an organization's hiring of a person thought to be outstanding based on his or her government or industry consultative or advisory experience, when the individual never has demonstrated good performance in a comparable private sector job elsewhere.

A good example of such a situation known to the author is a municipality's employment of a retired military officer to serve in a large department's number two position. The municipality in question found to its chagrin that the managerial style and habits which may lead to success in the military, at least in the case of the individual in question, were simply not transferable to the requirements of the municipality.

Human resources professionals doubtless have their own "horror stories" about their organization's employment of retired military officers, government officials, or consultants. Indeed, such a person's employment by a private sector organization or municipality probably should be considered fraught with hazard because the individual engaged must not only change from a prior organization to your organization, but must also mentally and on a performance basis alter roles, styles of conduct and communication, and habits of action (or inaction). Such a transition often appears to be exceedingly difficult.

All of this does not mean that such individuals should never be employed by your organization. However, hiring someone for the wrong reason is most definitely a risk factor in the "wrongful hiring" calculus and should require a different approach from the human resources professional. A written employment agreement with mutual "termination for any reason" provisions letting your organization terminate the individual for any reason or no reason, subject to stated termination pay, seems most advisable in this situation. It appears that the only reason the hiring of such individuals has not generated more "wrongful hiring" litigation is precisely because of the widespread use of such employment agreement provisions when such persons are engaged.

Hiring for Failure

While harshly titled, this topic is meant to encompass those situations in which a person is employed with an inadequate commitment by the hiring organization to the needs of the job the person is being asked to perform. Human resources professionals should ask whether any person can be successful with the commitment restraints, and whether the company is prepared to commit enough resources for the success of the job. This is often a problem when a new endeavor is being launched over significant internal opposition, such as a new product, marketing tactic, or sales territory.

The organizational commitment, of course, involves budget, training, staff, and the other physical and financial tools which one should have to do the job well. We suggest that whenever there is significant internal opposition to what anyone in a particular job would need to perform well, such opposition will not vanish the instant the job is filled but will continue. Disclosure to the applicant in this circumstance can be highly problematical. Too much disclosure can scare away the person your organization wants to hire for this job. No or inadequate disclosure may leave the employed individual hostile to your organization when all his or her efforts are doomed to failure by lack of your organization's lack of commitment to what that person needs to perform the job.

We suggest that the applicant be told shortly before the hire offer is made that the job in question may be tough, and that he or she may have to compete for necessary physical and financial resources needed. The applicant should also be told that as with any new project, product, or approach, some individuals in the organization may feel threatened by the applicant's success or the change such success may create for the organization. The goal here is for the human resources professional or line manager to describe enough of the internal opposition so that the employee later will not be hostile enough to launch litigation. You will want to be able to say: "You knew this job was difficult when you took it."

The job applicant also can be told that there is some internal disagreement or apprehension about certain aspects of the job, and that such disagreement means that he or she may have to work hard for the tools needed to get the job done. Since such internal pushing and pulling over budgets, staff, and other physical and financial resources is customary, and since most job applicants may suspect that such statements are designed to test their organizational coping skills, most such disclosures probably can be made without injecting too much apprehension into the applicant.

Some disclosure in this context is advisable not just to give the applicant a more accurate appraisal of the job's difficulty, but because organizational goals and tactics can and do change, often suddenly. Projects can be canceled, new products scrapped, and recently opened territories closed or marketing distribution concepts altered. These sudden surprises, and their resulting personnel changes, are especially likely to occur if your organization's industry in general, or your organization's financial well being in particular, is declining.

Declining Industry/Declining Firm Circumstances

Is the job for which you are hiring likely to be in existence in 3 months, 6 months, or 12 months? Is the recently opened plant at which the job applicant is to work going to remain open during the next economic downturn; or conversely, is the long-established plant for which you are hiring already scheduled to be closed once the current period of high demand for its output decreases? Similarly, is your company one that reshuffles its sales organization every year or two, from areas to districts to zones and back again? Has your organization been of two minds regarding your research and development staff: building it up, tearing it down, and now beginning a new buildup phase?

These organizational and industry growth and decline factors should play a significant role in the presentation of a particular job to applicants, especially shortly before a hire offer is extended. Few other factors are calculated to engender terminated employee hostility, or arouse the rage of juries, than a job applicant courted with glowing oral promises about the industry's future, the company's growth, and the important significance of the job in question only to find employment quickly ended by declining economic conditions or company cutbacks. Particularly calculated to upset the affected employee, as we will discuss, are those circumstances where the employee has relocated his or her residence.

At the very least, human resources professionals and line managers should be cautious in verbally decorating a job in a declining industry or a declining company with too many statements that suggest longevity of employment. This caution is especially advisable for companies that typically have multi-year growth plans, which may be discussed with the applicant. Instructive on this point is *Forman v. Bri Corp.*, 532 F. Supp. 49

(E.D. Pa. 1982). In that case, plaintiff Forman accepted a salaried position with the defendant company and moved at the company's expense to the location of her new job. Six months later she was terminated. She alleged breach of a multi-year oral employment contract, contending that the company entered into such an agreement with her pursuant to its five-year growth plan. The question of whether employment for a "reasonable time" was for the duration of the defendant company's five-year growth plan was held to be a question for the jury.

Residence Relocation

Wrongful hiring cases depend, of course, on unique characteristics particular to the employee's and the company's circumstance. Liability may vary greatly depending on whether the terminated employee finds another job, or a better job, and how quickly that occurs. The role of litigation does seem enhanced, however, if the terminated employee recently relocated his or her residence to accept the job at issue. For almost 100 years the relocation of an employee's residence has suggested the possibility of a contractual commitment beyond at-will employment. Such early cases exist as *Smith v. Theobald*, 86 Ky. 141, 5 S.W. 394 (1887); and *Schultz v. Simmons Fur Co.*, 46 Wash. 555, 90 P. 917 (1907). More recent decisions are to the same effect, such as *McIntosh v. Murphy*, 52 Haw. 29, 469 P.2d 177 (1970); and *Brawther v. H&R Block, Inc.*, 28 Cal. App. 3d 131, 104 Cal. Rptr. 486 (1972).

Common sense also suggests that an employee who has relocated his or her residence and who quickly loses a job will have greater hostility toward the terminating employer, and so will the employee's family. Indeed, terminated employees usually require significant personal feelings of hostility toward the terminating employer in order to launch wrongful termination litigation. Terminated employees who have significantly changed their lives, in particular relocating their residence, can be expected to more easily possess hostility sufficient to start a lawsuit.

Since many white collar employees, especially those who work in sales, management, and the professions, fear "burning their bridges" by starting wrongful termination litigation, many individuals in those categories who lose their job are unlikely to sue. However, those employees who have made a major change in their life in order to accept a new job, which quickly and unexpectedly ends, have fewer ties to the immediate community in which the terminating employer operates, have made a greater personal commitment to the job at issue, and should be expected by human resources professionals to be more willing to litigate their wrongful termination claims. Litigation seems especially likely if the terminated employee left a previous job at which he or she had substantial longevity of employment, as well as relocated residence to accept the new position.

In *Foley v. Community Oil Co.*, 64 F.R.D. 561 (D.N.H. 1974), plaintiff was employed for approximately 30 years before his employer was acquired by a larger company. Eight years after the acquisition, plaintiff's position was terminated and he was asked to fill an equivalent position in another state. Plaintiff accepted the offer, sold his home, and moved to the other state, purchasing a new house. Less than three years later that position also was eliminated. No other local position was available and the plaintiff's employment with the company was terminated.

The Federal District Court in New Hampshire noted that even in the 1800s, courts found that the relocation of a family was reason for finding a contractual employment relationship other than at-will employment. The court also noted the longevity of this plaintiff's employment period. Since the plaintiff alleged that the defendant company acted in bad faith and out of malice in terminating him, a motion for judgment on the pleadings was denied.

The giving up of secure employment elsewhere to take a new job, which quickly and unexpectedly is ended by the new employer, has been found to give rise to a cause of action by the affected employee. See, for example, *Scott v. Lane,* 409 So. 2d 791 (Ala. Sup. Ct. 1982). In that case, plaintiff *Scott* had resigned secure employment to take a position offered her of allegedly permanent employment. Scott alleged that the defendants had knowledge that she would resign her previous employment. The Alabama Supreme Court held that if the hirer knows that the person being employed is giving up current employment to take the hirer's offered position, then valuable consideration is shown sufficient to render a contract for permanent employment enforceable.

The Minnesota Supreme Court has held that employees who leave employment in one job to accept a new job can assume they will be given a good faith opportunity to perform their duties to the satisfaction of the new employer. *Grouse v. Group Health Plan Inc.,* 306 N.W.2d 114 (Minn. Sup. Ct. 1981).

In *Hodge v. Evans Financial Corp.,* 228 App. D.C. 161, 707 F.2d 1566 (D.C. Cir. 1983), the plaintiff left a position with his former employer in Pennsylvania to accept employment with defendant in Washington, D.C. Plaintiff had to relocate his residence and family to accept that position. The plaintiff alleged that he left his former employment because he had a commitment of "permanent" employment with the defendant. The U.S. Court of Appeals for the District of Columbia reversed the District Court's grant of summary judgment, finding that triable issues of fact existed regarding the plaintiff's job expectancies.

As can be seen from these and other decisions in the wrongful termination area, residence relocation and family uprooting are a significant risk factor in the wrongful hiring area.

What Are You Trying to Ignore? ("I Knew it Wasn't Going to Work Out")

Another significant risk factor in the wrongful hiring calculus are those personality traits or observable conditions of an applicant that normally would preclude employment, but which are ignored because of the need to fill the position quickly. Examples are the applicant's spouse working for a competitor, a prior covenant not to compete, or training, skill, and experience limitations articulated by the applicant.

It is less emotionally difficult for a former employee to commence wrongful termination litigation when he or she has been terminated for factors disclosed during the interview process, especially if the employee has relocated residence and family to accept the position. This ignoring of observable conditions or articulated limitations also occurs in such employment discrimination areas as physical handicap, race, and sex discrimination. An interviewer may be so eager to hire a particular candidate that the interviewer overlooks job-related shortcomings that only later become obvious that the applicant is not and could not have been successful on the job.

Terminated employees can present an attractive case to a judge or jury when the reason for their termination, such as lack of experience or skills in a particular area, was disclosed to the interviewer during the hiring process and the employer nevertheless hired that individual. Particularly if the employee in question was not given a sufficiently lengthy opportunity to perform well in the position at issue, or alleges inadequate training for the position by the employer, is liability potential enhanced.

This chapter hopefully will assist human resources professionals in recognizing risk factors in the interview and hiring process. The risk factors identified in this chapter have been hiring the replacement before the incumbent is terminated, hiring for the wrong reasons, hiring for failure (without disclosure to the applicant), declining industry or declining company circumstances, residence relocation, and ignoring observable or articulated shortcomings of the applicant because of a critical need to fill a position quickly.

Especially in combination, these risk factors should alert human resources professionals to the need for greater disclosure to the applicant about the difficulties of the position, or for a written employment agreement trading termination benefits for the company's ironclad privilege to terminate at will.

It is common to think of the wrongful termination upheaval in employment relations as a new phenomenon. However, the law of employment relations has reflected societal, legislative, and judicial changes for at least a century. As far back as 1898 the U.S. Supreme Court made a statement about the flexibility of the common law to adapt itself to new employer-employment relationships:

[I]n view of the fact that, from the day Magna Charta was signed to the present moment, amendments to the structure of the law have been made with increasing frequency, it is impossible to suppose that they will not continue, and the law be forced to adapt itself to new conditions of society, and, particularly, to the new relations between employers and employees, as they arise. *Holden v. Hardy*, 169 U.S. (1898).

Hiring organizations must continue to adapt themselves to the "new relations" of employer and employee created by developments in wrongful termination law. There is no doubt that the relationship of employer and employee previously characterized by the employer's broad privilege to terminate is fundamentally changing in much of the United States as conditions of decreased job mobility have occurred. As the U. S. Supreme

Court made clear by its unanimous decision in *Hishon v. King & Spaulding,* the employment relationship is a contractual one, and the significant contractual terms are formed at its creation. It is hoped that greater attention to the interview and hiring process, and the wrongful hiring risk factors discussed in this chapter, will decrease wrongful termination claims against your organization.

Chapter 13

EMPLOYMENT CONTRACTS
HOW TO PREPARE THEM

Stanley E. Tobin, J.D.
James G. Johnson, LL.M.

A contract is inherent in any employment relationship. Once an offer to employ is accepted, either by word or deed, a contract is formed. The employer is then obligated to pay the agreed-upon (stated or implied in fact or in law) rate for the services rendered under the contract until the contract is terminated.

Most employments neither have nor require a writing to memorialize the terms of the relationship. As the duties and responsibilities become more complex, however, both the employer and the employee often see the benefit of preparing a written agreement, defining either generally or specifically what the parties expect. As the title suggests, the purpose of this chapter is to assist prospective employers in the negotiation and drafting of employment contracts by identifying common concerns and by suggesting contract provisions that address those concerns.

As an initial caveat extreme care must be taken in drafting employment contracts. If drafted inartfully, the contract provisions may come back to haunt the employer in a subsequent traditional breach of contract or modern wrongful discharge lawsuit. In addition, since the laws of the 50 states differ, and sometimes significantly so, the advice of competent labor counsel is recommended so that any agreement negotiated will be found fully enforceable, as written, should the validity of its terms ever be challenged.

NEGOTIATION OF THE EMPLOYMENT CONTRACT

When to Use Them

Written employment contracts may, and sometimes do, cover every employee on an employer's payroll. Form contracts prepared in advance involve little or no administrative expense and are executed by the employees on their hire. Such contracts create a general atmosphere of stability and certainty, even though they often may be modified or terminated at will. Of necessity, however, they must be general in their terms to allow flexibility as conditions surrounding the employer's operation change or as the employee advances in his or her duties and responsibilities. In addition, time and circumstances inevitably alter the employment relationship. Employment contracts must be designed with this in mind.

Written employment contracts are a useful tool for all employers. They provide a solid framework upon which the employment relationship is built and offer a degree of protection or security to both the employer and employee should disputes arise. In most instances, however, employers forego the formalities of individual contracts for all but their executives and other highly compensated personnel; rank-and-file employment is usually governed by the employer's written and unwritten policies, practices and procedures, as well as by supervisory discretion. The written and unwritten factors in the latter situations are often deemed to constitute the "employment contract"; a written contract, however, usually leads to greater predictability and therefore protection.

Setting the Terms

Written employment contracts range from the simple "I agree to employ _____at $_____ per hour," to contracts as sophisticated and complex as any in the world of business. In setting or preparing to negotiate the terms, the employer must evaluate both its needs and the function that the contract will serve. Will the contract govern the entire employment relationship, or will existing policies, practices and procedures also apply? Is the contract to be written in general terms, allowing for the exercise of individual judgment and discretion as various circumstances arise, or is every contingency to be addressed and resolved? Regardless of how the contract is structured, obvious benefits and burdens attach to the agreement from both the employer and the employee viewpoints. The ultimate objective, of course, is to establish enforceable terms that satisfy the employer's needs and still result in an employee's signature at the bottom of the page.

Employment contracts are governed by the traditional principles governing the formation and enforcement of all contracts. To be binding there must be certainty as to the parties, the nature, and extent of the employee's duties and compensation. All other aspects of the employment relationship, including the term, may be left unstated, although the benefits of such a barebones agreement is usually virtually nil.

The following is a list of the subject areas that should at least be considered for inclusion in a written employment contract:

1. Identification of the parties
2. Term
3. Description of duties
4. Place of performance
5. Compensation
    a. Wage, salary or commission
    b. Overtime
    c. Basis for additional compensation
    d. Bonus
    e. Profit sharing
    f. Stock options
6. Employee benefits
    a. Vacations
    b. Holidays
    c. Personal leave
    d. Sick leave
    e. Insurance
        i. Medical
        ii. Disability
        iii. Life
    f. Retirement plan
7. Reimbursement of expenses
8. Limitation on outside activities
9. Confidentiality of trade secrets and customer lists
    a. Covenant not to disclose
    b. Covenant not to use
10. Covenant not to compete
    a. Length of time
    b. Geographic limitations
11. Covenant not to recruit
12. Ownership of inventions and patents
    a. Licensing
13. Return of property
14. Covenant to notify management of unlawful acts or practices

15. Termination of employment
    a. With cause
        i. Grounds
    b. Without cause
        i. Notice
16. Dispute resolution procedure
    a. Management rights
    b. Arbitration
    c. Court action
17. Remedies for breach
    a. Specific performance
    b. Liquidated damages
    c. Attorneys' fees
18. Waiver of breach
19. Severance
20. Illness, incapacity, or death
21. Cooperation after retirement or termination
22. Repayment of loans
23. Assignment by employer
    a. Merger, consolidation, or acquisition
24. Assignment by employee
25. Modification, renewal, or extension
26. Effect of prior agreements or understandings
27. Effect of existing employer policies and procedures
28. Zipper clause
29. Savings clause
30. Applicable law

Avoidance of an Unenforceable Contract of Adhesion

In recent years the courts have been increasingly inclined to examine the terms of agreements, not only as to the legality of their provisions, but also as to their basic fairness. Where the parties' bargaining power was not relatively equal at the time that the agreement was executed, the courts have exercised their powers to void some or all of the provisions on the grounds that they are fundamentally unconscionable.

Employment contracts are generally found to be unenforceable contracts of adhesion when the employer presents a present or prospective employee with a standardized agreement on a take-it-or-leave-it basis. Unfortunately that is precisely how most employment contracts are offered. The simple fact that an agreement is presented in that manner does not doom its enforceability, however. Rather, an adhesive employment contract is fully enforceable unless it fails to meet minimal levels of integrity, such as where the dispute resolution procedures are institutionally biased in favor of the employer.

The "secret" to drafting enforceable employment contracts, even if standardized, is to try to assure that the provisions are reasonably related to the employer's needs, yet even-handed in approach. If a contract as a whole, or any provision contained therein, is one that the drafter would not willingly enter into himself, the danger flag is raised; a drafter should consider alternate approaches to achieve the same end in order to preserve the agreement's integrity and enforceability.

What to do if the Employee Balks at the Terms

In the vast majority of cases, present or prospective employees will willingly execute any employment contract presented to them, either because the provisions are fair and fully acceptable or because the employee believes, correctly or not, that he or she has no ability to negotiate the terms. In some situations, however, an employee will question the meaning and intent of particular provisions. While others the employee will flatly object to the inclusion of a particular provision, or to its wording. (Typically such objections will occur with corporate officers or higher paid personnel, because their position and respective bargaining power is clearly greater than that of a rank-and-file or lesser-ranked managerial employee.)

When questions or objections arise, a response is obviously due. The company's reasons for the inclusion of any provision must be thought out in advance and artfully articulated in the event a question is raised. Not only is it insufficient to say "It's there because we want it," but it also decreases the employee's contentment with both the contract and his or her employment situation in the event that he or she signs; moreover, it obviously decreases the likelihood that the contract will be accepted in the first place. Of a greater concern, however, is the possibility that such a response will be used against the employer in a subsequent wrongful termination lawsuit as evidence that the employment contract is one of adhesion. Moreover, as noted in the previous section, the provision will be subject to much greater judicial scrutiny if a court becomes convinced that the provision became a part of the employment contract only because of the employer's superior bargaining strength. Further, it should be noted that as a general precept of law, contract language is construed against the party that caused its inclusion. Courts, thus, tend to achieve "equity" by interpreting "tough" contract provisions against employers.

When questions arise, it is advisable from an overall employer perspective to address each question or objection individually with the same care and concern that one would wish one's own questions or objections would be treated. This is true not only from the practical standpoint of enhancing employee morale, but also to establish that the terms of any agreement, as presented, are not necessarily written in stone. The greater that an employer is able to establish that it is flexible in the negotiation of employment contracts, either individually or on a company-wide basis, the greater the prospects are that any particular contract will not be deemed a contract of adhesion.

Necessarily following from the idea that the employer is willing to at least consider modifications to the contract terms in response to employee questions or objections, is the amenability of the employer to negotiate individual changes. Assuming that flexibility is acceptable, reasonably detailed notes, either during or immediately following the discussions, should be kept and maintained. Such notes will be of assistance in the future to establish the employer's amenability to modification by negotiation as to that or any other employment contract. In addition, in the event that modifications are negotiated, they can be accommodated either by interlineation and initialing, or by drafting side letters or other addenda to the contract. If the changes proposed by the employee are not acceptable, again detailed notes memorializing the arguments both pro and con *that were discussed* are highly advisable.

The Effect of Personnel Handbooks, Manuals, Policies, and Other Employment-Related Documents

In most companies where employment contracts are considered, the employer has already promulgated written employee handbooks, manuals, or policies. At the very least, personnel policies and procedures have been established by the company's past practices. The question then arises: to what extent do those policies and procedures, whether written or established by past practices, affect the employment contract, or vice versa? Often personnel manuals or handbooks are written with the rank-and-file in mind. Indeed, some manuals are explicitly so delimited. In any event, employee handbooks, as well as other employment-related documents, such as stock options, pension plans, and so on, must be drafted carefully as they may directly affect or tacitly modify express provisions of a written employment contract.

It must be emphasized that in wrongful discharge litigation, the employer's policies or procedures will almost certainly be argued as being binding policies or procedures for upper level employees despite specific statements to the contrary. Of course, the thought is that if the policies and procedures are good enough for rank-and-file employees, they are certainly minimum standards to which the employer must adhere in dealing with its management personnel—not an unreasonable assumption. Careful drafting is only real protection against any such unwanted result.

Written or established policies or practices often provide procedures by which employee complaints or discharges are handled. Notwithstanding a specific provision in the employment contract negating the applicability of such policies and practices, the courts are presently inclined to engraft those procedures into the employment relationship. Again, the theory of what is good for the goose is good for the gander prevails, and that if the company is willing to provide certain protections (although possibly illusory) to a rank-and-file employee, such protections generally must be available to management level employees as well. Indeed only the clearest and most explicit expression to the contrary will likely be enforced.

THE HIRING LETTER

The hiring letter is not uncommon in employment relationships. The letter written to confirm an offer of employment, or to confirm an employee's acceptance of an offer, is often given the same weight as a fully executed employment contract. Not infrequently, the hiring letter is overly effusive in its stated glee of the employee's acceptance. That effusiveness, as with poorly drafted employment contracts, can come back with devastating consequences in subsequent breach of contract or wrongful discharge litigation. The reason, of course, is obvious: the letter can make damaging statements that are not wholly accurate or can make either express or implied promises of lifetime or long-term employment.

As with an employment contract, the hiring letter must be drafted with care and precison. The employer must decide whether the hiring letter shall define the full parameters of an individual's employment, or whether it will merely confirm the rudiments of an individual's hire, position, rate of pay, and starting date. In the latter situation, all other aspects of the individual's employment may be left subject to the employer's established policies and practices, or to a subsequent employment contract.

Although an employer may be delighted that an individual has accepted employment, expressions of such delight ought to be reserved. A simple statement that the employer is "pleased" that the individual has accepted the employer's offer of employment is sufficient; anything more can and will be argued to establish that the individual was a real "catch," even though his or her subsequent performance proves to be otherwise, resulting in termination. *Absolutely nothing* should be said or intimated concerning a "long and prosperous" relationship, for such statements arguably constitute implied promises of long-term employment. By the same token "guarantees" of advancement, or increased compensation or benefits should be avoided whenever possible.

INDEPENDENT CONTRACTOR V. EMPLOYEE

Is an Independent Contractor Relationship Feasible?

In drafting an employment agreement consideration should be given to whether the required duties could be performed by an independent contractor, rather than by an employee. If an independent contractor relationship is feasible, the employer's liabilities arising out of an employment relationship *may be* avoided.

The determination whether an individual is an employee or an independent contractor is not predicated on the label used in denominating the relationship as one or the other. In some contexts employment will be presumed, and it will be up to the purported employer to rebut the presumption by establishing that the individual possessed the necessary indicia of independent contractor status. Indeed, in virtually any context, the employer will bear the burden of establishing the nature of the relationship should it ever become an issue.

For this reason, the drafting of an independent contractor agreement with care and precision is just as important—indeed sometimes more important—than the employment agreement, since the purpose served by the former is to minimize potential liability below that which would otherwise flow from an employment context. In addition, the provisions in an independent contractor agreement must be more than mere words; the operative provisions establishing an independent contractor relationship must be followed, lest the agreement be disregarded in favor of a finding that the individual is an employee-in-fact.

The Standard For Independent Contractor Status

As a general rule, an employee works for wages or salaries under direct or indirect supervision. An independent contractor, on the other hand, generally undertakes a job for a set price, sometimes payable in installments, and retains the right to decide how the work will be performed, whether by the individual or by others. The key determinant is *control* over the manner and means by which a job will be performed.

In addition to control, the entrepreneurial aspects of the independent contractor's business must be considered. Is there a risk of loss or an opportunity for profit? Can the individual increase his or her profit by being efficient and completing the assigned task in less than the expected or allotted time? Conversely, is the individual at risk for loss or reduced profitability if the manner and means of his or her performance is not efficient? Does the independent contractor have a capital investment in their business? Is the individual free to delegate the duties by hiring others to perform the work, while still maintaining primary responsibility over the ultimate completion of the assigned tasks? If the answer to most of these questions is affirmative, an independent contractor relationship may be feasible and ought to be considered.

Even in the presence of the foregoing factors, most businesses considering the use of an independent contractor to perform a task either have or perceive a need to retain some control over the individual's performance. Uniformity of result is often important to preserve goodwill, and performance guidelines, thus, are deemed to be necessary. As long as those guidelines are result-oriented, leaving the individual more or less free to establish on their own the manner and means by which those uniform results are obtained, with little or no supervision, a bona fide independent contractor relationship may still exist. The greater that the business intrudes on the individual's right to determine on their own the manner and means of their performance, the more likely it will be that their independent status could be successfully challenged.

The determination whether an individual is an independent contractor or an employee may be one that is decided on fine-line distinctions. The question is one that is resolved on a case-by-case basis in which all of the aspects of the relationship will be explored.

ENFORCEMENT OF EMPLOYMENT CONTRACTS

Are They Enforceable?

An employment contract obviously has no value to the employer unless its provisions are enforceable. The courts and arbitrators, when called on to enforce an agreement, look to both the stated terms of the agreement and the parties' application of those terms, or deviations therefrom, in the actual experience of their relationship. If the agreement says one thing and experience says that something entirely different occurred, the agreement may be deemed to be modified so as to be consistent with the parties' practice.

Also of concern is the question of overreaching. Is the agreement reasonable on its face, or are the terms so one-sided that equity would compel that they be disregarded? So long as the agreement is even-handed in approach, reasonable in effectuation of bona fide business purposes, and acted upon in fact during the course of the employment experience, the agreement will likely be found to be fully enforceable.

Specific Performance

Certain aspects of an employment contract are subject to specific performance either by judicial or arbitral determination. Under certain circumstances, such as where the employee's performance is unique, the employee may be compelled to complete his or her assigned tasks. Specific performance of the employee's job duty functions is rare, however, for it smacks of involuntary servitude that is prohibited under the U.S. Constitution. Negative covenants, however, such as covenants not to compete, covenants not to disclose or utilize confidential information, and the like, are frequently litigated and specifically enforced.

Since specific performance is a matter of equity, all equitable considerations will come into play in determining whether an employee's adherence to the terms of an employment agreement is to be compelled. An employer will not be given judicial assistance where it is a wrongdoer itself, or where the employer failed to assert its claim in a timely fashion. In addition, for specific performance to lie, the remedy at law (i.e., damages) must be both uncertain and inadequate. Further, equities must dictate that the burden of nonperformance outweighs the burden that would be imposed by a specific performance order.

Problems and Pitfalls

The question which often arises on an individual's termination of employment, whether voluntary or not, concerns when and if an action should be instituted to enforce the employment agreement's continuing obligations. For an action to lie, the former employee must be suspected of acting in derogation of the agreement. Additionally the suspicion must be based on the presence of objective facts on which a court or arbitrator may make a finding that a violation is either likely to occur or has occurred and is liable to continue unless enjoined.

Where the facts suggest that the former employee is being unfaithful to the agreement, consideration must be given to the damage that the employer has suffered and is likely to continue to suffer in the event that the agreement is not enforced. If the damages are inconsequential and the estimated costs of litigation high, the benefits to be expected from a successful effort obviously dictate that no action should be taken unless other strong considerations exist.

Where the issue, indeed, is important, consideration must be given not only to the likelihood of success, but also to the negative impact of failure. For example, covenants that are subject to specific performance may be found to be unenforceable as a matter of law. If the risk of unenforceability is relatively high, prudence will likely be the best tact, for if a provision is ruled to be unenforceable, the deterrent value of the provision's simple existence is wiped out and the proverbial flood gates opened; the individual will then have virtual carte blanche to do that which he or she agreed not to do. However, if untested, a provision may well have the practical effect of compelling adherence to its terms. Therefore, care must be taken to avoid jumping the gun on any minor or suspected violation.

Comment

The sample hiring letter is obviously rudimentary in form. It could contain all of the specifics that might be contained in a full employment contract, but need not do so. Indeed, if an employment contract is intended to be detailed, it is best to obtain the employee's signature on it, rather than having his or her acceptance merely inferred by acquiescence through subsequent performance. In addition, unless all of the terms of a detailed contract have been discussed and agreed to in advance, it is *not recommended* to set forth in the hiring letter anything other than the most basic outline of employment. To do otherwise would invite the inference of over-reaching (and consequent unenforceability of the stated terms) in the event that the hiring letter is received by the employee after he or she has already given notice to their then-existing employer of his or her intented to quit.

If a detailed hiring letter is desired as an alternative to a full-written employment contract, all details of the employment relationship discussed and agreed to should be addressed in the letter, with probably no less formality than would be set forth in a formal employment contract. The letter should then conclude with a statement such as this:

If a detailed hiring letter is the preferred vehicle, it is recommended that the prospective employee be advised not to give notice of intent to quit his or her then-current employment or to take any other significant action (e.g., travel, list home for sale, etc.) until he or she receives either the hiring letter or a detailed employment contract. Of course, this is to protect against the argument that an employer offered employment, without limitations or conditions, only to find out after quitting his or her employment that new terms and conditions have been attached to that employment. Although the individual may be so advised in writing before the hiring letter or contract is actually prepared and sent, it is probably sufficient that a warning to that effect be memorialized in the individual's personnel file.

In the event that the prospective employee does object to or question some of the provisions set forth in the detailed hiring letter, the general manager or other responsible individual should take notes of the conversation and confirm the results therof in a written memorandum to the file. In the event that the employee has not returned the executed detailed hiring letter prior to reporting to work, it should be presented to and executed by him or her before commencing work.

SAMPLE PROVISIONS WITH COMMENT

Suggested Hiring Letter

XYZ CORPORATION
123 Main Street
Los Angeles, California

Mr. John Smith
456 Frontage Road
Los Angeles, California

Dear Mr. Smith:

This will acknowledge, with pleasure, your decision to accept the company's offer of employment as _____ (e.g., general manager) at the company's facility located at 123 Main Street, Los Angeles, California. As agreed, your employment will commence on January 2, 1986, at the rate of $_____ per month.

I trust that the foregoing satisfactorily sets forth the agreements that we have reached. Of course, if there are any questions or comments, or if the foregoing does not fully or accurately set forth the agreements reached, please do not hesitate to give me a call. In addition, if the foregoing is acceptable and conforms to the agreements reached, please execute and return to me at your earliest convenience a copy of this letter in the envelope provided.

I look forward to seeing you on January 2.

Very truly yours,

XYZ CORPORATION

By _____
FRED JONES
General Manager

ACCEPTED

_____   _____
John Smith   Date

Short-Form Employment Contract

Most employment contracts, especially for the lower level or rank-and-file employee, will be standardized short-form agreements designed for general application. Such contracts will not normally abrogate existing policies and procedures and, in fact, usually refer to such policies, practices, and procedures as governing the employment relationship. As noted, a short-form employment contract should contain the rudiments upon which the employment relationship is based. It should name the parties, describe the position, establish the compensation, and establish a *maximum* term, subject to renewal, extension or modification. A sample short-form agreement is set forth below:

OPTION 1

EMPLOYMENT AGREEMENT

This agreement is made and entered into this _____ day of _____, 19 _____, by and between XYZ Corporation ("XYZ") and John Smith ("Smith"). This Agreement is to memorialize the terms of the agreement between the parties as follows:

1. XYZ agrees to employ Smith as a _____ (e.g., general manager) at its facility located at 123 Main Street, Los Angeles, California.
2. Smith's employment with XYZ shall commence on _____, 19 _____.
3. This Agreement shall be terminable by either party upon 30 days' notice to the other for any reason whatsoever.
4. This Agreement shall be interpreted and governed in accordance with the laws of the State of California.

XYZ CORPORATION

By: _____
    Fred Jones
    General Manager

_____
JOHN SMITH

OPTION 2

EMPLOYMENT AGREEMENT

XYZ Corporation (hereinafter the "Employer"), located at 123 Main Street, Los Angeles, California, hereby agrees to employ John Smith (hereinafter the "Employee") as _____ (e.g., general manager) to serve and perform such duties at such times and places, and in such manner as the Employer may from time to time direct.

The Employee agrees to perform the duties assigned to him to the best of his ability. The Employee further agrees to devote his full and complete attention to the Employer's business, to make prompt, complete and accurate reports of his work and expenses, when requested, to promptly remit to the Employer any and all monies or property collected by him or coming into his possession in connection with the performance of his duties, and not to engage or be engaged or be interested in any other business during the existence of this agreement without the Employer's prior written consent thereto.

In consideration for the Employee's services, the Employer agrees to pay to the Employee a salary of $_____, and to reimburse the Employee for any necessary and reasonable expenses incurred in the performance of his assigned duties, supported by such appropriate documentation thereof as the Employer may require.

The Employee agrees that he will not utilize or disclose any confidential information that he may acquire during his employment, such as, but not limited to, the Employer's customer lists, manufacturing processes and other trade secrets, for a period of _____ years following the termination of this agreement for any reason whatsoever.

This agreement shall be in effect from _____, 19 _____, until _____, 19 _____, or until this agreement is terminated by either party at any time and for any reason on _____ (e.g., 30) days' written notice to the other party. Upon termination of this agreement, the Employer shall pay to the Employee all salary earned by the Employee up to and including the date of such termination, and shall reimburse the Employee for all business expenses reasonably incurred; such payment shall be in full satisfaction of all claims that the Employee may have against the Employer under this agreement.

Executed this _____ day of _____, 19 _____ at Los Angeles, California.

XYZ CORPORATION

By: _____
FRED JONES
General Manager

_____
JOHN SMITH

OPTION 3

EMPLOYMENT AGREEMENT

This agreement is made and entered into between XYZ Corporation (the "Employer") and Jane Smith (hereinafter the "Employee"). This agreement is intended to embody the terms of the Employee's employment with the Employer as follows:

1. The Employer agrees to employ the Employee on the terms and conditions set forth below.

2. Subject to the conditions set forth herein, the Employer agrees to employ the Employee commencing on _____, 19 _____, which employment shall be for a period not to exceed one year.

3. The Employee shall be employed as the _____ (e.g., general manager) at the Employer's facility located at 123 Main Street, Los Angeles, California. The Employee's duties and responsibilities may be increased or reduced at the Employer's discretion at not less than the compensation set forth in this agreement, unless the Employee agrees in writing to a different level of compensation commensurate with her position.

4. The Employer agrees to pay to the Employee a salary of $_____ per month, payable in equal installments of $_____ every _____ (e.g., two weeks).

5. The Employee agrees that she will devote her entire time, attention and energies to the Employer business during her employment and that she will not engage in any other business activity, regardless of whether such activity is pursued for profit, gain or pecuniary advantage without the express written consent of the Employer. By this provision, the Employee is not prohibited from making personal investments in any other business, so long as those investments do not require her to participate in the operation or activities of any business in which she invests.

6. The Employee acknowledges that certain information which may come into her possession is both confidential and critical to the success of the Employer's business. As a result thereof, the Employee agrees that she will not, during or after the term of her employment, reveal or otherwise utilize any such information to or on behalf of any person, firm, corporation, or other business enterprise, whether or not for pecuniary advantage. If the Employee reveals or threatens to reveal, or utilizes or threatens to utilize any such information, the Employee agrees that the Employer shall be entitled to an injunction restraining her from disclosing or utilizing any such information for any purpose whatsoever. The right to secure injunctive relief shall not be exclusive, and the Employer may pursue any other remedies that it may have against the Employee for breach of this agreement, including the recovery of damages resulting to the Employer as a result thereof.

7. The Employee shall be entitled to _____ weeks of vacation with pay. The Employee shall accrue no rights to vacation benefits, or

any proration thereof, unless and until she has completed _____ (e.g., six) months of employment.

8. The Employee shall be entitled to the following paid holidays: _____ (or such holidays as the Employer traditionally recognizes).

9. Upon receiving authorization therefor, the Employee may incur reasonable expenses for promoting the Employer's business, including expenses for entertainment, travel and related items. The Employer shall reimburse Employee for any such business expenses, provided the Employee presents to the Employer acceptable itemization and documentation therefor.

10. This agreement may be terminated by either party for any reason whatsoever upon 30 days' written notice to the other. In addition, the Employer may terminate this agreement, and the Employee's employment thereunder, immediately upon any or all of the following:

   a. The Employer's termination, merger, consolidation or sale;

   b. The Employee's termination for cause, which shall include, but not be limited to, the following:

      i. Incompetence

      ii. Insubordination

      iii. Carelessness

      iv. Failure or refusal to perform his assigned duties:

      v. Intoxication or being under the influence of alcohol, narcotics, or other controlled substances during working hours

      vi. Commission of immoral or illegal acts during working hours or in connection with the performance of duties under this Employment Contract

      vii. Conviction of a felony

      viii. Violation of the Employer's established rules and regulations governing employment.

11. In no event shall liability under this agreement resulting from termination of the Employee's employment for any reason whatsoever exceed 30 days' pay, unless specifically agreed in writing to the contrary.

12. This agreement supersedes any and all prior agreements or understandings between the Employer and the Employee concerning the subject matter hereof and this agreement constitutes the entire agreement between the parties with respect thereto. This agreement may be modified in writing only, duly executed by each of the parties.

13. Any claim or controversy that arises out of or relates to the interpretation, application or enforcement of this agreement shall be submitted to final and binding arbitration in accordance with the voluntary Labor Arbitration Rules of the American Arbitration Association.

14. Each party agrees that a breach of any provision of this agreement by either party shall not constitute a waiver of any subsequent breach of the same or any different provision.

15. If, for any reason, any provision of this agreement is determined by an arbitrator or a court of competent jurisdiction to be illegal or otherwise invalid, all other provisions of this agreement shall remain in full force and effect, insofar as they are consistent with existing law.

16. This agreement shall be governed by and interpreted in accordance with the laws of the State of California.

XYZ CORPORATION

By: _____
FRED JONES
General Manager

_____
JOHN SMITH

Comment

Obviously, the short-form agreements set forth above are inherently different. The first is extremely general in nature, and either inferentially incorporates the employer's existing practices to fill out the provisions, or leaves the remaining aspects of the employee's employment to subsequent negotiation. The second agreement, while more comprehensive, is still relatively short in nature, yet addresses many of the areas of typical concern. The third agreement contains even more detail, including a zipper clause which provides that no other agreements or understandings (or existing policies, practices or procedures) shall be deemed to modify the provisions set forth therein. Of course, if such an extended "short-form" agreement is utilized, other existing benefits, such as health insurance, sick leave, retirement and the like, probably should be discussed, if even in general terms.

The Long-Form Employment Contract

IDENTIFICATION OF THE PARTIES

OPTION 1

This Employment Agreement is made and entered into this _____ day of _____, 19 _____, between _____, a _____ [e.g., California] corporation, whose principal business is located at _____ ("Employer", and _____ _____ ("Employee"). Employer agrees to employ Employee on the terms and conditions set forth herein.

OPTION 2

XYZ Corporation hereby agrees to employ you, subject to the terms and conditions contained in this Employment Agreement. You hereby accept such employment and agree to perform to the best of your abilities the duties and functions described in this agreement or such other duties and functions as may be assigned hereafter.

Comment

Most forms for employment agreements refer to the parties as "Employer" and "Employee." As a result, final employment contracts are often written with those same sterile references. Where feasible, the parties should be referred to by name, such as "XYZ" and "Smith" to give the agreement a more personalized appearance. The more that an agreement appears to be individually prepared for the employee, rather than a standardized form, the better. If a standard-form employment contract is utilized, questions or comments should be solicited, with the fact of such solicitation, plus a description of those questions, comments, and any responses thereto, memorialized in the employee's file.

Term

OPTION 1

The term of this agreement shall commence on _____, 19___, and shall terminate on _____, 19_____. In the event the Employer elects to employ the Employee beyond the stated term of this agreement, the Employer will notify the Employee in writing of that election not later than 30 days prior to the expiration date for purposes of negotiating and entering into a successor employment agreement.

OPTION 2

Your employment shall commence on _____, 19_____, and shall continue for a period of _____ (e.g., 12 months). Your employment may be extended for additional periods upon mutual agreement. This agreement and any extensions thereof may be terminated by either party for any reason upon 30 days' notice to the other.

OPTION 3

The term of your employment shall be for a period of _____ (e.g., one year), but may be extended beyond that term upon mutual agreement. Nothing in this agreement, whether extended or not, shall be construed as an agreement for permanent employment; both you and the company have the option of terminating this agreement for any reason whatsoever upon 30 days' notice.

Comment

In wrongful discharge and breach of employment contract litigation, probably the two most important provisions from an employer's standpoint are those specifying the term of the agreement and the conditions upon which the agreement may be terminated prior to the stated expiration date. The stated term should be for a reasonably realistic period, such as one year, but with the proviso that it may be terminated for any reason on 30 days' notice. In this way, a strong argument can be made that if the employment agreement was wrongfully terminated, the maximum damages for any breach thereof should be limited to either one month's salary or possibly the employee's salary for the balance of the agreement's term.

In the second option, there is a provision that the employee must be notified in writing if the agreement is to be extended beyond the stated term. The benefit of such a provision is that it underscores the need for positive action for the agreement to be extended. On the downside, however, the employer is put to the affirmative burden of notifying each employee in writing that it wishes to extend the employee's employment and to cover that employment under the terms of the employment agreement. If no written notice is sent, and employment continues beyond the stated termination date, the employer risks losing all of the protections otherwise afforded by the employment agreement.

Description of Duties

OPTION 1

The Employee shall be employed in the capacity as _____(e.g., general manager). By way of illustration, and not as limitation, the Employee's duties and responsibilities are described as follows:

(Specify).

OPTION 2

During the term of this agreement, you shall be employed as a _____ (e.g., general manager), or in such other capacities as you and the Employer hereafter may agree. As _____ (general manager), your duties and responsibilities are generally described as follows:

(Specify).

Comment

The description of an employee's duties and job functions should be as general or as specific as the particular circumstances demand. If specific duties and functions are described, the specifics should be followed by a general catch-all provision that the employee shall perform such other duties and functions as may be assigned or otherwise necessary to carry out the employer's operations.

If an employee is promoted or transferred, consideration should be given to prepare either an entirely new employment agreement, or an addendum thereto, to describe the new position, along with its particular duties and functions that the employee has assumed. If a new agreement is not to be prepared, a review of the existing agreement should be made to make sure that the description of duties is sufficiently broad to encompass those required by the employee's new position.

Place of Performance

OPTION 1

The Employee shall be employed at the Employer's business facility located at _____, or at such other location as the Employer hereafter may designate.

OPTION 2

You shall be employed at the company's facility located at _____, or at such other facility as you and the company hereafter may agree.

Compensation

OPTION 1

The Employee shall receive as full compensation for all services rendered and hours of work performed under this agreement a monthly salary of $_____, payable in equal installments of _____ every _____ (e.g., two weeks). The Employee shall not receive, nor shall he be entitled to receive, additional compensation for his services, unless specified in writing by the Employer.

OPTION 2

The company shall pay you a monthly salary of $_____, payable in equal installments on the first and fifteenth of each month. You shall not be entitled to additional compensation for any services rendered under this agreement unless such additional compensation is agreed to in writing by the company. You understand that the compensation paid under this agreement shall be for all hours of work performed by you.

OPTION 3

As compensation for the services rendered under this agreement, the Employee shall be entitled to a commission calculated on the following basis:

(Specify).

In the event the Employee receives an advance on his commissions from the Employer, any amounts so advanced shall be deducted from the commissions earned.

OPTION 4 (to be used in conjunction with one of the provisions set forth previously)

In addition to the compensation set forth above, the Employee shall be entitled to the following: (set forth the basis for any additional compensation, such as overtime entitlement, bonuses, stock options, profit sharing, etc.).

Comment

The terms of the employee's compensation should be clearly specified. Where the employee's compensation is subject to certain factors, such as sales, performance, profitability, and so forth, the specific formula or means by which the compensation may be calculated should be detailed in full wherever possible.

In setting forth the employee's compensation, it is suggested that a monthly salary, rather than an annual salary, be utilized. A monthly salary strengthens the oft-stated and highly emphasized provision that the agreement and employment thereunder may be terminated upon 30 days' notice for any reason whatsoever.

Employee Benefits

VACATION

OPTION 1

Following the completion of _____ months of employment under this agreement, the Employee shall be entitled to receive a paid annual vacation of _____ weeks. In the event that this agreement is terminated prior to its stated expiration date, the Employee shall be entitled to a proration of any vacation benefits due; provided, however, that if the Employee has received the full vacation benefits prior to the expiration of this agreement, the Employer shall be entitled to a prorated credit to be applied against any other amounts that may be owing.

OPTION 2

You shall be entitled to receive an annual vacation of _____ weeks. In the event that you have not taken the full vacation to which you are entitled during the term of this agreement, you may receive a cash payment in lieu of such vacation or may carry such vacation forward into any additional or extended term of this agreement, provided that such vacation carried forward into a successive term of this agreement shall not exceed _____ weeks.

HOLIDAYS

OPTION 1

The Employee shall be entitled to receive the following paid holidays:

(Specify).

OPTION 2

The Employer recognizes the following holidays:

(Specify).

Comment

Obviously, employee benefits are an important part of the employee's total compensation package. Where the long-form agreement is utilized, a full description of the employee's benefit package either should be set forth in the agreement itself, or an appropriate reference to existing benefits or policies should be made. In addition to vacations and holidays, a description or reference to personal leave, sick leave, medical, life and disability insurance coverages, retirement plans, and other employee benefits, if applicable, should be made.

Reimbursement of Expenses

OPTION 1

The Employee shall be entitled to reimbursement of all expenses authorized and reasonably incurred in the performance of his duties under this agreement.

OPTION 2

You will be reimbursed for all expenses incurred by you, provided that such expenses are reasonably related to the performance of your duties under this agreement and are consistent with the company's established policies and practices. To receive reimbursement, you must provide the company with an itemized account of all expenditures, along with suitable receipts therefore.

Comment

The specifics of business expense reimbursement need not be set forth in the employment agreement if the details thereof are contained in well-articulated policies or written guidelines that are distributed to the employees. Occasionally the guidelines for employee business expense reimbursement are set forth on the face of the forms which employees must fill out and submit in order to obtain reimbursement.

Limitation on Outside Activities

OPTION 1

The Employee agrees that he will devote his entire time, attention, and energies in the performance of his duties and responsibilities under this agreement. The Employee shall not engage in any other business activity, whether or not pursued for profit (other than personal investments which do not require active participation in other business enterprises), unless specifically authorized by the Employer in writing.

OPTION 2

You understand that during the term of this agreement, your working time and efforts shall be devoted exclusively to the company. You further agree that you will not actively engage in any other business or employment other than that for the company without prior written authorization therefor.

Confidentiality of Trade Secrets and Customer Lists

OPTION 1

During the course of employment, the Employee may learn or have access to certain trade secrets and proprietary information belonging to the Employer. Such trade secrets and proprietary information include, but are not limited to, confidential customer lists, manufacturing processes, and other information relating to the Employer's operation which is not generally known and/or disclosed to the public. The Employee acknowledges that such trade secrets and proprietary information are important and unique assets of the Employer. The Employee agrees that during the life of this agreement, and for a period of not less than _____ (e.g., five) years thereafter, the Employee will not disclose to others or utilize for his own benefit, or for the benefit of another, any such trade secrets or proprietary information, without the express prior written consent of the Employer.

OPTION 2

The Employee agrees that any trade secrets or confidential information acquired by him during the course of his employment is both confidential and essential to the Employer's success. The Employee agrees that he will not utilize or reveal such information to others, either during the life of this agreement or at any time thereafter, except where such use and disclosure is necessary for the performance of his duties and functions as an employee under the terms of this agreement or authorized in writing by the Employer.

OPTION 3

During the course of your employment, you may have access to certain information which is both confidential and important to the company's operation. You agree that you will not disclose or utilize such information at any time, whether during the life of this agreement or thereafter, except where such use or disclosure is authorized by the express written consent of the company.

Comment

The covenant not to use and/or disclose confidential information is often one of the more important provisions in an employment agreement, especially where the employee is a top level manager or has unique access to the company's trade secrets. The more critical the confidential information may be to the employer's success, the more important it is to protect that information from unauthorized use either during the life of the agreement or following the employee's termination.

Some information, such as a particular manufacturing process, is useful only as long as it may be on the cutting edge of technology. Other information, similarly, may have value only if it is relatively recent, such as a customer's buying habits and history, the names of "current" contacts within a customer's operation, and so forth. Where a company's trade secrets are of a limited or decreasing value over time, it is recommended that the covenant not to utilize or disclose such information be similarly limited in time (e.g., one year, two years, five years).

Since this covenant and the covenant not to compete are probably the two most frequently litigated issues in suits to enforce employment agreements (excluding wrongful discharge cases), care should be taken to assure that the restriction on use or disclosure is reasonably related to the employer's business needs. This is especially true where the distinction between a trade secret and an employee's development of experience and expertise in a particular field may be fuzzy. If the provision can be interpreted or construed to limit the employee's use of his or her own developed expertise, the provision will likely be invalidated to that extent as being overly restrictive upon the employee's ability to earn a living, unless the provision is reasonably limited in time and geographic area.

It is also recommended that the covenant include a provision that the use or disclosure of confidential information may be authorized by the employer on request. In this way, the employer can better argue that the restrictions are reasonable, even though questionable in terms of duration or scope, because they explicitly provide a means by which the employee may escape the potentially harsh consequences of the provision's restrictions. Indeed, if the employee has not sought written authorization from the company, the burden will likely shift to him or her to establish the reasonableness of his or her actions.

Covenant Not to Compete

OPTION 1

The Employee agrees that for a period of _____ years following the termination of this agreement for any reason whatsoever, he will not engage in business activities, whether directly or indirectly, that compete with the Employer's business, unless such business is located outside _____ [specify geographical area]. The Employee agrees that the term directly or indirectly engaging in business includes ownership in, employment by, or contracting with any person, firm, partnership or corporation that is engaged in competition with the Employer by manufacturing, selling or providing the same or similar products or services as are manufactured, sold or provided by the Employer within the geographical area set forth above.

OPTION 2

You agree that for a period of _____ years following the termination of this agreement for any reason whatsoever, you will not own, be employed by or be connected with, whether directly or indirectly, any other firm, company, or business enterprise that competes with the company within _____ (specify geographical area; for example, a radius of 50 miles, Southern California, etc.).

Comment

To be enforceable, a covenant not to compete must be reasonably limited both in duration and geographic area. If the covenant is overbroad in either respect, it will be held to be unenforceable as an unwarranted and unreasonable intrusion upon the employee's ability to earn a living following the termination of his or her employment. If the employee is a relatively low-level manager who has little or no access to confidential information, a covenant not to compete will probably be deemed to be unenforceable, even if restricted in scope. Instead the covenant should be utilized only for those individuals whose contributions to the company's business are unique or particularly critical to the company's success, or who have significant access to the company's trade secrets or other confidential information.

The scope of the geographic limitation in a covenant not to compete should be carefully considered. The geographic limitation should be only so broad as is required to protect the company's legitimate interests, but no more. For example, if the company's business is local in scope, it is unreasonable to prohibit an employee from engaging in the same type of business in another city or county, unless the company had established plans to move into those areas in the immediate future. If the company's business is either statewide or nationwide, however, and where the employee could seriously affect the company's position by engaging in a competitive business within the company's territory of operation, a broad covenant is more likely to be enforced, again provided it is reasonably limited in time (e.g., one year, two years, five years).

Covenant Not to Recruit

OPTION 1

The Employee recognizes that the Employer's workforce constitutes an important and vital aspect of its business. The Employee agrees, therefore, that for a period of _____ (e.g., two) years following the termination of this agreement for any reason whatsoever, he shall not solicit any of the Employer's then-current employees to terminate their employment with the Employer and to become employed by any firm, company or other business enterprise with which the Employee may then be connected.

OPTION 2

If you should leave your employment with the company for any reason whatsoever, you agree that you will not recruit or solicit any of the company's employees in favor of employment with another firm or business at any time within _____ (e.g., 12 months) following the termination of your employment.

Comment

The covenant not to recruit is a little-used provision which is probably enforceable, again provided it is reasonably limited in duration. Since the employer's work force is a principal and significant asset, the covenant should be considered for inclusion to protect the company's managerial and technical work force, especially where the individual may be in a position to effectively entice others to leave their employment.

Ownership of Inventions and Patents

OPTION 1

All right, title and interest in and to any inventions, patents, trademarks, copyrights, ideas, and other developments or improvements conceived by the Employee during the term of this agreement shall be the sole and exclusive property of the Employer for any and all purposes and uses whatsoever, provided such inventions, patents, and other items constituting intellectual property shall have been created, developed, or conceived in connection with or arising out of the Employee's employment under this agreement. Inventions, patents and other items constituting intellectual property that are created or developed outside the course of the Employee's employment hereunder shall be submitted to the Employer for review and consideration; the Employer shall have the right of first refusal to purchase or otherwise obtain the rights thereto.

OPTION 2

During the course of your employment under this agreement, you may create or develop certain ideas, products, programs or processes that are subject to protection under the patent, trademark, copyright, and related laws. You agree that any and all such items deemed by the company to be of value shall be the sole and exclusive property of the company.

Comment

It is not uncommon for provisions relating to the ownership of inventions and patents to go beyond those items developed during the course and scope of employment and to cover items conceived during the employee's personal "free time." Although such provisions have been enforced, they smack of overreaching and unnecessarily intrude on the individual's non-working time creativity. If a broad provision is desired to take advantage of the individual's innovative talents, it is suggested that inventions unrelated to the company's normal operations and developed during the employee's free time be subject to the employer's right of first refusal to purchase the rights thereto or to the employer's right to enter into a licensing agreement concerning their use.

RETURN OF PROPERTY

OPTION 1

The Employee agrees that within five days of the termination of this agreement for any reason whatsoever, the Employee will return to the Employer all property in the Employee's possession belonging to the Employer, including but not limited to manuals, business documents, reports, memoranda, computer print-outs, customer lists, credit cards, keys, identification, product, and automobiles.

OPTION 2

You agree that all company property in your possession of any kind or nature whatsoever, shall be returned to the company immediately on termination of this agreement for any reason whatsoever.

Covenant to Notify Management Regarding Unlawful Acts or Practices

OPTION 1

It is the Employer's policy and practice to comply in full with all governmental laws and regulations. In the event that the Employee is aware of or believes that the Employer, or its officers or employees have violated or are violating any such laws or regulations, the Employee agrees that he shall immediately bring all such actual or suspected violations to the company's attention in writing in order that the situation may be properly investigated and appropriate action be taken, if necessary.

OPTION 2

The company endeavors to assure full compliance with all governmental laws and regulations. If at any time you believe or suspect that a violation has occurred or is likely to occur, it is in the best interests of all that you report the facts to the company so that an investigation and appropriate corrective action, if necessary, may be taken; you agree to do so.

Comment

Although covenants to notify management have not been widely used, they can be useful to nip problems in the bud. In addition, the covenant can be useful to establish that certain conduct (e.g., sexual harassment) did not occur because the employee failed to complain or notify management of the facts at or about the time that they allegedly occurred.

Some commentors have suggested that the covenant go so far as to preclude an employee from filing a complaint with the governmental agency having jurisdiction over particular alleged wrongful conduct unless the employee first notifies management of the facts and permits it to investigate and correct the asserted problem. Such a restriction is probably unenforceable on its face, however, and may negate any presumptions that otherwise might apply in the event an employee fails to notify management of actual or suspected violations.

Termination of Employment

OPTION 1

This agreement and employment hereunder may be terminated by either the Employer or the Employee at any time and for any reason whatsoever upon giving 30 days' written notice to the other of such termination.

OPTION 2

The parties hereto agree that employment under this agreement is employment at will and that this agreement may be terminated by either party at any time on notice to the other, with or without cause.

OPTION 3

This agreement and the Employee's employment hereunder may be terminated by the Employer, at its option, at any time upon the occurrence of any of the following:

1. Termination, reorganization, or fundamental change in the Employer's operations
2. Misconduct of the Employee, including, but not limited to, any of the following:
   a. The commission of any act or acts of dishonesty
   b. The willful failure or refusal to perform assigned duties and functions

    c. Failure or refusal to comply with established policies, practices and procedures

    d. Failure or refusal to comply with the terms of this agreement

    e. Insubordination

3. Carelessness or incompetence by the Employee in the performance of assigned duties and functions

4. Death

5. Retirement

6. Illness or disability rendering the Employee incapable of performing his assigned duties and functions for a period of _____(e.g., four) months

In the event that this agreement is terminated for any of the reasons stated above, the Employer's sole liability to the Employee shall be the payment of all salaries, wages, and other monies earned by the Employee, and the reimbursement of all reasonable business expenses incurred by the Employee up to and including the date of termination. The Employer's exercise of its right to terminate this agreement shall be without prejudice to any other remedy to which it may be entitled at law, in equity, or under this agreement.

This agreement and the Employee's employment hereunder may be terminated for any reason not specified above upon 30 days' notice.

Comment

The termination provision, as with the provision defining the term of the agreement, is of primary importance to the employer in wrongful discharge or breach of contract actions. The provision may be either general or very specific in defining the conditions upon which employment may be terminated. It may specify that employment, notwithstanding the agreement, is employment at will and may be terminated at any time and for any reason upon notice to the other. Such provisions have been enforced.

At the other end of the spectrum, the agreement may enumerate each and every ground or condition authorizing termination. If specific conditions are enumerated, the provisions have an even greater likelihood of being enforced, and a proper termination upheld, provided the conditions are met. Whether or not those conditions are met, however, often becomes a question of fact which almost certainly can be placed before a jury or other trier of fact to determine. Accordingly, wherever specific provisions authorizing the termination of employment are included in an employment agreement, the more general provision authorizing termination for any reason upon 30 days' notice should also be included as a safety valve against second-guessing by a jury or the failure of any particular condition.

Dispute Resolution Procedure

OPTION 1

Any claim or controversy arising out of or relating to this agreement, or any asserted breach thereof, shall be resolved in accordance with the following procedures:

1. All claims, disputes, or controversies relating to the interpretation, application or enforcement of this agreement, including any asserted breaches thereof, shall be reduced to writing and submitted to the other party no later than _____ (e.g., 10) days following the acts, occurrences or omissions giving rise to the claim, controversy or dispute.

2. The parties shall meet within _____ (e.g., five) days of the submission of any such claim, controversy or dispute in an effort to informally resolve the same.

3. In the event that the parties are unable to settle the claim, controversy or dispute informally among themselves, either party shall have the option of submitting the same to final and binding arbitration not later than _____ (e.g., 10) days thereafter in accordance with the Voluntary Labor Arbitration Rules of the American Arbitration Association. If so submitted, the arbitrator shall have no authority to alter, amend, change or modify any provision of this agreement.

4. Any claim, controversy or dispute not submitted to the Employer and/or to arbitration within the time limits set forth above shall be deemed to be waived and abandoned for all purposes.

5. It is expressly agreed and understood that the procedures set forth herein for the resolution of claims, controversies or disputes shall be exclusive, and neither party shall have the right to institute judicial proceedings for damages or enforcement of this agreement, except as may be necessary to compel specific performance of this provision.

6. In the event judicial action is instituted to compel specific performance of this provision, the prevailing party thereto shall be entitled to recover its costs of suit and reasonable attorney's fees incurred. The costs of arbitration, including the fees of the arbitrator, shall be split equally between the parties.

OPTION 2

Any disputes or differences arising between the parties concerning the interpretation, application or enforcement of this agreement shall be submitted to final and binding arbitration in accordance with the Voluntary Labor Arbitration Rules of the American Arbitration Association; such arbitration shall be the parties' exclusive remedy. In rendering his decision, the arbitrator shall have no authority to alter, amend, modify or disregard any provision of this agreement. All costs of arbitration, including the arbitrator's fees, shall be borne equally between the parties, unless the arbitrator finds that any claimed breach was willful and in bad faith, in which case the arbitrator may order that all such costs and fees be borne by the losing party.

OPTION 3

Any and all claims, controversies or disputes arising out of the interpretation, application, or enforcement of this agreement, including alleged breaches thereof, shall be reduced to writing and submitted to the other party within _____ (e.g., 10) days of the acts, events, occurrences or omissions, or the party's initial knowledge thereof, giving rise to the claim, controversy or dispute. Any such matter not reduced to writing and submitted to the other party within said time period shall be deemed waived for any and all purposes, and thereafter may not be the basis of any action at law.

The parties shall meet within _____ (e.g., five) days of the submission of any such written claim or dispute in an effort to informally settle the same and/or to narrow the issues.

In the event that the parties are unable to informally resolve the dispute among themselves, either party may refer the matter to final and binding arbitration in accordance with the Voluntary Labor Arbitration Rules of the American Arbitration Association or may institute an action at law or equity in any court of competent jurisdiction, provided, however, that in the event an action at law is instituted, the defendent may, at its option, demand that the action be dismissed and that the dispute be referred to final and binding arbitration in accordance with the provisions hereof. If submitted to arbitration, the arbitrator shall have no authority to alter, amend or modify any term or provision of this agreement.

Comment

A comprehensive and impartial dispute settlement mechanism is perhaps the best means to control the forum in which disputes with employees, including disputes involving alleged wrongful terminations, are heard and resolved. Certainly, a comprehensive procedure will not bar an employee from enforcing statutory rights and pursuing statutory remedies in the courts or before appropriate governmental agencies. Findings resulting from an impartial arbitration conducted under an employment agreement's dispute resolution procedures, however, may be determinative of the statutory claims under the doctrine of collateral estoppel.

In order to ensure impartiality, it is recommended that the resources and procedures of the American Arbitration Association, or some other acceptable format providing for final and binding arbitration, be utilized. If the grievance procedure is biased in favor of the employer, or does not provide for a final and binding resolution of disputes, the benefit of having a procedure is greatly minimized; the employee will likely be permitted to pursue his or her remedies in court, leaving the employer open to all of the dangers of being second-guessed by a sympathetic jury.

Some procedures expressly provide that attorneys may not participate at any stage. This is unwise, for it places the employee at an actual or perceived disadvantage, especially if the company representatives have particular skills or experience in handling matters, such as arbitrations.

Finally, although the arbitration of disputes involves definite costs, those costs are insignificant when compared with the costs of litigation in the event an employee pursues court action. It is best, therefore, not to be penny-wise and dollar-foolish when it comes to implementing a full and impartial procedure for the resolution of employee disputes.

Remedies for Breach

OPTION 1

The parties agree that the breach of any term of this agreement, other than the payment of money, is one that would cause immediate and irreparable injury and damage to the other party. The party so injured, in addition to any other remedies available under this agreement, may obtain specific performance of the provisions hereof, and any other equitable relief from either an arbitrator or a court of competent jurisdiction.

OPTION 2

The parties agree that the Employee's performance under this agreement is of a special, unique, extraordinary and intellectual character and that a breach by the employee of any of his duties and obligations will cause the Employer serious and irreparable injury which cannot be adequately compensated in damages. The parties agree, therefore, that in the event of the Employee's breach, the Employer shall be entitled to specific performance and any other equitable relief deemed to be appropriate by a court of competent jurisdiction to prevent further breaches of this agreement by the Employee. Any action for specific performance or other equitable relief shall be without prejudice to any other rights that the Employer may have to recover damages or other appropriate remedy for such breach.

OPTION 3

The parties agree that if the Employer terminates the Employee's employment in violation of this agreement, the damages sustained by the Employee would be difficult to ascertain. The parties agree, therefore, that in the event of such a termination, the Employer shall be liable to the Employee for a sum of money equal to the lesser of the Employee's salary for _____ (e.g., three) months, together with estimated bonuses, or the Employee's salary and estimated bonuses to the end of the term of this agreement which the Employee might have earned had he been permitted to fully perform his obligations hereunder. Such monies shall be paid as liquidated damages and not as a penalty for such breach. The payment or award of such amounts shall be the exclusive monetary remedy to which the Employee may be entitled in the event of the Employer's breach.

OPTION 4

The parties agree that in any action or arbitration to enforce the terms of this agreement the prevailing party shall be entitled to recover its costs, including reasonable attorney's fees, incurred in maintaining or defending any such action.

Comment

In some situations, the remedies for breach provision may be inconsistent with the dispute resolution procedures. Care should be taken to assure that the provisions are either consistent, or any inconsistencies resolved. For example, it is appropriate to except certain breaches (such as breaches of the covenants not to compete, not to disclose or utilize information, not to solicit employees, etc.) from the mandatory arbitration provisions. In this manner, the employer is free to pursue its legal and equitable remedies in a court of law. Of course an arbitrator has the authority to issue injunctive relief if the agreement so provides; the procedures involved in obtaining equitable relief from an arbitrator, however, may not be as swift as the procedures available in the courts. The main concern, of course, is to cover all potential disputes arising out of the employment relationship, to the extent permitted by law, under either the dispute resolution procedure or the remedies for breach provision, or some appropriate combination thereof.

Waiver of Breach

OPTION 1

It is agreed and understood that either party may waive a breach of this agreement by the other party; provided, however, that any such waiver shall not be deemed to constitute a waiver of any subsequent breach.

OPTION 2

Either party may waive or excuse the failure of the other party to perform any provision of this agreement. Any such waiver shall not preclude the enforcement of this agreement on any subsequent breach, whether or not similar in character.

Cooperation After Retirement or Termination

OPTION 1

In the event the Employee retires or is terminated, the Employee agrees that he will cooperate fully with the Employer on any or all of the following matters:

1. The return of all books, records, or other property belonging to the Employer;
2. Providing the Employer with all necessary information related to the completion and/or orderly transfer of work in progress; and
3. Cooperating with the Employer in all such other matters as are necessary and reasonable.

In the event that the Employer requires the Employee's assistance following retirement or termination, the Employer shall pay to the Employee an amount equal to the Employee's salary upon retirement or termination for the time spent performing such additional duties and functions as are requested.

OPTION 2

On termination or retirement, you agree that you will cooperate with the company in order to effect an orderly transfer of your work in progress to such other employee or employees as the company may designate. In return, the company shall compensate you for all time spent by you in accordance herewith at an hourly or daily rate computed on the basis of your salary at the time of your termination or retirement.

Modification, Renewal, or Extension

OPTION 1

This agreement may be modified, renewed or extended at any time upon the mutual agreement and consent of the parties all modifications hereto shall be reduced to writing and signed by the parties.

OPTION 2

Unless expressly terminated in accordance with the provisions hereof, this agreement may be modified, renewed, or extended for an additional term of _____ (e.g., one year) on mutual agreement of the parties.

OPTION 3

This agreement shall not be renewed, modified, or extended, except upon written agreement of the parties. In the event that the Employee remains employed by the Employer beyond the stated term of this agreement, or any written renewals or extensions thereof, the Employee's employment shall be terminable at will upon notice for any reason whatsoever, but shall be subject to all other provisions set forth herein.

Comment

Although employment agreements are often renewed or extended simply by continuing employment beyond the stated term, it is recommended that the employer establish a practice of executing either new agreements or written extensions of expiring agreements, again for a specific term. Option 3 perhaps gives the employer greater protection in the event of a subsequent wrongful discharge or breach of contract suit by the employee; however, the employer, as a matter of practice, should implement an affirmative procedure whereby employment agreements are automatically reviewed shortly before their stated termination dates and new written agreements prepared.

Effect of Prior Agreements or Understandings

OPTION 1

This agreement constitutes the entire agreement between the parties. Any and all prior agreements or understandings between the parties that are not embodied in this agreement shall be of no force or effect.

OPTION 2

This agreement constitutes the entire agreement between the parties and supersedes all prior agreements or understandings concerning the subject matter hereof. The terms of this agreement may not be modified, except by written agreement signed by the party against whom enforcement of any such modification is sought.

OPTION 3

This agreement supersedes any and all prior agreements or understandings between the parties and constitutes the entire agreement concerning the subject matter set forth herein. Modifications of the terms or conditions of this agreement shall be of no force or effect unless the same shall have been reduced to writing and signed by the parties.

Comment

The sample provisions above obviously differ somewhat in scope. Options 1 and 2 are standard "zipper" clauses, whereas Option 3 provides that the agreement is complete only as to the subject matter covered therein. Option 3, therefore, leaves open the possibility that unarticulated policies and procedures, such as those contained in a company manual, may apply to the extent that they are not inconsistent with or covered by the express provisions of the employment agreement. This provision, if one is to be included, therefor must be drafted with the foregoing consideration in mind.

Savings Clause

OPTION 1

It is the intent of the parties that this agreement be in compliance with all governing laws and regulations. In the event that any provision hereof is unenforceable, all remaining provisions of the agreement shall not be affected thereby, and shall remain in full force and effect.

OPTION 2

Should any provision of this agreement be determined to be invalid or unenforceable by any final decision of a court of competent jurisdiction or by any final determination of a state or federal agency having jurisdiction over the subject matter, such provision or provisions shall be construed to the extent feasible to conform with applicable law or regulation. Any decision invalidating any provision of this agreement shall not affect the validity or enforceability of any other provision of this agreement.

Applicable Law

OPTION 1

This agreement shall be interpreted and construed in accordance with the laws of the State of _____.

Comment

The choice of applicable law may well be an important consideration for employers having interstate operations. The choice of law must be reasonably related to the employment and is generally limited either to the state in which the employer's primary operations are located, or the state in which the employee is expected to perform his or her services under the employment agreement. As some states recognize numerous exceptions from the employment-at-will doctrine and/or permit the imposition of punitive damages for breaches of contract, whereas other states are still extremely conservative in their approach, it is wise to consult with a knowledgeable labor attorney in advance to determine which body of law will be the most advantageous from the employer's point of view.

TABLE OF CASES

Abella v. Foote Memorial Hospital, Inc. 79
Abron v. Black & Decker Mfg. Co. 304
Adair v. United States 6–7
Adler v. American Standard Corp. 27
Albermarle Paper Co. v. Moody 313
Alexander's, Inc. 136
Amalgamated Meat Cutters, Local 540 v. Neuhoff Brothers Packers, Inc. 125
American Airlines 275–276
Arie v. Intertherm, Inc. 100
Associated Gen. Contractors of Mass., Inc. v. Altshular 325
Bauer v. Bailar 313
Becket v. Walton Becket & Associates, Inc. 24
Bender Ship Repair, Inc. v. Stevens 19
Blaisdell v. Lewis 5
Blau v. Del Monte Corp. 79
Bodewig v. K-Mart, Inc. 138
Bondtex Corp. 140–141
Bravo v. Board of Educ. of Chicago 317
Brawther v. H&R Block, Inc. 362
Britton v. South Bend Community Schood Corp. 323
Brockmeyer v. Dun & Bradstreet 8, 11, 30
Buscemi v. McDonnell Douglas Corp. 23
Cancellier v. Federated Department Stores 31
Carney v. Memorial Hospital 144
Carter v. Gallagher 311
Chamberlain v. Bissell 99–100
Clearly v. American Airlines, Inc. 30–31, 80, 101, 102
Cloutier v. Great Atlantic & Pacific Tea Co. 17
Commonwealth Oil Refining Co. v. EEOC 305
Conboy 78
Consolidated Rail Corp., v. Darrone 58
Contractors Ass'n of E. Penn. v. Secretary of Labor 325
Copeland v. Usery 314
Cordle v. General Hugh Mercer Corp. 20
Cort v. Ash 47
Cort. v. Bristol-Meyers Co. 25–26, 138

403

Craik v. Minnesota State Univ. Bd.	306
Crosier v. United Parcel Service, Inc.	26, 32
Crossen v. Foremost-McKesson, Inc.	13–14, 107–108
Daniel v. Magma Copper Co.	30
De Briar v. Minturn	5–6
De Funis v. Odegaard	325
Delancy v. Taco Time International, Inc.	9, 10
Deveraux v. Geary	323
Diaz v. American Tel. & Tel.	322
Dockery v. Lampart Table Co.	16
Donahue v. Shoe Corp. of Am.	313
Dothard v. Rawlinson	312
Drzewiecki v. H&R Block, Inc.	34
Duncantell v. Universal Life Ins.	144
EEOC v. Local 638	322
Firefighters Local Union 1784 v. Stotts	321–322, 323
FMC Corp.	132
Foley v. Community Oil Co.	362–363
Forman v. Bri Corp.	361–362
Fortune v. National Cash Register Co.	30
Frampton v. Central Indiana Gas Co.	16
Garibaldi v. Lucky Food Stores, Inc.	13, 22
Gates v. Life of Montana Ins. Co.	31, 93, 101–102, 106
Geary v. United States Steel Corp.	19, 28
General Motors Corp. v. Piskor	140, 147
Glenn v. Clearman's Golden Cock Inn	21–22
Goodnough v. Alexanders	134
Great Am. Fed. Sav. & Loan Ass'n v. Novatny	43
Green v. Missouri Pac. R.R.	311
Gregory v. Litton Systems, Inc.	311
Griggs v. Duke Power Co.	311
Grouse v. Group Health Plan Inc.	363
Hansrote v. Amer. Industrial Techologies, Inc.	13
Harless v. First National Bank of Fairmont	13, 27
Harmon v. La Crosse Tribune	15
Harrison v. Arrow Metal Products Corp.	144–145
Harrison v. Lewis	310
Hathaway v. Bennett	6
Hedrick v. Center for Comprehensive Alcohol Treatment	97–98
Heideck v. Kent General Hospital, Inc.	94
Hentzel v. The Singer Company	17–18, 22
Hepp v. Lockheed-California Co.	97
Hicks v. Crown Zellerbach Corp.	314
Hillsman v. Sutter Community Hospitals	75–76, 107
Hishon v. King & Spaulding	353–356
Hodge v. Evans Financial Corp.	363
Hodgson v. First Fed. Sav. & Loan Ass'n of Broward County	312
Huskie v. Griffen	148
International Nickel Co.	139
Jackson v. Kinark Corp.	20
Johnson v. National Beef Packing Co.	94
Johnson v. Pike Corp. of Am.	312
Johnson v. Railway Express Agency	43
Johnson v. Trans World Airlines, Inc.	23
Jones v. Cleland	301
Kalman v. The Grand Union Co.	15
Kavanaugh v. KLM Royal Dutch Airlines	24
Khanna v. Microdata Corp.	24, 32
Kromnick v. School Dist. of Philadelphia	322
La Fleur v. Cleveland Bd. of Educ.	317
La Rivera v. EEOC	322
Larsen v. Motor Supply Co.	20
Lewis v. Equitable Life Assurance	143
Local 53 v. Vogler	312

Lo Re v. Chase Manhattan Corp. 305

Maddaloni v. Western Massachusetts Bus Lines 31

Magnan v. Anaconda Industries, Inc. 10

Mallard v. Boring 19

Martin v. New York Life Insurance Co. 6

McCullough Iron Co. v. Carpenter 6

McDonnell-Douglas Corp. v. Green 317

McIntosh v. Murphy 362

McNulty v. Borden, Inc. 12

Meredith v. C.E. Walther, Inc. 11, 24

Merkel v. Scovill, Inc. 10

Midgett v. Sackett-Chicago, Inc. 23

Miskotoni v. Michigan National Bank-West 19

Mitford v. DeLasala 108

Monahan v. Sims 146

Monge v. Beebe Rubber Co. 29–30

Montalvo v. Zamora 10–11, 25

Moore v. Home Insurance Co. 23

Munoz v. Kaiser Steel Corp. 355

National Labor Relations Board v. J. Weingarten, Inc. 252, 277–278

Nees v. Hocks 19

Newfield v. Insurance Company of the West 36

New York State Div. of Human Rights v. New York-Pennsylvania Professional Baseball League 312

Novosel v. Nationwide Insurance Co. 9, 25

Olquin v. Inspiration Consolidated Copper Co. 23

Orr v. Ward 6

Ostrofe v. H.S. Crocker Co. 12

Palmateer v. International Harvester Co. 27–28

Palmer v. District Bd. of Trustees 301

Parham v. Southwestern Bell Tel. Co. 301

Parnar v. Americana Hotels, Inc. 9, 11, 30

Payne v. Western & Atlantic Railroad 4

Payton v. City of Santa Clara 119, 149

Peller v. Retail Credit Co. 136

Perks v. Firestone Tire & Rubber Co. 20

Perry v. Hartz Mountain Corp. 12, 13

Perryman v. Johnson Products Co. 317

Petermann v. International Brotherhood of Teamsters 7–8, 9, 10, 12

Petrik v. Monarch Printing Corp. 27

Picker X-Ray Corp. 131

Pierce v. Ortho Pharmaceutical Corp. 14–15

Pine River State Bank v. Mettille 35, 95–96, 98–99

Portillo v. G.T. Price Products, Inc. 16–17

Prentiss v. Ledyard 6

Price v. Carmack Datsun, Inc. 23

Pugh v. See's Candies, Inc. 34–35

Rabago-Alvarez v. Dart Industries, Inc. 358

Redgrave v. Boston Symphony Orchestra 25

Robinson v. Lorillard Corp. 314

Rowe v. General Motors Corp. 312

Rulon-Miller v. International Business Machines Corp. 26, 31, 101, 102, 156

Salimi v. Farmers Insurance Group 104

Schipani v. Ford Motor Company 107

Schultz v. Simmons Fur Co. 362

Schwartz v. Michigan Sugar Co. 18

Scott v. Gulf Oil Corp. 79

Scott v. Lane 363

Shapiro v. Wells Fargo Realty Advisors Inc. 8, 31, 78, 83

Sheets v. Teddy's Frosted Foods, Inc. 13, 28

Sheriff v. Revell, Inc. 355

Simpson v. Western Graphics Corporation 104–105

Smith v. Atlas Off-Shore Boat Service, Inc. 24

Smith v. Theobald 362

Smith v. Union Oil Co. of Cal. 301

Smith v. Western Elec. Co.	317
Southern Ill. Builders Ass'n v. Ogilvie	325
Southwest Gas Corp. v. Ahmad	96–97
Speciale v. Tekronix, Inc.	104
Staggs v. Blue Cross of Maryland, Inc.	99
State v. Community Distributors, Inc.	121
Strauss v. A.L. Randall Co.	21
Suchodolski v. Michigan Consolidated Gas Co.	15, 28
Sugarman v. Dougall	311
Tameny v. Atlantic Richfield Co.	11–12, 37
Thomas v. Basic Magnesia	302
Thompson v. St. Regis Paper Co.	14, 99, 106
Tiranno v. Sears, Roebuck & Co.	100, 106
Toussaint v. Blue Cross & Blue Shield of Michigan	35, 95, 102, 104, 105–106, 107
Trombetta v. Detroit, Toledo & Ironton Railroad	18
United States v. County of Fairfax	308, 313
United States v. Household Finance Corp.	305, 313
United States v. St. Louis-San Francisco Ry. Co.	314
United States v. U.S. Steel Corp.	308
United States v. Virginia Elec. & Power Co.	308, 310, 311
United Steelworkers of Am. v. Weber	323, 325
Van Aken v. Young	322
Vanguards of Cleveland v. Cleveland	322
Walker v. Northern San Diego County Hospital District	100
Waters v. Olinkraft	301
Watkins v. L.M. Berry & Co.	130–131
Weiner v. McGraw-Hill, Inc.	35, 97
Wheeler v. Caterpiller Tractor Co.	18–19, 28
Whirlpool Corp. v. Marshall	59
Witt v. Forest Hospital, Inc.	28
Women's Comm. For EEO v. National Broadcasting Co.	316
Wygant v. Jackson Bd. of Educ.	322, 323–324
Yartzoff v. Democrat-Herald Publishing Co.	96, 99

INDEX

Administrative hearing, 208
  preparation for, 221–224, 224–232
Administrative law judge, 208, 225–226, 227,
  228–229, 232, 233
Affirmative action plan, 300–352
  announcement of, 343
  checklist for, 331–332
  committee for, 351
  compliance officer for, 349
  current status of, 321–324
  EEO audit system monitoring, 318–320
  equal employment opportunity, differing
    from, 300, 351
  goals and timetables set for, 306–307, 351
    data sources for developing, 340–341
    worksheet for, 334–339
  implementation, 302–303, 349–351
  instituting, 300–301
  letter to outside sources for, 345
  manager of, 302–303
  positive action programs for, 307–318
    benefits and employment conditions,
      316–317
    disciplinary action, 317
    recruitment, 308–309
    selection procedures, 309–313
    termination policy, 317
    union contracts, 317–318
    upward mobility system, 313–316
    wage and salary structure, 316
  problem area and deficiency questionnaire
    for, 333
  publication of, 303–305, 348
  references sources for, 342
  sample, 346–347

  supportive company and community
    programs for, 320–321
  terms pertaining to, 328–330
  workforce assessment and utilization for,
    305–306
  written equal employment opportunity
    commitment needed for, 302, 344, 348
  see also Discrimination charges
Age discrimination, wrongful discharge based
  on, 20–21. *See also* Discrimination
  charges, wrongful discharge based on
Age Discrimination in Employment Act of
  1967 (ADEA), 2, 44, 46, 53–56, 164–
  165, 168, 169, 177, 178, 181–183, 299,
  326
AIDS, tests for, 128
Alcohol tests, restrictions in, 125–128
Antitrust violations, as basis for wrongful
  discharge claims, 13
Application to reopen, 208–215
Arbitrary discharges, risk of wrongful
  discharge reduced by avoiding, 37–39
Arbitration:
  electronic surveillance and, 131–132
  as internal review procedure, 85–86
  intrusive policies and, 138–139
  lie detector program and, 125
Arbitration grievance, as internal review
  procedure, 85
Arrest records, disclosure of, 141–142, 155
At-will doctrine, 1–40
  contractual exceptions to, 33–39
    express or implied, 33
    independent consideration rule and, 33–
      35

At-will doctrine, contractual exceptions to (*Continued*)
  statute of frauds and, 36
  employer reserving right of, 106–108
  history of, 4–7
  implied covenant of good faith and fair dealing and, 29–33
  judicial erosion of, *see* At-will doctrine, public policy exception
  public policy exception, 7–9. *See also* At-will doctrine, refusal to commit unlawful act; At-will doctrine, retaliation for exercising lawful right; At-will doctrine, "whistleblower" cases
    definition of, 8–9
    Petermann decision and, 7–8
  refusal to commit unlawful act, 9–16
    antitrust violations, 11–13
    bribery and dishonest conduct, 13–14
    ethics code violation, 14–15
    perjury and false statements, 9–10
    truthful testimony against employer, 10–11
  retaliation for exercising lawful right, 9, 16–26
    constitutional rights, 25–26
    fair employment laws, 20–21
    jury duty, 19–20
    lie detectors, 20–21
    occupational safety and health, 17–19
    pension and employee benefit rights, 23
    public policy suits by union employees, 22–23
    right to sue employer, 24–25
    union or other collective activities, 21–22
    workers' compensation cases, 16–17
  traditional, 4
  "whistleblower" cases, 9
  wrongful dscharge risk reduction, 36–39
    bad faith or arbitrary discharges avoidance, 37–39
    based on implied contracts, 39
    public policy violation avoidance, 36–37

Bad faith discharges, risk of wrongful discharge reduced by avoiding, 37–39
Behavior problems, *see* Progressive discipline
Blackstone, 5
Breach of employment contract, 398–399
Bribery, wrongful discharge from employee's refusal to engage in, 13–14
Business records, as documentation for termination, 254–255

Changes, employees notified of, 83
Civil Rights Acts:
  of 1820, 162
  of 1866, 47, 162, 302
  of 1871, 47, 56–58, 162, 302
  of 1886, 56–58
  of 1964
    Title VI, 58

    Title VII, 2, 11, 21, 43, 44, 47, 51–53, 54, 55, 58, 162–164, 168–169, 170, 177, 178, 181–183, 300, 322–323, 325, 326
Civil Rights Attorney's Fees Award Act of 1976, 56
Civil Service Reform Act, 27
Clean Air Act, 45
Codes of ethics, wrongful discharge based on refusal to violate, 14–15
Collateral estoppel, after termination, 88–89
Collateral proceedings, after termination, 88–89
Collective bargaining:
  intrusive policies and, 138–139
  lie detector program and, 125
Common law defamation, employer's privilege under, 143–144
Community programs, affirmative action plan supported by, 320–321
Company programs, affirmative action plan supported by, 320–321
Competition, employment contract limiting, 390–391
Conciliation, discrimination claim resulting in, 204
Conciliation agreement, discrimination claim resulting in, 204–206
Confidential information, employment contract stipulating, 389–390
Conflicts, agreements prohibiting, 82–83
Constitutional rights:
  employee privacy and, 118–119
  wrongful discharge and, 25–26
Constructive discharge, 83
Consumer Credit Protection Act, 44, 47
Consumer protection, as basis for wrongful discharge claims, 13
Consumer Protection Act, 162
Consumer protection legislation, limitations on employer information gathering in, 132–137
Consumer reports:
  employee information from, 133, 134
  investigative, 133, 135
Continuing employment relationship, wrongful termination litigation avoided by, 79
Contracts, *see* Employment contract
Conviction and arrest records, disclosures of, 141–142, 155
Covenant not to sue or release, termination conference including, 290
Credit reporting agencies, employee information from, 132–137
Customer complaints, as documentation for termination, 255
Customer lists, employment contract stipulating, 389–390

Defamation:
  alleged in wrongful termination cases, 67
  to redress wrongful disclosure of false information, 142–145, 146–147

Defamation liability, internal company
    communications creating, 146–147
Deferred compensation, termination at will
    not restricted by, 83
Demotion, as option to termination, 280–281
Discipline, in employee handbook, 111–113.
    See also Progressive discipline
Disclosure of information, *see* Employee
    privacy, disclosure of information
Discovery, preparation for court trial and,
    221
Discrimination charges:
    administrative procedure regarding, 167–
        206
        conciliation agreement, 204–206
        information and document requests,
            197–200
        investigatory conference, 201–206
        investigatory questionnaire, 189–197
        notice of charge, 176–180
        private settlement with complainant,
            184–189
        statute of limitations, 180–184
        subpoenas, 200–201
    defending, 207–242
        administrative hearing, 224–232
        administrative hearing preparation, 221–
            224
        application to reopen, 208–215
        employer's answer, 218, 220–221
        issuance of notice of hearing, 216–217
        motion for more definite statement, 217–
            218, 219
        notice of hearing, 209, 211, 214
        recommended decision and objections,
            232–241
        settlement prior to notice of hearing,
            215–216
    probable cause, 167, 204, 206. *See also*
        Discrimination charges, defending
    wrongful discharge based on, 20–21
    see also Affirmative action plan
Discrimination law, 202
    on equal employment opportunity, 162–
        165, 167–174
    on labor relations, 161–162
Dishonest conduct, wrongful discharge from
    employee's refusal to engage in, 13–14
Dispute resolution:
    as posttermination procedure, 85–86
    procedure for employment contract, 396–
        398
Documentation, as step of progressive
    discipline, 252, 253–256
Document review, as posttermination
    procedure, 87–88
Drinking Waste Act, 45
Drug tests, restrictions in, 125–128

Education Amendments of 1972, Title IX, 44
Electronic surveillance, restrictions on, 129–
    132
Emotional distress, alleged in wrongful
    termination cases, 67

Employee benefits:
    in affirmative action plan, 316, 350
    in employment contract, 387–388
    wrongful discharge claims and, 23
Employee file, 256
    discrimination claim utilizing, 197–200
    independent review of, 256–257
    limitations on release of, 151–153
    review of as posttermination procedure,
        87–88
Employee handbook, 33, 91–114
    awareness of employee of, provision in for
        enforcement, 103–104
    as binding policy, 92–98
    decision as to violation of, 104–105
    discretion of employer retained in, 105–106
    employment contract and, 372–373
    implied covenant of good faith and fair
        dealing and, 100–102
    provisions of, as enforceable contracts, 98–
        100
    revising, avoiding wrongful termination
        litigation, 80–82
    right to terminate at will indicated in, 106–
        108
    standard of performance in, 253, 267–268
    termination of employment policy in, 262–
        267
    wrongful discharge avoided by format of,
        108–114
        conforming other documents, 113
        discipline and discharge, 111–112, 258–
            262
        fundamental rule of, 113–114
        introduction, 109–110
        merger clauses, 113
        performance reviews, 111
        probationary clauses, 110–111
        seniority clauses, 111
Employee privacy, 115–159
    constitutional right to, 118–119
    disclosure of information, 142–155
        of arrest and conviction records, 141–
            142, 155
        defamation and, 142–145, 146–147
        of lie detector tests, 155
        of medical records, 140–141, 153–154,
            159
        of nonemployment activities, 142
        of personnel records, 151–153
        service letter statute and, 142, 145–146,
            153
        wrongful disclosure of truthful but
            private information, 147–155
        wrongful disclosure of wrong
            information, 142–147
    electronic surveillance, 129–132
    employee testing restrictions, 120–129
        AIDS tests, 128
        drug and alcohol tests, 125–128
        genetic testing, 128–129
        lie detectors, 120–125, 158
    false imprisonment and, 139–140
    information gathering and, 120

Employee privacy (*Continued*)
  intrusion, 137–140
  investigative or credit agency reports and,
    132–137
  wrongful discharge and, 25–26
Employee representation, at termination
  conference, 277–278
Employee Retirement Income Security Act of
  1974 (ERISA), 2, 23, 44–45, 79, 162,
  285
Employee testing, in affirmative action plan,
  315. *See also* Employee privacy,
  employee testing restrictions
Employee Warning Report, 245, 246
Employer rules and policies, *see* Employee
  handbook
Employment agreement:
  locating and preserving, avoiding wrongful
    termination litigation, 80
  wrongful termination litigation avoided by,
    77–78
  see also Employment contract
Employment applications, wrongful
  termination litigation avoided by, 77–
  78
Employment contract, 367–402
  breach of, 398–399
  compensation in, 386–389
  confidentiality of trade secrets and
    customer lists stipulated by, 389–390
  cooperation after retirement in, 399–400
  covenant not to compete in, 390–391
  covenant not to recruit in, 391–392
  dispute resolution procedure in, 396–398
  duties described in, 385–386
  employee benefits in, 387–389
  employee manual and, 372–373
  enforcement, 375–376
  hiring letter, 373, 376–377, 378
  independent contractor status *vs.* employee,
    373–375
  inventions and property ownership in, 392–
    393
  outside activities limited by, 389
  place of performance in, 386
  prior agreements or understandings and,
    401
  reimbursement of expenses in, 388
  renewal or extension of, 400–401
  return of property stated in, 393
  savings clause of, 401–402
  short-form, 378–383
  termination provision in, 394–395, 399–
    400
  terms, 368–370
    employee balking at, 371–372
  as unenforceable contracts of adhesion,
    370–371
  unlawful acts reported to management
    stipulated in, 393–394
  use of, 368
  see also Employment agreement
Energy Reorganization Act of 1974, 45

Engagement letters, wrongful termination
  litigation avoided by, 75–77
English law, at-will employment and, 4, 5
Equal employment opportunity, 207
  affirmative action plan differing from, 300,
    351
  laws on, 161–165, 167–174, 326–327
  policy on, 344, 348
  see also Affirmative action plan;
    Discrimination law, or equal
    employment opportunity
Equal Employment Opportunity (EEO)
  agencies, 168–174, 181, 183, 184, 185,
  186, 208, 209, 210, 214, 215, 217, 218,
  224
Equal Employment Opportunity (EEO) audit,
  318–320
Equal Employment Opportunity Commission
  (EEOC), 43, 52, 54, 163–164, 168, 169,
  180, 182, 185, 186, 207, 254, 301
Equal Pay Act of 1963, 299, 326
Executive Orders:
  11246, 300, 326
  11375, 300, 326
Exit interview:
  in affirmative action plan, 317
  by human resource/personnel staff, 84–85
Explanations, as posttermination procedure,
  86
Explanatory memo, application to reopen
  and, 215
External mediation, as alternative to
  conventional litigation, 296

Fact finders, for dispute resolution, 86
Fact-finding conference, *see* Investigatory
  conference, discrimination claim and
Factual arguments, 210
Fair Credit Reporting Act (FCRA), 133, 134–
  135, 136–137
Fair employment laws, wrongful discharge
  and, 20–21. *See also* Equal Employment
  Opportunity (EEO)
Fair Employment Practices Committee, 44
Fair Labor Standards Act (FLSA), 43, 50, 51,
  162
False imprisonment, 139–140
False statements, wrongful discharge cases
  from employee's refusal to make, 9–10
Federal Employers' Liability Act, 45
Federal Railroad Safety Act, 45
Field, David Dudley, 6
Field Code, 6
Final order, 238, 241
Formal severance plan, 285
Frauds, statute of, 36
Free speech, wrongful discharge and, 25

Genetic testing, restrictions on, 128
Golden handcuffs, termination conference
  negotiating, 286–288
Golden parachutes, termination conference
  negotiating, 286–288

Good faith and fair dealing, wrongful discharge and, 26. *See also* Implied covenant of good faith and fair dealing
Grievance procedure, lie detector program and, 125
Guideline, of EEOC, 310

Headhunters, investigative consumer report and, 135
Healthful workplace, wrongful discharge in retaliation for demanding, 17–19
Hearing *de novo*, 227
Hiring letter, 373, 376–377, 378
Hiring practices, wrongful termination litigation avoided by, 74–79. *See also* Employment contract; Wrongful hiring
Holidays, in employment contract, 390
Human resource/personnel staff development, *see* Wrongful termination litigation, defending against, human resource/personnel staff development
Human Rights Law, in New York State, 183–184

Implied contracts, avoiding wrongful discharge suits based on, 39
Implied covenant of good faith and fair dealing:
   at-will employees recovering from wrongful discharge based on, 29–33
   employee handbooks and, 100–102
   as termination restriction, 67
Implied-in-fact contract theory, as termination restriction, 66–67
Imprisonment, false, 139–140
Independent consideration, rule of, 33–35
Independent contractor, employee status *vs.*, 373–375
Internal dispute resolution, as alternative to conventional litigation, 295–296
Internal review, as posttermination procedure, 85–86
Intracompany communications, defamation liability for, 146–147
Intrusion, protection against, 137–140
Inventions, employment contract stating ownership of, 392–393
Investigative consumer report, 133, 135
Investigative services, employee information from, 132–137
Investigatory conference, discrimination claim and, 201–206
Investigatory questionnaire, regarding discrimination charge, 189–197
Involuntary transfer, as wrongful discharge, 83

Job application, for affirmative action plan, 311–313
Job interviews, in affirmative action plan, 313
Job references, *see* References
Jury duty, wrongful discharge for serving on, 2–3, 19

Jury System Improvements Act of 1978, Section 1875, 45

Labor arbitration, *see* Arbitration
Labor Management Relations Act (LMRA), 47, Title I, *see* National Labor Relations Act (NLRA) of 1935
Labor relations, laws respecting, 161–165
Layoffs, in affirmative action plan, 317
Legal arguments, in application to reopen, 210
Libel, 143
   alleged in wrongful termination cases, 67
Lie detector:
   disclosure of results of, 155
   restrictions on, 120–125, 158
   wrongful discharge for refusal to submit to, 19–20
Litigation, *see* Wrongful termination litigation, defending against
Long-form employment contract, 383–385

Management development program, *see* Wrongful termination litigation, defending against, management development program
"Master and servant," law of, 5
Mediation, for dispute resolution, 86
Medical information:
   acquisition of, 140–141
   disclosure of, 153–154, 159
Merger clauses, in employee handbook, 113
Mini-trial, as alternative to conventional litigation, 296
Misconduct, termination for, 68–69
Mitigating damages, 87
Motion for more definite statement, 217–218, 219

National Labor Relations Act (NLRA) of 1935, 2, 18, 22, 43, 47, 48–51, 52, 252
   privacy and, 118
   Section 8, 161
   Taft-Hartley amendments, 43, 48
National Labor Relations Board (NLRB), 11, 18, 21–22, 43, 48, 49, 50, 51, 52
New York State Human Rights Law, 183–184
Nonemployment activities, information as to, 142
Notice of hearing, 209, 211, 214
   issuance of, 216–217
   settlement prior to, 215–216
Notices:
   changes indicated by, 83
   in progressive discipline, 245–250

Objections to recommended order, 232–241
Objectives, performance review conference establishing individual, 84
Occupational Safety and Health Act of 1970 (OSHA), 17, 45, 50, 58–59, 161–162
Omnibus Crime Control and Safe Streets Act of 1968, Title III, 129–130

One last chance, as option to termination, 283–284

Open door policy, as internal review procedure, 85

Oral notice, in progressive discipline, 244–245

Order preparation unit, 233

Out placement, 87, 294–295
  termination conference discussing, 295

Outside activities, employment contract limiting, 389

Patents, employment contract stating ownership of, 392–393

Peer-group review, for dispute resolution, 86

Pension rights, wrongful discharge claims and, 23

Performance evaluations:
  discrimination claim utilizing, 197–198
  in employee handbook, 111
  in progressive discipline, 245

Performance review conferences, individual goals and/or objectives set in, 83–84

Perjury, wrongful discharge cases from employee's refusal to, 9–10

Personnel department, *see* Wrongful termination litigation, defending against, human resource/personnel staff development

Personnel file, *see* Employee file

Personnel policies, *see* Employee handbook

Photographs, as documentation for termination, 255–256

Placement:
  as posttermination procedure, 87. *See also* Out placement
  termination conference discussing, 294

Polygraphs:
  disclosure of, 155
  restrictions on, 120–125, 158
  see also Lie detector

Poor performance, termination for, 69

Positive action programs, *see* Affirmative action plan, positive action programs for

Posthearing brief, 229–232

Posttermination, 293–297. *See also* Wrongful termination litigation, defending against, posttermination risk management

Preemployment inquiries, wrongful termination litigation avoided by, 74–77

Preemption, 46

Pregnancy Discrimination Act of 1978, 165

Pretermination checklist, for management, 70–73

Pretermination review, human resource/personnel staff and, 84

Privacy, *see* Employee privacy

Private dispute resolution, as alternative to conventional litigation, 296

Private information, public disclosure of, 147–150

Private settlement, of discrimination charge, 184–189

Probable cause, 167, 204, 206. *See also* Discrimination charges, defending

Probation:
  in employee handbook, 110–111
  as option to termination, 281–282

Probation period, 247

Progressive discipline, 243–268
  employee file for, 256
  steps of:
    documenting, 252, 253–256
    oral notice, 244–245
    suspension, 250–251
    termination, 251–252
    written notice, 245–250
  termination policy for, 251, 262–266
  union representation during, 252–253

Property, employment contract and return of, 393

Protection of Jurors' Employment Act, 162

Protective laws, affirmative action plan superseding, 316–317

Psychologic stress evaluators, as lie detector test, 123

Public disclosure of private facts, 147–150

Public hearing, *see* Administrative hearing

Public policy:
  risk of wrongful discharge reduced by avoiding violations of, 36–37
  termination in violation of, 65–66

Public policy exception, *see* At-will doctrine

Railway Labor Act (RLA), 45, 46–47, 48

Recommended decision and objections, 232–241

Recruitment:
  affirmative action plan's policy for, 308–309
  employment contract limiting, 391–392
  wrongful termination litigation avoided by policies on, 74–77

References:
  defamation and, 144–145
  as posttermination procedure, 87
  resignation in lieu of termination and, 279–280

Refusal to commit unlawful act, *see* At-will doctrine, refusal to commit unlawful act

Rehabilitation Act of 1973, 44, 58, 327

Reimbursement of expenses, in employment contract, 388

Release or covenant not to sue, termination conference including, 288

Relocation, hiring requiring, 362–363

Request for redetermination, *see* Application to reopen

Resignation, in lieu of termination, 278–280

Res judicata, after termination, 88–89

Resource Conservation and Recovery Act, 45

Retaliation for exercising lawful rights, *see* At-will doctrine, retaliation for exercising lawful rights

Retirement, employment contract stipulating cooperation after, 398–400
Reverse discrimination liability, 325
Revised Order No. 4, 165, 324
Rightful termination, guidelines for, 68–70
Right to sue letter, 207

Safety, wrongful discharge in retaliation for demanding, 17–19
Salary structure, in affirmative action plan, 316, 350
Savings clause, of employment contract, 401–402
Selection, affirmative action plan's policy for, 309–313. *See also* Hiring letter
Seniority clauses, in employee handbook, 111
Separation agreement, inadequate performance of, 69–70
Service letter laws, personnel information disclosure and, 153
Service letter statute, to redress the wrongful disclosure of false information, 142, 145–146
Severance benefits, *see* Termination conference, severance benefits discussed in
Short-form employment contract, 378–383
Slander, 143
  alleged in wrongful termination cases, 67
Solid Waste Disposal Act, 45
Standards of conduct, policy on, 253, 267–268
State action, privacy and, 118
Statute of frauds, 36
Statute of Limitations:
  as posttermination event, 293–294
  regarding discrimination charges, 180–184
Statutes of Laborers, 4
Subpoenas:
  discrimination claim and, 200–201
  preparation for hearing, 222
Supervisor's manual, reviewing avoiding wrongful termination litigation, 80–82. *See also* Employee handbook
Supplemental benefits, termination conference negotiating, 286–288
Supremacy Clause, 46
Suspension:
  as option to termination, 282–283
  in progressive discipline, 250–251
Sworn testimony against employee, wrongful discharge based on, 10–11

Taft-Hartley amendments, 43, 48
Termination conference:
  employee representation at, 277–278
  location of, 289
  participants, 290
  severance benefits discussed in, 284–289, 292
    covenant not to sue or release, 288
    formal severance plan, 285
    supplemental benefits, 286–288
  substantive elements of, 290–293

timing of, 289–290
  see also Termination terms
Termination decision:
  human resource/personnel staff and, 84
  implementation of, 70
  review of, 70
Termination interview, 251
Termination policy, 251, 262–266
Termination terms, 269
  confirmation of asserted basis for termination, 271–273
  confirmation of compliance with employer procedure, 275–276
  confirmation of equal treatment of all employees, 273–275
  legal *vs.* practical determinants, 269–271
  options:
    one last chance, 283–284
    probation, 281–282
    resignation in lieu of termination, 278–280
    suspension, 282–283
    in termination conference, 288–289
    transfer and demotion, 280–281
  see also Posttermination; Termination conference
Testing, *see* Employee testing
Title VII, of Civil Rights Act of 1964, 2, 11, 21, 43, 44, 47, 51–53, 54, 55, 58, 162–164, 168–169, 170, 177, 178, 181–183, 300, 322–323, 325, 326
Tort theories, alleged in wrongful termination cases, 67–68
"Totality of the circumstances" approach, 5
Toxic Substances Control Act, 45
Trade regulation, as basis for wrongful discharge claims, 13
Trade secrets, employment contract stipulating, 389–390
Training, in affirmtive action plan, 350
Transfer policy:
  in agreement, 83
  as option to termination, 282–283
A Treatise on the Law of Master and Servant (Wood), 5
Truth verification devices, restrictions on, 120–125, 158

Underutilization, affirmative action plans and, 305–306, 324, 335
Unenforceable contracts of adhesion, 370–371
Union activities, wrongful discharge based on, 21–22
Union contract, in affirmative action plan, 317–318
Union employees, wrongful discharge and public policy suits by, 22–23
Union representation, during progressive discipline meetings, 252–253
Unions:
  electronic surveillance and, 131–132
  intrusive policies and, 138–139
  lie detector program and, 125

U.S. Code, Title 42:
  Section 1981, 56–57
  Section 1985, 57–58
Unlawful acts, employment contract
    stipulating reporting of, 393–394
Upward mobility system, in affirmative action
    plan, 313–316
Utilization, affirmative action program
    studying, 340–341

Vacation, in employment contract, 387
Veterans Administration, 44
Veterans Re-employment Act of 1974, 44,
    326–327
Video display terminals (VDTs), for electronic
    surveillance, 129, 130
Vietnam-Era Veterans' Readjustment
    Assistance Act of 1974, 165, 327
Voice stress analyzers, as lie detector test, 123

Wagner Act, *see* National Labor Relations Act
    (NLRA) of 1935
Water Pollution Control Act, 45
"Whistleblower" cases, 9, 27–29, 45–46
Witness statements, as documentation for
    termination, 255
Wood, Horace Gay, 5, 6
Workers Compensation Appeals Board, 162
Workers' compensation claim, wrongful
    discharge based on workers filing, 16–
    17
Written customer complaints, as
    documentation for termination, 255
Written notice, in progressive discipline, 245–
    250

Wrongful hiring, 353–365
  in declining industry and firm, 361–362
  employee relocation, 362–363
  hiring for failure, 360–361
  hiring replacement before terminating
      other, 357–358
  hiring for wrong reasons, 358–360
  ignoring undesirable traits, 363–364
  state statutory protection against, 352–354
Wrongful termination litigation, defending
      against, 61–89
  human resource/personnel staff
      development, 73–85
    continuing employment relationships in,
        79–84
    exit interview in, 84–85
    hiring practices in, 74–79
    pretermination decision making in, 84
    termination decision and, 84
  management development program, 63–73
    balanced approach in, 64–65
    changing rules in, 63–64
    implementation of termination decision
        in, 70
    pretermination checklist in, 70–73
    restricted termination reasons in, 65–68
    review of termination decision in, 70
    rightful termination guidelines in, 68–70
  posttermination risk management, 85–89
    collateral proceedings in, 88–89
    explanations, references and placement
        in, 86–87
    file and document review in, 87–88
    internal review and dispute resolution in,
        85–86